Rulemaking

Rulemaking

HOW GOVERNMENT AGENCIES WRITE LAW AND MAKE POLICY

Fourth Edition

Cornelius M. Kerwin
American University

Scott R. Furlong
University of Wisconsin–Green Bay

CQ PRESS

A Division of SAGE
Washington, D.C.

CQ Press
2300 N Street, NW, Suite 800
Washington, DC 20037

Phone: 202-729-1900; toll-free, 1-866-4CQ-PRESS (1-866-427-7737)

Web: www.cqpress.com

Cover design: Blue Bungalow Design
Typesetting: C&M Digitals (P) Ltd.

♾ The paper used in this publication exceeds the requirements of the American National Standard for Information Sciences—Permanence of Paper for Printed Library Materials, ANSI Z39.48-1992.

Printed and bound in the United States of America

14 13 12 11 10   1 2 3 4 5

Library of Congress Cataloging-in-Publication Data

Kerwin, C. M. (Cornelius M.)
  Rulemaking : how government agencies write law and make policy / Cornelius M. Kerwin, Scott R. Furlong. — 4th ed.
      p. cm.
  Includes bibliographical references and index.
  ISBN 978-0-87289-337-5 (pbk. : alk. paper) 1. Administrative procedure—United States. 2. Administrative regulation drafting—United States. I. Furlong, Scott R. II. Title.

  KF5411.K47 2010
  342.73'066—dc22

                                                              2010019523

To Ann, Paul, Michael, Alex, Kara, and Violet
—Cornelius M. Kerwin

For Debbie, Kyle, and Darcy Furlong
and all they do to make my life complete

and

For Neil Kerwin, my colleague, mentor, and friend,
who spurred my interest in rulemaking
—Scott R. Furlong

Contents

Tables and Figures   ix
Preface   xi

Chapter 1   THE SUBSTANCE OF RULES AND THE REASONS FOR
RULEMAKING   1

The Definition of Rulemaking   2
The History of Rulemaking   7
Categories of Rules   21
The Reasons for Rulemaking: What It Has to Offer   28

Chapter 2   THE PROCESS OF RULEMAKING   39

Process and Substance   43
The Core Elements of Rulemaking: Information, Participation,
Accountability   53
Information: Increased Legal Requirements   57
Participation: Expanded Opportunities Mandated by Law   65
Mechanisms of Accountability   70
How the APA Model Has Changed   71
Exceptions, Exemptions, and Evasions   72
The Stages of Rulemaking   75

Chapter 3   ISSUES AND CONTRADICTIONS   89

The Volume of Rulemaking   91
Quality in Rulemaking   96
Timeliness   105

Participation   114
Bureaucratic Discretion   116
The Effects of Rulemaking   117
Inseparable Issues   118

Chapter 4   THE MANAGEMENT OF RULEMAKING   122

Presidential Management   122
Management on the Agency Level   129
Managing Individual Rules   152
Conclusion   163

Chapter 5   PARTICIPATION IN RULEMAKING   167

The Purposes of Participation   168
The Origins and History of Participation   170
Actual Patterns of Participation   189
Does Participation Matter?   210

Chapter 6   OVERSIGHT OF RULEMAKING   221

Accountability and Congress   222
Accountability to the President   232
Accountability to the Courts   247

Chapter 7   RULEMAKING: THEORIES AND REFORM
PROPOSALS   269

The Value of Theory   269
The Elements of Rulemaking Theory   270
The Reform of Rulemaking   292

Appendix   Titles and Chapters in the *Code of Federal
Regulations*   297

Index   301

Tables and Figures

Tables

1-1 Reagan Administration Final and Proposed Rules, Number and *Federal Register* Page Count, 1981–1988   17

1-2 Bush I Administration Final and Proposed Rules, Number and *Federal Register* Page Count, 1989–1992   17

1-3 Clinton Administration Final and Proposed Rules, Number and *Federal Register* Page Count, 1993–2000   19

1-4 Bush II Administration Final and Proposed Rules, Number and *Federal Register* Page Count, 2001–2008   19

1-5 Obama Administration Final and Proposed Rules, Number and *Federal Register* Page Count, 2009   20

1-6 *Code of Federal Regulations* Page Count by Selected Presidencies   22

2-1 An Outline of Rulemaking Activity   76

5-1 Comparative Importance to Interest Groups of Involvement in Rulemaking   192

5-2 Devices Employed by Interest Groups to Influence Rules, by Frequency of Use   197

5-3 Ratings by Interest Groups of the Effectiveness of Techniques   198

5-4 Frequency of Changes by Agencies to Rulemakings Based on Participation by Interest Groups, by Type of Organization   214

6-1 Frequency and Effectiveness of Oversight Techniques, Ninety-fifth Congress   229

6-2 Legislative Vetoes Passed by Congress, by Decade   230

6-3 Types of Actions Taken by the OMB on Agency Rules, 1981–2009   235

6-4 Average Review Times by the Office of Information and Regulatory Affairs   241

6-5 Percentage of Rules Approved by OIRA without Change   245

Figures

2-1   Sample of the Hazardous Materials Regulations in the *Federal Register*   40

3-1   Percentage of Significant Rules Finalized within Certain Time Periods after the Close of the Public Comment Period by FAA and Other Selected Regulatory Agencies, Fiscal Years 1995–2000   107

3-2   Rulemaking Timelines from Initiation to Final Rule for Sixteen Case Studies   108

4-1   Rulemaking Process Flowcharts, Federal Aviation Administration   138

5-1   Exceptions Used by Agencies to Publish Actions without Notices of Proposed Rulemaking (NPRMs)   191

Preface

In the preface to the first edition of this book, Kerwin explained the significance of rulemaking in the American system of government:

> Rulemaking is the single most important function performed by agencies of government. Some readers may find this a surprising, if not outrageous, assertion. But consider the breadth and depth of influence that rulemaking has on our lives.
>
> Rulemaking refines, and in some instances defines, the mission of every government agency. In so doing it provides direction and content for budgeting, program implementation, procurement, personnel management, dispute resolution, and other important government activities. Rules provide specific, authoritative statements of the obligations the government has assumed and the benefits it must provide. It is to rules, not to statutes or other containers of the law, that we turn most often for an understanding of what is expected of us and what we can expect from government. As a result, intense political activity surrounds the contemporary rulemaking process, and effective political action in America is no longer possible without serious attention to rulemaking.
>
> The centrality of rulemaking in our public policy system has placed it under considerable stress. The demand for rules created by hundreds of new government programs and the intense scrutiny of the process by which they are developed give rise to persistent questions from the business and academic communities about the quantity of rules, their quality, and the time it takes to write them. Whether the problems the questions address are real or perceived, the questions themselves raise doubts in the public's mind about the ability of rulemaking to play its vital role. These doubts—and the failures they sometimes reflect—often reduce the effectiveness of public programs and reverberate throughout the political system.

Since the initial publication of this book sixteen years ago, crisis has been a recurrent presence in the American experience. The third edition was completed shortly after the attacks of September 2001 forever shattered our illusions of physical invulnerability to external threats. This edition arrives in the wake of the most dramatic economic downturn since the Great Depression, fueled by meltdowns in the housing market, exotic financial instruments often related to the mortgages that fueled the housing boom, and the collapse of previously iconic financial institutions that had become hostage to transactions whose risk they failed to fully grasp or care enough about. In between these deeply traumatic events the country experienced more mundane but still disturbing threats to the safety of our food and water, physical environment, and workplaces. The integrity of governance of private and nonprofit institutions has been called into question. The health care system continues to disappoint with high costs, insufficient coverage for some, and weaker than desired results. Similar complaints have been heard about our institutions of higher education. Throughout it all, the one constant has been the call for government action or intervention, and with that call the inevitable resort to rules developed in the complex and dynamic systems that are the topics of this book. The agenda of important issues changes constantly, and with it the cast of players in and out of government who determine the outcomes of rulemaking efforts. But rulemaking is a constant.

We write this preface just slightly more than one year into the presidency of Barack Obama, a historic administration in many respects and one for which there are few rivals in the mix of vexing problems and high expectations that greeted its arrival. If there is consensus on anything, it is that regulation will be a centerpiece of the Obama program. His election was viewed in part as a repudiation of the policies of the preceding administration. Among those policies was a fairly typical Republican skepticism about interventions into the market and the value of social regulation. Liberals see in the president a believer in government as a force for positive change across a wide range of social issues and are determined to push their causes through the use of formidable policy tools like rulemaking. Conservatives see Obama the same way, but with markedly less enthusiasm, and they have expressed fears that the country is in for another round of government intervention comparable to the era of the late 1960s and 1970s. What is yet to be determined is whether the much-anticipated rulemaking will be undertaken to implement new authorities created in a wave of landmark statutes in the areas of health, environment, labor, financial services, and food safety, or whether it will be undertaken in lieu of new statutes blocked or stalled by an uncooperative Congress. In the pages that follow, we will comment on various pieces of empirical evidence that are available to measure the frequency, complexity, and impact of rules. They paint a complex picture of a function that waxes and wanes over time. However, it is plain that without an understanding of rulemaking our grasp of the dynamics of both American policymaking and politics is woefully incomplete. This book is our contribution to a complete education.

When a book survives to a fourth edition there are many people to thank. At American University, Kerwin remains in debt to his now coauthor, whose contributions to earlier editions were important, as well as to colleagues such as Laura Langbein, David Rosenbloom, Jeff Lubbers, Andy Popper, Bernard Ross, and James Thurber. In addition, there are the entire faculty and generations of students in American University's School of Public Affairs, who provided the type of intellectual atmosphere and high expectations that helped him grow as a scholar. Michael Kerwin provided important research and insights for earlier editions. Meg Clemmer, Shavana Gonzales, and Maria Bueno assisted with the preparation and editing of the manuscript, exhibiting both wisdom and an undeserved level of patience throughout. Furlong would also like to thank many of the School of Public Affairs faculty who encouraged his scholarship in rulemaking, particularly his coauthor, who introduced him to this area and provided a number of scholarly opportunities. He also thanks his colleagues at the University of Wisconsin–Green Bay, who have supported his efforts and career, and the students who make the teaching of rulemaking fun and exciting. Both authors would like to thank Kay Hofer of Texas State University, Glenn C. Smith of California Western School of Law, and Kelly Tzoumis of DePaul University for their many helpful comments on the manuscript.

With all this help and encouragement, errors of omission or commission are difficult to justify. But where they have happened, the fault is ours alone.

Cornelius M. Kerwin
Washington, D.C.

Scott R. Furlong
Green Bay, Wis.

CHAPTER 1

The Substance of Rules and the Reasons for Rulemaking

"Outcry Builds in Washington for Recovery of AIG Bonuses" read the March 17, 2009, headline in *The New York Times,* one of many that followed the recent and historic collapse of financial institutions, credit markets, and the larger economy. In a time when outrage had become commonplace, the reaction to this particular story was extraordinary. The American Insurance Group (AIG), a very large and established firm that required hundreds of billions of dollars of taxpayer money in 2008 to avoid a collapse feared to be catastrophic to the broader economy, had entered into contracts with employees that required the company to pay hundreds of millions of dollars in bonuses. When the news broke it threatened to undermine the credibility of all involved in the efforts to forestall systemic financial failure. How could people who ostensibly participated in one of the most astounding financial collapses in history and accepted unprecedented amounts of public assistance be rewarded in such a fashion? Congress had already enacted President Barack Obama's proposed framework for restoration of the American economy, the American Recovery and Reinvestment Act. With the new developments from AIG, one of the act's nonspending provisions—an amendment to the executive compensation provisions of 2008—took on new and compelling significance.

Just three months after news of the AIG bonuses was revealed the Department of the Treasury issued a set of regulations that severely restricted compensation for executives working in firms that received bailout funds from the Troubled Asset Relief Program (TARP). The rules were the direct result of the authority granted to the secretary of the Treasury through the American Recovery and Reinvestment Act.[1] They provided specificity on the new requirements essential to the affected companies, the personnel covered by the new rules, and enforcement officials in the government. The Treasury-issued rules covered the full range of compensation issues raised in the statute, including limits on salary, bonuses, and payment of "golden parachutes and so-called 'clawback' regulations that allowed the federal government to recoup compensation awarded on the basis of"[2] materially inaccurate performance criteria. In addition, they added a number of other requirements the department viewed as important to the goals Congress intended in the legislation but not specifically included in the statute. These included mandatory reporting of "perks" over $25,000; prohibition of the practice of providing additional compensation to cover tax liability and the appointment of a special master with broad powers to review and approve the compensation structure for the executive officers and one hundred top earners in any affected firm; and the authority to negotiate repayments by firms to the Treasury for improper payments made previously to covered employees. The Treasury rules covered 123 pages in the *Federal Register* on the day they were issued, including references to earlier rules they had issued on the same topic. This compares to the four pages devoted to the executive compensation issue in the parent legislation. The rules conclude with the qualification that some would consider a warning that Treasury would issue additional rules as conditions merit.

Throughout our history, in crisis and in the normal course of the public's business, Congress deferred to the expertise, management, and administrative capabilities of an agency to carry out what they, as elected representatives, perceived to be the will of the people.

Rulemaking has been used in this case, and countless others, because as an instrument of government it is unmatched in its potential for speed, specificity, quality, and legitimacy. Rulemaking is a ubiquitous presence in virtually all government programs. For a variety of reasons Congress is unwilling or unable to write laws specific enough to be implemented by government agencies and complied with by private citizens. The crucial intermediate process of rulemaking stands between the enactment of a law by Congress and the realization of the goals that both Congress and the people it represents seek to achieve by that law. Increasingly, rulemaking defines the substance of public programs. It determines, to a very large extent, the specific legal obligations we bear as a society. Rulemaking gives precise form to the benefits we enjoy under a wide range of statutes. In the process, it fixes the actual costs we incur in meeting the ambitious objectives of our many public programs.

Rulemaking is important for many reasons. The best place to begin a discussion of those reasons is with a definition of rulemaking and an explanation of why it is crucial to our system of government.

The Definition of Rulemaking

Colin Diver, former dean of the University of Pennsylvania Law School and one of the most thoughtful observers of rules and rulemaking, defines the term in a paraphrase of the great jurist Oliver Wendell Holmes: A "rule is the skin of a living policy ... it hardens an inchoate normative judgment into the frozen form of words. ... Its issuance marks the transformation of policy from the private wish to public expectation. ... [T]he framing of a rule is the climactic act of the policy making process."[3] This definition underscores the pivotal role that rules play in our system of government, but more light must be shed on their key characteristics.

More than sixty years after its enactment into law, the Administrative Procedure Act of 1946 (referred to henceforth as the APA) still contains the best definition of *rule*. The act was written by Congress to bring regularity and predictability to the decision-making processes of government agencies, which by the mid-1940s were having a profound influence on life in this country. Rules and rulemaking were already important parts of the administrative process in 1946. Both, however, required careful definition so that the procedural requirements established in the act would be applied to the types of actions Congress intended to affect.

The APA states: "[R]ule means the whole or part of an agency statement of general or particular applicability and future effect designed to implement, interpret, or prescribe law or policy."[4] At first reading this statement does not appear to reveal much. On closer examination, however, it surrenders several elements crucial to understanding contemporary rulemaking. Not the first element mentioned but a good place to start is a single word—*agency*—because it identifies the source of rules.

The Source of Rules: Agencies

We learn first from this definition that rules do not come from the major institutions created by the Constitution. They are not products of Congress or some other legislature. Rules are by-products of the deliberations and votes of our elected representatives, but they are not themselves legislation. Congress does have its own institutional rules, but they apply only to its members and committees. Under the APA definition, rules do not originate with the president or some other chief executive. As we will see, the actions of the president of the United States and chief executives at the various levels of government have a profound effect on the rulemaking process. These officials employ executive orders and directives in the course of their management responsibilities, but rarely, if ever, do they write rules of the type considered in this book.[5]

Various and sundry courts may have reason to consider rules. Their actions may result in rules being changed or eliminated. But judges do not write rules in the first instance either, except, like Congress, to establish procedures for their colleagues and the operation of the courts over which they preside.

Rules are produced by bureaucratic institutions entrusted with the implementation, management, and administration of our law and public policy. We view bureaucracies as inferior in status to the constitutional branches of government—Congress, the president, and the judiciary. We do so because the authority of these agencies is derived and patterned after and drawn from the three main branches. In one important respect, however, agencies are the equal of these institutions. The rules issued by departments, agencies, or commissions are law; they carry the same weight as congressional legislation, presidential executive orders, and judicial decisions. An important and controversial feature of our system of government is that bureaucratic institutions are vested with all three government powers established in the Constitution. Through a device called delegation of authority, government agencies perform legislative, executive, and judicial functions. Rulemaking occurs when agencies use the legislative authority granted them by Congress.

It is significant that agencies are the sources of rules, because it means that rulemaking is subjected to the external and internal influences that have been found to affect decision making in our public bureaucracies. Agencies behave differently from the constitutional branches of government. Their decisions cannot be explained simply by reference to the admittedly strong pressures they continually feel from Congress, the White House, the courts, interest groups, and the public at large. As one group of scholars put it, "Public agencies are major political actors in all phases of the policy process."[6]

The organization, division of labor, culture, professional orientation, and work routines of bureaucracies affect the way they make decisions. So too do the motives of individual bureaucrats. These themes will be developed further in the book's final chapter. We must expect the law and policy embodied in rules written by agencies to be different from what would be developed by Congress, the president, or the courts. So the very source of rules makes them immediately distinctive from other instruments of law and public policy.

Agency can mean any one of a number of organizational arrangements used to carry out law and policy. Public bureaucracies have many names. There are departments, such as the Department of Transportation; commissions, such as the Federal Trade Commission (FTC); administrations, such as the Federal Aviation Administration (FAA); and agencies, such as the Environmental Protection Agency (EPA). However organized or named, most of these bodies have the authority to issue rules and use a rulemaking process to carry it out.

The Subject Matter of Rules: Law and Policy

Having specifically identified the source of rules, the APA definition, interestingly, does not refer to subject matter other than "law" and "policy." In this respect, the definition could not be written more broadly. No area of public policy is excluded. This was not intended by the drafters of the APA as an invitation or authorization to engage in rulemaking in any area that a given agency found interesting or attractive. On the contrary, authority to issue rules can derive only from the statutes that establish the mission of agencies and set their goals and objectives. The definition simply acknowledges that rules can be developed in any area in which Congress adopts a valid statute that is signed by the president.[7] Our experience since the time this definition was framed makes it plain that the decision to put no substantive limits on the potential reach of rules was wise. Rules covered a large range of topics in 1946; in the early twenty-first century the scope is virtually limitless.

The Range of Influence of Rules over Law and Policy: Implement, Interpret, Prescribe

The definition clearly establishes an expansive relationship between rules, law, and public policy. The terms *implement, interpret,* and *prescribe* describe the fullest range of influence that a rule could have. Rules merely *implement* when law or policy has been fully developed in a statute enacted by Congress, an executive order of the president, or a judicial decision. Hence, rules need provide no additional substantive elaboration. In these cases rules give instructions to administering officials and the public in the form of procedures but add nothing else of substance to the direction already provided by Congress.

Rules *interpret* when law and policy are well established but confront unanticipated or changing circumstances. Statutory terms, clear and precise when written, may require adaptation when new business practices or technologies appear. Legislation implemented by the Federal Trade Commission, for example, seeks to eliminate improper restraints on competition. This creates tasks in the present time that are very different from those created in the era of the robber barons and the trusts. Similarly, statutes mandating air or water quality clearly require agencies to be attentive and respond to industry structure and production processes that may, in turn, alter the sources and types of pollution to be regulated. Currently, the rapid innovation in financial products such as collateralized debt obligations, interest rate swaps, and other "products" challenges the reach and grasp of regulators.

Rules *prescribe* when Congress establishes the goals of law or policy in statutes but provides few details as to how they are to be put into operation or how they are actually to be achieved. The Occupational Safety and Health Act stated its ambitious goals in this way: "to assure so far as possible every working man and woman in the Nation safe and healthy work conditions."[8] Although it provided some additional guidance, it left to the administering agency, the Occupational Safety and Health Administration (OSHA), the job of defining through rules key legal terms such as *so far as possible, safe,* and *healthy.* And once these terms were given an authoritative, legal meaning the huge task of finding the ways that health and safety could be protected was left to the agency as well. Similarly, it was not uncommon for statutes dealing with economic regulation to set agencies off in search of "the public interest" as the criterion for their actions.[9] The APA definition allows agency rulemaking to fill whatever vacuum has been left by Congress, the president, and the courts in the formation of public policy or law. The greater the demands on these institutions, the more likely that the role of rules will expand.

The Range of Circumstances Affected by Rules: General and Particular Applicability

Rules affect persons or activities in the widest possible range of circumstances. The phrase "general or particular applicability" in the APA allows rules to range from those that affect large segments of the population and economy to those that produce changes in a single individual, group, firm, or government unit. Some may find this element of the definition confusing, even troubling. We tend to think of legislative action as being concerned with general issues and problems that affect groups of people and activities. The judicial process is generally thought to be better designed for dealing with individual circumstances.[10]

So, should not a reduction in number of activities or persons affected by a government action cause an agency to shift from a quasi-legislative process to a quasi-judicial mode of decision making? Should not an agency use other delegated authority to act in a judicial capacity? The short answer is that, although the number of persons affected might influence the specific procedures used to make a decision, this characteristic alone does not determine whether an action that is contemplated is best classified as a rule. The underlying purpose of the action is a key element in this regard, and it is addressed directly in the APA definition.

The Importance of Future Effect

Rules, like legislation, attempt to structure the future. By creating new conditions, eliminating existing ones, or preventing others from coming into being, rules implement legislation that seeks to improve the quality of life. The term *future effect* is thus a crucial element in the definition of rules because it allows a clear contrast to situations in which agencies issue decisions, acting in their judicial capacity.[11]

Agencies are often concerned with determining the legal implications of current or past events and conditions. This occurs when an individual challenges an adverse regulatory decision, such as a denial of his or her petition for a benefit provided by some government program, or applies for a license. In these instances the government is being asked to issue an *order,* the term used when agencies are acting in a judicial capacity. An order applies existing rules to past or existing circumstances. Although an order may have a future effect, such as granting benefits to an individual or permission to operate a particular type of business, its primary purpose is not the creation of policy or law to establish new conditions. Again, although the type of *procedures* an agency uses to issue rules may at times resemble those used by courts, the *purpose* of rules is clearly distinct from that of other forms of administrative actions.

The key features of rules, then, are that they originate in agencies, articulate law and policy limited only by authorizing legislation, and have either a broad or a narrow scope but are always concerned with shaping future conditions. This tells us what rules are. Now we must examine the growth of rulemaking through time to determine why it has come to play so central a role in our system of government.

The History of Rulemaking

Rulemaking is a direct consequence of the demands the American people make on government. By persuading elected officials to improve health care, clean the environment, or protect them from deceptive or dangerous business practices, the American people inexorably set in motion the rulemaking process. But it would be hard to agree that there is enthusiastic, explicit, or even conscious public support for rulemaking. The support for rulemaking is implicit in the public's seemingly insatiable appetite for new public initiatives and programs. Virtually all new laws enacted by Congress to deal with real or perceived problems bring with them the need for additional rulemaking. It has been this way since the dawn of the Republic, so the American people have had ample time to learn about this unavoidable relationship.[12]

The evolution of rulemaking is best understood in parallel with the historical development of American statute law. The symbiotic relationship between legislation and rulemaking was established in the earliest days of the very first Congress. Put simply, statutes and rules depend on one another. Statutes provide the legal authority for rules and the various processes by which they are made. Rules provide the technical detail so often missing in statutes, and rulemaking brings a capacity for adaptation to changing circumstances that the letter of the law alone would lack. These two vital elements of American public policy and law have been growing and diversifying throughout our history.

The Early Sessions of Congress

In its very first sessions, Congress enacted laws that delegated to the president of the United States the authority to issue rules that would govern those who traded with Indian tribes.[13] The law had scant content, relying instead on the president's rules to provide the substance.[14] Subsequent Congresses continued to delegate the power to write rules to officials of the executive branch. For the most part, these powers were confined to matters of trade and commerce.[15] In 1796, for example, the president was given the authority to develop regulations that set duties on foreign goods. Twenty years later, these powers were expanded considerably when Congress granted sweeping rulemaking powers to the secretary of the Treasury to regulate the importation of goods into the United States. This particular statute is notable because it recognizes a subordinate official of the executive branch—a cabinet officer—as the authority to whom rulemaking power is delegated. This is the norm in contemporary legislation. The vague and sweeping language used in the legislation—"to establish regulations suitable and necessary for carrying this law into effect; which regulations shall be binding"—became common in the many statutes that followed.[16]

The Late Nineteenth and Early Twentieth Centuries: An Expanding National Government

During the twentieth century the government of the United States experienced two periods of extraordinary growth. Each was a response to crisis, real or perceived. The New Deal was an attempt to plan and regulate the economy out of depression during the 1930s; the 1960s and early 1970s saw much broader and deeper efforts to eliminate poverty, pollution, injury, and inequity. These were, indeed, pivotal periods in our political and legal history. Their legacies with regard to rulemaking are extremely important. But a careful examination of legislative activity demonstrates that, although these were extraordinary periods of expansion, government and rulemaking have been growing steadily since the late nineteenth century.

In the earliest days of the Republic, rulemaking was limited. The reach of federal government powers for much of the nineteenth century was comparatively modest. This began to change in the late nineteenth century, however, when Congress turned its attention to domestic issues and problems and sought solutions. The 1880s, for example, saw the creation of the Interstate Commerce Commission (ICC), which would serve as a model for serial interventions by the federal government into many other sectors of the economy.[17] Programs to protect American agriculture and livestock production from contamination were authorized by legislation. Statutes designed to protect wildlife were passed in this same decade as well. These laws required varying numbers of rules to be issued by the responsible agencies to implement important provisions. By the beginning of the second decade of the twentieth century, rulemaking had become prominent enough to attract serious academic attention. Legal scholars began to study what one termed "delegated legislation."[18] These early works did not suffer any illusions about what rulemaking was: It was, and is, lawmaking by unelected administrative officials.

From roughly 1900 to the onset of the Great Depression in 1929, Congress created public programs that affected a wide variety of previously private activities.[19] Many were designed to protect consumers from dangerous or unfair practices. The creation of the FTC, the passage of the Clayton Act to extend its jurisdiction, enactment of legislation to ensure the quality of food and the efficacy of drugs, the creation of a federal program to inspect meat, and the establishment of the Federal Reserve System all occurred during this period. Agriculture was also a frequent target for new legislation during this time. Included among the many statutes were laws designed to ensure the purity of milk and the quality of grain, to extend existing powers of quarantine, and to regulate the operation of stockyards and packing houses. Congress ventured into the energy arena by passing the Federal Water Power Act and increased the powers of the ICC with the Hepburn Act. The nation's natural resources got considerable legislative attention as well through statutes that emphasized the importance of conserving and protecting wildlife and migratory birds and managing public lands effectively. The congressional actions undertaken during these thirty years resulted in a broader and deeper federal role in the affairs of the American people. The authority of existing laws was amended and usually extended into new areas, and wholly new types of commitments were made.

The New Deal: New Roles for Government and New Repositories for Rulemaking

The most casual student of this country's political history knows that the election of Franklin Delano Roosevelt and the coming of the New Deal brought an outpouring of legislation unprecedented in its volume and implications for the role of government. In response to an economic crisis and an aggressive presidential agenda, Congress enacted laws that greatly increased the powers and responsibilities of the federal government. The centerpiece of the New Deal was the National Industrial Recovery Act (NIRA), enacted in 1933. The act authorized the president to create bodies of rules, called "codes," that would establish fair competition in many sectors of the economy.[20] The legislation was breathtaking in its scope—very few significant industries or economic activities were unaffected. The reliance the NIRA placed on rulemaking and other forms of administrative action was near total. Although it fell to a constitutional challenge in 1935 and was subsequently amended extensively by later Congresses, the act stands as an important milestone in the history of rulemaking.

The New Deal is properly thought of as a period of intense economic regulation, but many forms of new public policy appeared during this time. Agriculture, labor relations and employment conditions, assistance for the aged and disadvantaged, housing and home ownership, transportation, banking, securities, consumer protection, rural electrification, natural resources, wildlife, energy, and transportation were all profoundly affected by the statutes of the New Deal.[21]

If we assume a direct relation between statutes and the rules needed to implement them, rulemaking had become a major government function by the height of the New Deal. But there was no way accurately to assess the volume and significance of rulemaking done by agencies. For example, until 1934 there was no single authoritative way to publish and make available the rules and related decisions made by federal agencies. This situation was corrected by the creation of the *Federal Register.* With the *Register* came the *Code of Federal Regulations* (CFR), which was organized functionally by agency and program and will be considered in more detail later. A remarkable study by a committee appointed by the attorney general at that time, Robert Jackson, inventoried rulemaking by the federal government. Completed during the closing days of the New Deal, the study reveals that all agencies were actively engaged in rulemaking but that there was considerable variation in both substance and volume.

The State of Rulemaking at the Close of the New Deal

The magnitude of delegated authority granted to agencies during the New Deal and the manner in which certain agencies used these new powers caused a great deal of concern. It was perceived that these administrative processes were not only growing at an alarming rate but were operating in violation of basic legal principles. As described by the Brownlow Committee, a group empowered by Franklin Delano Roosevelt to examine government management, they were a "headless fourth branch of government."[22] In response to mounting criticisms and calls for change, President Roosevelt created a committee to study administrative practices in force in the main agencies of the federal government. It was intended to be FDR's answer to the Brownlow Committee.[23] Called the Attorney General's Committee on Administrative Procedure, it conducted a series of case studies that today provides us an invaluable historical record on the status of rulemaking almost seventy years ago. It demonstrates conclusively that frequent and highly significant rulemaking was occurring in most agencies, and that it was often the result of legislation that predated the New Deal. The following examples from the committee's research, published in 1941, will help put contemporary rulemaking into the proper historical perspective.

The committee found that nearly thirty administrative entities were empowered to issue rules that had significant effects on the public. Some of these agencies were delegated rulemaking authority under multiple statutes. Of all the agencies studied by the committee, the one with the greatest accumulation and annual production of rules was the Department of the Interior. The committee wrote that other agency functions were "obscured" by the "momentousness" of rulemaking at the department. It was estimated that at the time of the study several thousand rules were in effect and several hundred new rules were issued each year. The rules dealt largely with the department's responsibilities for the protection of fish, wildlife, and birds, and its stewardship of the many uses of public lands. But wildlife and public lands were not the sole concern of the rulemakers. The program that regulated the coal industry had a rulemaking task that was described as "monumental." The making of one rule alone involved the participation of 387 people, including more than 200 lawyers, and generated more than 700 supporting documents.[24]

The volume of rules issued by the Department of the Interior was rivaled by the various agencies that at different times were responsible for veterans' affairs. The program had been in operation in some form since the late 1700s, so it is not surprising that a large body of rules had accumulated. In fact, rules affecting veterans filled several thousand pages, and the matters they covered ranged from minor administrative details to policies of considerable substance. The study group found them so comprehensive and specific that they left little discretion for agency administrators.[25]

The ICC was also heavily engaged in rulemaking under the Motor Carrier Act. It prepared "a dozen sets" of rules from one five-year period following passage of the act. In another area of its statutory responsibilities, the ICC was involved in constant rulemaking from 1908 to 1940, issuing seven full revisions of rules governing the transport of explosive materials.[26]

Apparently as active in a related area was the Bureau of Marine Inspection and Navigation, an agency performing functions that had been conducted under one administrative arrangement or another since the earliest days of the Republic. The bureau's rules were described as "voluminous" and covered all aspects of vessel constitution and operation to ensure safety.[27]

Rulemaking, although clearly established as a crucial government function in the late 1930s, was not undertaken uniformly in all major policy areas. In some instances rulemaking was avoided; in others the agencies wrote rules but added little to what Congress had provided in legislation. Notable among the agencies that did not undertake large programs of rulemaking were the FTC and the National Labor Relations Board (NLRB). Both agencies chose to proceed largely in a quasi-judicial manner, dealing with individual cases brought to them by individuals or groups with complaints. Their policies and law evolved through the accumulation of individual decisions.

The Social Security Administration (SSA), then called the Social Security Board, undertook a considerable amount of rulemaking after passage of amendments to the Social Security Act in 1939, but little of it was legislative, or substantive, in nature.[28] In this instance, the agency adopted rulemaking but chose to exercise little or no discretion in the process. This would change as the programs administered by the agency grew and diversified.

The legislative history of the statutes of the FTC indicates that Congress intended it to be a vigorous rulemaker. But it was not until the 1970s that political forces and significant reforms forced the FTC to undertake rulemaking.[29] The NLRB continued to eschew rulemaking, and it does so to this very day, despite frequent entreaties from those who believe more rules are badly needed.[30]

By the time the *Code of Federal Regulations* began publication in 1938, the legislative phase of the New Deal was winding down. Organized in fifty titles, which correspond to different areas of law and public policy, the CFR of 1938 provides a summary, albeit incomplete, of the results of rulemaking up to that time. Several titles were reserved for Congress, the judiciary, the president, the *Federal Register,* and "government accounts." A substantial portion of the CFR was devoted to national defense and the conduct of foreign relations. Other elements of the 1938 CFR contain material that has since been superseded or subsumed by more recent legislative activity. Some programs are notable by their absence. The "Public Welfare" title contained chapters devoted to an office of education in the Department of the Interior, the Civilian Conservation Corps, the Works Progress Administration, and the National Youth Administration. There was no mention of Social Security; in 1938 the regulations mentioned earlier were still being developed. As one would expect from the previous discussion of statutory developments, there were titles devoted to agriculture and meat production, labor, banking, commerce, transportation, housing, public health, pure food and drugs, telecommunications, public lands, public resources, and wildlife. Some constituted larger bodies of rules; others were small. The rules pertaining to agriculture filled eight chapters and nearly 1,200 pages, whereas those devoted to labor could be contained in just 39 pages.

From the End of World War II to the Mid-1960s

From the end of World War II to the mid-1960s, combined effects of legislation and rulemaking continued to expand the reach of the federal government. As in the past, we see here the amendment of existing statutes as well as the creation of new programs. The CFR grew and was periodically reorganized to reflect these changes. The count of fifty titles in the *Code* has remained relatively constant. Chapters and volumes rapidly expanded in numbers, reflecting the growing reach of the government. For example, what began as a publication of fifteen volumes in 1938 filled forty-seven volumes in 1949.

In the 1950s and 1960s, legislative attention focused heavily on ways to provide basic rights, benefits, and services to the American people.[31] Statutes established national standards for unemployment insurance, aid to veterans, health care for the elderly and indigent, food stamps, and support for urban mass transit systems; they also established programs to protect consumers from dangerous products, ineffective vaccines, food additives, and unscrupulous lenders. Laws were passed to prevent or punish discrimination based on age, race, or sex. Existing statutes to protect fisheries were extended, and new programs to preserve wilderness areas, scenic trails, and wild rivers were created. The 1950s saw the federal government's first tentative incursions into the areas of air and water quality; and the close of the 1960s brought the landmark National Environmental Policy Act, which required rulemaking in every agency whose actions directly or indirectly disturbed the ecology.

The Decade of the 1970s: Rulemaking Ascendant

By 1969 the crucial importance of rulemaking in our system of government was unmistakable. Rulemaking had developed into a major force in our legal, political, and economic lives. The volume of rules was formidable, and the range of areas covered by the rules was enormous. Why, then, is it the decade of the 1970s that is frequently characterized as the "era of rulemaking"?[32] Although such characterizations tend to underestimate the importance of earlier periods, there are good reasons why the 1970s deserve their special reputation.

In the 1970s the content of congressional delegations of authority, and the general political environment in which they occurred, brought fundamental changes to rulemaking. The number of statutes that established major programs requiring extensive rulemaking was unprecedented. By one count, 130 laws establishing new programs of social regulation were enacted during this one decade.[33] Proposals dealing with virtually all types of environmental problems, health and safety hazards in most workplaces, and comprehensive consumer protection became law. Congress also enacted broad-ranging reforms in worker pensions. The rulemaking tasks created by legislation like this differed from those that accompanied earlier statutes in many ways.

To be sure, agencies operating under earlier statutes often faced formidable obstacles when writing rules. After the invalidated New Deal legislation, however, rarely did their delegations of rulemaking authority sweep so broadly across the economy in the manner that became commonplace in the regulatory legislation of the 1970s. Environmental legislation, taken as a whole, required rulemakers to identify, locate, prevent, control, or mitigate virtually every form of harmful pollutant or dangerous substance in the air, water, and ground. The health and safety of the majority of American workers, regardless of industry or occupation, and the safety of most consumer products were similarly entrusted to newly created programs and agencies.

For the most part, the rulemaking authority granted to agencies prior to the 1970s was more narrowly confined, affecting specific industries and activities.[34] Those agencies actually granted broadly based powers, such as the National Labor Relations Board and the Federal Trade Commission, used their rulemaking authority quite parsimoniously. Furthermore, industry-specific programs of regulation had grown incrementally, giving the agencies an extended period of time to develop working relationships with those they regulated or served. Even when dealing with multiple constituencies, as in the areas of natural resources and employment conditions, the agencies could trade on long-term relationships and work at a pace that they largely dictated. These conditions would change, however.

The authorizing legislation of the 1970s represented sudden and radical shifts in the federal role, creating agencies from whole cloth or through the consolidation of programs from numerous departments. These new agencies could neither avoid nor delay rulemaking; the authorizing statutes frequently mandated that rules be developed in specified areas.[35] The same laws often contained mandatory deadlines by which rules were to be completed.

The relationships between the rulemakers and affected parties were given no time to mature. Instead, the rulemaking agencies were immediately positioned between well-organized, aggressive environmental, labor, and consumer groups on one side and threatened, equally aggressive business interests with plentiful resources on the other.

These pressures produced a period of extraordinary rule production. From 1976 to 1980, a time when we would expect to see the cumulative effect of the statutory explosion, 36,789 rules were added to the *Code of Federal Regulations,* and agencies of government proposed 23,784 rules, averaging roughly 9,200 and 6,000 per year, respectively.[36] As the decade of the 1980s began, the government's rulemaking engines were well stoked; to reverse them would require extraordinary action.

To the volume of work, accelerated pace, and inevitable conflict contained in their delegations of rulemaking authority, the statutes of the 1970s added several layers of substantive and procedural complexity. Environmental and workplace safety programs are good examples of statutes that sent rulemaking routinely to the edge of human knowledge and technical capabilities and beyond. Agencies were expected to create information (for example, information on "safe" levels of various chemicals and substances, like benzene and asbestos, in the workplace) while simultaneously incorporating that information into a rule that could be implemented, complied with, and enforced. Furthermore, Congress became increasingly concerned with the process by which rules were being written by agencies. As we will see in the next chapter, the rulemaking provisions of new statutes created more complex and difficult processes for rulemakers to use.

The breadth of the new legislation brought about the potential for conflict between new rules and those of more established programs. The responsibilities of OSHA with regard to all American workers appeared to overlap considerably with those of agencies having jurisdiction over specific industries, such as transportation, food and drug production, and even nuclear power plants. Conflict could occur within a single agency as well. Actions taken as a result of the rules put forth by one office of the EPA to protect the air could result in pollution of the water, which was the responsibility of another office. The need for coordination between agencies of the federal government was dwarfed by intergovernmental issues created by these new statutes. Many laws created partnerships between federal and state governments in which standards were set in Washington but supplemented and enforced in the fifty states.[37] The federal legislation of the 1970s set off considerable rulemaking activity in the states as well.[38]

The rulemaking of the 1970s was also more important than that which had come before. If we assume that Congress had properly identified real threats in the wave of protective legislation it passed in the 1970s, then to a remarkable extent the health, safety, financial well-being, and general quality of life of Americans would hinge on the success of rulemaking by agencies. These rules would also impose unprecedented costs, transfer huge amounts of wealth across our society, and affect our capacity to vie in increasingly competitive world markets.

The Reagan and Bush I Administrations: A Modest Retreat

As a period in the history of rulemaking, the 1980s are more difficult to characterize. On the one hand, much of the massive agenda for rulemaking established in legislation of the 1970s remained to be completed in the 1980s. Exacerbating this backlog of work were important amendments to existing environmental, workplace safety and health, and consumer statutes that added even more responsibilities and caused the revision of rules already in existence. In the face of these formidable pressures, however, powerful political forces were at work to eliminate some rules, to prevent others from being made, and to impose new decision-making criteria on those that remained.

During his presidential campaign Ronald Reagan was aggressive in his opposition to government regulation. His administration introduced the most significant changes since the basic process for rulemaking was established in the Administrative Procedure Act of 1946. These changes will be considered at length in two subsequent chapters.

The years of the Reagan presidency were generally ones of reductions in rulemaking activity, beginning with a sixty-day moratorium at the outset of his first term. Table 1-1 contains information on the numbers of rulemaking documents published in the *Federal Register* during the Reagan presidency. The number of final rules declined throughout 1987. Proposed rules followed a more erratic course but were not significantly changed over the eight years. There were 28 percent fewer new final rules in 1988 than at the outset of Reagan's presidency. The numbers of rules alone do not tell the entire story. The volume and complexity of requirements of new rules are better captured, albeit imperfectly, in the page count in the *Federal Register* and *Code of Federal Regulations*. For both final and proposed rules, annual page counts were larger at the end of the Reagan presidency than at the beginning, although there was much volatility in this metric as well.

During his presidency, George H. W. Bush was stung by critiques that he was soft on regulation, and he instituted several moratoriums on rulemaking. The number and volume of rules issued during the first Bush administration are reflected in Table 1-2. Here we see a decline in the number of final

TABLE 1-1 Reagan Administration Final and Proposed Rules, Number and *Federal Register* Page Count, 1981–1988

Year	Final rules		Proposed rules	
	Number of rules	*Number of pages*	*Number of rules*	*Number of pages*
1981	n.d.		n.d.	
1982	6,329	15,300	3,745	10,433
1983	6,056	16,196	3,897	12,772
1984	5,290	15,473	3,459	11,972
1985	5,182	15,460	3,670	13,772
1986	4,991	13,904	3,455	11,186
1987	4,935	13,625	3,653	14,179
1988	5,141	16,033	3,606	13,892
Average	5,417	15,151	3,640	12,620

Source: Office of the Federal Register; Regulatory Information Center, United States General Services Administration.

n.d. = data not available.

TABLE 1-2 Bush I Administration Final and Proposed Rules, Number and *Federal Register* Page Count, 1989–1992

Year	Final rules		Proposed rules	
	Number of rules	*Number of pages*	*Number of rules*	*Number of pages*
1989	5,157	16,489	3,451	13,219
1990	4,765	14,179	3,258	12,694
1991	4,852	16,793	3,351	16,759
1992	4,525	15,921	3,351	15,174
Average	4,824	15,845	3,352	14,461

Source: Office of the Federal Register; Regulatory Information Center, United States General Services Administration.

rules over the term. Little change, however, is seen in proposed rules and page counts, which generally exceed the numbers in the Reagan years, particularly for proposed rules.

It is interesting to note that the page count for final rules during the Reagan years is similar to that of the first two years of the Carter administration. With regard to proposed rules for these blocks of years, the Reagan administration page counts are actually larger. However, the data also confirm the remarkable volume of activity in the last two years of the Carter administration and the jolt of the emergency brake pulled by Reagan in 1981.

Characterizing the Reagan/Bush years as a "modest retreat" is, on balance, fair. There were significant reductions early in the Reagan administration in both final and proposed rules, as well as in pages in the *Federal Register*. Indeed, in the latter category the reduction in pages from 1980 to 1981 was the greatest percentage decrease in terms of pages in any single year. The frequency of rulemaking was lowered, but the new levels that emerged were hardly insubstantial. During the full twelve years of this era agencies produced, on average, eight thousand proposed and final rules per year. The momentum coming out of the Carter administration was slowed, not arrested, and despite the small government intentions and rhetoric of these two Republican leaders, the reality of government, as measured by rulemaking activity, remained prominent.

The Clinton Years

The statistics related to rulemaking during the Clinton presidency are mixed. Annual averages for the numbers of both final and proposed rules were slightly less than the first Bush administration—surprising, given what one might reasonably expect from a Democratic president following more than a decade of conservative Republican rule. Page counts in the *Federal Register* devoted to final and proposed rules are quite a different matter, however, and these dramatically increased from the previous administrations, as shown in Table 1-3. Any conclusions drawn from the appearance of a comparatively modest number of rules issued during the Clinton administration compared to their predecessors must be approached with care. First, Bush did not leave an inactive rulemaking process for Clinton to resurrect from the dead. Indeed, Bush was roundly criticized by members of his own party for failing to slow the pace of new rules. Second, when we look beyond the gross numbers of rules we find that the Clinton administration was much more active in areas of regulation identified with an activist Democrat agenda. For example, during the years of his presidency, rules related broadly to environmental protection and safety increased very substantially, with rules issued by the EPA increasing nearly 40 percent per year.

The Bush II Presidency

The presidency of George W. Bush will always be framed by the war on terror, and its dominating presence is evident in the rulemaking record. As Table 1-4 demonstrates, there is no question that the Bush II administration can be characterized as a time of fewer final and proposed rules, but it was

TABLE 1-3 Clinton Administration Final and Proposed Rules, Number and *Federal Register* Page Count, 1993–2000

Year	Final rules		Proposed rules	
	Number of rules	*Number of pages*	*Number of rules*	*Number of pages*
1993	4,614	18,016	3,330	15,410
1994	4,868	20,385	3,628	18,184
1995	4,828	18,047	3,339	15,982
1996	4,963	21,639	3,266	15,352
1997	4,615	18,992	3,035	15,289
1998	4,898	20,029	3,169	18,258
1999	4,660	20,201	3,414	19,447
2000	4,477	24,482	2,850	17,943
Average	4,740	20,223	3,253	16,982

Source: Office of the Federal Register; Regulatory Information Center, United States General Services Administration.

TABLE 1-4 Bush II Administration Final and Proposed Rules, Number and *Federal Register* Page Count, 2001–2008

Year	Final rules		Proposed rules	
	Number of rules	*Number of pages*	*Number of rules*	*Number of pages*
2001	4,100	19,643	2,635	14,166
2002	4,147	19,233	2,758	18,640
2003	4,225	22,670	2,732	17,357
2004	4,074	22,546	2,552	19,332
2005	3,956	23,041	2,631	18,260
2006	3,713	22,347	2,461	19,794
2007	3,569	22,771	2,391	18,611
2008	3,775	26,320	2,449	18,648
Average	3,944	22,308	2,576	18,163

Source: Office of the Federal Register; Regulatory Information Center, United States General Services Administration.

more active when measured by pages in the *Federal Register* and the numbers added to the *Code of Federal Regulations*. But more important to note is the changing composition of rulemaking activity during these Bush years. When compared to the Clinton presidency and measured by the activities of two of the traditionally most active rulemaking agencies—the Environmental Protection Agency and the Department of Transportation—rulemaking declined significantly. The Bush II presidency, however, also saw the rise of the Department of Homeland Security as a major rulemaking force; indeed, it became the third most active rulemaking agency in the entire federal government. This underscores an important point learned eventually by all presidents: Rulemaking is a versatile tool; it has no inherent political tilt. It can serve both liberal and conservative agendas.

The overall assessment of the Bush II period is that rulemaking in many areas declined in frequency but in others remained essentially unchanged. In one area important to the safety and quality of our lives it was very prominent: homeland security.

The Obama Presidency

This edition of *Rulemaking* appears after one year of the Obama administration. While its campaign and early legislative initiatives presage dramatic increases in rulemaking, it is too early for any reliable evidence to accumulate. Nevertheless, Table 1-5 does contain data that may appear mildly surprising. The first year of the Obama administration compared to the last year of the Bush II presidency saw declines in both proposed and final rules. Given the campaign rhetoric of then-candidate Barack Obama, one might have expected more activity in his first year. Furthermore, given the data on final and proposed rules, one would then expect page counts to be down as well, and they were. However, with the last transition from a Republican to a Democratic president (Bush I to Clinton), both rules and page counts increased. Time will tell whether the expectation that the Obama administration will be a much more active rulemaker proves accurate.

President Obama, like his predecessors, moved immediately to assert management and policy control of rulemaking, including a hold on last-minute

TABLE 1-5 Obama Administration Final and Proposed Rules, Number and *Federal Register* Page Count, 2009

	Final rules		*Proposed rules*	
Year	*Number of rules*	*Number of pages*	*Number of rules*	*Number of pages*
2009	3,388	20,782	2,035	16,651

Source: Office of the Federal Register; Regulatory Information Center, United States General Services Administration.

regulations issued by the outgoing Bush team and elimination of some of its directives. We will review the Obama program for management and oversight of rulemaking in subsequent chapters.

Some have argued that rulemaking is actually in decline as a method for making law and policy. In the next chapter we will explore the process of rulemaking and how it has developed through time. For some rules, especially those with the greatest potential effects on the economy and society, the rulemaking process can be complex, expensive, time-consuming, and risky. Several prominent scholars have concluded that these and other factors have led agencies away from rulemaking to other mechanisms for implementing programs.[39] Rulemaking will certainly not disappear, but its avoidance or mutation by agencies is a serious issue that will be covered at length in subsequent sections of this book.

Rulemaking is a direct, if not always desired, consequence of legislation. More to the point, rulemaking, as a mechanism for refining law and policy, has been essential to the government's efforts to assume responsibility for the range of activities demanded by the voters. It was and remains an inevitable and indispensable extension of any significant legislative activity. As long as the American people demand new or altered public policies, and as long as Congress responds to these demands, rulemaking will remain a basic and determining element of our political and legal systems.

Categories of Rules

If nothing else is evident from this brief history or rulemaking, it should be apparent that defining or categorizing the substance of rulemaking is very difficult. All topics, issues, and activities touched by public policy are or will be the subject of a rule. Still, there are ways to categorize rules that capture certain key characteristics, if not their full richness.

Policy Area and Agency of Origin

The *Code of Federal Regulations* organizes rules in fifty distinct categories called titles and chapters, which correspond to distinct public programs, policies, or agencies. For example, the rules for banks and banking can be found in Title 12; those for protection of the environment, in Title 40; and those governing acquisition of goods and services by the federal government, in several dozen chapters of Title 48. The subject matter of rules contained in the fifty titles of the CFR is vast; any attempt at classification based on substance is not likely to improve on the categories found in it. The current index of the CFR's titles and chapters is included in the

TABLE 1-6 *Code of Federal Regulations* Page Count by Selected
Presidencies

President	*Average annual number of pages in the* Code of Federal Regulations			
	At start of presidency	*At end of presidency*	*Difference in number*	*% change*
Carter	72,308	102,195	29,887	41.3
Reagan	102,195	117,480	15,285	14.9
Bush I	117,285	128,344	11,059	9.4
Clinton	128,344	138,049	9,705	7.5
Bush II	138,049	157,974	19,925	14.4

Source: Office of the Federal Register and *Code of Federal Regulations.*

appendix. Table 1-6 charts the growth of the CFR during each presidency from Carter through Bush II, providing more evidence that rulemaking was and remains a potent source of law and policy.

Functions Performed by Rules

There are alternative ways to look at the total body of rules that convey other important dimensions of their status, purpose, and effect on our society. The oldest method for classifying rules is suggested in the definition cited earlier from the Administrative Procedure Act of 1946. The first and most important category consists of "legislative" or "substantive" rules. These are instances when, by congressional mandate or authorization, agencies write what amounts to new law. In the terms of the APA definition, legislative rules "prescribe" law and policy.

A second category consists of "interpretive" rules. As suggested earlier, these occur when agencies are compelled to explain to the public how they interpret existing law and policy. Although interpretive rules may stretch law or rules to fit new or unanticipated circumstances, they do not impose new legal obligations.[40] A good example of this type of rule is the "Uniform Guidelines on Employee Selection," issued by the Equal Employment Opportunity Commission in conjunction with other agencies that have responsibilities for enforcing Title VII of the 1972 Civil Rights Act.[41] Like all interpretive rules, these guidelines were intended to advise the public how the agencies interpreted their legal obligations under the act and assorted court cases that it had stimulated. The agencies issued interpretive rules in this case because civil rights was one of the few areas of statutory development in the 1960s and 1970s in which Congress failed to grant authority to write legislative rules. Because they are advisory in nature, interpretive rules can be developed in any way the agency sees fit, but they are generally published in the *Federal Register.*

The third category consists of "procedural" rules that define the organization and processes of agencies. Although they are often regarded as little more than bureaucratic housekeeping, they do deal with matters of importance to the public. Among other things, they inform the public how they can participate in a range of agency decision making, including rulemaking. As we will see in the next chapter, external forces have taken much of the initiative in the rulemaking process away from agencies. Nevertheless, procedural rules provide essential road maps for those attempting to find their way around the decision-making pathways of our massive and complex bureaucracies.

This way of classifying rules actually predates the APA by many years. Studies of administrative processes in federal agencies conducted in the 1930s refer repeatedly to these different types of rules and suggest that the distinctions had been commonly understood for some time.[42] The distinctions are still important. Many agencies, for example, still use variations on interpretive rules to supplement legislative rules. These come in a variety of forms—guidelines, policy statements, technical manuals—and some suspect that agencies use them to avoid the procedural rigors of legislative rulemaking.[43]

What and Whom Rules Affect

Another way to consider the body of rules is to classify them by the segment of our society they influence and direct. Some rules deal with private behavior. Others guide those individuals, groups, or firms that are approaching the government to obtain a payment, a service, or permission to engage in some activity. Finally, there are rules that deal with the way the government conducts its business. Most if not all rules can be placed in one of these three categories.

Rules for Private Behavior. One good way to appreciate the scope of rules directed at the private sector is to consider how they might affect a business.[44] Quite literally, rules govern American businesses from their very beginning to beyond their demise. Virtually every business decision of any substance is affected by rules written in government agencies. Rules can have a determining effect on the decision to go into business in the first place. Before one enters certain businesses or occupations, a license is required. The granting of a license, the qualifications needed to obtain one, and the conditions that are attached to it are determined by rules. Money is needed to start most businesses, and banks are often the providers. Banking rules determine in large part the availability of funds and the manner in which financial institutions make business loans. Assuming the owners of the business are prudent, they will want to protect their business from claims of damage arising from negligence or faulty products. Insurance regulations will determine whether they can get coverage and what it will cost.

Where a business is located is not a decision that can be made without reference to rules. Environmental and zoning rules have a significant influence on where businesses are established. Companies whose operations substantially pollute the air and water may find it difficult to locate in areas where rules set tight limits on new sources of pollution. The zoning authorities of local areas use rules to implement land-use plans that restrict, sometimes severely, where new businesses can locate.

Once the decision to go into business is made and a location is selected, rules may affect who is employed and how they are treated by the new concern. If the firm expects to do business with the federal government, it will be required, under a variety of rules, to have an affirmative action program. Those doing no government business must still take care not to discriminate in hiring. The "Uniform Guidelines on Employee Selection," mentioned earlier, provide direction to employers in this area. These guidelines affect virtually all employment decisions, from initial interviewing of candidates to termination of those who fail to meet expectations.

What a new business produces and how that product is made are governed by a multiplicity of rules, some designed to protect workers, others to protect consumers, and still others to protect the environment. Industrial operations are constrained by rules that are designed to ensure safety in the workplace and to prevent or minimize pollution of the air, water, and land. These rules frequently specify the types of equipment that can and cannot be used and how the machinery is to be designed or operated. The service sector is similarly affected by rules that govern how it will operate. The energy, banking, insurance, securities, transportation, and even education sectors are governed by industry-specific rules that dictate finances, employee qualifications, service quality, and even internal management.

Once the business has a product to sell, rules may determine how it will be sold, how it will get to consumers, the price that is charged for the good or service, and the company's obligations after it has been bought. The potential consumers of goods and services are protected by rules intended to prevent deceptive advertising. Other rules require that information be provided, on labels or packaging inserts, informing the public about the content, purpose, and potential hazards of consumer products. Rules written to regulate airlines, railroads, trucks, telecommunications, pipelines, and electricity transmission facilities profoundly affect how and at what cost goods and services get in the hands of consumers. Some commodities and services are still affected by rate making done by agencies. Agricultural commodities and energy transmission are two major areas of the economy where rules directly or indirectly set the price that consumers will pay. Once a good is sold, rules establish the producer's obligations. Rules can require that products, such as automobiles, be recalled by the manufacturer if defects are found that threaten safety or environmental quality. Similarly, rules outline the types of information consumers should have regarding warranties provided by the manufacturer or vendor of products should the product or service they purchase fail to provide what was promised.

Rules determine the conditions under which a firm can go out of business. Here two types of rules are notable. One governs the ongoing obligations that firms and businesses have to their retirees. Under the Employee Retirement Income Security Act (ERISA), rules have been developed to secure the pension rights of retirees even when a firm decides to go out of business. We need not belabor the importance of these protections in light of the devastating effects of corporate failures and corruption. The rules written under laws governing the disposal of hazardous waste also carry obligations for companies to clean up the mess they might otherwise leave behind, and try to forget, after they cease operations.

How Rules Affect Private Behavior. When considering rules that affect private parties it is also useful to think of the kinds of requirements they contain. Although the scope of government activity is virtually limitless, the instruments at the disposal of agencies to accomplish these varied tasks are not. We can observe many common instruments in rules of agencies with profoundly different missions, clienteles, and resources.

A relatively infrequent but nonetheless significant instrument is outright prohibition of certain substances, products, or activities. The number of rules that include unconditional prohibitions is comparatively small, but these rules attract considerable attention because of the consequences to affected parties and society at large. Recall the hue and cry that accompanied the 1970 ban on cyclamates, which had been used to sweeten soft drinks, and other actions that took suspected carcinogens off the market. Agencies with responsibilities to protect the traveling public impose prohibitions on key personnel working for airlines, railroads, and interstate buses. Frightening reminders of the need for these types of rules occurred in 1990 by the criminal prosecution of two Northwest Airlines pilots charged with violating the

Federal Aviation Administration's ban on alcohol consumption during the twenty-four-hour period prior to takeoff; and in 2002 of two America West pilots, who, suspected of being under the influence, were called back from a runway on which they were about to take off. A much more recent and troubling example involved two distracted pilots who, in 2009, flew over their intended destination and were out of contact with air traffic controllers while they discussed their airline's corporate policies. Each lost his license to fly.[45] There are rules prohibiting certain types of advertising, such as the ban on television ads for cigarettes. Other rules proscribe activities on wild and scenic rivers, national parks, and wilderness areas. Rules governing benefit programs prohibit recipients from engaging in certain types of activities. Various types of political action are off limits to the recipients of some federal grants and contracts.

More common than outright prohibitions are rules that place limitations on substances, products, and activities. Most of us have heard of, and have probably been revolted by, the rather disgusting forms of foreign matter that can find their way into processed foods. Hundreds of environmental regulations impose limits on the production of and exposures to toxic substances of various kinds and uses. The Occupational Safety and Health Administration has struggled since its creation to set limits on the amounts of certain types of chemicals that are potentially harmful to workers. The ordeal of setting standards for occupational exposure to the chemical benzene spanned more than a decade. The crisis in the savings and loan industry in the 1980s, the home mortgage industry more recently, and the shakiness of banks focused attention on rules of various agencies that limit the high-risk investments these types of institutions can make. The FAA places limits on the number of hours airplane pilots and attendants can work. Perhaps the most common form of rule is the one that sets standards for products and activities. Limits and standards are different versions of the same instrument of government control. They allow the private sector to do what it wants, but only within certain boundaries.

The importance of these boundaries was brought home by the serial revelations of massive misrepresentations of corporate earnings and profits. Enron, WorldCom, Global Crossing, and other such companies may be fading from memory. But the activities of banks and financial institutions and their products that brought our and other economies to the verge of depression are not. Rulemaking related to these dangers has just begun.

A common form of rule that serves as an adjunct to regulations that prohibit, impose limits, or set standards is the one that establishes information requirements. It is increasingly common for rules to contain requirements that private individuals, groups, and firms collect, analyze, retain, and report information about their activities. Information rules provide agencies an unparalleled mechanism for monitoring the behavior of persons who fall under their programs. In some instances, programs could not be managed and requirements could not be enforced if agencies were required to develop these data on their own. Labels, package inserts, requirements to conduct tests and report the results, and rules requiring recipients of government assistance or licensees to report periodically are all forms of information rules on which the integrity and success of many government programs depend.

Rules for Those Who Approach the Government. Private individuals, groups, or firms approach the government for many reasons, but usually to obtain a payment or service or to gain permission to conduct an activity that requires official sanctioning of some sort. The types of rules that apply in such circumstances establish the criteria for eligibility to receive the assistance or benefit offered under a government program. Social security programs of various sorts, welfare, medical care, educational assistance, housing benefits, and a host of other public programs operate on the basis of these eligibility rules.

A substantial number of activities conducted by private individuals, groups, or firms require various forms of permission from the government. Licenses and permits are required for a wide variety of activities, ranging from operating nuclear power plants to flying airplanes. When requesting licenses or permits, individuals must meet the standards set in rules. For example, the applicant for a license to operate a hydroelectric power plant must demonstrate that he or she can meet financial, engineering, and environmental standards established by the responsible agency, in this case the Federal Energy Regulatory Commission.[46]

Rules for Government. Purely governmental activities are guided by rules as well. These are—broadly defined—the procedural rules mentioned earlier. The *Code of Federal Regulations* has titles devoted to the management of government accounts, administrative personnel, administration of the judicial branch, public contracts and property management, and the acquisition of goods and services. In addition, the other titles of the CFR contain procedural rules that apply to the operation of individual programs. These detail, among other things, how the agency intends to comply with laws governing public and private information, how agency hearings and other proceedings involving the public will be conducted, and who within the agency has authority to make various types of decisions.

Two statutes, the Freedom of Information Act and the Privacy Act, require agencies to issue regulations about how and why information is being used. Under the Freedom of Information Act, the agency must explain to members of the public how they can obtain information. The Privacy Act requires the agency to describe personal information it has collected and is holding, how people can get access to records that agencies maintain on them, and how personal information is being protected from unwarranted disclosure.

We see, then, that the targets of rules include the private and public sectors. Whether regulated entities or potential beneficiaries of the federal government's largesse, individuals, groups, firms, states, and local governments must look to rules for refinements of their rights and obligations and for procedures by which the programs with which they are concerned will operate. The vast range and diversity of subject matter that rules now touch have been mentioned. It is also important to note the remarkable variations in the complexity of rules, the numbers of persons or activities they affect, and the duration of their effects.

Differences in Scope and Importance. Most rules published in the *Federal Register* are brief and deal with a very narrow range of activities. They may be based on complex technical or scientific information, such as regulations issued by the Federal Communications Commission to allocate radio frequency bands to individual stations and the Federal Aviation Administration rules dealing with flight paths at airports. Other rules, fewer in number, are enormously long and complex and cover vast areas. But the length of the rule is not always an accurate indicator of the rule's effects. An "airworthiness directive," the type of rule the FAA issues to correct potential safety problems on aircraft, will affect every person who flies on the affected planes. Similarly, an "agricultural marketing order" that limits the amount of a commodity that can be shipped to sellers will affect every consumer who buys the affected vegetable or fruit. Both types of rules usually take up no more than a single page in the *Federal Register.*

Rules, then, vary greatly in their purpose and significance. Why do we rely on them for so much law and policy?

The Reasons for Rulemaking: What It Has to Offer

However they are categorized and classified, rules accomplish most of the ambitious goals we set for ourselves as a society. Up to now we have discussed rulemaking as a constant force in our political and legal history and as an inescapable contemporary reality. But this history inevitably requires further explanation. Rulemaking has the place it does in our system of government for many reasons.

The number and diversity of rules written in this country are evidence that rulemaking is, at least, a common form of government decision making. We have not yet fully explored why rulemaking has attained so central a position in the policy process. In general, it has achieved its prominence because of the contributions it makes to the conduct of government and the benefits it provides, as described in the next sections. But it also has disadvantages.

The Capacity of Bureaucracy and the Limits of the Legislature

If we examine the body of laws enacted by Congress, it is immediately apparent that those laws touch virtually every aspect of human life. Consequently, every known professional discipline must be drawn upon for the knowledge needed to achieve its ambitious goals. This range and depth of expertise have never been present among members of Congress or the staff that supports legislative operations. Congressional staffs are large and diverse but still limited. Many staffers are concerned with matters other than crafting new legislation, such as the constituency-related work that is so close to the hearts of elected officials. Committee staffs and those in the Government Accountability Office are preoccupied with oversight, the importance of which is magnified by the way Congress writes law. More about this in a moment.

In the Progressive Era there was faith in the neutral competence of a professionalized bureaucracy. The public had confidently expected bureaucrats to carry out the will of the people efficiently and effectively.[47] However diminished, this confidence, combined with the principle of separation of powers, has provided considerable justification for Congress to rely on rulemaking to supplement legislation rather than attempt to enact laws that answer all questions and anticipate all circumstances associated with a new program. In one view, since it is the task of the executive branch in our constitutional system to see that the law is carried out, bureaucracies, as instrumentalities of the executive branch, can be expected to clarify what the law means and take the steps necessary to ensure that its goals are achieved. Our laws require the constant application of knowledge and expertise to varied conditions and circumstances, so it makes sense to concentrate specialists in the administrative agencies that execute them rather than in the legislature.

This view begs the fundamental constitutional question of who writes the law. We saw that under the APA definition the term *rule* can have many different meanings. Each has different implications for lawmaking. When a rule merely "implements" a law, there is no constitutional dilemma, because it will restate, perhaps in more functional language, what Congress has already enacted. When a rule "interprets" legislation, the rulemaking activity may be more substantial, bordering on lawmaking. But here there is no pretension of making new law. Rather, the agency is answering questions that have arisen about the law's reach and meaning in particular instances. It is when a rule "prescribes" law that conflict between the constitutional roles of the executive and the legislature is most evident.

The depth of concern about rulemaking hinges to a considerable extent on whether agencies are agents of the legislature or the executive branch. If bureaucracies are merely extensions of Congress, then we should be no more alarmed by rulemaking than we are by reports that congressional staff members play a vital role in drafting statutes. If, however, these agencies are properly viewed as extensions of the president, then their exercise of substantial rulemaking powers threatens the constitutional design. But the question of who runs the bureaucracy is by no means settled; Congress and the president have long struggled to gain the hearts and minds of bureaucrats.[48] Both have formidable powers at their disposal to influence the course of bureaucratic decision making. The president prepares budgets, appoints senior officials, and issues executive orders that profoundly affect how agencies manage their work. Congress is the ultimate decision maker on budgets and appointments, conducts oversight and investigations, and engages in casework on behalf of constituents. In the battle for influence over the bureaucracy, congressional powers are at least as substantial as those of the president. Congressional power to define an agency's mission and fix its budget is more determinative than the transitory and fragmented sources of presidential influence. Therefore, when delegating the power to interpret and prescribe law, Congress does it in the secure knowledge that it retains sufficient power and opportunity to redirect rulemakings that go astray. We will examine control of rulemaking through oversight in Chapter 6.

Expertise situated in a constitutionally acceptable relationship to Congress is not the sole reason why rulemaking by agencies is beneficial. One of the great advantages of rulemaking by agencies is their ability to respond in a timely manner to unanticipated and changed conditions, most especially emergencies. Agency officials who administer and enforce programs may be the first to learn that an existing program is flawed in some way, or that conditions affecting the program, or conditions that programs are intended to affect, have changed significantly. As James Landis wrote in 1938, "The Administrative [process] is always in session."[49]

A good illustration of this capacity is evident in the rulemaking of the Federal Aviation Administration. Through its inspection and regulatory enforcement programs, the FAA regularly discovers problems in the design, operation, or maintenance of airplanes. Some of these problems are trivial;

others pose serious threats to the flying public. The organization of the FAA allows for swift communication from the field staff to those in the Washington headquarters that a new rule is required. For example, should a review of maintenance records or a series of inspections reveal excessive corrosion in the fan blades of a particular type of jet engine, the FAA technical staff can decide how serious the problem is, the steps that must be taken to correct the problem without endangering passengers and crew, and how quickly these actions should be taken. The rule in this case is the "airworthiness directive," mentioned earlier, hundreds of which the FAA issues each year.

Consider the same situation without rulemaking. To establish the new obligations borne by manufacturers or carriers for their jet engines, an amendment to the existing statute would be required. For such an amendment to come to pass, the information would have to work its way up the FAA organization and be communicated to the appropriate House and Senate subcommittees; legislation would have to be drafted; hearings would have to be held; votes would have to be taken in subcommittee, full committee, and the floors of both houses; possibly conference committee deliberations and another round of votes would be required; and then the president would have to sign the legislation. If real danger existed, a tragedy could occur long before action of this sort was completed. Those of us who are averse to risk are especially so when we step through the doors of an aircraft being readied for takeoff. Rulemaking to those flyers is a godsend.

Rulemaking supplements the legislative process in another significant way. Subsequent chapters will demonstrate that the waves of interest in public participation that swept through public administration since the 1960s affected rulemaking. It is not surprising that the proponents of increased public involvement in the decisions of agencies would focus on a function as crucial as the development of rules. Rulemaking adds opportunities for and dimensions to public participation that are rarely present in the deliberations of Congress or other legislatures. It is often difficult for interested parties to determine exactly what a bill under consideration means to them. The more vague the proposed provisions, the more difficult it is for the public to decide whether participation is worth the effort and, if so, what position to take.

In rulemaking the decisions regarding participation become much clearer because the issues are better defined, the actions the government is contemplating are more specific, and the implications for affected parties are much easier to predict. Positions are thus easier to formulate and articulate. There are many ways for the public to get involved in rulemaking and to influence the content of rules. The cost of effective participation in rulemaking may be lower, and the chances of success in rulemaking greater than those that confront the public during legislative deliberations.

A Means of Containing Administrative Discretion

Rulemaking is an important tool in limiting the power and discretion of bureaucrats. Since the mid-twentieth century the growing power of the bureaucracy has been viewed by many with considerable alarm. Armed with vast but poorly defined authority delegated to them by Congress, bureaucrats are seen as able to exercise discretionary powers that threaten the rights and security of individuals.[50] Many critics have claimed that administrative officials with the power to deny or rescind benefits and licenses, impose regulatory requirements and sanctions, and force the reporting of all types of information do so without adequate standards to guide them and to protect the public. But rulemaking is a potential remedy for the unchecked abusive bureaucratic discretion.

Some discretion is essential if the administrative process is to operate effectively, efficiently, and fairly. In his highly influential book *Discretionary Justice,* Kenneth Culp Davis acknowledged this but concluded that "our ... systems are saturated with excessive discretionary power which needs to be confined, structured and checked."[51] The problem, he argued, was not the then-common prescription that Congress and other legislative bodies work harder to specify limits in legislation. "Legislative bodies do about as much as they reasonably can do in specifying the limits on delegated power," he stated. And he was quite specific about the tool in which he placed the most faith: "Altogether, the chief hope for confining discretionary power does not lie in statutory enactments but in much more extensive administrative rulemaking, and legislative bodies need to do more than they have been doing to prod the administrators."[52]

Whether Congress heard this plea is unclear, but it certainly acted as if it had. Professor Davis was writing at the threshold of the 1970s, the so-called "era of rulemaking." The statutes since expressed a clear preference for rulemaking as a device for administering the programs they created. Many mandated rulemaking and added deadlines on agencies for completing this work. Although they are often viewed from the perspective of the private citizen or firm whose behavior is constrained, rules control agencies and bureaucrats as well. Rules set limits on the authority of public officials in all areas of their work, identifying what they can know, how they can learn it, when they must act, what they must do, when they must do it, and actions they can take against those who fail to comply. A violation of rules puts the bureaucrat no less at risk than the private scofflaw. Fears of unfettered discretion in the hands of willful or ignorant bureaucrats are largely unfounded in a system in which citizens can trust that rulemaking will occur subsequent to any legislative enactment and set effective and reasonable limits on the use of discretionary power. Again, this is not to say that rulemaking is the font of wisdom and uniform success for public programs. Like most human activities, it is beset with problems. But rulemaking clearly provides advantages over the legislative process, which is overloaded with demands for action but impeded by shortages of time and expertise. There are reasons other than these institutional considerations why rulemaking has assumed a position of such importance in our government system: It serves the interests of the most powerful players in our public policy process.

Rulemaking and Self-Interest

In all matters determined by politics the self-interest of the major participants is a major determinant. Rulemaking is certainly no exception. Its other advantages notwithstanding, rulemaking delivers clear benefits to the main actors in our political system. Consider what rulemaking provides Congress, the president, the judiciary, interest groups, state and local governments, and the bureaucracy itself.

Congress. By resorting to widespread delegation of legislative power to the rulemaking process, Congress both frees and indemnifies itself. Rather than spending all their available time in drafting, debating, and refining statutes, members of Congress are free to engage in other activities, like getting reelected. Of course, rulemaking promotes reelection in more ways than just generating free time. If we examine contemporary statutes, it is clear that members of Congress are routinely faced with the legislative equivalent of a catch-22. Squeezed by powerful and contending interests—environmentalists and industry, workers and management, program beneficiaries and taxpayers—members of Congress realize that their votes on very specific legislative proposals that clearly identify winners and losers can erode support or foster outright opposition. As others have noted, this provides powerful incentives for Congress to remain vague, leaving the specific, painful, and politically dangerous decisions to the agencies.

Congressional self-interest is served by rulemaking for reasons other than the "responsibility avoidance" that accompanies the delegation of authority.[53] Congress remains free to intervene in ongoing rulemakings and to review completed rules using a variety of devices that will be discussed presently. Some of these devices allow members to perform services to individual constituents, an always-popular reelection activity.

Presidents. It took a long time for presidents to learn how to make the most of it, but rulemaking provides extraordinary opportunities to influence the direction and content of American public policy. President Reagan instituted changes that gave the White House the power to review and influence all rules written by federal agencies. Viewed from one perspective, this reform gave the president a new weapon in the ongoing struggle with Congress to define public policy. In a period of divided government, presidential management of the rulemaking process is especially significant. Because it is based in the White House, it avoids some of the perennial problems presidents have had in gaining control of their own executive machinery in departments and agencies. With the power of review, even presidents who take a dim view of big government and regulation will favor controlled use of rulemaking, since it allows them to influence the full range of public policy in a manner that does not directly entail negotiations with Congress.

Judges. Although it is less common to think of the judiciary as dominated by self-interest, there is no question that at least some judges relish an active role in the public policy process, and that most hold strong views on the proper scope and channels for government action. As an opportunity for the exercise of authority and power by the courts, rulemaking makes it much easier for judges to supervise and impose their will on the operations of bureaucracies. This is true whether judges seek to impose their personal beliefs about law and policy or the more common situation when attempting to meet the obligations of the judicial branch in the political system.

Clearly articulated rules offer judges an efficient way to review and determine agencies' stewardship of the law and public policy. When lawsuits challenge the results of rulemaking, judges are able to evaluate the content of a rule to determine whether it is consistent with the statutes from which they derive their sole claim to authority and legitimacy. Furthermore, judges can review the process by which rules were developed to determine if the obligations to allow for meaningful participation and to conduct required analyses were met. Judges have developed numerous devices to correct deficiencies in the substance or development process of the rules they review. Many of these vest in the judges themselves the equivalent of supervisory power over rulemaking, giving them the potential for great influence over the ultimate content of laws and policies. Other forms of administrative action, notably case-by-case decision making, are theoretically as susceptible to judicial review but are labor intensive in the extreme. Given the limited resources of the judiciary, review of rules is by far the more cost-effective path for judges to pursue personal power and institutional influence, or merely to fulfill their constitutional responsibilities.

Interest Groups. Interest groups could find few modes of government decision making better suited to their particular strengths than rulemaking. Here and throughout the book, *interest group* will refer to organizations of any sort, including individual companies that attempt to influence the decisions of government. Their size, longevity, and issues of interest are not important. Because rulemaking is specialized it allows these groups to focus their attention and use their resources to influence decisions they know will affect their members. As we have already noted, rulemaking often requires a considerable amount of substantive (often technical) information. Agencies are rarely in possession of all the information or insights they require to write sound, defensible rules. Frequently, interest groups and the individuals or firms they represent have ready access to the information that agencies need. This gives such groups a considerable amount of leverage in the development of rules. Unlike legislative deliberations, in which political considerations frequently overwhelm or obscure operational issues and technical details, the outcome of rulemaking often hinges on the amount and quality of information available, which is a stock-in-trade for interest groups.

State and Local Governments. The explosion of rulemaking that began in the late 1960s and has continued ever since is of great consequence to state and local governments. Not only are they affected directly—becoming, in effect, regulated parties under environmental, workplace safety, equal employment, and other programs—they also have become more active rulemakers in their own right. Many statutes allow states to be the primary rulemaker as long as their rules are at least as strict as those developed by the federal agency with primary jurisdiction for the program. Thus, state and local governments cannot avoid federal rulemaking, and they must await its results before exercising their own rulemaking powers. Because of these powers, state and local governments can have considerable influence over the federal rulemaking process simply by virtue of what they might do subsequently. For example, if state agencies are selected to enforce or otherwise implement rules, federal rulemakers must be attentive to their needs and preferences. Even when states and localities do not write rules, they are often responsible for enforcing the federal ones. By successfully influencing the content of federal rules, state and local governments can ease the burdens of subsequent implementation.

Bureaucrats. An equivocal position on rulemaking by bureaucrats would not be surprising. For many agencies, rulemaking represents a daunting workload that curtails their discretion and exposes them to scrutiny and pressure from Congress, the president, courts, and interest groups. Such a situation would seem sufficiently unattractive to put off even the most mildly self-interested bureaucrat. Although some may consider it nothing more than an unavoidable chore, rulemaking does bring certain benefits to at least some bureaucrats. Those "zealots" identified four decades ago by Anthony Downs, a scholar of bureaucratic behavior, have in rulemaking the possibility of putting their indelible mark on public policy and law. His "climbers" find rulemaking presents an excellent opportunity to advance careers in and out of the agency. The author of a major rule gets considerable visibility in an agency and may become marketable on the outside. Even Downs's "conserver," who avoids risk in favor of a more predictable existence, sees in rules the opportunity to stabilize and regularize the working environment.[54]

In short, rulemaking has something for every key institution and actor in our political system. For this reason alone we should expect it to be a permanent feature of the way we govern ourselves.

The objective of this first chapter was to convince the reader that rulemaking is a significant government function that has, since the start of the Republic, played an increasingly pivotal role in the definition of American public policy and law. In the hope that this case has been made, the next task is to explain how rules are written. The process of rulemaking has been evolving since the enactment of the first statute that delegated the authority to develop rules to the first president. Today it can be highly complex. The way it is conducted has important implications for the nation's well-being and the functioning of our democracy. It is to the process of rulemaking that we turn next.

Notes

1. American Recovery and Reinvestment Act of 2009, Public Law 111-5.
2. Department of the Treasury, Press Room, "Interim Final Rules on TARP Standards for Compensation and Corporate Governance," www.treas.gov/press/release/tg165.htm.
3. Colin Diver, "Regulatory Precision," in *Making Regulatory Policy,* ed. Keith Hawkins and John Thomas (Pittsburgh: University of Pittsburgh Press, 1989), p. 199.
4. 5 United States Code 551 (4) (hereafter cited as U.S.C.).
5. For discussion of these instruments of presidential power, see Phillip J. Cooper, *By Order of the President: The Use and Abuse of Executive Direct Action* (Lawrence: University Press of Kansas, 2002).
6. Charles Levine, B. Guy Peters, and Frank Thompson, *Public Administration: Challenges, Choices, Consequences* (Glenview, Ill.: Scott Foresman/Little, Brown, 1990), p. 99.
7. One scholar would argue that this broad definition is just an example of the APA's rulemaking provisions in which "Congress' delegation of vast lawmaking power was acknowledged and legitimated." See Martin Shapiro, "APA: Past, Present, Future," *Virginia Law Review* 72 (1986): 453.
8. 29 U.S.C. 553, 651–678.
9. Florence Heffron and Neil McFeeley, *The Administrative Regulatory Process* (New York: Longman, 1983), p. 152.
10. Stephen Breyer and Richard Stewart, *Administrative Law and Regulatory Policy,* 2nd ed. (Boston: Little, Brown, 1985), pp. 466–467.

11. Ibid. The relation between rules and future effects has been accepted in the literature for a long time. See Ralph Fuchs, "Procedures in Administrative Rulemaking," *Harvard Law Review* 52 (1938): 261.

12. As James O'Reilly puts it, "Rules are as old as the republic." See O'Reilly, *Administrative Rulemaking* (Colorado Springs, Colo.: Shepard's/McGraw-Hill, 1983), p. 4.

13. Gary Bryner, *Bureaucratic Discretion: Law and Policy in Federal Regulatory Agencies* (New York: Pergamon, 1987), p. 10.

14. Attorney General's Committee on Administrative Procedure, Administrative Procedure in Government Agencies, S. Doc. 8, 77th Cong., 1st sess., 1941, p. 97. Hereafter cited as Attorney General's Committee.

15. Ibid.

16. Ibid.

17. David Rosenbloom, "Public Law and Regulation," in *Handbook of Public Administration*, ed. Jack Rubin, Bartley Hildreth, and Gerald Miller (New York: Marcel Dekker, 1989), pp. 544–545.

18. See Attorney General's Committee, p. 98, at n. 17.

19. Many sources cover the historical development of public policy in the areas mentioned in the text. Various authors consider successive "eras" of growth and diversification in public policy, regulation, and rulemaking. An accessible list of major statutes that established programs and authorities for a wide variety of agencies that issue rules can be found in the *Federal Regulatory Directory,* 14th ed. (Washington, D.C.: CQ Press, 2010).

20. Ernest Gellhorn and Barry Boyer, *Administrative Law and Process in a Nutshell,* 2nd ed. (St. Paul, Minn.: West Publishing, 1982), p. 17.

21. Rosenbloom, "Public Law and Regulation," pp. 553–555.

22. Phillip J. Cooper, *Public Law and Public Administration* (Palo Alto, Calif.: Mayfield, 1983), p. 75. In a subsequent chapter we will review Supreme Court decisions that invalidated much of the legislative basis for the New Deal. Although these cases hinged on perceived defects in the NIRA, the way agencies conducted rulemaking and other program functions was prominent in the Court's opinions.

23. Ibid.

24. Attorney General's Committee, part 7, Department of the Interior, p. 57, and part 10, Bituminous Coal Division, Department of the Interior, pp. 12–13.

25. Ibid., part 19, Veterans Affairs.

26. Ibid., part 11, Interstate Commerce Commission, p. 67.

27. Ibid., p. 99.

28. Attorney General's Committee, part 3, Social Security Board, p. 23.

29. William F. West, "The Politics of Administrative Rulemaking," *Public Administration Review,* September/October 1982, pp. 421–423.

30. Susan Estreicher, "Policy Oscillation at the Labor Board: A Plea for Rulemaking," *Administrative Law Review* 37 (1985): 163.

31. This summary of legislation draws on material found in Rosenbloom, "Evolution of the Administrative State," in *Handbook of Public Administration,* pp. 563–564, and the *Federal Regulatory Directory.*

32. Antonin Scalia, "Making Law without Making Rules," *Regulation,* July/August 1982, p. 25.

33. Theodore Lowi, "Two Roads to Serfdom: Liberalism, Conservatism, and Administrative Power," *American University Law Review* 36 (1987): 298.

34. A. Lee Fritschler, "The Changing Face of Government Regulation," in *Federal Administrative Agencies,* ed. Howard Ball (Englewood Cliffs, N.J.: Prentice Hall, 1984); Bryner, *Bureaucratic Discretion,* p. 13.
35. Bryner, *Bureaucratic Discretion,* p. 13.
36. These data were provided by the Office of Federal Register.
37. See, for example, Harvey Lieber, *Federalism and Clean Waters* (Boston: Lexington Books, 1974).
38. Arthur Bonfield, *State Administrative Rule Making* (Boston: Little, Brown, 1986), pp. 19–20.
39. Jerry Mashaw, "Improving the Environment of Agency Rulemaking: An Essay on Management, Games, and Legal and Political Accountability," report to the Administrative Conference of the United States, August 1992; Thomas McGarrity, "Some Thoughts on Deossifying the Rulemaking Process," *Duke Law Journal* 41 (1992): 1385–1462; Robert Anthony, "Interpretive Rules, Policy Statements, Guidances, Manuals, and the Like— Should Agencies Use Them to Bind the Public?" *Duke Law Journal* 41 (1992): 1311–1384.
40. Anthony, "Interpretative Rules," p. 1312.
41. 29 CFR, part 1607.
42. Attorney General's Committee, p. 100.
43. Anthony, "Interpretive Rules."
44. The effects of government rules and regulations on American businesses are summarized in a large number of texts and reports. See, for example, Murray Weidenbaum, *Business, Government, and the Public,* 4th ed. (New York: Prentice Hall, 1990).
45. "Northwest Pilots Are Found Guilty of Drunken Flying," *New York Times,* August 21, 1990; "America West Fires Pilots Accused of Drinking," July 3, 2002, www.cnn.com; Mike Ahrens, "Pilots of Wayward Jet Lose Licenses," October 27, 2009, www.cnn.com.
46. Cornelius M. Kerwin, "Transforming Regulation," *Public Administration Review* 50 (January/February 1990): 91–100.
47. See Marver Bernstein, *Regulating Business by Independent Commission* (Princeton: Princeton University Press, 1955).
48. There are many treatments of the struggle between the White House and Capitol Hill for control of the bureaucracy. See, for example, Louis Fisher, *The Politics of Shared Power,* 3rd ed. (Washington, D.C.: CQ Press, 1993), chap. 4, and James A. Thurber, *Rivals for Power* (Washington, D.C.: CQ Press, 1996).
49. James Landis, *The Administrative Process* (New Haven: Yale University Press, 1938), p. 69.
50. Lowi, "Two Roads to Serfdom."
51. Kenneth Culp Davis, *Discretionary Justice: A Preliminary Inquiry* (Urbana: University of Illinois Press, 1969), p. 27.
52. Ibid., p. 55.
53. Morris Fiorina, "Legislative Choice of Regulatory Forms: Legal Process or Administrative Process," *Public Choice* 39 (1982): 46–47.
54. Anthony Downs, *Inside Bureaucracy* (Boston: Little, Brown, 1967), chap. 9.

CHAPTER 2

The Process of Rulemaking

Return with us now to one of those countless times you have found yourself driving behind a large truck. A sign on its rear with a familiar diamond shape and markings triggers the recognition that you are sharing the roadway with something dangerous. As you strain to make out the message of the sign, you goose the accelerator to get a bit closer. You are attracted to those hurtling explosives, corrosives, or combustibles like a moth to a flame. Finally you can read the dire warning and it says, "Drive Gently: Have a Nice Day."

Empty tanker trucks with their banal messages notwithstanding, the amount of hazardous cargo transported on the road and rails, by water and air, and the dangers they pose are no joke. The volume is impossible to estimate, but we know that the government has established more than twenty different classes of dangerous cargo. The substances that fill these various categories number in the thousands. And we are routinely treated to the depressing sight of overturned tractor-trailers, punctured railroad cars, or tankers with gaping holes surrounded by emergency response personnel outfitted like something out of a low-budget science fiction film. The threat is real, and for over a century government has been attempting to deal with it.

With passage of the Explosives and Combustibles Act of 1908, the federal government assumed regulatory authority over dangerous substances and material moving through interstate commerce. The rules written to implement this legislation and the amendments to it that followed grew in number until 1994, when they filled 1,400 pages in the *Code of Federal Regulations*. Known collectively as the Hazardous Materials Regulations (HMR), these rules by the government's own admission have evolved incrementally and disjointedly, as noted in Figure 2-1; by the 1970s the rules were being roundly criticized for being too long, too complex, too difficult to use, and too hard to enforce.

The work of revising the HMR began sometime in 1981, and in April 1982 the first public notice that the Department of Transportation (DOT) was developing new regulations appeared in the *Federal Register*. The notice invited the public to comment on the new rules. Many supplemental public

FIGURE 2-1 Sample of the Hazardous Materials Regulations in the *Federal Register*

DEPARTMENT OF TRANSPORTATION

Research and Special Programs Administration

49 CFR Parts 107, 171, 172, 173, 174, 175, 176, 177, 178, and 179

[Docket Nos. HM-181, HM-181A, HM-181B, HM-181C, HM-181D and HM-204; Amdt. Nos. 107-23, 171-111, 172-123, 173-224, 174-68, 175-47, 176-30, 177-78, 178-97, and 179-45]

RIN 2137-AA01, 2137-AB87, 2137-AB88, 2137-AA10, and 2137-AB90

Performance-Oriented Packaging Standards; Changes to Classification, Hazard Communication, Packaging and Handling Requirements Based on UN Standards and Agency Initiative

AGENCY: Research and Special Programs Administration (RSPA), DOT.

ACTION: Final rule.

SUMMARY: This final rule comprehensively revises the Hazardous Materials Regulations (HMR; 49 CFR parts 171–180) with respect to hazard communication, classification and packaging requirements. The changes are based on the United Nations Recommendations on the Transport of Dangerous Goods (U.N. Recommendations) and RSPA's own initiative. They are made because the existing HMR are: (1) Difficult to use because of their length and complexity; (2) relatively inflexible and outdated with regard to non-bulk packaging technology; (3) deficient in terms of safety with regard to the classification and packaging of certain categories of hazardous materials; and, (4) generally not in alignment with international regulations based on the U.N. Recommendations. This action will: (1) Simplify and reduce the volume of the HMR; (2) enhance safety through better classification and packaging; (3) promote flexibility and technological innovation in packaging; (4) reduce the need for exemptions from the HMR; and (5) facilitate international commerce.

DATES: Effective October 1, 1991. However, compliance with the regulations as amended herein is authorized on and after January 1, 1991. The incorporation by reference of certain publications listed in these amendments is approved by the Director of the Federal Register as of October 1, 1991.

Petitions for reconsideration must be received on or before March 21, 1991.

ADDRESSES: Address comments and petitions for reconsideration to the Dockets Unit, Research and Special

Programs Administration, Department of Transportation, Washington, DC 20590-0001. Comments should identify the docket and be submitted in five copies. If confirmation of receipt is desired, include a self-addressed stamped postcard showing the docket number (i.e., Docket HM-181). The Dockets Unit is located in room 8421 of the Nassif Building, 400 Seventh Street SW., Washington, DC 20590-0001. Public dockets may be reviewed between the hours of 8:30 a.m. and 5 p.m., Monday through Friday, except holidays.

FOR FURTHER INFORMATION CONTACT: Delmer Billings, telephone (202) 366–4488, Office of Hazardous Materials Standards, or Charles Hochman, telephone (202) 366–4545, Office of Hazardous Materials Technology, U.S. Department of Transportation, 400 Seventh Street SW., Washington, DC 20590-0001.

SUPPLEMENTARY INFORMATION:

Special Notices

The amendments presented in this document entail changes, both editorial and substantive, to substantial portions of the existing HMR. In a rulemaking project of this magnitude it is inevitable that errors and omissions will come to light subsequent to publication. Comments addressed to such errors and omissions are requested, so that they may be corrected in future rulemaking action under this docket.

For this final rule, the 30-day limitation for the receipt of petitions for reconsideration (49 CFR 106.35) is hereby waived and 90 days is provided in consideration thereof.

Preamble Outline

I. Overview of the HMR
II. Problems with the HMR
III. The International System
IV. History of HM-181 Proposals
V. Related Rulemakings
VI. Major Features of the Final Rule
VII. Shipper/Manufacturer Responsibility
VIII. Transition Period
IX. Impact on Exemptions
X. Enforcement of Performance-oriented Packaging Standards
XI. Public Input to International Standards-Issuing Entities
XII. Section-by-section Review
  Preamble Outline
  A. Part 107
  B. Part 171
  C. Part 172
  D. Part 173
  E. Part 174
  F. Part 175
  G. Part 176
  H. Part 177
  I. Part 178
  J. Part 179
XIII. Administrative Notices
  A. Executive Order 12291
  B. Executive Order 12612
  C. Impact on Small Entities

D. Paperwork Reduction Act

I. Overview of the HMR

The Hazardous Materials Regulations (HMR) apply to the interstate (and in some cases intrastate) transportation of hazardous materials in commerce. They have their origins in the Explosives and Combustibles Act of 1908, originally administered by the Interstate Commerce Commission. The HMR are currently issued pursuant to the Hazardous Materials Transportation Act (HMTA) of 1974, administered by DOT, and are found in the Code of Federal Regulations (CFR), title 49, subtitle B, chapter 1, subchapter C, parts 171 through 180.

The HMR govern the safety aspects of transportation. They include requirements for classification of materials, packaging (including manufacture, continuing qualification and maintenance), hazard communication (i.e., package marking, labeling, placarding, and shipping documentation), transportation and handling, and incident reporting.

Subchapter C occupies approximately fourteen hundred pages of the CFR. The largest parts, part 173, entitled "Shippers—General Requirements for Shipments and Packagings," and part 178, entitled "Shipping Container Specifications, occupy about three hundred and fifty and four hundred and fifty pages, respectively.

Part 171 of the HMR includes definitions, reporting requirements, a listing of matter incorporated by reference, and procedural requirements, including provisions which permit use of other regulations, such as the ICAO Technical Instructions and the IMDG Code. Part 172 of the HMR contains a listing of hazardous materials in the Hazardous Materials Table (§ 172.101) and various communications requirements for shipping paper descriptions, marking and labeling of packages, placarding of vehicles and bulk packagings, and emergency response communication.

Part 173 contains various hazard class definitions for classifying materials, lists the DOT packagings authorized for specific materials and references the appropriate sections of part 178 when DOT specification packagings are required. Parts 174 through 177 contain requirements applicable to specific transport modes: Part 174 for transport by rail car, part 175 for transport by aircraft, part 176 for transport by vessel, and part 177 for transport by motor vehicle. Part 176 will now include provisions for the transportation of military explosives by vessel. These

FIGURE 2-1 *(continued)*

were previously contained in 46 CFR part 146, which is being revoked in a separate rulemaking.

Part 178, addressed primarily to container manufacturers, contains detailed construction specifications for a wide variety of packagings. The specification packagings found in part 178 range from paper bags to cargo tanks (tank trucks). The major portion of part 178 is devoted to non-bulk packagings (authorized capacities of 110 gallons or less) and includes approximately 100 specifications for carboys, drums, barrels, boxes, cases, trunks, tubes, bags and various sorts of inside containers or receptacles designed to be enclosed by larger containers. Not included in these 100 specifications are those covering cylinders for compressed gases and packagings designed solely for radioactive or explosive materials, none of which are addressed under this final rule.

Part 179 addresses specifications for tank cars. Part 180 contains requirements for the continuing qualification and maintenance of packagings.

Beginning with the creation of the Department of Transportation in 1967, the Department assumed responsibility for the HMR and embarked on a long-range effort to simplify and improve the regulations. In 1968, under Docket HM-7 [33 FR 11862; August 21, 1968], DOT stated its intent to revise the HMR to make them uniform for the various modes of transport and easy to understand and apply. DOT also stated it would improve hazard classification of materials to better describe their hazards and relate classification to appropriate handling and packaging designs, improve hazard communication through labeling, placarding and emergency response provisions, and prescribe packaging requirements in terms of performance standards rather than manufacturing specifications.

Major accomplishments of this effort to simplify and improve the HMR include adoption of labels and placards (1974) based on the United Nations Committee of Experts' Recommendations on the Transport of Dangerous Goods (U.N. Recommendations), development and widespread distribution of DOT's Emergency Response Guidebook, and adoption of identification numbers for hazardous materials (1980) based on the U.N. Recommendations. Numerous other rulemaking projects have addressed improvements to classification, hazard communication, and packaging. Docket HM-181 and related rulemaking projects represent the culmination of RSPA's

efforts since 1968 to improve the HMR and align them with an internationally-based performance standards system.

The importance of this rulemaking initiative has been recognized in the Department's National Transportation Policy which states that it is Federal transportation policy to:

• Adopt hazardous materials packaging standards that are based on performance criteria rather than detailed design specifications, to accommodate technical innovation, and

• Implement Federal hazardous materials standards for movements by the various modes that are, to the maximum extent consistent with safety, compatible with international standards, in order to facilitate foreign trade and maintain the competitiveness of U.S. goods.

II. Problems With the HMR

The development of the HMR has been an evolutionary process. Regulations originally were addressed only to the most acute transportation safety hazards such as the risks of explosives and flammable materials. As new materials presenting different risks entered the transportation system, new hazard classes were added. The HMR now address over 20 different classes of hazardous materials. Hazard communication and packaging requirements were added as the need arose, based on the occurrence of accidents or the development and adoption of industry standards. Packaging requirements were based on industry standards, with economic considerations sometimes taking precedence over safety considerations, rather than on a systematic assignment of packagings based on the hazards of the materials to be packaged and the suitability of the packaging. By the same token, hazard classifications were often made based on subjective criteria, with economic considerations occasionally taking precedence over safety considerations.

Because of the non-systematic and piecemeal fashion in which they were developed, the HMR tend to be unnecessarily complex and difficult to use. RSPA believes there is a need to amend the HMR to address deficiencies related to safety, complexity of the regulations, inflexibility of packaging standards and incongruities between the HMR and international regulations for hazardous materials transport.

With regard to safety, correct classification of materials is essential for determining the hazards posed, appropriate hazard communication, and packaging. Classification procedures in the HMR were developed in a piecemeal

fashion over an eighty-year period and tend to be imprecise and subjective. The classification scheme proposed in Docket HM-181, based in large part on the U.N. Recommendations, is more precise than the existing system and would replace subjective hazard class definitions with objective criteria, particularly with regard to gases which are toxic by inhalation and flammable solids. Other safety initiatives embodied in Docket HM-181 involve enhancements to general packaging provisions for both bulk and non-bulk packagings, and improvements to the integrity of packagings for extremely hazardous materials such as those which are poisonous by inhalation.

The HMR have long been criticized as being too lengthy (1400 pages), complex, and difficult to use and enforce. It is impossible to eliminate complexity in regulations which, of necessity, must address the legal, technical and operational concerns for classification, hazard communication and packaging for thousands of hazardous chemicals. However, a new format and use of performance standards rather than detailed design specifications will make the HMR more "user friendly" and substantially reduce the number of HMR pages.

With regard to packaging flexibility, the detailed design specifications which are found in the HMR are generally based on industry standards, many of which were incorporated into the regulations in the 1920's and 1930's. They tend to be overly specific and are outdated in many respects, thereby stifling innovation and resulting in the need for numerous burdensome exemptions. Authorizations to use specific packagings for specific hazardous materials were often made based on economic considerations, operating convenience or historical precedence, rather than by assessing the risks posed by the hazardous material and selecting a packaging suitable for the material. Typical specifications found in part 178 include requirements for materials of construction, thickness, fastenings, capacity, coatings, openings, joints and carrying devices. Much of the information contained in a specification is given in great detail and is repetitious. For example, there are fourteen specifications for wooden boxes. Most wooden box specifications list each acceptable type of wood from which the box must be constructed. This list may be repeated in the next specification for a similar, but slightly different box. In addition to listing the acceptable types of wood, the regulations also specify the thickness and width of boards, kinds

Source: Federal Register, December 21, 1990, 52402–52403.

notices were issued during the development process, and members of the public took full advantage of each of these opportunities to influence the rulemaking. It is estimated that the last notice before the new regulations became official generated more than 2,200 written comments from interested parties. Controversy, sometimes intense, occurred often. There were disagreements in the department, disagreements between the DOT and other agencies, and opposition from those affected by the rules. During the more than ten years it took to develop the new regulations, dozens, if not hundreds, of DOT personnel were involved in some way in writing them. In the final two and one-half years of intensive work, more than twenty employees were engaged in a "core workgroup," concentrating on completing the regulations. Dozens of individual analyses and studies were conducted. The department did evaluations of the effect of the new rules on the environment, small business, federalism, paperwork, and the economy in general. Countless individual decisions were made, some large, some small, that determined the final content of the rules. The Office of Management and Budget (OMB), a staff organization serving the president, reviewed all these analyses. The rules were cleared by the OMB before they were published in both draft and final form. On December 21, 1990, the Department of Transportation announced its comprehensive revision of the HMR, dealing with packaging, classification, communication, and handling. Of more interest to us here than the specific contents of these rules is the way in which they were developed.

It would be misleading to suggest that the long, complex, and resource-intensive process by which the new HMR were developed is typical of contemporary rulemaking. Alternatively, consider the response of the Federal Aviation Administration (FAA) when imminent dangers to the public are discovered. The FAA's airworthiness directives program can issue the equivalent of an emergency rule in twenty-four hours or less.[1] Still, the HMR, now nearly two decades old, are by no means unique and continue to hold powerful lessons. Some of the more recently completed rules or ongoing rulemaking efforts took longer to write, generated more interest and conflict, involved more studies and negotiations, and occupied the time and talent of more agency personnel. For example, food safety rules issued in July 2009 can trace their origins to proposed rules first issued during the Clinton administration, and labeling requirements for human prescription drugs begun during the first Clinton term were issued in 2006, more than thirteen years later.[2] So, the HMR and similar rules have much to tell us about rulemaking and the current state of our democratic government. The process by which rules are written is a critical element in our legal and political system. The contemporary rulemaking process is the evolutionary product of forces at work for many decades. The attention it has attracted through the years confirms its status as a prime element of government decision making.

Process and Substance

Given the vast scope of rules and the importance of their content, it should not be surprising that the process used to write them draws attention. During the past sixty years rulemaking has been the focus of considerable professional and political controversy. The way rules are written profoundly affects what they contain, and the content of rules determines, to a very large extent, the quality of our lives.

The substance of rules and the process of rulemaking are linked in many important ways. The elements of the contemporary rulemaking process are reactions to great expansion in the substantive reach of rulemaking. We have seen that the New Deal and the 1970s and 1980s were periods of explosive growth in government programs that required massive rulemaking to meet ambitious objectives. Even the Bush II administration—reputed to be skeptical about, if not hostile to, regulation—found it useful to dramatically expand the use of rulemaking and the number of rules related to homeland security. These expansions of the subject matter of rulemaking stimulated intense interest in the manner in which rules were developed by the responsible agencies. In each period there was concern about how agencies were making decisions about the contents of rules. What were agencies taking into account? To whom were they listening? To whom were they responsible? These concerns led to many proposals—some successful, others not—to change the way rules were written.

Rulemaking is a highly developed process, subject to a complex web of legal requirements. Nevertheless, the subject matter of a particular rule can still exert a powerful effect on how the rule is developed. The types and amount of information needed and the persons affected by a rule determine which of a large set of legal requirements will actually apply in a particular rulemaking. As important, the technical, administrative, and political dimensions of each rulemaking are determined almost entirely by the topic and scope of the rule to be written. A few simple examples highlight the differences.

A rule that deals with important aspects of the transport of hazardous materials necessarily involves a large number of issues, some of which require major research efforts to resolve. The rule will affect large and diverse segments of the population, each interested in it for different reasons. Those who ship goods, transport them, and consume them will all be concerned with the effect of the rule on them, as will environmental groups and organizations representing the workers who come in contact with the dangerous materials. Because the rule will have a large overall effect on the economy, certain legal requirements that would otherwise not apply must be met. Similarly, the rule's potential effect on the environment and small businesses triggers other specific legal requirements. Because the provisions of the rule mandate the keeping of records and periodic reporting to the government, a law that seeks to limit paperwork for regulated parties must also be considered. The number and diversity of interests affected by the rule alter rulemaking procedures in less formal ways as well. The agency writing the rule must provide for participation by those affected, and this will be determined in part by what the law requires in this regard and in part by the agency's assessment of the political environment. Within and outside of the agency there are systems to review and approve rules before they take effect. Given the scope of the rule, the costs it will impose on regulated parties, and the inevitable controversy it will generate, it is certain that all parties in a position to affect its content will scrutinize it closely.

Contrast this with the making of a much less prominent and more common rule. The Marketing Service of the Department of Agriculture issues rules that affect the handling and sale of specified commodities. The "rule"— actually termed "order" or "agreement"—is initially developed by a committee of producers and other experts and affected parties with an interest in the commodity in question, and the decision is based on the clearly stated goal of supporting and facilitating the marketing of lemons, oranges, or the other half-dozen fruits and vegetables affected by this program.[3] The interests most immediately and substantially affected are narrow and comparatively few in number. Even more frequent and less visible are rules establishing classes of airspace for purposes of navigation and air traffic control. These rules are certainly important, but any one of them has a very limited effect, both in terms of physical area and affected parties.[4] Their limited scope and impact allow the agency to routinize procedural and analytical requirements that require extensive work in the writing of the rule for transportation of hazardous materials.

Substance and process are inextricably linked in rulemaking. The missions established for agencies in authorizing legislation determine what rulemaking must accomplish. These goals, in turn, determine the types and amount of information that must be collected. The legal requirements that apply to rulemaking do so on a contingent basis, triggered by the size and type of populations or activities affected by the rule being developed. For virtually every procedural requirement imposed on rulemaking, exceptions may be granted, an acknowledgment that few elements of process make political or economic sense in all rulemaking situations. Process is so modulated for reasons of politics and efficiency.

Most actions classified as rules deal with narrowly defined subjects or affect only a small number of activities and people and are temporary in their effects. Their content may hinge entirely on technical considerations about which there is no debate. Such rules are not likely to stimulate affected parties to invest considerable time and effort to change the process by which they are written. Furthermore, additional procedures will not sufficiently improve or alter the decisions made during rulemaking to justify the additional costs imposed on the agencies that write the rules. The substance of rules determines the extent and intensity of political attention to a given rulemaking, driving oversight by Congress, the White House, and the courts. All of these, in turn, influence the administrative and management systems that support and oversee rulemaking in the agencies. When considering the rulemaking process, we must always be aware of the leavening effects of a given rule's subject matter.

From the First Congress to the Administrative Procedure Act

Not much is known about how our early presidents actually wrote the rules they were authorized to issue under the laws enacted by the first Congresses. Clearly, George Washington and many of his successors lacked the formidable executive office and massive bureaucracies that now support rulemaking. The function of rulemaking eventually migrated from the direct control of the president to cabinet secretaries, but it was not until the latter part of the nineteenth century that sizable bureaucracies were available to put their collective expertise to the task of rulemaking. From the start of the Republic, however, presidents and cabinet secretaries issued rules, sometimes numerous and complex. Take, for example, the extensive rules governing customs duties that the president was required to issue. Washington was an accomplished man, but was he sufficiently expert to fix the level of duties on so large a number of goods?

Until the 1930s none of the main government institutions—Congress, the president, the courts—paid serious or sustained attention to rulemaking as a general public function. In particular instances, however, Congress did provide guidance on how rulemaking in specific programs should work, and in some agencies it was remarkably well developed by the time of the New Deal. Consider the rulemaking techniques used by the Wage and Hour Division of the Department of Labor under the Fair Labor Standards Act. A study conducted in the late 1930s revealed a five-step process to establish rules governing wages. An "industry committee" consisting of representatives

This too was ruled an unconstitutional delegation of authority by Congress. In these cases the Court questioned not only basic grants of authority but also how they were exercised by the various instrumentalities that arose under the NIRA. Cited were instances of rules being written with little or no advance warning, of their being written with minimal consultation with affected parties, and even of their being unpublished or otherwise unavailable to the regulated parties.

The New Deal was shaken by this judicial assault, and the question of what constituted an acceptable delegation of legislative authority was opened.[10] Since much of the NIRA and other New Deal law were based on similarly broad grants of power, the prospects for a rapidly expanding government were very much in doubt. The implications for rulemaking, as a general government function, were particularly ominous. Each of the cases touched some aspect of rulemaking and left a clear message. In the future, rulemaking might be severely limited because Congress would be required to be more specific and restrictive in its grants of authority. Furthermore, the rulemaking that remained to be done would be scrutinized closely on both substantive and procedural grounds.

As it happened, however, the threat was short-lived. The Court's decisions triggered a firestorm of protest from the supporters of the New Deal, and Franklin Delano Roosevelt personally led the charge. Most students of American government are familiar with the constitutional crisis that ensued. President Roosevelt argued that an out-of-touch, overworked, and thoroughly unresponsive group of five of the nine Supreme Court justices was thwarting the will of the American people, and he launched an offensive to recoup what had been lost. His "Court-packing plan" would add to the Court one justice for every sitting justice over age seventy, giving him an immediate 10–5 majority. Congress, outraged at the judicial decimation of its handiwork, was not willing to countenance this wholesale manipulation of another constitutional branch of government.[11] The Court-packing plan failed, but Roosevelt still prevailed. Shifts in voting by two members of the Court changed a bare 5–4 majority against the New Deal into a vocal minority. Departures of sitting judges delivered FDR the opportunity he needed to remake the Court in his own image. He succeeded in the transformation; the New Deal and rulemaking were quickly restored to their previous states of health and influence.

The loss of their judicial ally hurt but by no means destroyed the critics of the new administrative state. On the contrary, the action shifted to the legislative arena, and the bar took the lead in attempting to recast the rulemaking process in a form more consistent with traditional lawyerly practices. In this political arena the tenor of the debate shifted from careful, scholarly arguments regarding the proper "channels" for legislative powers to politically charged and less subtle accusations that rulemaking and other administrative functions were manifestations of a creeping "socialism." The specter of unelected and essentially invisible bureaucrats writing, in virtual secrecy, laws that could curtail freedom and confiscate property was a compelling, if somewhat melodramatic, argument for reforming the administrative process.

The ABA's original proposals for reform focused on the elimination of independent regulatory commissions and the transfer of all adjudicatory powers from the remaining agencies to the federal courts. Furthermore, it argued that all administrative actions that stayed with agencies be subjected to judicial review in a special federal administrative court. Rulemaking would be transformed into a quasi-judicial activity, with each proposed rule subjected to a formal public hearing. The content of rules would be determined using standards of evidence like those used in civil trials. Many of these proposals were contained in the Walter-Logan bill of 1940, which, surprisingly, passed both houses of Congress. The bill "attempted to enforce common law due process, applicable only to adjudication, to the legislative process of administrative agencies."[12] Support for the Walter-Logan bill in the wake of the New Deal was apparently not seen by members as contradictory, perhaps because they failed to see the link between the substance of programs and the processes by which they were administered. Clearly, however, the immobilization of the administrative state was again at hand. Intended or not, the Walter-Logan bill would calcify the administrative process and render rulemaking on a large scale virtually impossible.

If Congress did not see the threat, Roosevelt most certainly did. He vetoed the bill, and the veto was not overridden by Congress. But the president knew he had a problem that would not go away. There was widespread belief, justified or not, that the administrative process needed attention. Rulemaking procedures were well developed in many agencies, but that was not uniformly the case. No generally applicable procedural standards had been authoritatively established by legislation or any other means. What those standards should be was not immediately clear to FDR, but his recent experience with the Walter-Logan bill probably convinced him that Congress should not be let loose on the task. So he did what all presidents have done when they faced difficult and politically dangerous decisions. He bought time, and prayed for answers, from an advisory commission.

The extraordinary work of the Attorney General's Committee on Administrative Procedure was discussed in the previous chapter. Its case studies of the practices in force in more than two dozen agencies in the late 1930s constitute an invaluable resource for scholars. More important, its findings laid the foundation for one of the landmark statutes of the twentieth century. The report of the Attorney General's Committee, *Administrative Procedures in Government Agencies,* was issued in 1941, and the recommendations developed in it became the springboard for what became the Administrative Procedure Act of 1946. World War II delayed its passage, but enactment followed soon thereafter. Its enduring importance to contemporary rulemaking is debatable, but the act remains a historic statement of the principles of government for a bureaucratic age.

Martin Shapiro has characterized the APA as a "deal struck between opposing political forces" at a pivotal stage in the development of the national government.[13] On the one hand were the New Dealers, who were not quite yet the dominant force in American political life, and on the other were conservatives, who probably saw the handwriting on the wall but wanted to delay reading it for as long as possible. The New Dealers sought a large and active government capable of defining and refining policies quickly and able to implement them with dispatch. The conservative forces held on stubbornly to the notion that the common law and judicial processes were the best, if not the only, way to protect private property, individual rights, and capitalism itself from a rapacious public sector. The compromise struck was perfectly logical, but lopsided. In the APA the proponents of big and easy government won a great victory.[14] They failed to rout the enemy thoroughly, however, and over the next several decades would lose the war.

Shapiro has observed that the APA divides all administrative procedure into three categories: rulemaking, which is when agencies act like legislatures; adjudication, which is when agencies act like courts; and everything else.[15] The final category is hardly trivial, since it contains the classic bureaucratic task of administering all manner of public programs. In the simplest terms, the APA requires agencies to behave like a legislature when they write rules and like courts when they adjudicate disputes. Everything else is left essentially to the discretion of the agencies. Looked at from this perspective, the New Dealers succeeded in capturing much of the making and all of the implementation of policy and law for their political philosophy. America's historical penchant for an independent judiciary, with its distinctive and elaborate methods for making decisions, however, was preserved. Adjudication in agencies would be conducted in the manner of a civil trial presided over by a judicial officer whose objectivity would be guaranteed through his or her structural and functional separation from the other activities and personnel of the agency. The APA is vague concerning the situations in which adjudication is the required method for decision making, defining them only as "matters other than rulemaking ... but including licensing."[16] For decades the struggle to define a clear and bright line between situations appropriate for rulemaking and those appropriate for adjudication has produced few hard and fast generalizations, leaving a substantial number of government actions in a procedural twilight zone. It is safe to say that adjudication is the preferred method when the rules or standards to guide decision making already exist. Hence, it is best used in situations when the status of an individual (as a petitioner, potential beneficiary, or regulated party) is in question, and the application of known rules depends on facts about that individual or his or her activities that may be in dispute or in need of elaboration.

Adjudication works best with two-sided issues. Rulemaking, as a legislative process, is designed to sort through facts from multiple sources in order to select standards that will apply generally. That said, it does not take much imagination to think of situations in which "individual fact" might have a strong influence on the rule that an agency is considering. This is especially true when a regulated or beneficiary community is very small, or when the risk to the public posed by incorrect or incomplete facts is great. The APA takes these situations into account by leaving room for Congress to require formal adjudicatory procedure on certain classes of rulemaking when it authorizes agencies to carry out programs. In reality, Congress has used this option infrequently. The key rulemaking provisions of the APA, found in section 553, are very different:

553 Rule Making

(a) This section applies, according to the provisions thereof, except to the extent that there is involved—

   (1) a military or foreign affairs function of the United States; or

   (2) a matter relating to agency management or personnel or to public property, loans, grants, benefits, or contracts.

(b) General notice of proposed rule making shall be published in the *Federal Register,* unless persons subject thereto are named and either personally served or otherwise have actual notice thereof in accordance with law. The notice shall include—

   (1) a statement of the time, place, and nature of public rule making proceedings;

   (2) reference to the legal authority under which the rule is proposed; and

   (3) either the terms or substance of the proposed rule or a description of the subjects and issues involved.

Except when notice or hearing is required by statute, this subsection does not apply—

   (A) to interpretative rules, general statements of policy, or rules of agency organization, procedure, or practice; or

(B) when the agency for good cause finds (and incorporates the finding and a brief statement of reasons therefor in the rules issued)
that notice and public procedure thereon are impracticable, unnecessary, or contrary to the public interest.

(c) After notice required by this section, the agency shall give interested
persons an opportunity to participate in the rule making through
submission of written data, views, or arguments with or without
opportunity for oral presentation. After consideration of the relevant
matter presented, the agency shall incorporate in the rules adopted a
concise general statement of their basis and purpose. When rules are
required by statute to be made on the record after opportunity for an
agency hearing, sections 556 and 557 of this title apply instead of this
subsection.

(d) The required publication or service of a substantive rule shall be made
not less than 30 days before its effective date, except—

(1) a substantive rule which grants or recognizes an exemption or
relieves a restriction;

(2) interpretative rules and statements of policy; or

(3) as otherwise provided by the agency for good cause found and
published with the rule.

(e) Each agency shall give an interested person the right to petition for the
issuance, amendment, or repeal of a rule.

The procedures framed in section 553 have come to be known as
"notice and comment" or "informal" rulemaking. Kenneth Culp Davis, one of
the most influential voices in the history of American administrative law,
describes them as one of the "greatest inventions of modern government."[17]
What made administrative rulemaking so attractive to him was its speed, its
economy, and that "it can be, when the agency so desires, a virtual duplicate
of the legislative process."[18] In fact, as contemplated in the APA, administrative rulemaking was considerably less encumbered than the legislative process. Rulemaking authority, safely ensconced in the bowels of agencies, was
the province of specialized staffs with narrow responsibilities and without
the presence of constituencies holding the big stick of reelection in their
hands. The most remarkable feature of rulemaking was the extraordinary
freedom of action it appeared to grant the bureaucrat. History has shown it
to be just that, an appearance. Freedom of action for bureaucrats is not rulemaking's most prominent characteristic. A grasp of the APA's original provisions is nonetheless an important foundation for understanding current
process.

The Core Elements of Rulemaking: Information, Participation, Accountability

The core elements of rulemaking as put forth in the Administrative Procedure Act can be expressed in three words: information, participation, and accountability. These are familiar principles, basic to our constitutional democracy. In the context of rulemaking, however, they assume forms and meanings different from those in other political settings.

Information

The most basic element of "information" in rulemaking is the notice provided to the public at large when a rule is being developed and when it becomes final and binding. Generally these notices appear in the *Federal Register*. Under the provisions of the APA the notice varied, depending on the stage of the rulemaking. For proposed rules, agencies needed only to tell the public, in general terms, what it was proposing to do and the authority under which it was taking action. The agencies had the option to serve the notice on persons individually and directly rather than using the *Federal Register*. For proposals, agencies could give the public either a description of what it had in mind or the actual intended language of the rule. In the absence of other statutory mandates these decisions were left unequivocally to the discretion of the rule writers. The agencies also were expected to provide information on the time and place of rulemaking, and for final rules a "concise, general statement of basis and purpose" and at least thirty days warning before their requirements took effect.

Another dimension of information is implied in the statement of basis and purpose. That is the information the agencies rely on to develop the rule. Beyond acknowledging its existence and the need to disclose it, the APA says little about what must be considered. We will see in the upcoming chapters devoted to the management of problems and the oversight of rulemaking that this aspect of information has since received a lot of attention.

An argument can be made that the information thus provided the public during rulemaking was at least the equal of what we have access to when Congress or a state legislature is considering a new law. What we learn of pending legislation comes from the selective and often superficial accounts in the media or from direct inquiries we make of our elected representatives, or from their increasingly frequent newsletters. There is no equivalent of a *Federal Register* notice for pending legislative votes. Still, agencies enjoyed considerable discretion when deciding how much information to disclose.

All they needed to reveal was a general description of the rule they had in mind and, once it was complete, the statute that it was designed to implement and some discussion of the "basis" for the action they took. In 1946 much discretion was left to agencies when determining the quantity and quality of the information that the public would have to work with as they decided if and how they would participate in rulemaking.

Participation

Agencies enjoyed considerable freedom when structuring public participation under the provisions of the APA. The agencies were obliged to allow written comments, but participation in any other form was not a matter of right. Surprisingly, the agencies were not instructed anywhere in the act to take heed of what they learned from the public in written comments or whatever other form of participation they allowed. Participation was included in the APA for some purpose, but from the language of the act one cannot conclude that it was for any reason other than the education of the agency. No explicit linkage was drawn, for example, between the participation provisions of the act and the requirement that agencies briefly describe the "basis" for their decisions. In like fashion the APA allowed the public to petition agencies to write a rule but provided no additional mandates or guidance to agencies on how to handle or dispose of these petitions.

It is interesting that the framers of the APA chose to codify the least intrusive mechanisms for public participation that were already in use in rulemaking agencies. As noted earlier, by the time the act was passed in 1946 many agencies, clearly a majority of those writing a significant number of rules at the time, used a variety of procedures to interact with the public they were affecting. In some instances constant and intense interactions between the rulemakers and regulated parties were common. By establishing a floor, below which no agency could fall in its interactions with the public, the APA left it to existing or future legislation to add additional, general procedural requirements. Nothing in the act prevented the agencies themselves from innovating in their dealings with the public during the course of the development of regulation. On reflection, this approach is quite consistent with the views of some in the New Deal coalition that placed such great faith in the capacity of government. If agencies were up to the myriad technical tasks required to produce a better society, they were certainly capable of fashioning the proper structures and procedures for public participation within the loose constraints of the APA. Those who fashioned the legislation were comfortable with entrusting the stewardship of public participation to the agencies in which they had such faith.

Accountability

The APA's substitute for the accountability fostered by the ballot box was the specter of judicial review. The act does not explicitly mention other, more powerful mechanisms for accountability. Congress and the president exert influence over rulemaking. These influences were not treated in the APA other than by limited references to Congress. As outlined in section 706 of the act, judicial review is paradoxical. On the one hand, the act made the courts available to those who wished to challenge rules, repudiating earlier theories of judicial review that made the courthouse threshold difficult to cross. On the other hand, the standard against which agencies' rulemaking decisions would be judged was anything but strict. Rulemaking could be judged on both substantive and procedural dimensions, but in neither were agencies given difficult criteria to meet.

The substance of rules could not constitute an "arbitrary or capricious abuse of discretion."[19] According to definitions found in Webster's *New Collegiate Dictionary*, arbitrary behavior and capricious behavior should be very rare and difficult to establish when they did occur. *Arbitrary* means "at random," an "unreasonable act"; *capricious* means "impulsive," "unpredictable." Taken literally, few rules could be so devoid of "basis and purpose" that their contents would not pass so easy a test. The other avenue established in the APA for challenging a rulemaking was procedural. Given the rather minimal procedures outlined in the act, agencies should have had little difficulty meeting these standards as well. Of course, if Congress had increased procedural requirements for a particular program, or if the agency itself had adopted more elaborate procedures, these would have become the standards against which the rulemaking would have been judged. In this sense, the procedural basis for judicial review was potentially more formidable than the standards for review of the substantive content.

The New Dealers had reason to rejoice over their success in fashioning a rulemaking process that could serve as the vehicle for a rapidly expanding government. As noted earlier, however, the conservatives took firm control of agency adjudication. Based on long-standing principles of common law, and embodying the adversary model of decision making, adjudication in the provisions of the APA was structurally separated from other agency functions, including rulemaking. This was accomplished through the creation of an independent corps of hearing examiners, later to be called administrative law judges. Preserved was the principle that adjudication was special; when it was the appropriate form of government action, the full complement of administrative due process was essential to ensure the accuracy and fairness of the result.

The fundamental rulemaking principles of the APA have not changed since passage over sixty years ago, but we should not conclude that the act as written in 1946 thoroughly dominates the making of rules today. In fact, most important rulemaking is not conducted according to the minimalist model of the APA, if it ever was. Minor and routine rulemaking is also not carried out in tight accordance with the APA, but for different reasons. The fact that the basic principles of the APA have never been altered does not mean that Congress, the president, the courts, and the agencies themselves have not been busy changing rulemaking, including amending the APA itself.

The political coalition that produced the rulemaking provisions of the APA has long since disappeared. The seeds of change the authors planted in the original legislation are the act's most enduring legacy. The three fundamental elements of rulemaking procedure contained in the APA—information, participation, and accountability—have remained dominant themes throughout the past thirty years of virtually constant change. Again, the APA allows for forms of rulemaking other than the notice-and-comment provisions of section 553. Specifically, if Congress indicated that rulemaking was to be conducted "on the record," the procedures that normally apply in adjudication would come into force.[20] In addition, when this type of rulemaking is invoked, the standard of review shifts from the permissive "arbitrary and capricious" standard to the considerably more demanding requirement that agencies demonstrate "substantial evidence" for the decisions embodied in the rule. Formal judicialization of rulemaking, which the ABA and its conservative allies fought so hard for in the late 1930s, was not strongly promoted by this provision in the APA, nor has Congress frequently exercised this option. The fact that it was retained as an option to exercise is significant nonetheless, perhaps betraying some nagging doubt about the adequacy of the procedures in section 553.

Whether or not the equivocation in the APA was from discomfort over informal rulemaking is little more than an academic question at this point. For important rules, the events of the 1960s, 1970s, 1980s, 1990s, and 2000s have rendered the pure notice-and-comment rulemaking of 1946 a historical artifact. What happened to the rulemaking process during these years could be described as creeping judicialization: "creeping" because many small, often uncoordinated alterations were enacted; "judicialization" because their net effect has been to push rulemaking from a purely legislative mode of operation to one with more of the elements we have come to identify with decision making in courts. The forces pushing rulemaking in this direction are both external and internal to the agencies. Some were motivated by a profound mistrust of government regulation of private activity and the rulemaking that made it possible. Others were motivated by a concern for more rational and comprehensive decision making. Like the APA, all are united by their emphasis on information, participation, or accountability as preferred devices for changing rulemaking into a process more to the liking of reformers. Concentration on these three elements has been remarkably consistent over time.

In rulemaking, information and participation cannot be separated. Effective participation is simply impossible without accurate and complete information on what the agency intends to do, the reasons the agency has for doing it, and the likely effect a new rule will have. Through the years Congress, the president, and the courts have dramatically increased the information that may be generated and shared with the public during the course of rulemaking. They have taken a similar approach to participation. In fact, these institutions have rarely expanded information requirements without simultaneously increasing the opportunities for the public to participate in the larger rulemaking process. Every increment of information on the need and justification for, and implications of, rules under development increases the ability of interested and affected parties to consider their position and present fully informed views to the rulemaking agency. It should not be surprising, then, that the very vehicles that vastly expanded the information requirements in rulemaking also opened the process to additional involvement by the public.

Information: Increased Legal Requirements

Information is a crucial element in any rulemaking. How it is handled by an agency profoundly influences the content of the rule that is ultimately produced. Information in two general forms must be considered. The first is the information that any agency must collect, or develop, and then consider during the course of a rulemaking. The second is the information that the agency must provide to the public during and after the rulemaking. Both dimensions of rulemaking have changed dramatically since passage of the APA.

Up to 1946, authorizing statutes provided agencies the sum and substance of the direction regarding information they were expected to use when writing rules. Except for its single reference to the "basis" for a rule an agency is about to adopt, the APA provides no additional guidance to the agency on how it is to go about assembling the information on which a rule will be based. Authorizing statutes varied considerably in the direction they provided agencies, but until the 1960s, laws mandating or allowing rulemaking were usually vague as to the specific types of information to be used and the way it was to be collected.

Information That the Agency Must Consider

Authorizing Statutes. Since the late 1960s, regulatory statutes have become increasingly concerned with the type of information an agency considers when deciding whether and how to write a rule. The pattern is most evident in the statutes that establish major programs of social regulation and, to a lesser extent, those dealing with economic institutions and transactions. The section of the Occupational Safety and Health Act (OSHA) that grants the secretary of labor authority to promulgate rules to protect American workers is illustrative. After setting out the goals that OSHA's rules are to promote, the statute turns to the types of information that should be used during rulemaking:

> Development of standards ... shall be based on research, demonstrations, experiments and such other information as may be appropriate. In addition to the attainment of the highest degree of health and safety protection for the employee other [information] considerations shall be the latest available scientific data in the field, the feasibility of the standards and the experience gained under this and other health and safety laws.[21]

Congress established formidable information collection and analysis responsibilities for the Occupational Safety and Health Administration when it writes rules. It is obliged not only to rely on what is already known about health and safety aspects of substances and activities. There also is a clear mandate to create and use new knowledge when what is available is insufficient. Furthermore, information that relates to health and safety must be supplemented by information about "feasibility," which means, in this instance, what is possible technologically, operationally, and financially.

Rulemaking to control the threat posed by toxic substances in the environment is the responsibility of the Environmental Protection Agency (EPA) under the Toxic Substances Control Act (TSCA). A key element in the TSCA scheme is the testing of substances that may pose a risk. These tests are to be performed in accordance with regulations governing testing facilities promulgated by the EPA. The information that Congress expects the agency to develop when writing test rules includes "the relative costs of the various test protocols and methodologies which may be required under the rule and the reasonably foreseeable availability of the facilities and personnel needed to perform the testing required under the rule."[22] But the TSCA supplements these bits of practical information with an imposing list of considerations related to the core purpose of the statute. When writing test rules on substances, the EPA is required to consider a range of health and environmental effects that are produced by various characteristics of the chemical under examination. These characteristics include its "persistence, acute toxicity, subacute toxicity, chronic toxicity." In addition to information on these characteristics, the act requires the EPA rulemakers to consider a range of risks posed by the chemicals that are tested. Risks that testing must be attentive to are expressed in the form of effects such as "carcinogenesis, mutagenesis, teratogenesis, behavioral disorders, cumulative or synergistic effects and any other effect which may present an unreasonable risk to health or the environment."[23]

The information provisions in the Occupational Safety and Health Act and the Toxic Substances Control Act that relate to the physical well-being of individuals are examples of a general approach to regulation known as "risk assessment." Many other statutes explicitly or implicitly require some form of risk assessment as a basis for rules.[24] Not all statutes treat the risk assessment issue identically. In fact, different statutes administered by the same agency often establish different criteria for risk assessment, which require different approaches to information collection. This inconsistency is evident in different programs administered by the same agency: the EPA. Compare the standards set for risk assessment in the Safe Drinking Water Act; the Federal Insecticide, Fungicide, and Rodenticide Act (FIFRA); and the Toxic Substances Control Act. The Safe Drinking Water Act, under which the EPA writes rules governing the quality of potable water from public water supplies, requires establishment of "maximum contaminant levels ... [at which] no known or anticipated adverse effects" could happen and that allow for an "adequate margin of safety." The pesticides law requires the agency to develop the information needed to set standards that result in "no unreasonable adverse effect" but that take "into account the economic, social and environmental costs and benefits." The TSCA adopts a similar approach. It calls for the control of toxic substances to the extent that "unreasonable risk" is eliminated but using the "least burdensome requirements" to accomplish this goal.[25]

By authorizing agencies to protect the public from risks in the environment, the workplace, and consumer goods, Congress necessitated the development or collection of other types of information. Information requirements of the sort listed above reflect Congress's strong desire to please all affected constituencies. By mandating that rules be based on such information, Congress encourages, and sometimes requires, agencies to balance information on risks to health and safety with risks to economic well-being. This sets the stage for a rulemaking process characterized by the same types of trade-offs and compromises that dominate congressional lawmaking.

Information Statutes. The information requirements established through individual authorizing statutes are significant because they give structure to the specific analytical tasks that rulemakers must perform. Rivaling this source of collection and analytical requirements, however, is what can be termed the *information statute.* This type of law does not apply to a single program or agency. Rather, these statutes apply generally to all agencies that write rules. The National Environmental Policy Act (NEPA), the Regulatory Flexibility Act (RFA), and the Paperwork Reduction Act (PRA) are good examples of congressional insistence that a particular type of issue be considered in all rulemakings undertaken by the federal government.[26] The vehicles to ensure adequate consideration of these issues are statutory provisions that mandate the collection or development, analysis, and use of information about the effects of a rule on particular interests or populations.

NEPA is a landmark statute in many ways. Passed in 1969, it is often viewed as the symbolic start of a period of environmental policymaking that continues unabated to the present day. It has many notable provisions, but the ones most pertinent here are those that require agencies to consider the effect of rules on the environment. The law calls for what could be two stages of information collection and analysis on environmental issues that arise in the making of a single rule. First, there is a threshold assessment of whether the actions contemplated in the rulemaking, such as the setting aside of public lands for certain types of activities or the relaxation of emissions standards for nuclear power plants, constitute a potentially significant impact on the environment. If they do not, the agency issues a "finding of no significant impact." If the agency reaches the opposite conclusion, it must then prepare an environmental impact statement (EIS), which is a report on the likely effects of the rule and the steps the agency will take to eliminate or mitigate damage to the environment. The EIS is also prepared in two stages, draft and final, a system that is strikingly similar to that of proposed and final rules established in the Administrative Procedure Act.

The Paperwork Reduction Act and the Regulatory Flexibility Act are remnants of an ambitious but failed effort, primarily by the U.S. Senate, to overhaul the regulatory process with a single, massive statute.[27] The originally proposed legislation, which went through many iterations, ultimately failed to attract the support needed to make a new law. These two statutes emerged in 1980 as the progeny of those efforts. The PRA requires agencies to develop information on the extent of the paperwork burdens that will accompany new rules. It also requires agencies to obtain White House permission, in advance, for all new collections of information. The legislation was intended to reduce these burdens by forcing agencies not only to analyze the information collection and reporting costs they were imposing on the private sector but also to use the studies to minimize the costs. Essentially the same approach was taken in the Regulatory Flexibility Act. Here the protected class was less global than that embraced by the Paperwork Reduction Act. The RFA sought to protect small businesses and organizations from the ravages of federal rulemaking by requiring agencies to develop and analyze information on the effect of rules on small entities. When the effects of a rule are likely to be substantial, the agency is expected to take steps that will reduce the burden. The agency can fashion devices that will scale back the actual requirements or somehow make it easier for the smaller entity to comply.

In the 1990s Congress again attempted to pass general statutes to reform the entire rulemaking process. In 1995 President Bill Clinton vetoed the Comprehensive Regulatory Reform Act, which would have greatly expanded the use of certain analytical techniques in all rulemaking. In 1995 and 1996, respectively, Congress did amend the Paperwork Reduction Act and the Regulatory Flexibility Act, strengthening their information provisions and increasing responsibilities for agencies that write rules.

In 2000 Congress, with no fanfare, enacted an amendment to the Paperwork Reduction Act that came to be known as the Information (or Data) Quality Act. Plenty of fanfare followed, however. Agencies struggled to comply with the provisions of this statute, which included the development of policies to ensure that information "disseminated" by them met high standards of "quality, objectivity, utility, and integrity." The act also empowered private parties to petition agencies to correct what they considered to be deficiencies in information quality.

Each of these information statutes represents an effort by Congress to minimize the negative effects of rulemaking and other government activities on resources, activities, and individuals deemed worthy of special protection by Congress. Their basic designs are very much alike. Development and analysis of information is central to each statute. There is an unexpressed but obvious intent that the information will alone be a substantial force in altering the rulemaking behavior of agencies. We will see shortly, however, that Congress was not so naive as to think that information alone would be sufficient. In these and other statutes, Congress combined information with participation and accountability to ensure that the desired results were achieved.

Information Requirements by Executive Order. Congress, although it has been the major source of expanding information requirements for rulemaking, has not acted alone. Presidents since Richard Nixon have burdened agencies and departments under their direct authority with additional information requirements. With time these requirements have become broader and more rigorous. The major device that enables presidents to intervene in the rulemaking process is the executive order. More than 13,500 executive orders have been issued by our presidents since the start of the Republic. Several of these have had important effects on rulemaking; one may be the most important reform of rulemaking since passage of the Administrative Procedure Act of 1946.

President Nixon started the process when he imposed a "quality of life" analysis on new rules, the meaning of which was never particularly clear. This gave way to President Gerald R. Ford's executive order requiring an analysis of a rule's impact on inflation. President Jimmy Carter wrote a more extensive set of reforms into his Executive Order 12044. Among the requirements in this executive order was a mandatory analysis of "regulatory alternatives" to force agencies to consider innovative and less restrictive and burdensome ways to achieve regulatory objectives. President Ronald Reagan followed the tradition with Executive Order 12291, arguably the most significant incursion by any president into the core processes of rulemaking. This order mandated a regulatory impact analysis for all rules whose estimated effect on the economy was $100 million or more. This amounts to full cost-benefit analysis with the additional feature that the proponents of any new rule were required to demonstrate a net gain to society prior to its promulgation. Like Carter's Executive Order 12044, Reagan's Executive Order 12291 had a reformist dimension. It was accompanied by a set of regulatory principles that exhorted agencies to adopt nonregulatory options for accomplishing public policy objectives whenever possible and to use the least intrusive and burdensome regulatory devices when government intervention was the only realistic alternative.

President Reagan did not stop with Executive Order 12291. During the course of his presidency he signed numerous other executive orders requiring the development of specific types of information during rulemaking. In 1983 the president signed Executive Order 12498, which required agencies semiannually to assemble and send to the White House agendas of the significant rulemaking that was under way or contemplated in the near future. Executive Order 12612 required agencies to conduct a "federalism assessment" of rules under development, a requirement that was strengthened in subsequent years in Executive Order 13175. The intention here was to ensure that federal rulemaking did not interfere with the "sovereignty" of the states. In effect, this executive order forced agencies to consider whether action by the states was a legal and feasible alternative to federal action and, even when it was not, how the rule could be structured to minimize disruption to the authority and financial integrity of those governments.

The federalism initiative was followed by executive orders requiring consideration of the effects of rules on private property and on the family. These additional executive orders, like the more prominent and controversial Executive Order 12291, were manifestations of the mandate that President Reagan believed he had received from the American people in both 1980 and 1984. The types of information required to be collected and analyzed by these executive orders are predicated on a deep respect for the free market and private property, states' rights, and the family. Is there a better summary of the domestic policies of the Reagan presidency?

President Clinton followed the same tradition of influencing rulemaking through executive order. Executive Order 12866 replaced Reagan's Executive Order 12291 but embraced many of the same information principles. It endorses cost-benefit analysis and mandates agencies to analyze regulatory circumstances to find both innovative and less burdensome ways to accomplish public objectives.

President George W. Bush operated partially under the Clinton executive order, but he issued several new interpretations of the order's requirements that were binding on agencies. He also issued two related executive orders, 13258 and 13422. Executive Order 13258 amended Clinton's executive order by reducing the role of the vice president of the United States in the rulemaking process. Executive Order 13422 was more significant in that it extended the power of the president's Office of Management and Budget to include the review of "guidance" documents issued by federal agencies—a category of governmental actions that, in the view of the White House and others, were being used in lieu of rulemaking in order to avoid both procedural requirements and presidential scrutiny. That same order also directed each federal agency to name a regulatory policy officer who would act, in effect, like a local OMB for the purposes of regulation development.

It is notable that when President Barack Obama took office he issued his own order, revoking both Bush executive orders and setting in motion a process for establishing his own rulemaking directives. He issued an invitation to the public to comment on ways his administration should manage federal rulemaking.[28]

Information That Agencies Must Provide the Public

There is, of course, another side to information. The information the agency is required to produce to educate itself during the course of rulemaking is undoubtedly important. Information that agencies are required to disclose, and to whom, establishes the crucial link between information and participation and accountability. The Administrative Procedure Act requires disclosure of information about rulemaking to the public through the vehicle of notice in the *Federal Register*. To this day the *Federal Register* remains the primary, but not the sole, official mechanism for communication with the public regarding rules under development. Today, the content of notices of proposed rulemaking and notices of final rules is vastly different from what was contemplated by the drafters of the APA and by those who were initially involved in its interpretation and implementation. The APA appeared to allow agencies considerable flexibility in what went into a rulemaking notice. A manual prepared by the attorney general shortly after passage of the act went so far as to advise agencies against publication of the actual text of proposed rules. The attorney general instead recommended that agencies publish general descriptions of what they were intending to do, based on the dubious proposition that the actual text might simply confuse the public.[29]

The content of notices has developed in a very different manner and now routinely includes material that could not have been contemplated by the drafters or early interpreters and implementers of the APA. Notices of proposed rulemaking nearly always contain not only the full text of the rule that the agency has developed to that point but a preamble as well, which is frequently as informative as the rule itself. The publication of the full rule in the notice is mandated by some statutes, but is more often a matter of agency practice. Agency practice, in turn, is a result of intense pressure from the public, the White House, and the courts for rulemakers to be precise about what they are proposing to do. Preambles, in contrast, are mandated by rules of the *Federal Register,* which dictate the format for all proposed and final rules. Issued by the administrative committee of the *Federal Register,* these rules call for a "preamble which will inform the reader who is not an expert in the subject area of the basis and purpose for the rule or proposal."[30]

Notices of proposed and final rules often contain a great deal of additional information arising from the statutes and executive orders discussed earlier. For example, agencies report in preambles the results of the reviews they are required to conduct under a variety of statutes and executive orders. Illustrations of this type of reporting can be found daily in the *Federal Register.*

Beyond the disclosure of information of this sort in proposed and final rules, agencies are required to summarize the "basis" for their decisions. This entails, in the preambles of rules, explanations of the information, data, and analyses the agency relied on when developing the regulation. As noted earlier, the information, data, and analyses that are given depend on what the authorizing statutes require and are either in the form of specified studies or the objectives they are expected to achieve. These sections can be quite extensive. Preambles are frequently longer than the rules they precede, and those for major rules can be several hundred pages long.

Although the preambles of rules can be lengthy and detailed, they do not contain every bit of information that the agency reviewed and relied on during its deliberations. For this purpose agencies maintain "dockets" or "records" into which all material pertinent to a rulemaking is placed. In some instances the docket or record is mandated by an agency's authorizing legislation. Such requirements can be found in legislation establishing environmental regulation, notably clean air and toxic substances regulations, and consumer protection programs. Much of the widespread maintenance of records and dockets in other programs arises from the fear of litigation, during which agencies would be expected to document their actions.[31] The rulemaking docket or record, like the information it contains, is a vital element in participation and accountability, and new technologies have diversified their accessibility.

We know from the records of the period that the writers of the Administrative Procedure Act consciously decided to leave to the agencies decisions about the type, quantity, and means of disclosure of information on which their rules were based. As Kenneth Culp Davis observed: "In making rules of general applicability agencies were generally free, in the absence of a special statute, to develop factual materials or not to develop them as they saw fit.... Such freedom for the agencies was understood at the time of enactment in 1946. Nothing in the APA changed that presumption."[32]

What we have experienced since 1946 is a repudiation of this approach to information collection and use in rulemaking through the enactment of many special statutes, the imposition of numerous executive orders, and the adoption of a defensive posture by agencies because of the possibility of litigation. Agencies engaged in significant rulemaking today usually do not enjoy anything near the discretion Davis alludes to; a high threshold for information collection, use, and disclosure is now set for rulemakers by these actions of Congress, the president, and the courts. The agencies are free to exceed these requirements if they wish. The laws, executive orders, and judicial decisions constitute a floor below which the agencies cannot fall unless specifically exempted from their legal requirements. As we will see, however, such exemptions are not rare, and their use appears to be more frequent.

Participation: Expanded Opportunities Mandated by Law

The opportunity to participate in the development of rules lends the process an element of democracy not present in other forms of lawmaking. In Chapter 5 we will examine actual patterns of participation in rulemakings, the perceptions of those involved as to the effectiveness of various forms of participation, and the relationships that exist between public participants and the agencies that write rules. We also will take up the troublesome but crucial question of the efficacy of participation from the perspectives of other scholars, the agencies, and the participants themselves. In this chapter we deal with participation in rulemaking solely as a legal requirement. The objective here is to demonstrate how the opportunities for participation have grown and diversified since they were codified in the Administrative Procedure Act.

Participation in rulemaking began long before the passage of the APA. The Attorney General's Committee that studied administrative practices in agencies in the late 1930s discovered that significant and apparently highly effective programs of public participation supported rulemaking in many agencies. The Department of Labor, which administered the wage and hour laws, used an especially interesting form of such participation. A "conference" of affected parties, including representatives from both business and labor, met regularly with the agency to set and adjust rules governing wages and hours. This conference approach, both formal and informal, was not uncommon among the agencies that wrote rules.[33] These and many other early mechanisms for participation are discussed in Chapter 5. But when the drafters of the APA decided on the form public participation would take, they chose instead a much less direct and substantial approach. Except for those rare circumstances when formal, trial-type proceedings were mandated by authorizing statutes, agencies could limit public participation to written comments in response to notices of proposed rulemaking.

The legislative history of the APA reveals at least some concern for the adequacy of written comment as a means for rulemaking agencies to educate themselves and for the public to be able fully to articulate its concerns or opinions. The record shows that the framers of the APA expected agencies to reach out to the public in different ways when issues of great importance or difficulty were under consideration.[34] They did not, however, define those circumstances in the act, nor did they mandate the use of more elaborate forms of participation. They were satisfied to leave it to the informed discretion of agencies or to subsequent Congresses to add to the basic framework. Later Congresses, as well as presidents and courts, accepted the implicit invitation in the APA with considerable enthusiasm.

Contemporary authorizing statutes, particularly those creating or amending regulatory programs, are replete with examples of the conscious and aggressive expansion by Congress of opportunities for public participation to accompany new information requirements. The practice became so commonplace that by the 1970s academic and professional journals were acknowledging and generally endorsing the rise of a "hybrid" form of rulemaking.[35] This new form displays a variety of options for public participation located somewhere between the minimal model of notice-and-comment rulemaking and the full-blown trial procedures of "formal" rulemaking. Indeed, diversity in modes of participation became the norm in laws establishing new programs. Some authorizing statutes built on the APA by specifying the amount of time that the public would have to comment on proposed rules. Invariably, the allowed time in these statutes was more generous than what had become the norm of thirty days among the agencies. The amount of time given the public to respond to a proposed rule can be crucial for several reasons. It takes time to assemble the essential information needed to evaluate and then respond to what can be highly technical and complex rules. As important in the contemporary political environment, time allows people to get organized, build coalitions, and orchestrate a response to the agency's proposals. As we will see in Chapter 5, timing is so crucial that both agencies and participants find ways to share information long before a proposed rule is published.

An interesting and highly significant question is what the agency does with the comments it receives from the public. On this the APA is essentially silent, except for the required statement of basis and purpose that must accompany the final rule. Obviously, Congress would not have required agencies to, at minimum, solicit written comments if they expected the rule writers to ignore what the public had to say. If public comments raise significant issues related to statutory objectives or requirements, the agency can ignore them only at its peril. Reviewing courts are responsive to arguments from the public that a matter of central importance to a rule was missed or mishandled by the responsible agency. In a subsequent chapter we will discuss this form of judicial review. Agencies include a discussion of public comments in the preambles of rules. Not only are the nature and number of public comments reviewed, the actions the agency has taken, or chosen not to take, in response to them are detailed. The amount of attention paid to comments depends on the volume and seriousness of the comments received, but in many instances they dominate the preamble. There is little question that agencies take public comments seriously.

Other statutes sought to diversify participation by mandating that agencies give the public different types of opportunities to express its views during rulemaking. Perhaps the most common of these means is the "legislative hearing," during which witnesses present testimony orally to those responsible for the rulemaking in much the same manner as congressional committees do their work. This allows for a give-and-take not possible through written comments. The legislative hearing was required in rulemakings authorized or mandated in statutes dealing with occupational safety and health, safe drinking water, toxic substances, clean air and water, endangered species, consumer products, energy conservation, and trade practices. Some statutes went even further, virtually to the edge of formal trial-type proceedings, by allowing for either rebuttal comments or actual cross-examination of agency personnel. The former is an option in rulemakings dealing with toxic substances and drinking water; the latter also occurs in rulemaking for toxic substances and in that for certain trade practices regulated by the FTC.

Many laws allow for or require a more institutionalized form of participation through the use of advisory committees. The role of advisory committees in rulemaking can vary considerably. In some instances the committee may be nothing more than a sounding board for agency ideas; in others it may help the agency set the rulemaking agenda; and in a few instances, such as the Safe Drinking Water Act, consultation with advisory groups is mandatory. Although the use of advisory committees is widespread and highly varied, several features of their operations are standard. The Federal Advisory Committee Act of 1972 (FACA) established strict requirements that agencies must meet when using these types of groups during rulemaking. The provisions of the FACA govern the composition of advisory committees by requiring that they be "chartered" in the *Federal Register* to inform the public of their functions and activities. Furthermore, agencies must ensure that the committees are balanced in regard to the interests that will be affected by their rules, and the meetings of the committees must be open to the public.[36]

Some have commented that the FACA has a chilling effect on the use of advisory committees. But it is important to acknowledge that a primary intent of the statute was to ensure that principles of public participation were observed in the operation of these highly influential groups. The model established in the FACA was essentially duplicated in the Negotiated Rulemaking Act of 1990, a statute that establishes the basic procedural requirements that agencies must use when they develop rules using what amount to collective bargaining techniques. This too will be reviewed in Chapter 5.

Other general statutes promote participation in rulemaking by expanding it in certain subject areas. The National Environmental Policy Act and the Paperwork Reduction Act are prominent examples of how this indirect approach to participatory rulemaking works. NEPA requires public input at two critical stages in the development of environmental impact statements. At the outset the agency preparing the EIS is required to conduct a "scoping session," at which plans for the study are discussed with the public. The public has the opportunity to help set the agenda for the research and analysis by identifying those environmental resources and values that might be significantly affected by the rule being written. The agency then prepares a draft EIS, which is made available for public comment. At this stage the public comments on the adequacy and accuracy of the agency's plans for avoiding or mitigating the potential environmental damage associated with the rule. The comments must be addressed in the final EIS that accompanies the final rule. In this sense, public comments on a draft EIS are treated in a manner quite similar to the public comments made on a draft rule.

Participation fostered by the PRA is different. In this case the public has no role in the preparation of the paperwork analysis or in the review conducted by the Office of Management and Budget. But where pertinent and required, the agency's assessment of the paperwork burden is contained in the notice of proposed rulemaking, as is information on the availability of the analysis on which the estimates are based. The public is then free to review the agency's studies and conclusions, consider the estimated burdens, and comment on both along with the draft rule.

In general, executive orders promote participation as an important by-product of the information they require agencies to develop and disclose. The regulatory impact analysis required by Executive Order 12866 is available to the public. So too are the results of the OMB's review of the rule. These pieces of information can facilitate informed comment and other forms of participation by the public in a rulemaking that is under way. Other executive orders provide different types of aids to participation or other forms altogether. Executive Order 12372 required consultation with the states when agencies undertake actions that affect the management of intergovernmental fiscal affairs. Executive Order 12866 requires agencies to develop and publish a planning document that outlines their future regulatory actions, most of which require rules. This assists participation by giving the public an advance look at what is in store for them and allowing them time to plan for effective participation in those rules that carry a high priority. All this presumes, of course, that critical information is accessible and used by those with an interest in participation.

Judicial review of rulemaking can promote participation as well. When an aggrieved party convinces a court that an agency has failed to take into account important information during the course of a rulemaking, the judge(s) may order several remedies. One is to require the agency, in effect, to work with the successful plaintiff to correct the deficiencies in the rule. A court's finding that a rule is defective and its agreement with the plaintiffs as to the reasons why will compel an agency to be quite attentive to the parties that brought the lawsuit when it returns to the rulemaking to try again. The patterns we observe in participation are essentially the same as those that emerge in the information dimension of rulemaking. The actions of Congress, the president, and the courts have increased and diversified the opportunities for participation. Information and participation are linked inextricably. Information has no practical significance unless it is used by those who wish to contribute to and influence the course of rulemaking, whether it is before the rule is issued or after, as in litigation and oversight. Participation cannot be effective unless people have the information that is needed to determine if, how, and to what extent a rule under development will affect their lives.

We will see in Chapters 5 and 6, however, that there are other sources of information and paths of influence that are less formal and more numerous than those discussed above. Taken together, the formal and informal dimensions mean that the development of important roles is open, rich in information sources, and replete with opportunities to influence the outcomes.

Mechanisms of Accountability

A strong case can be made that the elements of information and participation outlined above would be of questionable significance if they stood alone with no mechanisms to hold agencies accountable for the rules they ultimately write. Like participation, these mechanisms of accountability are so crucial to contemporary rulemaking that an entire chapter of this book is devoted to them. At this point, however, it is important to establish the main forms of accountability. Like information and participation, they too have grown and diversified since passage of the Administrative Procedure Act.

Rulemakers are accountable to three constitutional authorities. These are the primary institutions created in the Constitution. The actual mechanisms of accountability used by Congress, the president, and the courts take many forms. Some are direct and explicit; others are indirect and subtle. At times the line between participation and accountability blurs, as members of the institutions to whom rulemakers answer become active players in the development of rules. What is clear, however, is that Congress, the president, and the courts review and routinely pass judgment on the products of the rulemaking processes. The institutions vary in the criteria they employ, which creates a situation in which an agency in attempting to respond to the wishes of one may run afoul of another. In days of divided government the stresses placed on rulemakers attempting to respond to their squabbling sovereigns can be substantial.

Two fundamental aspects of this accountability network are worthy of note. First, those who write rules are expected to be responsive to multiple superior authorities, each of which wields considerable power over the agency. Second, the priorities and objectives of each of these authorities differ. Congress is driven by the interests of constituents and expects those who write rules to be responsive to them as well. The power exerted by Congress is fragmented and incoherent as many members of the House and Senate jockey for influence in the rulemaking process. House and Senate jurisdictions, drawn as they are, can result in agencies' reporting to multiple committees and subcommittees. The president is driven by what he perceives to be his mandate from the entire electorate or at least those segments that supported him. His priorities are more focused, as are the mechanisms he uses to ensure responsiveness. Judges have no constituents as such. Their purpose is to see that the law is observed and to resolve disputes accordingly. But in their behavior judges resemble Congress more than the president because of the varied backgrounds and judicial philosophies they bring to the bench. Although presidents have put their clear stamp on the judiciary through the appointment process, there is never any guarantee of consistency or predictability in a federal court system as diverse as ours.[37]

How the APA Model Has Changed

It is evident from this review of contemporary developments in the process of rulemaking that the model established in the Administrative Procedure Act has been altered profoundly. The changes have been observed and documented more fully by other scholars.[38] It is true that for virtually all the requirements outlined above there are exceptions when the rulemaking agency is freer to act. Every case of rulemaking is distinctive in some way. Many rules are sufficiently minor and routine that the speed and flexibility contemplated by the APA actually characterize the process used by the agency. But there is no mistaking the general direction in procedural requirements for those rules that are not considered routine or minor, or for the once rare instances of emergency action: Congress, the president, and the courts have come to prefer a more elaborate and procedurally encumbered model for rulemaking than that which was outlined in the APA.

It is striking how far we have moved from the model outlined in the APA, particularly in the category of information. One could argue that the net effect of the various legal developments related to information is the creation of a legislative equivalent of "open discovery"—when litigants can learn about the facts in each other's possession—and the deposition processes so familiar in civil litigation. As noted, numerous statutes and executive orders require the agency to produce information and documents on a range of standard questions, just as the attorney for the plaintiff might do during a deposition. This information, once developed, is placed with all the other information the agency considered during the course of a rulemaking into a formal record, or docket, which is then completely open for review by the public. The docket and the records it contains must, on examination, explain the decisions that led to the rule.[39] While critical features found in trial proceedings are missing, information requirements and the intensity provided by public participation, particularly when information in the record is challenged and agency witnesses are cross-examined, have gone so far as to transform some rulemakings into quasi-judicial proceedings.

We can see from these decades of legal developments that the coalition that embraced the simple and flexible requirements of section 553 of the APA soon lost its salience. The rulemaking process simply became too crucial, visible, and potentially dangerous. The political coalition that had advocated big government was able, for a time, to dominate both the substantive and the procedural dimensions of the debate. In order to extend the reach of government further, as occurred in the 1960s and 1970s, an implicit trade-off of substance for process was made. The advocates of more government got new laws and programs; those who opposed these initiatives or feared their negative consequences got new procedural requirements for rulemaking, which they could use to constrain, channel, and delay this crucial stage in the policy process. As James O'Reilly notes, these "procedural victories took the sting out of substantive regulation."[40]

Exceptions, Exemptions, and Evasions

At this stage the reader may feel as though he or she is sitting at a railroad crossing waiting for a freight train with no end in sight to pass. But before reaching what would be the eminently reasonable conclusion that contemporary rulemaking is hopelessly encumbered by massive and stultifying legal requirements, one must remember, there are no absolutes in government. Not all rulemakings entail every one of the legal requirements outlined above. In fact, only a minority do. Although the rulemaking process has become generally more complex than the minimum standards outlined in the APA, most rules can be developed without attention to all the analyses, reviews, and opportunities for public involvement mentioned earlier.

There are three ways that some or most of the legal requirements outlined can be suspended. First, some types of rules were exempted when some of these requirements were first enacted. Second, the subject matter of some rules makes certain legal requirements irrelevant. Third, if they are so inclined, agencies can evade certain requirements by engaging in pro forma compliance or by finding a way to characterize their actions so that the requirements do not apply.

Exemptions and exceptions have been written into many of the statutes that established the requirements now associated with rulemaking. The practice began with the Administrative Procedure Act itself. Provisions of the APA allow agencies to develop procedural and interpretive rules without prior public notice or participation. When, in the opinion of the agency, there is a compelling public interest, these same requirements, which are the core of the APA's rulemaking provisions, can be suspended for legislative rules as well.[41] The National Environmental Policy Act has been interpreted to allow for "programmatic exemptions" when a given type of frequent or routine agency action can be shown to carry no significant environmental effects.[42] Rulemaking apparently qualifies broadly for such exemptions, because one can read final rules published in the *Federal Register* for many days without once encountering a reference to NEPA. The Paperwork Reduction Act also allows exemptions for certain types of frequent, minor, and routine rulemakings.

Executive orders also exempt certain types of rules from their analysis and review requirements. Executive Order 12866 specifically exempted regulations dealing with "emergency situation(s)" and regulations where OMB involvement would interfere with the ability of the agency to meet statutory or judicially imposed deadlines. Executive Order 12866 also allowed for exemptions of entire classes of rules, a privilege that is extended to several programs administered by the Environmental Protection Agency, the Department of Agriculture, the Federal Aviation Administration, and others.[43]

As noted earlier, the subject matter of a rule can effectively eliminate many legal requirements. If a rule has no environmental effects, has no serious implications for smaller entities, has no effect on state and local government powers and prerogatives, or involves no new collections of information, then the procedural obligations that would otherwise apply have no bearing on the rulemaking process. Of course, each of these conditions involves some degree of interpretation. What constitutes a significant effect on state and local government or smaller entities is a matter of judgment. Agencies applying a liberal threshold for what constitutes "significance" will find themselves burdened with additional work; those with a more restrictive view will find the rulemaking task substantially eased.

The effects of evasion through interpretation can be seen in the case of the intended regulatory impact analysis requirements put forth in Executive Order 12291. The order required an analysis only if the costs of complying with a rule equaled or exceeded $100 million or if compliance had "major" or "significant" effects on other levels of government or on various aspects of the economy. In fact, regulatory impact analyses were done infrequently by rule-writing agencies. Ostensibly, this was because they estimated that the rules they wrote would not have effects of the magnitude set out in the executive order. Although there was no hard evidence to suggest that agencies were engaging in minimal or pro forma compliance, it is true that economic impact, federalism, and small entities are frequently dealt with in the preambles of rules with language that can only be described as boilerplate. Those who would evade these types of analytical requirements faced a tougher task under Clinton's Executive Order 12866. Under his order OMB review was more selective; ostensibly it allowed the president's staff to scrutinize regulatory analyses more closely in order to ensure that they were done and done well.[44]

Another form of evasion is the avoidance of rulemaking altogether. Because of the difficulties agencies face in rulemaking, some have resorted to the use of "guidelines," "interpretations," and technical manuals and other vehicles to state or refine policy.[45] Less easy to characterize is the "direct final rule" that turns the normal rulemaking process on its head. In direct final rulemaking the agency publishes its new requirement without benefit of prior notice or public comment, but invites participation and the possibility of amendment after the first effective date for compliance.[46] In the next chapter we will consider the controversy that has resulted from the use of these devices, in lieu of rulemaking. Suffice it to say that the frequency of their use is testimony to the formidable task that rulemaking has become because of multiple procedural requirements.

The variable applicability of the procedural obligations that have accumulated since passage of the Administrative Procedure Act should underscore for us some important points about the state of contemporary rulemaking. First, rulemaking is an enormously diverse form of government action; no single set of procedures is appropriate or even feasible in all circumstances. Although we are correct to be concerned about the right to participate in a crucial legislative process, most of us also acknowledge that in some circumstances even that cherished value must give way to the need for prompt action to preserve life or property. Second, we must acknowledge that bureaucratic routines and the sheer magnitude of the rulemaking process require attention to enforcement if procedural requirements are to be consistently observed. The pressures on rulemaking agencies are considerable, especially when powerful external or internal constituencies are clamoring for regulations. In Chapter 6 we will explore how the review of rules and other forms of oversight by the White House, the courts, Congress, and even other agencies contribute to compliance with procedural requirements.

The best way to illustrate the decisions and steps that are commonly associated with rulemaking is to leave this discussion of formal legal requirements and take a more practical look at how a substantial rulemaking might proceed from inception to conclusion.

The Stages of Rulemaking

Having established the legal dimension of the rulemaking process, we can now take a more practical, operational look at how rules come into being. The rulemaking process is easier to understand by conceiving of it as a sequence of activities, each of which is affected by ones that precede it. As in past editions of this book, James O'Reilly's conceptualization of the stages of rulemaking provides our framework (see Table 2-1).

Stage 1: Origin of Rulemaking Activity

Although not part of the actual rulemaking process, the writing of law by Congress is the true origin of rulemaking. No rule is valid unless it is authorized by law and is promoting a statutory purpose of some kind. Key features of such legislation are the substantive mission it establishes for rulemaking, the number and timing of rules the agency will be required to write, the degree of discretion the agency enjoys in determining the content of rules, and the procedural requirements imposed on the agency.

Stage 2: Origin of Individual Rulemaking

Although all rules can ultimately be traced to statutes, specific rules often have more proximate origins. Statutes vary considerably in the degree to which they mandate that particular rules be written. Laws may be very explicit and specific. They may also contain deadlines and provisions that will take effect if the agency fails to meet the schedule. These provisions are called *hammers* and will be discussed further in Chapter 6. When rules are not explicitly mandated, the potential sources of ideas for new rules are many. Some are internal to the agency; others are external. The political leadership of the agency may bring with it policy agendas that can be implemented only through rulemaking. Advisory committees attached to an agency can also be the source of ideas for rules, although their authority in this area varies markedly. Those closest to program operations in an agency are in the best position to spot the need for new or revised rules. Many agencies have well-developed systems for analyzing new legislation or amendments to existing statutory authorities in order to determine what rules will be required to carry out the new provisions.

TABLE 2-1 An Outline of Rulemaking Activity

Stage 1   Origin of Rulemaking Activity: Rules Mandated or Authorized by Law
  Degree of agency discretion
  Procedural requirements
  Volume and frequency of rules to be produced

Stage 2   Origin of Individual Rulemaking
  Content of legislation
   Deadlines
   "Hammer provisions"
  Internal sources
   Political leadership
   Senior career service
   Advisory committees
   Program office staff
   Office of general counsel
   Field staff
   Enforcement officials
   "Advance Notice of Proposed Rulemaking"
  External sources
   White House
   Congress (other than legislation)
   Other agencies
   Public petitions

Stage 3   Authorization to Proceed with Rulemaking
  Priority-setting system
  Agency approval process

Stage 4   Planning the Rulemaking
  Goals of the rule
  Legal requirements
  Information requirements—technical and political
  Participation plan
   Internal agency constituencies
   Affected groups, firms, and individuals
  Securing necessary resources
  Assigning staff

Stage 5   Developing the Draft Rule
  Collection of information
  Analysis of information
  Impact studies (paperwork, small business, environmental, etc.)
  Internal consultations
  External consultations (informal)
  Draft language of preamble and rule
  Implementation plan

Stage 6   Internal Review of the Draft Rule
  "Horizontal" review
   Other program offices

Stage 6   Internal Review of the Draft Rule *(continued)*
                General counsel
                Policy analysts
                Research and development
                Field and enforcement offices
                Advisory groups
            "Vertical" review
                Management chain
                Political leadership of office and agency

Stage 7   External Review of the Draft Rule
                Office of Management and Budget
                Congress (informal)
                Interest groups
                Other agencies

Stage 8   Revision and Publication of a Draft Rule
                Notice of Proposed Rulemaking transmitted to *Federal Register*

Stage 9   Public Participation
                Receipt of written comment
                Conduct of hearings or public meeting
                Review and analysis of public input
                Draft responses to public input

Stage 10   Action on the Draft Rule
                Choice of alternatives
                    (a) Prepare final rule with no change
                    (b) Prepare final rule with minor change
                    (c) Another round of public participation
                    (d) Prepare final rule with major change
                    (e) Abandon rulemaking and start over
                    (f) Abandon rulemaking altogether
                    If (f), prepare appropriate notice for *Federal Register*
                    If (e), return to Stage 3
                    If (d), return to Stage 5
                    If (c), return to Stage 8
                    If (b), draft revisions, repeat Stages 6 and 7 with formal
                        congressional review; prepare Notice of Final
                        Rulemaking for *Federal Register* and transmit
                    If (a), repeat Stage 7 with formal congressional review, and
                        prepare and transmit Notice of Final Rulemaking for
                        Federal Register
                    [See a reproduction of an actual rule in Figure 2-1]

Stage 11   Post-Rulemaking Activities
                Staff interpretations
                Technical corrections
                Respond to petitions for reconsideration
                Prepare for litigation

Source: Adapted from James O'Reilly, *Administrative Rulemaking: Structuring, Opposing, and Defending Federal Agency Regulations* (Colorado Springs, Colo.: Shepard's/McGraw-Hill, 1983), with the permission of West Group.

A good example of this is the work done by a task force within the Environmental Protection Agency in advance of passage of the Clean Air Act Amendments of 1990.[47] Months before the bill was signed by President George H. W. Bush, the EPA had in hand a detailed plan that contained information on the number, content, and scheduling of the rules by the new legislation. Similar planning was undertaken by the Federal Communications Commission to implement the complex and numerous provisions of the historic Telecommunications Act of 1996.[48] Efforts like these are usually led by a team of agency lawyers and technical staff in the affected program areas. Finally, the agency officials in the field actually implement, administer, and enforce rules and come into direct and constant contact with regulated or benefiting communities and representatives from other agencies and levels of government. They are a likely source of ideas for new or revised rules to improve program operations.

There are many potentially important external sources for ideas for rules as well. The most visible is the White House. The Vice President's Task Force on Regulatory Relief, which functioned during the Reagan administration, was a frequent source of ideas for elimination of rules and alterations in others to make them less burdensome to the private sector. This body took a new form in 1991 and was called the Council on Competitiveness. It was abolished by President Clinton early in 1993. He replaced it with the Regulatory Working Group (RWG), composed of representatives of the major departments and agencies, and chaired by the director of the OMB's Office of Information and Regulatory Affairs. Clinton also directed the focus to regulatory issues that cut across the government. President George W. Bush did not establish a new body but created a mechanism by which new ideas for rules were communicated to agencies by the OMB. Both he and President Clinton were aggressive in identifying rules in need of change or elimination.[49]

In addition to the White House, federal agencies can be a source of ideas, and pressure, for new rules. For many years the Federal Energy Regulatory Commission (FERC) failed to develop regulations that established its approach to complying with the National Environmental Policy Act. In this it was virtually alone among the major agencies of the federal government whose work had environmental consequences. In time, pressure on FERC from numerous federal and state environmental and natural resource agencies mounted. FERC conceded and in 1988 implemented its first comprehensive rule outlining how it intended to comply with NEPA.[50]

External sources of ideas for rules need not be confined to the public sector. The Administrative Procedure Act allows anyone to petition an agency to make a rule. There is scant empirical evidence on the number of petitions received and how they are ultimately disposed of. It is safe to assume, however, that they vary considerably in quality and seriousness. Agencies are required only to acknowledge the petition and consider the request. The attention these requests are given depends on the agency's views on the salience of the issue presented, the evidence provided with the request for a new rule, and the support for and source of the petition.

There is an important variation on the petition process. Several agencies use permanent committees on an ongoing basis to recommend new rules or revisions to existing ones. Prominent examples of these—in very different areas—are the Aviation Rulemaking Advisory Committee of the Federal Aviation Administration and the National Organics Standard Board of the Agriculture Marketing Service.[51]

Stage 3: Authorization to Proceed with Rulemaking

Given the multiplicity of sources and large number of potential rulemaking projects that most agencies could undertake, mechanisms may be in place to authorize the start of work on a new rule. Because the investment by an agency in the development of a rule can be substantial, senior management may want to be sure that available resources, which are always limited, are put to work on those projects of greatest importance. The priority-setting process for rulemaking in federal agencies is discussed at length in Chapter 4. Mechanisms to authorize rulemaking vary dramatically. This stage marks the transition in a rulemaking from ideas to action.

Stage 4: Planning the Rulemaking

Some type of planning is needed for all rules, regardless of their scope or complexity. Whether it is done consciously or unconsciously, formally or informally, planning for rulemaking forces agencies to confront important questions. The first order of business is to determine who in the agency will be responsible for developing the rule. Assigning responsibility for a particular rulemaking is determined by a variety of methods in government agencies. Usually the responsibility is shared by several components of an agency. The importance of rules, the variety of issues that must be resolved during rulemaking, and the variety of perspectives within an agency affected by the results will determine whether the rule is written by an individual or small group from a single office or whether it will be a collective exercise involving many people from throughout the entire agency. Whatever the form, these staff members must be found and assigned to the task. The selection of individuals is obviously based on their expertise and areas of responsibility, but the availability of key people at any point in time may be an issue. Conflicting demands on available expertise is a chronic problem, so agencies must have some method for assigning people to rulemaking projects.

Once personnel are selected and assigned, the task itself becomes the focus of planning. What is the objective of the rule being written? To answer this question, the agency must review the statutory language and, perhaps, the legislative history to determine what Congress sought to accomplish with the legislation. Then the agency must determine which of the numerous potential procedural requirements apply to this particular rulemaking. By sorting out the objectives of the rule and the legal requirements that must be satisfied during its development, the agency can begin to comprehend the information needed to complete the rulemaking. Knowing what information is required, the agency can then consider where and how to obtain it. This may well raise new resource issues. This review may lead the agency to conclude that internal staff and information resources are insufficient to complete the rule and that additional information must be collected. For this the agency may choose to use contractors. Sufficient monies must be available and the agency must set about to structure a separate process to meet the extensive legal requirements that apply when the government procures services from the private sector.

This stage is not too early to begin thinking about how the public will be involved. Each form of public participation requires different support. If the agency opts for written comments only, it must establish a system for docketing what it receives. If it intends to use an advisory group not already formed, the requirements of the FACA, discussed earlier, must be considered and arrangements made for the conduct of the group's meetings. Similarly, public hearings require considerable advance work. Sites and formats for the meeting must be determined, arrangements must be made to secure transcripts of the proceedings, and travel plans need to be worked out.

At this planning stage of the rulemaking process, the responsible staff may also receive guidance from senior officials and political leaders in the agency. Although it may be confined to only the most important rules, policy guidance from the agency's leadership can establish both the substantive and procedural direction for the rulemaking. If such guidance occurs early enough, it can foreclose certain options and prevent investments of time and effort on alternative approaches to a rule that would be unacceptable to those in the agency with ultimate authority.

Clearly, this is an important stage in the rulemaking. Although the content of the rule may not be determined with any degree of specificity, the quality of work done at this point influences the ease and speed with which the rulemaking is conducted. Advance planning of this sort, especially in determining major policy issues, obtaining guidance from senior officials, and clarifying how essential information can be obtained can prevent delays later.

Stage 5: Developing the Draft Rule

The content of a rule is determined during this stage. So too is the agency's compliance with many of the procedural requirements we have already discussed. There is a simple sequence that must be followed during this stage, since those working on the rule must determine to some extent what the rule will contain. Until some general idea of the content is formed, one cannot fully determine which of the myriad potential legal requirements will apply. Will the rule have an effect on the physical environment? Will it have a disproportionate impact on small businesses and other entities? Does it curtail in any way the normal legal prerogatives of state and local governments? Will it necessitate the collection and reporting of additional information? The answers to these basic questions, and many others, determine whether particular types of analyses and external reviews will be needed. In any event, the work to determine the content of the rule and to meet the legal requirements that apply is done during this stage.

This is a period of intense activity for those engaged in writing the rule. Extensive internal and external consultations are likely to occur for at least two important reasons. First, those responsible are combing known sources for the expertise and information needed to complete a draft of the rule. At the same time they are attempting to keep key constituencies informed of the direction and progress of the rule. Even though formal requirements for public participation usually do not take effect until a draft rule is completed, there is evidence of substantial contact between the agency and interested or affected parties well before this point in the process.[52] Informal contacts of this sort will be explored at length in Chapter 5.

At the end of this stage the agency will have completed work on drafts of key elements of the rule. It will have a draft rule that contains the actual language it is proposing. It will also have completed the studies and reports needed to satisfy whatever other legal requirements apply. Finally, it will have a draft preamble to the draft rule that is a narrative explanation of the rule and its compliance with applicable procedural requirements. At this stage, although the rule may not be formalized, the agency has also considered how it will be implemented, administered, and enforced. In some cases the agency expends considerable effort attempting to assist those affected by the rules in their efforts to comply. A regular feature of the EPA's rulemaking process is the preparation of a draft "communications strategy" that outlines how the regulated community will be informed of its new responsibilities.[53]

Amendments to the Regulatory Flexibility Act of 1996 require certain agencies to develop "compliance assistance" materials to aid small businesses.[54] The Nuclear Regulatory Commission routinely prepares a technical assistance manual to help the operators of regulated facilities to comply with new regulations. These documents would be prepared in draft form during this stage as well.

Stage 6: Internal Review of the Draft Rule

The ease or difficulty of conducting internal reviews depends quite heavily on how Stage 5 was conducted. Internal reviews of draft rules occur horizontally and vertically.[55] *Horizontal review* takes place across the agency, allowing the various offices to determine if the rule has any effect on the areas under their jurisdiction and, if so, whether they agree with (or at least can accept) what is being proposed. The role of offices in an agency during this internal review varies considerably, in no small part because of the relative power each enjoys in the bureaucratic pecking order. The office of the general counsel, or its equivalent, usually plays a major role, since its lawyers are charged with ensuring that everything the agency does is legally permissible. What other offices will be involved depends entirely on the scope of the rule and the issues raised during its development.

Vertical review involves supervisors and senior officials. Since rules are usually developed at a relatively low level of the agency, this review is conducted to ensure that what is being proposed is consistent with overall program operations and general agency policy. The number of levels of vertical review varies considerably across agencies. The number depends entirely on where in the agency responsibility for developing the rule lies and on the way in which an agency is organized.

The use of a team approach in developing a rule can expedite both horizontal and vertical reviews. If all the offices affected by a proposed rule are involved in its development and if their representatives reflect the views of their superiors, then the review process should be pro forma. This is especially true if the rule represents the consensus of the team. The role of these agency rulemaking teams is important and will be explored at greater length later in the book.

Stage 7: External Review of the Draft Rule

A wide variety of agencies may be asked to review a draft rule, and those especially affected by its contents may have been consulted extensively during its development. In certain instances an agency may have a special role to play for a particular aspect of the rulemaking. This is the case for the reviews by the Council on Environmental Quality of environmental impact statements and the role of the Small Business Administration in the Regulatory Flexibility Act. It is widely agreed, however, that the most consistently important external review of draft rules is conducted by the Office of Management and Budget under the authorities granted it by the Paperwork Reduction Act and a variety of executive orders.

The OMB affects both the substance and process of rules. All the reviews take time, the amount varying according to the size of the rule and the policy issues it raises. The OMB has the authority to return rules that do not meet the administration's standards to the agencies involved. At this stage, Congress is consulted.

Stage 8: Revision and Publication of a Draft Rule

The revision and publication of a draft rule may appear to be a routine matter, but in fact the *Federal Register* is particular about the format and content of the proposed rules it publishes. Its guidelines are quite stringent, and agencies must frequently revise their original submissions to meet the specifications in the *Register*.[56] Most agencies employ personnel who have expertise in *Register* publication guidelines—clear evidence that this step is both substantial and taken seriously.

Stage 9: Public Participation

As mentioned earlier, the views of the public can be received in a variety of ways. The agency can call for written public comments or decide to conduct some form of public meeting or hearing or embrace some combination that involves all these options. Authorizing legislation may require a particular form of participation. When it does not, decisions with regard to the form and management of public participation depend heavily on the amount and intensity of interest the proposed rule is likely to generate. There is little reason to structure elaborate opportunities for public participation when the agency is confident that it is noncontroversial. The choice between written comment and the conduct of public hearings often has more to do with politics and public relations than it does the quality of the input anticipated. In instances of complex or highly controversial rules, the public hearing may be selected because it allows agency personnel to go to the field and explain what they are doing to affected parties and make a case for it. At other times the opposition may be so intractable, and predictable, that public meetings would serve little purpose other than catharsis.

It is at this stage that the agency must actually manage the receipt of comments, ensuring that those that are submitted are retained and made available in a location accessible to the public. The content of public input must be reviewed and analyzed. The agency often prepares summaries, and it develops responses to the comments, which will ultimately appear in the rule's preamble. If the comments are limited in number and call only for clarification or further refinement of what is already in the rule, the task is relatively simple. The task grows more complex and difficult when numerous substantive issues are raised by commentators who are seriously involved or when this type of input comes from particularly influential or important constituencies. Access to these documents has improved with the development of e-rulemaking and e-dockets, which provide Internet access to the general public.

Stage 10: Action on the Draft Rule

This is obviously a crucial stage. All essential information—technical and political—has been collected, and all constituencies—internal and external—have been heard from. The still-unfinished rule has several alternative paths it might take:

(a) When no changes are needed, the agency has succeeded in producing a draft that can stand as is. All that remains is the preparation of the appropriate notice for the *Federal Register* and final clearance by the OMB and Congress (see Table 2-1). We have already discussed OMB review. The Regulatory Flexibility Act was amended in 1996 to allow for congressional review. That statute requires agencies to submit all final rules to both houses of Congress and the General Accounting Office (now the Government Accountability Office). If the rule is considered "major," it cannot become legally binding for at least sixty days, during which time Congress may take action through legislation to repeal the rule.[57]

(b) When only minor revisions are needed, those drafting the rule may circulate it for another round of internal and external reviews. If the revisions are truly minor, they will be made as a matter of form. Review of the final rule by the OMB and Congress is required, however.

(c) Another round of participation is pursued only when comments by the public are unclear or raise issues that cannot be resolved within the rulemaking agency. Normally, the notice that is issued will ask the public to respond to a specific set of questions.

(d) When major revisions are needed the agency will, in effect, reproduce the process starting with Stage 5, because the changes constitute a new proposed rule.

(e) Abandoning the rulemaking and starting over is a more extreme version of option (d). Here the agency is convinced that all of its work was for naught and begins anew.

(f) A rulemaking is abandoned altogether if the agency is convinced that its decision to write a rule was wrong. Through a notice in the *Federal Register,* it will notify the public that no rule will be issued.

Stage 11: Post-Rulemaking Activities

If rulemaking works smoothly, this stage is not necessary. If it is flawed, however, once the rule is published in the *Federal Register* in final form the process of attempting to undo or revise it can take place almost immediately. The actions take a number of forms. The most dramatic is a lawsuit filed against the agency claiming that in issuing the rule it has somehow acted illegally. The potential grounds for such lawsuits are numerous.

Many post-rulemaking revisions are less dramatic. Staff may be called on to interpret key provisions of the rule that are vague or unclear. Petitions for reconsideration may be filed by parties affected by a new rule who want some element of it changed or clarified. These are treated in a manner that most closely approximates petitions for rulemaking. Frequently, the agency itself will issue technical corrections or amendments to rules when it discovers shortcomings arising from omission or commission. Suffice it to say that it is unwise to consider rulemaking as a process that has a definite start and finish. Elements of rules can be challenged and changed at any time.

Variations in the Sequence of Activities

Rulemaking does not always occur in the sequence presented here. Some stages may be undertaken simultaneously, others reversed in order. The model captures the decisions and tasks that confront rulemakers; not all apply in all cases. In fact, the majority of rules are developed without one or more of the stages or sub-elements present. Very minor or routine rules are exempt from many if not most of the requirements. The content of others obviates the need for the steps related to planning, staffing, and public participation. Still, O'Reilly's basic design, as amended, provides an accurate and full description of a significant rulemaking.

Rulemaking may be relatively simple or highly complex, depending on the issues involved and the parties affected. Rulemaking during the past fifty years has accumulated requirements arising from concerns of the three branches of government, which in turn reflect a more active and sophisticated citizenry. The analyses, reviews, and opportunities for public participation that now characterize the rulemaking process resulted from a growing recognition that what goes on during and emerges from rulemaking is at least equal in importance to any other element of our public policy process. Concerns expressed in the larger political system, be they about the quality of the environment, the burden of government regulation, the vitality of state government, or the integrity of the family, find their way sooner or later to the rulemaking process.

What can be surmised about the larger political system from the current state of the rulemaking process? The lesson is as plain as it is perplexing. We, as a people, are apparently willing to accept the growing reach of government as expressed in the thousands of rules and regulations issued annually by agencies of government. But the process that manufactures these agents of government expansion—rulemaking—is designed to be difficult and slow, at least for the most important rules that agencies issue. However consistent this is with the plan for government established in the Constitution, our inconsistent approach to rules and rulemaking is bound to raise issues. It is to these issues and the contradictions that we now turn.

Notes

1. Personal interview with official of the Federal Aviation Administration, September 8, 2002.
2. Both food safety and prescription drug rules also demonstrate the generational or sequential nature of rulemaking. As in the rules cited here, a significant percentage of rules can trace their origins to studies or earlier rules that were undertaken or enacted years, and in some cases decades, before. For example, see "Prevention of Salmonella Enteritis in Shell Eggs during Production, Storage, and Transport," *Federal Register,* July 9, 2009, and a recent regulation dealing with information requirements for human prescription drugs, *Federal Register,* December 22, 2000, and *Federal Register,* January 24, 2006.
3. James Anderson, "Agricultural Marketing Orders and the Politics of Self Regulation," *Review of Public Policy* 2, no. 1 (2005): 97–111.
4. There are literally thousands of examples of these types of rules. For an example, see "Modification of Class E Airspace: Freemont, MI," *Federal Register,* March 3, 2009.
5. Attorney General's Committee on Administrative Procedure, Administrative Procedures in Government Agencies, S. Doc. 8, 77th Cong., 1st sess., 1941, part 1, p. 5 (hereafter cited as Attorney General's Committee).
6. Ibid., part 7, p. 67.
7. David Rosenbloom, "Public Law and Regulation," in *Handbook of Public Administration,* ed. Jack Rubin, W. Bartley Hildreth, and Gerald Miller (New York: Marcel Dekker, 1989), p. 532. See also David Rosenbloom, *Building a Legislative-Centered Public Administration* (Tuscaloosa: University of Alabama Press, 2000), pp. 27–28.
8. Stephen Breyer and Richard Stewart, *Administrative Law and Regulatory Policy* (Boston: Little, Brown, 1985), p. 31.
9. *Panama Refining Co. v. Ryan,* 293 U.S. 388 (1935); *Schechter Poultry Corporation v. United States,* 295 U.S. 495 (1935); *Carter v. Carter Coal Co.,* 298 U.S. 238 (1936).

10. Rosenbloom, "Public Law and Regulation."

11. Harold Spaeth, *Supreme Court Policy Making: Explanation and Prediction* (San Francisco: W. H. Freeman, 1979), p. 89.

12. Peter Woll, *Administrative Law* (Berkeley: University of California Press, 1963), p. 18.

13. Martin Shapiro, "APA: Past, Present and Future," *Virginia Law Review* 72 (1986): 452.

14. Ibid.

15. Ibid., pp. 453–454.

16. 5 United States Code 551 (6) (hereafter cited as U.S.C.).

17. Kenneth Culp Davis, *Discretionary Justice: A Preliminary Inquiry* (Urbana: University of Illinois Press, 1976), p. 65.

18. Ibid.

19. 5 U.S.C. 706 2(a).

20. Phillip Cooper, *Public Law and Public Administration* (Itaska, Ill.: F. E. Peacock, 2002), pp. 151–153.

21. 29 U.S.C. 655(b)(5).

22. 15 U.S.C. 2603(b)(1).

23. 15 U.S.C. 2603(b)(2)(a).

24. Michael E. Kraft, "The Use of Risk Analysis in Federal Regulatory Agencies: An Exploration," *Policy Studies Review* 1 (May 1982): 666–675.

25. "Elements of Risk Assessment," in *Regulation Development in EPA* (Washington, D.C.: Environmental Protection Agency, 1988).

26. National Environmental Policy Act, 42 U.S.C. 4321–4347; Regulatory Flexibility Act, 5 U.S.C. 601–612; Paperwork Reduction Act, 44 U.S.C. 3501–3520.

27. James O'Reilly, *Administrative Rulemaking: Structuring, Opposing, and Defending Federal Agency Regulations* (Colorado Springs, Colo.: Shepard's/McGraw-Hill, 1983), pp. 14–16.

28. "Federal Regulatory Review" Request for Comments, *Federal Register,* February 26, 2009, p. 8819.

29. Jeffrey Lubbers, *A Guide to Federal Agency Rulemaking,* 3rd ed. (Chicago: American Bar Association, 1998), p. 183.

30. Ibid., p. 185.

31. William Pedersen, "Formal Records and Informal Rulemaking," *Yale Law Journal* 85 (1975): 66–70.

32. Benjamin Mintz and Nancy Miller, *A Guide to Federal Agency Rulemaking,* 2nd ed. (Washington, D.C.: Administrative Conference of the United States, 1991), p. 204 at n. 1.

33. Attorney General's Committee, pp. 103–105.

34. Lubbers, *A Guide to Federal Agency Rulemaking,* p. 6.

35. Stephen Williams, "Hybrid Rulemaking under the Administrative Act: A Legal and Empirical Analysis," *University of Chicago Law Review* 42 (spring 1975): 401ff.

36. 5 U.S.C. app., 1–15. See also Steven Croley, "A Practical Guidance on the Applicability of the Federal Advisory Committee Act," *Administrative Law Journal of American University* 10 (1996).

37. Charles Johnson and Bradley Canon, *Judicial Policies: Implementation and Impact,* 2nd ed. (Washington, D.C.: CQ Press, 1999), chap. 2.

38. For example, see Thomas McGarrity, "Some Thoughts on De-Ossifying Rulemaking," *Duke Law Journal* 41 (1992): 1385–1462.

39. Lubbers, *A Guide to Federal Agency Rulemaking,* part 3, chap. 5.

40. O'Reilly, *Administrative Rulemaking,* p. 335.

41. 5 U.S.C. 553(b)(1)B.
42. Richard Linoff, *A National Policy for the Environment: NEPA and Its Aftermath* (Bloomington: Indiana University Press, 1976), pp. 193–207.
43. Executive Office of the President, *Regulatory Program of the United States Government* (Washington, D.C.: 1991), pp. 648–649.
44. President, Executive Order No. 12866, Regulatory Planning and Review, sec. 6 (a) (3) (A), *Federal Register,* October 3, 1993.
45. Robert Anthony, "Interpretive Rules, Policy Statements, Guidances, Manuals and the Like: Should Agencies Use Them to Bind the Public?" *Duke Law Journal* 41 (1992): 1311–1384. See also Bryan Tahler and Mark Shere, "EPA's Practice of Regulating by Memo," in *Natural Resources and Environment* (Washington, D.C.: American Bar Association, 1990).
46. For discussions of the use of direct final rules, see Jeffrey Lubbers, *A Guide to Federal Agency Rulemaking,* 4th ed. (Chicago: American Bar Association, 2006); see also Ronald Levin, "Direct Final Rulemaking," *George Washington Law Review* 64, no. 1 (1995).
47. Environmental Protection Agency, *Implementation Strategy for the Clean Air Act Amendments of 1990* (Washington, D.C.: Office of Air and Radiation, Environmental Protection Agency, 1991).
48. "Draft FCC Implementation Schedule for the Telecommunications Act of 1996, Pub. L. No. 104–104, 110 Stat. 56" (Washington, D.C.: Federal Communications Commission, 1997).
49. See Lubbers, *A Guide to Federal Agency Rulemaking,* chap. 8; Office of Management and Budget, "Draft Report to Congress on the Costs and Benefits of Federal Regulation," *Federal Register,* March 28, 2002.
50. *Federal Register,* December 17, 1987, p. 897.
51. U.S. Department of Transportation, Federal Aviation Administration, National Policy, Order 1110.119K, Aviation Rulemaking Advisory Committee, effective March 20, 2008 (available at www.faa.gov/about/committees/advisory/media/order1110_119K.pdf); U.S. Department of Agriculture, Agricultural Marketing Service, National Organic Program (available at www.ams.usda.gov/AMSv1.0/NOSB).
52. William F. West, "Inside the Black Box: The Development of Proposed Rules and the Limits of Procedural Controls," *Administration and Society* 41, no. 5 (September 2009): 576–599.
53. Environmental Protection Agency, Communication Strategy Document Development, EPA Order 1510 (Washington, D.C.: Environmental Protection Agency, undated).
54. Office of Advocacy, "Small Business Regulatory Enforcement Fairness Act of 1996 (Washington, D.C.: Small Business Administration, 1997).
55. Fred Emery, *Rulemaking as an Organizational Process* (Washington, D.C.: Administrative Conference of the United States, 1982).
56. *Code of Federal Regulations,* vol. 1, parts 15–22.
57. 5 U.S.C. 803(2).

CHAPTER 3

Issues and Contradictions

The general condition of government provides the context for rulemaking. Today that general condition defies easy characterization because public and professional opinion on government performance is unstable and continues to be profoundly affected by the events of September 11, 2001, as well as by events associated with the more recent financial and home mortgage crises. In 2009 a poll by the Pew Research Center for the People and the Press found that in those functions of the public sector that are especially dependent on rules, notably regulation, large majorities of the American people believed that government controls too much of their daily lives and that the restrictions on business do more harm than good.[1] Shortly after September 11, however, general levels of public confidence had risen to 60 percent according to a Gallup Poll, but a few months later the number had again dropped to 45 percent and continued to fall into the end of the George W. Bush administration. One moderate think tank, Third Way, actually advocated for a trust in government initiative as part of the Obama agenda.[2] The Pew poll also found that 57 percent, a majority of Americans, believed that the public sector was inefficient and wasteful.[3] This number is an improvement over previous years, and one has to wonder what role the economic crisis and the election of President Barack Obama have had to affect this.

The American people have long decried government in the abstract but rushed to its waiting arms with their problems or dreams. Throughout the 1980s, the 1990s, and into the 2000s, when skepticism and outright hostility toward the federal government reached unprecedented levels, demands for specific public responses to private needs and desires continued unabated. The public response to September 11, however temporary, is not at all unusual. Perhaps the best analogy is that of the drug- or alcohol-dependent person who despises the object of his or her addiction but cannot resist for long the siren call of the bottle, needle, or pipe. However much faith Americans have lost in the ability of government to solve problems or act fairly, they have not enthusiastically embraced the only clear alternatives. We usually do not ignore problems, tough them out on our own, or rely solely on the dynamics of the free market or the munificence of charities and philanthropists, despite the championing of these alternatives by popular politicians. One need only look to the aftermath of the corporate scandals of the early 2000s and to issues regarding Wall Street's role in the recent financial crisis for validation of this point. In the wake of Enron, WorldCom, and Tyco, the Pew Research Center for the People and the Press found that from July 2001 until February 2002 the public who regarded regulations as necessary shifted from 41 to 50 percent, whereas those stating that regulations do more harm than good dropped from 54 to 41 percent.[4] Similarly, there was an immediate outcry for increased regulation of the home mortgage and financial markets following the recent meltdown.

And so it is with rulemaking. That a process so vital to government is a popular target of the legions of the dissatisfied should come as no surprise. Indeed, considerable criticism has been heaped upon rulemaking and its results. In the 1980s and 1990s prominent scholars used terms like *malaise, ossification,* and *atrophy* to describe the state of rulemaking.[5] This will no doubt be curious to those who remember hearing objections that the government was issuing far too many rules. A paradox is obvious. On one side, there are complaints that rulemaking has congealed into a state of disuse; on the other, there is concern that it is running amok.

The reader must remember that the demand for rules and the concomitant pressures on rulemaking have oscillated during the past several decades. The level of discontent, although indisputably high, has not been sufficient for us to abandon rules as primary instruments of government. Nor have we even decided to depend less on rulemaking as the primary process for establishing our legal obligations and giving form and specific meaning to our public policy. We must evaluate what follows as critiques of an indispensable government process that persists despite its frailties and imperfections.

Beyond the issues discussed in this chapter are larger and more fundamental problems related directly to rules and rulemaking. Debates about the role of government in citizens' lives and the way government should be conducted are as intense today as they were at the time of the founding of the country. These debates arise from contrasting visions of the purpose and proper scope of the public sector. They involve ideology, constitutional theory, and assessments of institutional capacity. As we focus on pragmatic and operational issues, we must keep the more fundamental ones in mind as well. Ultimately, they are more important.

Four general issues emerge from the scholarship on rules and rulemaking. They are the volume of rulemaking, the quality of rules, the time it takes to write them, and the involvement of the American people in their development.

The Volume of Rulemaking

The first general issue, the volume of rulemaking, has a number of sub-issues associated with it. Two of these, the strain on institutional capacity and how the volume of rules affects implementation, are addressed here.

The Strain on Institutional Capacity

The rules written each year number in the thousands. Their aggregate effect on the lives of Americans cannot be exaggerated; no instrument of government exerts such influence on the quality and conduct of our lives. A common complaint is that there are simply too many rules. Beyond this general discontent lie potentially serious operational problems. When the amount of rulemaking undertaken by a single agency increases, questions of institutional capacity arise.[6] We have known for some time that when the number of rules affecting a particular sector of the economy or society increases, similar questions about the ability and willingness of the private sector to comply loom large.[7]

Like so many important elements of rulemaking, the volume of rules written by a given agency is determined in substantial part by the legislation it is administering. Some agencies exercise statutory authority that requires relatively few rules, whereas others must issue hundreds every year and maintain a sizable backlog of rules in various stages of development. In addition to legislation, three additional sources of rulemaking were identified in the preceding chapter. First, the agency itself can decide to undertake a program of rulemaking to address emerging issues or to renovate regulations that have become obsolete or ineffective. Second, the public may petition an agency to make a rule, and the agency may respond positively. Finally, new rules may be required when regulations are challenged successfully through litigation. Still, legislation, new or amended, is a major determinant of the size of an agency's rulemaking agenda.

It is meaningless to consider just the number of rules written without regard for their scope and complexity or for the resources available to the agency responsible for writing them. Whether the amount of rulemaking done becomes a problem for a given agency is determined by situational factors such as the agency's resources, experience, expertise, and relations with external interests. Even a comparatively small number of rulemakings can put an agency with limited experience and resources under considerable stress. Conversely, agencies that issue hundreds of rules a year can manage with little difficulty, thanks to accumulated expertise, relatively smooth relations with affected parties, the development of effective and efficient bureaucratic routines, and the serial, if not routine, nature of the rules themselves. There is ample evidence that a mismatch between the volume of rulemaking and institutional capacity frequently becomes a real problem.

Programs of social regulation are especially susceptible to strains on institutional capacity, and the reasons are clear. Such programs are created to deal with problems that sometimes cut across the entire society and economy. They are often the first substantial undertaking for the national government in areas that have either been the preserve of states and localities or left entirely to private transactions or relationships. Usually enacted by Congress against a backdrop of widespread public approval and high expectations, these programs are expected to accomplish daunting tasks in a short period of time.[8] The legislation that establishes the program is often long on lofty rhetoric and ambitious objectives but quite short on operational details and budgets.[9] And, as noted in Chapter 1, the agenda that such legislation sets for rulemaking is massive. The difficulties these factors can create for the agency responsible for rulemaking, and the difficulties the rulemaking agencies can create for themselves, are well illustrated by two landmarks in the history of social regulation—workplace safety and health and the management of hazardous waste.

When the Occupational Safety and Health Act became law in 1970, it included an unusual provision that allowed the responsible agency, the Occupational Safety and Health Administration (OSHA), to adopt "consensus national standards" without using rulemaking procedures outlined in the Administrative Procedure Act.[10] The demands for action from powerful and vocal constituencies that had lobbied effectively for its creation were unremitting. In an apparent effort to establish itself as an aggressive regulator, OSHA issued nearly 4,500 regulations in a period of five months.[11] Those remotely familiar with the normal pace of government decision making will agree that this level of productivity in rulemaking is absolutely breathtaking. Those who were the ultimate consumers of OSHA's regulations were also impressed. Unfortunately, the impression was anything but favorable. The rules were met with cascades of criticism, outrage, and—worse—ridicule. More than one astute observer of the regulatory process has attributed much of OSHA's tortured history in rulemaking to this fateful approach that seemed to value volume over professionalism, relevance, and reason.[12]

In retrospect, this unprecedented outpouring of rules was the result of a too fond embrace of Congress's tempting invitation to adopt consensus standards. Certainly this was the quickest way for OSHA to drop a net of rules across its vast jurisdiction, but it was also one of the least effective. OSHA adopted as its rules thousands of standards set by professional organizations and trade associations. They had been developed through the decades in a process that muted potentially intense controversy by treating the resulting standards as nonbinding, advisory, and voluntary. In a rush to respond to a sweeping legislative mandate and a clamoring public, OSHA failed to study these standards carefully. Nor did it gauge the implications of transforming voluntary guidelines into government regulations that carried the threat of significant sanctions. Others have commented on the obsolescence, unnecessary complexity, and downright silliness that became part of our law because of the fateful decision to produce rules so carelessly.[13] OSHA had traded quality for volume. For the past thirty years the legacy of this massive blunder, certainly one of the greatest rulemaking fiascoes in American history, has haunted the agency in its pursuit of an unquestionably important mission.

The issue of hazardous waste management allows us to observe a related but different problem that can arise when agencies undertake a large number of rulemakings in a short period of time. The Resource Conservation and Recovery Act (RCRA) was passed by Congress in 1976 in an effort to regulate the generators, shippers, and ultimate disposers of waste materials, also known as garbage. For the rest of that decade and the first years of the next, the Environmental Protection Agency's Office of Solid Waste and Emergency Response (OSWER) focused its attention on trash collection and disposal services provided by local governments, since these activities and facilities accounted for the greatest amount of trash. The problems at Love Canal and the virulent pollution of ground water caused by leaching from hazardous waste disposal sites ultimately led Congress to attach major amendments to RCRA in 1980 and 1984. These were known as the Hazardous and Solid Waste Amendments, and they radically altered OSWER's mission and approach to rulemaking.

In *The Nation's Hazardous Waste Management Program at a Crossroads,* a report now two decades old but still highly relevant, the EPA noted that the amendments "greatly expanded the magnitude of waste types and … facilities requiring regulation … approximately 81,000 waste management units … [and] 211,000 facilities that generate hazardous waste."[14] In addition to a greatly expanded jurisdiction, OSWER received tight deadlines for the production of the many regulations needed to implement the new statutory mandates. As a result, OSWER became the most efficient rulemaking "machine" in the EPA, producing regulations faster than any other program office in the agency. The volume of hazardous waste regulations increased by 150 percent after the amendments. But in the course of responding to persistent pressure from Congress, OSWER, by its own admission, paid a high price.

In a chapter titled "The Regulations Machine: Too Many, Too Fast," the authors assess the consequences of OSWER's attempt to satisfy the external demands for rules. They state, "This success in developing regulations has been achieved at the expense of other important program objectives, and has resulted in high staff burnout and turnover in the RCRA program."[15] The "other objectives" that were sacrificed included an ability to define an over-all philosophy and direction for the hazardous waste program, control over the process of setting priorities for rulemaking, stable internal management of rulemaking, and an ability adequately to address issues related to compliance and enforcement in the rules that were produced.[16] The price of volume was dear.

The preoccupation with production of rules obscured the fact that rules are worse than useless if they result in an inconsistent, incoherent regulatory program that cannot be understood by the regulated community or enforced by government agents in the field. Nevertheless, Congress continued to legislate in the same manner well into the 1990s. The 1990 amendments to the Clean Air Act again presented the EPA with a massive agenda for rulemaking to be accomplished in accordance with strict and ambitious schedules.[17] In 1996 Congress passed the landmark Telecommunications Act, the first major overhaul of this vast regulatory arena since 1934. The act mandated sweeping changes, to be implemented largely through a program of rulemaking by the Federal Communications Commission (FCC). Again, tight deadlines were imposed for issuance of rules that would cover more than fifty discrete areas of telecommunications policy.[18]

This edition goes to print before the fate is known of many of the elements of one of the most sweeping legislative agendas in recent history. The Obama administration has introduced or called for legislation affecting health care, financial services, global warming, food safety, and labor reform, to name a few. The health care legislation enacted in March 2010 is instructive. The Congressional Research Service identified forty separate provisions of this new statute that either require or allow for rulemaking, and each of these provisions entails multiple new rules.[19] Whatever the ultimate results of the other legislative initiatives of the Obama administration, it is clear that all that pass will follow, to a greater or lesser extent, the path of the historic health care bill, and that agencies already straining under the weight of their regulatory obligations will confront an agenda for rulemaking the likes of which have not been seen since the 1970s.

Volume and Implementation

Sudden increases in the volume of rules can have enormously disruptive effects on the ability of programs to implement and enforce regulatory standards or deliver government benefits and services. Government agencies are not monolithic, omniscient entities. In most agencies the officials who write rules are not those who are charged with implementing and enforcing them. Furthermore, the rule writers are often separated both by physical distance and bureaucratic perspective from the implementers and enforcers. Those charged with producing regulations are rewarded for that activity, and they may not be particularly sensitive to the problems their work may create for other parts of the agency or their state and local counterparts.

Rules that alter existing program requirements demand learning and adjustments on the part of personnel in the field. Their job is to ensure that a regulated community is doing what the law requires or that a group of beneficiaries, applicants for benefits, and those that deliver services are treated appropriately and fairly under new standards. New rules that add to existing regulatory, eligibility, or service requirements imply the need for more resources in the field to ensure that the new obligations are met. Too often rule writers have no incentive to consider these resource issues, and they almost never have the authority to augment the staff and related budgets available to field offices. So the greater the volume of rulemaking, the greater the likelihood that the resultant rules are being passed on to implementation and enforcement staffs with inadequate training and resources. At times, agencies acknowledge that they are overwhelmed. The FCC, for example, announced in 1993 that the implementation of rules that could reduce the price of cable television would be delayed. The FCC chair stated bluntly that it was "too short staffed and too strapped for money to implement its new rules."[20] Time has not improved the situation. Recent reports related to programs as diverse as intellectual property and worker protection indicate that the resources of agencies in themselves are insufficient to carry out the full range of enforcement tasks.[21] It is safe to say the mismatch is a general condition of regulatory programs.

Delays in the implementation of new rules can be dangerous, particularly when they require reallocation of resources devoted to enforcement of other rules. High-volume rulemaking can cause the perverse situation in which the creation of new rules leads to less protection from whatever danger the overall regulatory or social welfare program was intended to reduce.[22] Overtaxing also occurs in the private sector when increases in rulemaking activity take place. Contemplate for a moment being on the receiving end of even a tiny fraction of thousands of regulations adopted in one grand, wrongheaded gesture by OSHA. The typical and now well-known problems of complying with government regulations are magnified and multiplied when volume increases suddenly. Smaller entities have complained that they are disproportionately affected by government requirements. A significant number have trouble learning what and how requirements apply to them. They must rely on accountants, lawyers, and other compliance professionals far more than they want or probably can afford to do. And some perceive their only choice as either being in compliance with the law or keeping their business open.[23]

The Environmental Protection Agency personnel summarized the problems associated with increased rulemaking in the following way:

> The current hazardous waste system is plagued by a number of rules that are both difficult for industry to comply with and difficult for the EPA and the states to implement—and the requirements continue to grow. In RCRA, *as in other programs,* a regulated hazardous waste handler *literally must do hundreds of things correctly to fully comply with the regulations, yet doing only one thing wrong makes the handler a violator.*[24] [Emphasis added.]

In this way the sheer volume of rules compounds more fundamental problems with government regulation. Many of those who must comply with the rules feel insecure and exposed because of numerous complex requirements that are difficult to understand. They harbor a seething resentment as they watch their freedom of choice and autonomy continually eroded by government mandates. The impact of the sheer weight of regulation can be mitigated, however, by rules that are well conceived and written. The quality of rules is therefore critical.

Quality in Rulemaking

Quality in rules, like so many other aspects of contemporary American government, is an elusive concept. The most exacting standard of quality in rulemaking is derived from the fundamental purpose of a rule. We should expect our rules to reflect perfectly their statutory purposes and to promote these legislative objectives in the most effective and efficient manner possible. Here "effective" would be defined as producing the program outputs, such as regulations and enforcement, that in turn produce the outcomes contemplated by the enactors of the statute being implemented.[25] High-quality rules would produce these intended effects in the proper amounts. "Efficient" means that the rule calls for spending up to the point that the costs of implementation and compliance equal the benefits that society enjoys from the new conditions it creates.[26] Since legislation often ignores or explicitly rejects this classical definition of the word *efficient,* another, less rigorous approach can be employed. *Cost-effectiveness* is achieved when the results of the program, however defined, are produced at the least cost.[27] The importance of these standards of quality in public policy is indisputable, but their study takes us to a level of analysis beyond the scope of this book. Our focus is a bit more fundamental. Public policy is a failure if it does not accomplish the objectives established by Congress on behalf of the American people. Equally important are standards that promote the best use of scarce resources.

One important problem is that of matching rules to their legislative origins. The intent of Congress is not always clear in either the language of the statute or the legislative history on which it is based. The meaning of key statutory terms can be obscure, subject to alternative constructions, or seemingly contradictory.[28] Also, rulemaking must be evaluated in a manner consistent with its important but limited role in our overall system of government. We cannot, for example, credit or blame rulemaking for errors committed during the legislative process. If Congress writes a law that is based on faulty premises or incorporates requirements that prevent rules from being effective or efficient, the fault cannot lie with rulemaking. Similarly, the work that follows rulemaking—implementation and enforcement—may undo good work embodied in rules. The converse is also true, of course. Legislation that is self-implementing reduces the significance of the rules that follow, since the rules do little other than mirror statutory terms. It is also possible for implementing and enforcing officials to correct, through interpretation and enlightened use of discretion, rules that would otherwise obstruct progress toward statutory purposes. Finally, there is the persistent problem of measuring the actual effects of public programs. Measuring the benefits and costs of entitlement or regulatory programs has proved difficult and controversial; our grasp of end results is tenuous at best.

This chapter focuses on more immediate and practical issues of quality. Rules from a wide variety of public programs have been severely criticized because they are unnecessarily difficult to implement, comply with, and enforce. No corner of the vast expanse of American rulemaking has escaped censure. Serious consequences can arise from rules that are difficult or impossible to put in force because of deficiencies in the way they were written. It is often a challenge for regulated parties or potential beneficiaries of public programs to meet their responsibilities when rules are unmistakably clear. When rules are obscure or subject to multiple interpretations, however, the task can be overwhelming. Flaws that lead to problems in implementation, compliance, and enforcement come in many forms.

Colin Diver argues that rules should have three qualities: transparency, congruency, and simplicity.[29] For a rule to be transparent, it must mean the same thing to everyone who reads it. All should draw from it the same understanding of their legal obligations and what will happen to them if they fail to comply. The enemy of transparency is vagueness. It "leaves the reader to guess at the meaning of the rule and its application in a particular case." As a prominent example of vagueness, Diver points to the standards used by the FCC when considering whether to renew a broadcasting license or award it to a competitor. The standards place heavy reliance on whether the current holder can demonstrate a record of service that is "substantially attuned to meeting the needs of and interests of its area." Repeated efforts to clarify and specify the meaning of terms like *substantially, needs,* and *interests* failed and the rules remain, in Diver's terms, "a paragon of administrative opacity."[30]

Vagueness in rules can lead to bickering within an agency responsible for an important public program or between the agency and its clients or regulated parties. When the rule is unclear, implementing and enforcing officials must spend time and resources to develop an operational definition of key terms and concepts. This effectively transforms the implementer into a rulemaker. In complex public programs administered through regional or field offices, such a situation raises the real possibility that a key term, poorly defined in a rule, will mean different things in different parts of the country, damaging consistency and perhaps raising questions about equal protection of the laws. Even if there is perfect consistency within the government in the way vague terms are being defined, it is highly unlikely that the same will hold with the external parties they serve or regulate. It is reasonable to assume that those in the private sector will adopt the interpretation of vague rules that best suits their interests. This difference in interpretation leads to inevitable conflicts with the agency and, in some instances, lawsuits challenging the agency's interpretations of its own rules. Such challenges, until they are resolved, cast doubt over the status of the program and, when successful, trigger a new round of rulemaking that is dominated by the views of the successful plaintiff or the judge in the case.

A rule is "congruent" when it states what the law it implements intended, nothing more, nothing less. To Diver, threats to congruence are "overinclusiveness" and "underinclusiveness." These conditions occur when the rule includes persons, things, or activities that should not be included or excludes those that should be included.[31] Perhaps the best example of both characteristics can be found—again—in the thousands of standards issued by the Occupational Safety and Health Administration shortly after its creation in 1970. These "overincluded" to such an extent that the agency was open to ridicule for issuing standards that governed in excruciating detail the characteristics of safety devices and mandated, with no humor intended, portable toilets for cowboys. The underinclusion was probably more serious than the derision that greeted these types of standards. In its headlong rush to protect workers' safety, the agency lost sight of the other dimension of its work. Among the thousands of standards issued, virtually all dealt with safety and hardly any with workers' health.

Overinclusive rules also have a corrosive effect on working relationships in the public sector and the posture of the private sector toward the program. Consider for a moment the inspectors responsible for enforcement of the blizzard of safety standards issued by OSHA in the early 1970s. If they were to take the regulations literally, they would be measuring the distance between the struts that attach hand railings to walls in every American workplace covered by the act. By pursuing these responsibilities aggressively, as research suggests they did, the OSHA inspectors were sure to encounter problems with the private sector.[32] Many in the private sector derided this approach to regulation and those who were attempting to force their compliance with it. The agency was soon dismissed as one far more concerned with bureaucratic standards of performance, such as the number of citations issued, than with the ultimate goal of protecting workers' safety in the most effective and efficient manner. For nearly three decades the agency has attempted to eliminate or modify its irrelevant, obsolete, or excessively prescriptive rules. It has attempted to establish outreach programs to assist employers in developing compliance programs for the rules that remain. Still, the initial, overwhelmingly negative impression lingers.

A significant variant on overinclusiveness is what we might call overspecificity. It is evident that the OSHA rules treated the characteristics of common objects, such as railings, ladders, and protective clothing, as mysterious forms of new technology that required descriptions as impenetrable as the assembly instructions that accompany Swedish furniture. OSHA's obsession with detail extended even to rules for its own employees. These rules contained excessively thorough instructions on how inspections were to be conducted, what would and would not be considered violations, and how citations were to be written when violations were observed. In its early years OSHA displayed what some would view as a deadly combination of failings: overinclusiveness and rigid enforcement.

In Diver's view, simplicity is achieved when relatively little information is needed to determine the applicability of a rule and compliance with it. Complexity is the threat to simplicity.[33] Complexity comes in many forms. It is manifested in contemporary rules that incorporate myriad qualifications, exceptions, exemptions, and considerations that complicate the processes of determining applicability and complying with their provisions. A previous example is illustrative: the EPA's own report on hazardous waste regulations describes a situation in which a regulated entity is expected to do "hundreds of things to establish compliance." Perhaps even more complex are the rules issued by the Internal Revenue Service that implement the tax code. What was once a joke—that each attempt at "tax simplification" leads inevitably to the opposite—is now accepted fact.

Complexity produces many of the same general effects as vagueness and the lack of congruence. The damage occurs for different reasons, however. Complex rules present considerable difficulties for the private sector, especially small entities and private individuals. As they struggle to understand what is required of them to benefit from a government program or to comply with a regulatory obligation, they find themselves increasingly dependent on others to tell them what must be done.

Matters do not appear to have changed much in recent years. Research presented by the Small Business Administration found that "two-thirds of small businesses faced moderate to substantial burdens from rules. The most frequently reported burdens were a lack of clarity in what is required, frequent changes in rules (and) information about compliance and cost."[34] The inability of small businesses to benefit from the positive effects of the scale found in larger workforces contributed to a 2005 finding that the cost per employee to small firms (defined as less than twenty employees) was 45 percent higher than large firms. Regulatory compliance is a major factor in such calculations.[35]

Complexity can be a tactic of government. For example, the rules governing eligibility for health care benefits under the federal Medicaid program were so complex and laden with qualifications that their effect, if not their intent, has been to make it easier for the government to find some basis on which to deny benefits.[36] Entitlement programs like Medicaid are not the only programs that have been accused of issuing rules so complex that small or poor entities and individuals are at a severe disadvantage. Licensing programs and other types of regulatory programs have been criticized in much the same way. For example, the rules governing the content of applications for hydroelectric power licenses have been cited as deterring all but the richest applicants because they contain requirements for environmental, engineering, and economic studies and a multiplicity of bilateral consultations with other federal and state agencies.[37]

Complex rules hurt the government as well. It may be no easier for government officials charged with implementation and enforcement to understand a complex rule than it is for those in the private sector who are supposed to be complying with it. As mentioned earlier, contemporary rules usually contain preambles that are longer than the body of the rule itself. As preambles and rules grow in length and complexity, the chances increase that a critical term or issue will be handled differently from one section to the next. When the complying community is left to decide which version is correct—the interpretation in the preamble or the actual language in the rule—the credibility of the program is damaged and the potential for challenges to the rule's enforcement increases.

How common are these qualitative problems that frustrate implementation, compliance, and enforcement of the rules written by the federal government? When they occur, what are their root causes? Two important causes are considered here: poor information and ineffectual rule writers.

The Limitations of Information

Rulemaking, in one sense, changes information into law. Sometimes the information is obvious or easy to obtain; at other times the information is difficult to secure or simply nonexistent. When the Federal Aviation Administration (FAA) prepares an airworthiness directive, it is usually based on information that has been provided through routine inspections of aircraft by its own personnel or those working in the regulated community. When a problem is discovered, there are usually well-established ways to determine how to solve it and to explain to the regulated community what needs to be done. This is not to say that the system is infallible or without problems of clarity or specificity. In general, however, the FAA's rules are developed in what we might call an information-rich environment.

Some rules require no information other than what the agency issuing them wants to do. Agencies regularly use rulemaking to change their internal procedures for all types of programmatic activities. These rules are based on what the agency determines to be expeditious, convenient, or otherwise beneficial to the operation of its programs. This type of rulemaking can also be found in programs in which the agency traditionally enjoys considerable authority to protect health or safety. Coast Guard rules designed to maintain safe and efficient use of navigable waterways are examples of rules for which the only information really needed is the knowledge that a potential hazard or obstruction exists. Once the hazard is identified, the solution does not require much, if any, information collection, since the rule will be based on well-established policies and practices. Rules in which information is not much of an issue are usually quite easy to implement, although communicating the new obligation or restriction to the regulated community may be difficult. For example, the Coast Guard's rules may be quite clear, but because the boating community is so diverse, the process of making it aware of the restrictions can be a problem.

Weaknesses in information can be a serious obstacle to writing high-quality rules. Certainly on occasion the responsible agency knows little about the nature of a problem, its causes, or the practices of the individuals, groups, or firms whose behavior it must change to accomplish the goals of a statute. This was and remains true in social regulation.[38] The causes and consequences of threats to the environment and to human health and safety are extremely difficult to determine. Perhaps even more problematical is the sheer number of behaviors, activities, and practices that social regulation seeks to affect. When one combines the elusiveness of the problem with the indeterminacy of its cause and multiplies that by the number and diversity of the people whose lives the agency is attempting to change, the probability of error is very high indeed. Examples of agencies attempting, unsuccessfully, to write rules with less than complete or accurate information are not uncommon.[39] The George W. Bush administration and Congress acknowledged these short-comings and took steps to improve the situation through the development of guidelines issued at both the White House and individual agency levels to ensure quality of information used by government for a variety of purposes.[40] As noted in the preceding chapter, the more recent Information (or Data) Quality Act was ostensibly directed to the same problem.

Stephen Breyer, a noted scholar and Supreme Court justice, has identified four generic sources of information available to rulemakers. First, industry, broadly defined, is the most reliable source of information on its own processes and products. Second, the agency has in-house research offices, but Breyer sees these staffs as limited in what they know or can learn in time to help on specific rules. Third, the agency has access to outside experts, but it may be difficult to find experts on the right subjects, and they can be expensive. Finally, there are "public interest" groups, but they often have less hard information than industry and carry with them a predictable point of view.[41] In general, Breyer sees information shortcomings as a "central and persistent problem" and concludes, "In technical areas the agency to some extent inevitably works in the dark."[42] Those words are as true today as they were when Justice Breyer wrote them.

The Limitations of Rulemakers

As significant as limitations in information are the limitations of the people using it. Most agencies report that they assign the task of rulemaking to individuals with expertise in the subject matter in question. We would be surprised and alarmed to find that the contrary was true. Nevertheless, expertise on the subject matter in a given area of regulation does not necessarily mean that an individual also possesses a comparable level of practical experience and sensitivity to the nuances of regulatory language. The expert may know a given technology or industrial process, but can he or she write a rule that can be implemented with minimal effort, understood and managed by the affected parties, and enforced should it be violated? Some agencies have discovered that those writing regulations lack the essential perspectives and experience. The EPA put it this way:

> Implementation and enforcement issues raised by regulations are not
> consistently identified or addressed as part of the rulemaking process....
> Staff writing ... regulations are often not familiar enough with or do not
> have enough exposure to the types of facilities and industrial groups that

they are trying to regulate.... Some staff members lack field experience
and exposure to industry that limits their ability to design regulations that
both are understandable and work in the field.... This is especially true,
given the high turnover rates.[43]

This problem is not confined to a particular type of agency or government program. Large programs dealing with environmental, health, and
safety issues are likely to be especially affected, however. The learning curve
for those writing these regulations can be quite steep, since they must simultaneously understand the nature and consequences of the problem they are
attempting to deal with and the operations of the particular industry that
must be regulated. There is no more compelling example of the issue identified by the EPA nearly two decades ago than our current corporate scandals.
Exotic financial instruments and labyrinthine transactions challenge the most
astute and experienced rulemaker, public or private, with consequences that
continue to fill newspapers, blogs, and the public agenda. The looming
retirements of a large percentage of the federal workforce, many the most
senior and expert, will exacerbate these information deficits.[44]

The regulations of most agencies are written at their headquarters in
Washington, D.C. Usually there is no requirement that those writing the rules
be experienced field personnel. Although these agencies have large field
staffs, some of which have had long and intense interaction with the segment
of the economy or society affected by a given rule, the rule writers may not
consult these staffs to the extent that they should.

Some field staffs may simply be too busy with the task of implementing
and enforcing an existing body of rules to worry about rules under development. Since they will have to live with the problems created by unrealistic or
poorly crafted rules, this attitude may seem quite shortsighted, but given the
dynamics of program management, it may be entirely rational. Field staffs are
evaluated on their performance in relation to existing rules. They are usually
not rewarded for their efforts to make future rules better. Furthermore, field
staffs know intuitively that they control the process by which rules are put
into effect. Field staffs must balance the benefits from their participation in
the rulemaking with the probability that they will be able to mold the meaning of the rule when they become responsible for enforcing it.

When enforcement staffs choose to become involved in rulemaking,
they can face several types of obstacles. Resources may not be sufficient to
allow for full participation in the rulemaking. Rules are often written by teams
of agency personnel who interact on a regular basis, sometimes intensely.[45]
The locus of this activity is almost always the agency headquarters. Although
technology can provide effective substitutes for the physical presence of

participants, the logistical problems can be formidable. Communication and scheduling, which are difficult enough in a single location, become much more problematical when the input is from multiple remote sites.

When field personnel are willing to participate, the resources are available, and the logistics are manageable, obstacles to incorporating the implementation and enforcement perspective into a given rule still may remain. Those responsible for writing the rule may not want suggestions or data from those in the field. Some argue that rule writers have a short-term perspective with little or no incentive to get it right.[46] The issues raised by those concerned with implementation and enforcement are often numerous and complex. The larger the number and the more difficult the issues presented during the development of a rule, the longer the process takes. More important, the resolution of the types of issues raised by field staff may require a level of specificity in the rule that would threaten the consensus among the headquarters personnel involved. Elements of the legislative process in Congress are present in rulemaking. By avoiding certain issues or using vague language that is open to multiple interpretations, rulemakers may be able to satisfy various agency offices with different responsibilities, concerns, and perspectives whose opposition would otherwise block or delay issuance of the rule. It has also been suggested that rule writers could make a career of interpreting a rule they have written badly.[47]

For a variety of reasons, those in headquarters writing rules may mistrust the input from the field. They may view the positions of the field staff as either too friendly or too hostile to the segment of the private sector that will be affected by the rule. Headquarters personnel may respond by writing rules that narrow the range of discretion, an approach that those in the field may find unrealistic or unworkable. Conversely, personnel in both regulatory and social welfare agencies have been accused of "going by the book" and rigidly applying the language of the rule with no effort to respond to unique or unanticipated situations.[48] In these instances, by writing general rules that must be molded to individual circumstances, headquarters personnel may force the field staff's exercise of discretion and at the same time give the regulated or benefiting community grounds to question the judgment of that field staff when adverse decisions are made. Clearly, this is not a situation always welcomed by those in the field, especially when the number of parties affected is large and their circumstances are diverse.

It is important to note that the information needed to write rules that facilitate compliance is not solely in the hands of the public sector. On the contrary, those who know the most about the area affected by the rule are those in the regulated or benefiting community. It is conceivable that rulemakers who ineffectively handle input from field personnel could still produce feasible and workable rules if they could gain the necessary insights from the private sector. The impediments to gaining these insights will be discussed in Chapter 5.

Timeliness

After noting that many believe there are far too many rules, the reader may be wondering how it can be argued that the process by which they are written takes too long. But consider the following statement by Neil Eisner, assistant general counsel for regulation and enforcement at the U.S. Department of Transportation:

> [A]ll three branches of government have been concerned with delay in the rulemaking process. Their efforts to eliminate or lessen it have been hampered because delay in decision-making is an age-old disease for which there is no cure; there is rarely agreement on whether the victim is … ill…. Part of the difficulty in attempting to cure the problem of delay in the rulemaking process is its wide variety of causes.[49]

The general view that the pace of rulemaking is a problem is supported by several committees of the U.S. Congress, the recently reauthorized Administrative Conference of the United States, the federal courts, and elements of the private sector. But before turning to the causes, we should first attempt to explain the apparent contradiction between the twin charges that there are too many rules and that their production is too slow.

Those who decry the time it takes to issue rules are likely to be the individuals, groups, or firms who view themselves as the beneficiaries of rules or in need of the guidance they provide. Certainly they are not the same people who complain about the volume of rules. For example, environmental groups of all sorts have turned to litigation against the EPA in an attempt to speed up the issuance of regulations favored by their members. If Congress has indeed identified a problem whose elimination would result in net gains to some members of our economic or social system, delays in issuing the regulations that detail how the problem will be solved may well constitute a loss to those who would benefit. In other cases, businesses may suffer because of the uncertainty created when regulations affecting their operations are not completed in a timely fashion. Businesses are understandably reluctant to move into new areas or make changes in their operations and practices if a new regulation might make the activity unattractive. The government itself, and the taxpayers who finance its operations, can be big losers when essential regulations are delayed. A report by the General Accounting Office (GAO) over thirty years ago estimated that delays in issuance of regulations that established cost-sharing in the Medicaid program resulted in a loss of more than $81 million in just one fiscal year.[50] In current dollars, that is a very big number.

On what basis is the claim made that rulemaking takes too long? There are many individual cases of long-delayed rules and some empirical analysis of larger sets of rules. There are hundreds of examples of rules that took extraordinarily long periods to complete or that were never finished at all. The Federal Energy Regulatory Commission's rule implementing the provisions of the National Environmental Policy Act in its hydroelectric power licensing program was nearly twenty years in the making.[51] The inability of the FAA to revise the rules that govern flight time for airline pilots and crews in a timely way has been documented by the GAO, which forced the agency to issue thousands of individual "interpretations" so that the industry could function under regulations that were obsolete but still remained in force.[52] A study of rulemaking in the EPA found that the average time that elapsed in rulemaking in the four major program areas—air, water, toxic substances, and waste—ranged from slightly more than two years to just under five years.[53] Congress grew so frustrated with the pace of rulemaking in the EPA that it imposed nearly one thousand deadlines for the issuance of rules under a variety of statutes. Congress's use of deadlines is not unrelated to the EPA's slow pace.[54]

A long list of individual examples could be developed, but would such a list be a fair characterization of all rulemaking? For every example of a seemingly endless rulemaking, there are many that would lead one to conclude that the process is quite brisk. One report by the GAO makes the same general point. The pie charts in Figure 3-1 show the number of rules completed within various time intervals from the close of public comment to completion of the rule. A very recent study found in an examination of sixteen representative rules by major rulemaking agencies the following regarding the duration of various rulemaking projects. These data are suggestive, but it is actually difficult to assess the extent and significance of delay in rulemaking.

First, it is hard to measure the actual time elapsed in rulemakings. Few systems within the government allow us to determine, without considerable effort, when a rulemaking actually began. The first public notice of a proposed rule in the *Federal Register* is usually preceded by weeks, months, or even years of work.[55] Although many agencies have a process to authorize the start of a rulemaking, we cannot know how much time and effort have been expended on a given rule prior to these formal authorizations. The

FIGURE 3-1 Percentage of Significant Rules Finalized within Certain Time Periods after the Close of the Public Comment Period by FAA and Other Selected Regulatory Agencies, Fiscal Years 1995–2000

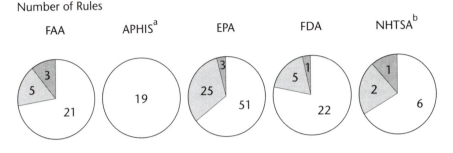

Number of Rules

FAA   APHIS[a]   EPA   FDA   NHTSA[b]

☐ Finalized within 24 months of close of public comment period

▨ Finalized from 24 months up to 60 months after close of public comment period

▨ Finalized from 60 months up to 120 months after close of public comment period

Source: The GAO's analysis of data from the Regulatory Information Service Center and the *Federal Register,* p. 46; U.S. General Accounting Office, "Aviation Rulemaking: Further Reform Is Needed to Address Long-Standing Problems," GAO-01-821 (Washington, D.C.: GAO, 2001).

Note: This analysis excludes interim final rules; rule count provided for each category/agency.

[a]Animal and Plant Health Inspection Service.
[b]National Highway Traffic Safety Administration.

data for Figure 3-2 related to time expended prior to the first notice were estimates obtained by GAO staff through a painstaking process. In some cases we can obtain partial measures of elapsed time, such as the duration between the notice of a proposed rulemaking and the publication of the final rule. Research discussed in Chapter 5 shows that a large number of final rules appear without benefit of a proposal, so in these many instances even a partial measure of elapsed time is not possible. A truly objective standard against which the timeliness of a rulemaking can be judged is even more difficult to ascertain. The circumstances surrounding a rule determine the length of development.

Complexity

Rules sometimes involve highly complex, difficult issues that take time to resolve. Writers of the flight-time rule mentioned earlier not only had to perform an analysis but also had to negotiate the treacherous shoals of collective-bargaining positions taken by pilots and airlines. The hazardous

FIGURE 3-2 Rulemaking Timelines from Initiation to Final Rule for Sixteen Case Studies

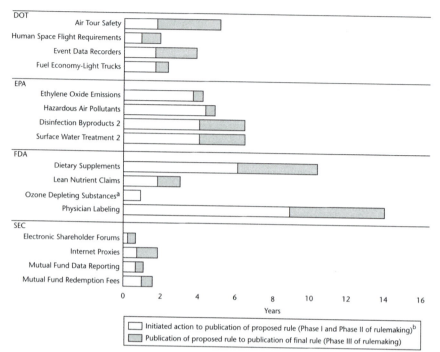

Source: U.S. Government Accountability Office, "Federal Rulemaking: Improvements Needed to Monitoring and Evaluation of Rules Development as Well as to the Transparency of OMB Regulatory Reviews," GAO-09-205, April 2009, p.18, www.gao.gov/new.items/d09205.pdf.

[a]FDA's Ozone Depleting Substances was a direct final rule, and as such, FDA published a proposed and final rule on the same day.
[b]Initiation was based on agencies' best estimates of when they initiated the rules. Also, because of the ambiguity in the early stages of rulemaking—only the end of Phase II of rulemaking, publication of a proposed rule, has a clearly defined milestone—[GAO] did not distinguish between the first two phases of rulemaking.

materials rule prepared by the Department of Transportation that was discussed earlier displays a different type of complexity. Rather than deal with a couple of difficult scientific and technological questions, the department was challenged to produce a single rule that addressed hundreds of distinct but interrelated issues in a coherent and consistent manner. Agencies of social regulation constantly deal with these types of complex tasks. This means that they are consciously or unconsciously balancing the quality of the rule they are writing with the timeliness of its issuance.

Controversy

Rulemaking agencies must accept and contend with controversy in the rules they write. The controversy can be internal to the agency, between external groups affected by the rule that the agency is writing, or between the agency and these external clients or constituents. Whatever the form, conflict can extend the time it takes to issue rules.

A given rulemaking may involve technical specialists in the program area or areas covered by a rule, lawyers who are responsible for interpreting the authorizing statute, policy analysts charged with finding innovative or economically efficient ways to achieve statutory objectives, and personnel who specialize in implementation and enforcement of completed rules. These varied concerns and backgrounds translate into significantly different views about rulemaking, differences that can lead to serious conflict.[56] The engineer's fondness for rules based on technology may run afoul of the preferences of the lawyers, who worry about whether such an approach is permissible under a statute. An economist working in a policy analysis unit may favor clear statements of objectives in rules but great freedom for the regulated community in how they are achieved. Consequently, he or she will oppose specific and rigid technology-based standards.

We have already noted the differences in perspective between those writing rules and those responsible for their enforcement. In addition, agencies now administer multiple statutes, and occasionally a single rule can cut across two or more of them. The EPA has long contended with the "multimedia" dilemma; for example, a possible solution to problems in air quality can create new problems for water quality or waste disposal. Each of these media is represented by different program offices in the EPA, and each office deals with statutes that have significantly different standards that guide its rulemakings. The same situation holds in other departments, such as Interior, Agriculture, and Transportation, that house multiple and distinct yet interrelated programs.

The degree to which internal sources of conflict lead to delay depends on the relative power of the various offices in a given agency and the organizational norms for rulemaking. If, for example, rulemaking authority is confined to the responsible program office and other offices have little or no opportunity to influence the process, then diversity of perspective will have little effect on the pace of rulemaking. If the agency has a process that allows for broad internal participation by interested offices, however, then the effect on timeliness can be significant.[57] Time will be spent in managing the mechanisms of participation and in circulating and obtaining comments on drafts. If this norm of participation is combined with the expectation that the rule will represent the consensus of the agency, further delay is likely. Here, time will be spent in each of the participating offices that must establish a position on the rule; negotiations to iron out differences may be extensive. When consensus is not achieved, the deadlock must be broken by senior agency officials, who may take time attempting to determine what should be done or who may force another round of lower-level negotiations.

We will see in Chapter 5 that participation has become the prevalent standard across the government. It is not confined to the formal avenues defined in the Administrative Procedure Act of 1946 and a myriad of other authorizing and general procedural statutes. A standard of consensus also exists, but not as constantly. Gaining consensus costs a great deal more than elapsed time. If the agency is committed to producing a rule with which everyone with a recognized interest can agree, the only way to break certain deadlocks is to produce a rule that ignores unresolved (or unresolvable) issues or deals with them through vague language whose meaning will be disputed during the implementation process. This is one potential cause of the qualitative problems that frustrate the enforcement of certain regulations and often lead to litigation that sends the issue in dispute back to agencies for clarification through—you guessed it—rulemaking.

There is another widely observed form of conflict within agencies that can delay the issuance of rules. The tension between career bureaucrats and the political appointees who lead the agencies is a persistent theme in the literature of public administration. It manifests itself in rulemaking when the approach favored by the program office specialists runs afoul of the policy priorities of the political leadership. This type of problem has been evident for several decades, but it reached its peak during the Reagan years. Policy differences aside, this type of conflict is especially damaging to timeliness when it is not anticipated or dealt with in the rulemaking process. If the career staff develop a regulation without early input from senior agency offi-cials, there is always the chance that it will produce a rule that is not accept-able. All or part of the time spent developing the proposal is wasted, and additional time will be spent reformulating the regulation, perhaps with a different cast of characters, or in what amounts to negotiation between the careerists and political appointees.

A special mention of an agency's relationships with its counterparts in the federal government and the states is in order. Comments referred to in the preambles of final rules confirm that agencies take great interest in the rulemakings conducted by other agencies. The jurisdictions of our national bureaucracies overlap and collide. Rules issued by the Federal Energy Regulatory Commission regarding environmental protection at hydropower facilities have implications for resources under the care of fish and wildlife, public lands, and agricultural agencies. Similarly, the EPA routinely issues rules that have an enormous impact on other federal agencies, such as the Departments of Defense and Energy, and all local governments. Other elements of the public sector—notably Congress, the White House, and the courts—are key players in rulemaking; when they are unhappy, they have means not always available to private organizations to exert influence. So it is reasonable to expect an agency engaged in rulemaking to attempt to accommodate its counterparts in the public sector. This takes time.

Harvard Law School professor Richard Stewart has written that the administrative process in government agencies is driven by the clash of external interests.[58] Those involved in decision making in a government agency, including decision making that is done during the course of rulemaking, strive for a result that can be embraced by the agency's external clients and constituents, whether they are beneficiaries or regulated entities. In order to satisfy external constituents, the agency staff must take the time to learn their preferences. Once learned, they must then be accommodated by the agency. When external parties are in conflict with one another, the task becomes more difficult and time-consuming. The same holds true when the positions of the external parties are at odds with what appears to be permissible under the statute or with the preferences of powerful interests inside the agency. Participation is the means by which the agreement of external parties is secured.

Procedural Requirements

The growth in procedural requirements, other than participation, is also responsible for delay in rulemaking. Certainly, each reform can be justified by a noble purpose, be it better-informed rulemaking or empowerment of those who will be affected by its results or a greater degree of management control by the president over a sprawling bureaucratic state. These stated goals notwithstanding, delay can also be an unspoken objective. In the case of Congress this amounts to a seeming contradiction. Our legislators enact programs of regulation or social welfare but then encumber them with procedural requirements that will almost certainly stall their implementation. This simply confirms that political decision making is multidimensional. The combination of an aggressive and ambitious substantive mission with a cautious and painstaking process of implementation can satisfy different sets of constituents.

Some presidents who have made incursions into rulemaking have been quite explicit and direct about their intentions to delay the process. When he took office in January 1981, President Ronald Reagan ordered a moratorium on new rules until the provisions of his executive order mandating Office of Management and Budget (OMB) review could become effective. Slowing the pace of rulemaking was a clear goal of his management program. President George H. W. Bush imposed a similar moratorium and then extended it during the waning days of his administration. His son's chief of staff issued a memo on the first day of their new administration delaying effective dates of rules sent to the *Federal Register* in the closing weeks of the Clinton administration. President Barack Obama upheld tradition by issuing a prohibition on publications of any pending regulations developed by the Bush II administration. His chief of staff issued this order within hours of Obama's inauguration. Presidents, like Congress, engage in the politics of mixed messages when it comes to timeliness in rulemaking.

In the context of administrative decision making generally, mandates about rulemaking from the president—or from Congress, the courts, or agency officials—are never neutral.[59] They elevate some interests or values over others. The value that is diminished by growth in procedure is timeliness.

Shortages of Resources

Rulemaking requires resources, human and financial, and when they are in short supply delay is an inevitable result. There are basic structural issues that lead to a situation of insufficient resources. Deficits have plagued the federal government for decades, and in the face of President Obama's massive stimulus package and the bailout expenditures, the balanced budgets of the late 1990s appear now to be anomalies that are unlikely to return anytime soon. There is also a lack of connection between the authorizing process that creates rulemaking responsibilities and the appropriations process that provides the resources agencies need to carry them out. The net effect of these and other factors is that rarely, if ever, are agencies with large agendas for rulemaking given the staff and access to the essential expertise that they think they need to get the work done. Agencies, consequently, set priorities in a variety of ways that will be covered in the next chapter. Priority-setting results in winners and losers in the competition for the attention of rulemakers. The latter group, depending on where they sit, will inevitably complain about other "overzealous regulators" or "bureaucratic foot-draggers."

Management Obstacles and Deficiencies

Another potential cause of delay is poor management of the rulemaking process by the agency. Although this is probably more likely in agencies that have relatively few rules or high staff turnover, it can occur anywhere. Rulemaking can require the organization and direction of many different people and activities. Personnel from different offices must be brought together, their work coordinated and supported by research, and their differences resolved. These things do not happen automatically or without substantial thought and effort. Breakdowns in communication, poor coordination of interrelated efforts, and inadequate supervision can lead to misunderstandings and oversights that ultimately delay the issuance of a rule.

Short supplies of resources for rulemaking are likely to persist as long as frugality in budgeting is perceived to be a political asset. President Bill Clinton set as a cornerstone of his government reinvention effort deep cuts in the number of federal workers. There was a slight increase in the federal workforce as a result of 9/11, but nowhere near the height of civilian employees in the early 1990s.[60] Much of this reduction was achieved by accelerated retirements and buyouts of long-term employees. Normal retirement cycles will reduce further the number of experienced, long-term public employees over the coming years. Like all other complex tasks, rulemaking benefits from experience, and we can be sure that the loss of these human resources has had an effect on rulemaking.

Changes in rulemaking priorities profoundly affect the resources available for rulemaking. A rule under development can be stalled or abandoned altogether when staff and money are reassigned to projects that are considered more important. Shifts in priorities occur for three reasons. First, Congress, through new legislation, amendments to existing statutes, and oversight activities, can cause the agency to undertake new initiatives. Given the proclivity of Congress to affix deadlines to these new rulemaking responsibilities, the shift of internal resources can be immediate.[61] Second, court decisions can have a similar, if less dramatic, effect. Studies have documented the impact that judicial rulings have had on the priority-setting process for rulemaking agencies.[62] These decisions can cause the agency either to redo a rule that the court has found somehow in error or to undertake the development of a rule that the agency has not yet started, or even anticipated.[63] While Congress can be faulted for a lack of generosity when handing out new rulemaking responsibilities, new resources never accompany a judicial decision of this sort. Third, decisions by the agency itself may lead to a reordering of rulemaking projects. New political leadership with a different vision of what is important, or staff work that uncovers serious problems or deficiencies that need attention, can lead to work on new projects, leaving others on hold.

Tactical Delays

Finally, delay can occur simply because the agency does not want to act. In many instances this type of delay is difficult to distinguish from that caused by conflict, be it internal or external. Realizing that any form of action will cause them untold grief, the responsible officials choose to wait, often using a study of some sort as a surrogate for action. For example, the chronology of the rule that set standards for benzene exposure, discussed in Chapter 1, showed a five-year period consumed by risk analyses. Stalling tactics are attractive because in time a conflict may dissipate on its own, the contending parties may reach an agreement that the agency can then ratify, or the burden may pass to an unlucky successor.

Any or all of the potential sources of delay could apply in a given case of rulemaking. Little systematic research has been undertaken on which of these many potential causes are the most common or serious. The authors of the only known empirical study of the variables affecting the passage of time in multiple rulemakings examined nearly two hundred rules and developed measures for complexity, internal and external conflict, procedural requirements, and participation. We found that taken together these variables could account for as much as 60 percent of the variation in elapsed time in rulemaking. The ways these variables were measured, however, were far from ideal. For example, complexity was measured by the length of the rule, and the number of comments received from the public served as the surrogate for external conflict.[64] At this stage it is hard to know whether better results could be obtained with better measurement of these variables or if some unobserved variables are also contributing to delay. We do know, however, that the problem of delay is generally accepted as a major issue in rulemaking and that few simple solutions for it exist.

Participation

Participation in rulemaking poses problems for both the public and the agency. In order to become involved in rulemaking in a way that holds some prospects for success, individuals, groups, and firms need resources, organization, and sophistication. These prerequisites are not distributed evenly. Consequently, some fail to participate in rulemaking because they lack the ability to do so or have little awareness of the problems. Rulemaking demands a keen sense of timing and a grasp of the subtleties of bureaucratic decision making. These skills are not necessarily related to the size of an organization or the amount of money it has to spend on public affairs. Size and money help, to be sure, but an understanding of the process of rulemaking is more important.

Problems arise, however, even when participation is both extensive and balanced. Sometimes the quality of participation is poor; the agency solicits and receives the views of the public, but the results do little or nothing to improve the rule. This occurs for several reasons. First, the information provided by the agency about the rule under development may be misleading or insufficient to allow interested parties to comment intelligently. As noted in earlier chapters, however, legal requirements and inbred agency caution make this a relatively minor problem. Second, given the fact that most rulemaking requires detailed and often technical knowledge, commenting parties may not possess the requisite expertise to be able to offer any additional information or constructive advice on rules. Finally, parties are often uninterested in improving a rule. They use the opportunity to participate to challenge the rule, per se, or to make their opposition a matter of public record that can be referred to in subsequent challenges to the rule.

The sheer number of participants can be a significant problem for the agency developing the rule. A system for collecting the comments must be established, and the comments themselves must be read and analyzed. Then the agency must have some mechanism to decide which of the comments have merit, which require changes in the rule, and what those changes will be. Finally, if the agency revises the proposed rule based on the comments it receives, it must prepare an analysis of the changes and why they were made. The magnitude of the task presented to the agency obviously depends on the number, length, and complexity of the comments.

There are near-legendary examples of rules proposed by federal agencies that generated massive outpourings of public comment. Several ill-fated efforts by the Department of the Treasury's Bureau of Alcohol, Tobacco, and Firearms to regulate handguns were greeted by tens of thousands of postcard responses, orchestrated by the National Rifle Association and related groups. Initial publication of proposed rules by the Department of Agriculture that would, among other things, define the term *organic* attracted more than 450,000 comments.[65] More recently, in 2008 a proposed rule by the Federal Reserve System dealing with business practices of credit card firms attracted 56,000 public comments, a record for that agency.[66] But lest it be thought that only politically charged issues like gun control, food labeling, or credit cards generate this level of interest, consider the proposed rule of the Animal and Plant Health Inspection Service (APHIS) on the importation of ostriches. When it was published it stimulated more than 2,000 written comments, an extraordinary number when one considers that ostriches are not normally considered an issue with high political salience.[67] Massive volumes of public participation in rulemaking strain agencies' resources. The rise of electronic communication exacerbates the problem and highlights the paradox of participation in rulemaking. Because rules bring specific effects to easily identified parties, there is a strong incentive to participate; technology makes this relatively easy. The volume of public comment, however, can slow the process and interfere with decision making.

Participation in rulemaking displays the same proclivity for conflict and deadlock that characterizes other key elements of the public policy process. Phillip Harter, an important figure in efforts to reform the rulemaking process, catalogued the problems that can beset the development of major rules under the general title "adversary process." He viewed rulemaking as too often characterized by the taking of extreme positions, both by the agency and by affected parties; waves of "defensive research"; and an inability or unwillingness of parties to the rulemaking to state and deal with "true concerns." Formal mechanisms for participation, such as written comment and public hearings, become stylized rituals from which neither side expects much more than an affirmation of what is already known. He noted that these forms are not conducive to the resolution of "polycentric" issues, and they are not well suited to the give-and-take between parties that is so elemental to dispute resolution.[68] Accommodation of contending positions, if it occurs at all, happens behind the scenes in quiet negotiations. When conflict persists and is not resolved, rules are issued, and the controversy spills into the federal courts, the halls of Congress, or the White House. Petitions for reconsideration are filed, and the initial rulemaking effort may be for naught.

Harter was careful to note that this description does not apply to all rulemaking. In fact, evidence will be presented in Chapter 5 that disputes this general view of rulemaking. Some external parties who participate actively in the rulemaking process find it a valuable and fruitful activity and find the agencies they deal with responsive. Nevertheless, at least some of the dysfunctions in participation of the sort Harter identified persist, and still others have appeared. They will be examined at greater lengths presently.

Involvement of the public in rulemaking may be the most complex and important form of political action in the contemporary American political system. When it is blocked or otherwise does not occur, there are profound constitutional and practical implications. As we will detail in Chapter 5, because rulemaking is a form of lawmaking, participation by the public is important to the maintenance of democracy. And because rule writers are not omniscient, the information that the public possesses is badly needed.

Bureaucratic Discretion

Like participation, the exercise of bureaucratic discretion is central to any consideration of rulemaking. Also like participation, bureaucratic discretion (or, more accurately, its containment) is a serious and persistent issue.[69]

When a function as basic as the making of law and policy is conducted by persons with no direct electoral link to any constituency, conflict with fundamental constitutional principles results. Furthermore, as we have seen in this chapter, the ability of a bureaucracy to perform well in the exercise of delegated authority through rulemaking has been questioned.

We have already established why the federal bureaucracy is entrusted with rulemaking initially. In subsequent chapters we will examine how the constitutional branches attempt to retain control, ensure the faithfulness of bureaucrats, and influence the results of rulemaking. Bureaucratic discretion as an abstract concept looms much larger than its actual occurrence in rulemaking. Far more important and interesting are the profound contradictions in our political system that express themselves so clearly in any serious consideration of rulemaking as a bureaucratic function. These contradictions deserve clarification.

The Effects of Rulemaking

None of the issues discussed in this chapter would attract much serious attention were it not for the effects of the rules themselves. These effects are determined by the balance of benefits and costs. We noted earlier that a majority of the American people believe that government regulation of business does more harm than good. The official assessment by the federal government indicates that regulation produces more good than harm. And these congressionally mandated estimates show that costs, taken alone, are considerably less than some prominent critics of regulation have argued.

In 1996 Congress added to an appropriations bill for several agencies a provision requiring the OMB to estimate the overall costs and benefits of regulatory programs, with particular attention to rules that impose compliance and other costs on the private sector in excess of $100 million per year. In what has come to be known as the Stevens Report (named after Sen. Ted Stevens, R-Alaska), the OMB drew on the best scholarship in the field as well as findings from its own analyses of the regulatory impact of major rules. The work is ongoing, but the results show that in 2007 the total cost of regulation was between $46 billion and $54 billion.[70]

The good news for supporters of regulation is that the study found the estimated annual benefits of regulation reviewed by the OMB between 1997 and 2007 was between $122 billion to $656 billion—significantly more than the estimated costs. As the Stevens Report acknowledges, the OMB cost estimates are lower, in some instances dramatically so, than those in other studies.

Inseparable Issues

The issues in rulemaking are serious, and their contradictions are perplexing. Presenting the issues as discrete problems is potentially misleading, because we must examine their interrelationships in order to expose their contradictions.

The most profound dilemma faced by those interested in rulemaking is how to address any one of these issues without further complicating another. If, for example, we seek to improve the quality of rules by ensuring that they anticipate and fully resolve implementation, compliance, and enforcement issues, it is difficult to imagine that the rulemaking process will be faster or the resultant rule will be less complex. If, instead, we make a concerted effort to accelerate the pace of rulemaking, it is likely that time will be gained at the expense of internal and external participation or the reasoned deliberation essential to high-quality rules. Many other examples of contradictory expectations can be offered.

In rulemaking we can observe the struggle between powerful and important values. The volume of rulemaking can be viewed as an agency's attempt to be responsive to legislative mandates. The quality of rules is linked to the faith, perhaps now dim, in the expertise and neutral competence of the bureaucracy. Concern for the speed of rulemaking is linked to responsiveness, but in addition it is linked to values, prevalent in the field of policy analysis, that delay is waste, and waste in a time of scarcity is a tragedy. Each of these values has merit, but the foregoing survey of problems in rulemaking should remind us that outsized and clashing expectations put our basic institutions and decision-making processes under considerable stress. Rulemaking is a process that demands trade-offs; each of these important values is thus threatened by compromise. The task of balancing these values falls to agencies and those who direct them. Management of rulemaking is a critical function. We turn to it next.

Notes

1. Pew Research Center for the People and the Press, Values Survey, March 2009, http://people-press.org/questions/?qid=1734728&pid=51&ccid=51#top.
2. William A. Galston and Elaine C. Kamarck, "Change You Can Believe in Needs a Government You Can Trust," Third Way (November 2008), www.thirdway.org/publications/133.
3. Pew Research Center for the People and the Press, Values Survey.
4. Pew Research Center for the People and the Press, "View of Business and Regulation Unchanged by Enron," February 21, 2002, www.people-press.org.
5. Phillip Harter, "Regulatory Negotiation: A Cure for the Malaise," *Georgetown Law Review* 71 (1982): 1; Thomas McGarrity, "Some Thoughts on De-Ossifying Rulemaking,"

Duke Law Journal 41 (1992): 1385–1462; Jerry Mashaw, "Improving the Environment of Agency Rulemaking," report to the Administrative Conference of the United States, August 1992.

6. Gary Bryner, *Bureaucratic Discretion: Law and Policy in Federal Regulatory Agencies* (New York: Pergamon, 1987).

7. Paul Sommers and Roland Cole, *Complying with Government Requirements: The Costs to Small and Larger Businesses* (Seattle: Battelle, 1981).

8. Bryner, *Bureaucratic Discretion*, chap. 9.

9. Ibid.

10. 219 United States Code 655(a) (hereafter cited as U.S.C.).

11. Albert Nichols and Richard Zeckhauser, "OSHA after a Decade: A Time for Reason," in *Case Studies in Regulation: Revolution and Reform,* ed. Leonard Weiss and Michael Klass (Boston: Little, Brown, 1981), p. 214.

12. Ibid., p. 203.

13. W. Kip Viscusi, "Reforming OSHA Regulation of Workplace Risks," in *Regulatory Reform: What Actually Happened,* ed. Leonard Weiss and Michael Klass (Boston: Little, Brown, 1986), p. 248.

14. Office of Solid Waste and Emergency Response (hereafter, OSWER), *The Nation's Hazardous Waste Management Program at a Crossroads* (Washington, D.C.: Environmental Protection Agency, 1990), p. 7.

15. Ibid., p. 31.

16. Ibid.

17. Office of Air and Radiation, "Implementation Strategy for the Clean Air Act Amendments of 1990" (Washington, D.C.: Environmental Protection Agency, 1991).

18. "Draft FCC Implementation Schedule for the Telecommunications Act of 1996, P.L. 104-4, 110 Stat. 56" (Washington, D.C.: Federal Communications Commission, 1997).

19. Curtis Copeland, "Regulations Pursuant to the Patient Protection and Affordable Care Act (P.L. 111-148)" (Washington, D.C.: Congressional Research Service, 2010).

20. Paul Farhi, "FCC Delays Reductions on Cable Television Rates," *Washington Post,* June 12, 1993, sec. D, p. 1.

21. U.S. Government Accountability Office, "Intellectual Property: Enhanced Planning by U.S. Personnel Overseas Could Strengthen Efforts," GAO 09-863, September 2009; U.S. Government Accountability Office, "OSHA's Voluntary Protection Programs: Improved Oversight and Controls Would Better Ensure Quality," U.S. GAO, 09-395, May 2009.

22. OSWER, *Nation's Hazardous Waste Management Program,* p. 87; see also John Mendeloff, "Does Overregulation Cause Underregulation?" *Regulation,* September/ October 1981, pp. 47–52.

23. Sommers and Cole, *Complying with Government Requirements,* p. 171, and more recently, Murray Weidenbaum, "Government Regulators and Medium-Sized Business," *Contemporary Issues Series* 77, Center for the Study of American Business, St. Louis, Mo., 1996.

24. OSWER, *Nation's Hazardous Waste Management Program,* p. 36.

25. Laura Langbein, *Discovering Whether Programs Work* (New York: Goodyear, 1980).

26. Edward Gramlich, *Benefit-Cost Analysis of Government Programs* (Englewood Cliffs, N.J.: Prentice Hall, 1981), chap. 2.

27. Ibid., p. 7.

28. David O'Brien, "The Multiple Sources of Statutory Ambiguity," in *Administrative Discretion and Public Policy Implementation,* ed. Douglas Shumavon and H. Kenneth Hibblen (New York: Praeger, 1986), p. 69.

29. Colin Diver, "Regulatory Precision," in *Making Regulatory Policy,* ed. Keith Hawkins and John Thomas (Pittsburgh: University of Pittsburgh Press, 1989), p. 200.

30. Ibid., p. 215.

31. Ibid., p. 200.

32. Peter Bardach and Robert Kagan, *Going by the Book* (Philadelphia: Temple University Press, 1982).

33. Diver, "Regulatory Precision," p. 200.

34. *The Changing Burden of Regulation, Paperwork, and Tax Compliance on Small Businesses: A Report to Congress* (Washington, D.C.: Small Business Administration, 1995), sec. II.

35. W. Mark Crane, "The Impact of Regulatory Costs on Small Firms," SBA Office of Advocacy, September 2005, www.sba.gov/advo/research/rs264tot.pdf.

36. "Maze of Medicaid Rules Forcing Painful Choices," *Washington Post,* August 18, 1991, p. 1.

37. 16 U.S.C. 661.

38. For example, see Mark Rothstein, "Substantive and Procedural Obstacles to OSHA Rulemaking: Reproductive Hazards as an Example," *Boston College Environmental Affairs Law Review* 12 (1985): 627.

39. Bryner, *Bureaucratic Discretion.*

40. Office of Management and Budget, "Draft Report to Congress on the Costs and Benefits of Regulation," *Federal Register,* March 28, 2002, pp. 15020–15021.

41. Stephen Breyer, *Regulation and Its Reform* (Cambridge: Harvard University Press, 1982), p. 109.

42. Ibid., p. 110. On this general point see also Peter Manning, "The Limits of Knowledge," in *Making Regulatory Policy,* ed. Keith Hawkins and John Thomas (Pittsburgh: University of Pittsburgh Press, 1989).

43. OSWER, *Nation's Hazardous Waste Management Program,* p. 37.

44. U.S. General Accounting Office, "Federal Employee Retirements, Expected Increase over the Next Five Years Illustrates Need for Planning," GAO-01-509, April 2001.

45. Cornelius M. Kerwin and Scott Furlong, "Time and Rulemaking: An Empirical Test of Theory," *Journal of Public Administration Research and Theory* 2 (1992): 118.

46. Barry Boyer, "The Federal Trade Commission and Consumer Protection Policy: A Post-Mortem Examination," in *Making Regulatory Policy,* ed. Keith Hawkins and John Thomas (Pittsburgh: University of Pittsburgh Press, 1989), p. 113.

47. Ibid.

48. Bardach and Kagan, *Going by the Book.*

49. Neil Eisner, "Agency Delay in Rulemaking," *Administrative Law Journal* 3 (1989): 7.

50. *Fundamental Improvements Needed for Timely Promulgation of Health Program Regulations* (Washington, D.C.: U.S. General Accounting Office, 1977), p. i.

51. See *Code of Federal Regulations,* vol. 18, chap. 1, subchap. W, sec. 380.

52. U.S. General Accounting Office, "Aviation Rulemaking: Further Reform Is Needed to Address Long-standing Problems," GAO-01-821, July 2001, pp. 22–23.

53. Kerwin and Furlong, "Time and Rulemaking," p. 117.

54. Benjamin Mintz and Nancy Miller, *A Guide to Federal Agency Rulemaking* (Washington, D.C.: Administrative Conference of the United States, 1991), p. 15 at n. 54.

55. U.S. Government Accountability Office, "Federal Rulemaking: Improvements Needed to Monitoring and Evaluation of Rules Development as Well as to the Transparency of OMB Regulatory Reviews," GAO-09-205, April 2009, www.gao.gov/new.items/d09205.pdf.

56. William F. West, "The Growth of Internal Conflict in Administrative Regulation," *Public Administration Review,* July/August 1988, pp. 773–782.

57. Kerwin and Furlong, "Time and Rulemaking," p. 118.

58. Richard Stewart, "The Reformation of American Administrative Law," *Harvard Law Review* 88 (1975): 1667–1711.

59. Mathew D. McCubbins, Roger G. Noll, and Barry R. Weingast, "Administrative Procedures as Instruments of Political Control," *Journal of Law, Economics, and Organization* 3 (1987): 243–277.

60. U.S. Office of Personnel Management, "Federal Civilian Workforce Statistics: The Fact Book" (2007), www.opm.gov/feddata/factbook/2007/2007FACTBOOK.pdf.

61. Lubbers, op. cit, pp. 15–16, 357–359; Jacob E. Gersen and Ann Joseph O'Connell, "Deadlines in Administration Law," *University of Pennsylvania Law Review* 156 (2008): 923.

62. Rosemary O'Leary, *Environmental Change: Federal Courts and the EPA* (Philadelphia: Temple University Press, 1993), p. 168.

63. R. Shep Melnick, *Regulation and the Courts* (Washington, D.C.: Brookings Institution, 1983), chap. 4.

64. Kerwin and Furlong, "Time and Rulemaking."

65. U.S. Department of Agriculture, "Food Safety Inspection Service Using the Claim 'Certified Organic By … ' on Meat and Poultry Labeling," March 2, 2002, www.fsis.usda.gov/oa/background/organic.htm.

66. Nancy Tregos, "Credit Card Industry Faces Reforms," *Washington Post,* August 10, 2009.

67. Personal interview with staff of the Animal and Plant Health Inspection Service, January 18, 1993.

68. Harter, "Regulatory Negotiation," p. 450.

69. Theodore Lowi, "Two Roads to Serfdom: Liberalism, Conservatism, and Administrative Power," *American University Law Review* 36 (1987): 295–322.

70. Office of Management and Budget, Office of Information and Regulatory Affairs, "2008 Report to Congress on the Benefits and Costs of Federal Regulations and Unfunded Mandates on State, Local, and Tribal Entities" (2008), www.whitehouse.gov/omb/assets/information_and_regulatory_affairs/2008_cb_final.pdf.

CHAPTER 4

The Management of Rulemaking

The volume of rules and the diversity and complexity of the rulemaking process pose serious management challenges. Rules are not equally important or equally advisable. Information for rulemaking is not always readily available, and it is never free. Personnel sufficiently expert and available to undertake a rulemaking do not appear magically. The multiple levels and types of review do not just happen; each requires attention and direction. Without such attention and direction the problems and dilemmas outlined in the previous chapter are not likely to be resolved. In fact, rulemaking is actively and aggressively managed, providing another indication of its central importance.

The management of rulemaking occurs at three distinct levels. The first level of management, and the one that has received the most scholarly and public attention, consists of government-wide programs operated out of the White House to coordinate and oversee key aspects of rulemaking. The second level of management is in the individual agencies. This level consists of structures and processes that have evolved in every agency, frequently over long periods of time, within the broader management frameworks established by recent presidents. Finally, management occurs at the level of the individual rule. Here, attention is focused on the techniques used to bring together the expertise and authorities needed to complete a particular rulemaking successfully. These efforts are strongly influenced by both presidential and agency management systems. Management exerts a powerful influence over the direction and content of rulemaking.

Presidential Management

"Herding cats" is now the standard description of the task facing someone trying to manage diffuse activities or people with diverse viewpoints. On a much grander scale this is akin to what a president confronts when he tries to manage rulemaking across the government.[1] Earlier we discussed rulemaking during the New Deal, when President Franklin Delano Roosevelt struggled with forces in Congress that appeared intent on transforming rulemaking into a pale version of judicial decision making. But beyond his successful efforts to resist extreme judicialization of the process, nothing FDR undertook during his terms could be properly called management of rulemaking. There is no evidence of any serious effort of this type in the years of Harry Truman, Dwight Eisenhower, John Kennedy, or Lyndon Johnson. During the presidencies of Richard Nixon and Gerald Ford, serious and sustained attention was given to the broader regulatory process. Both administrations called on agencies writing rules to conduct studies to predict the effect of new regulations on various segments of the population or economy. Nixon established a "quality of life review" and Ford an "inflation impact statement." Neither administration went much beyond these analytical devices in an attempt to direct or coordinate rulemaking across the full range of programs administered by the federal government.

Serious and formal programs to manage rulemaking from the White House are, then, a relatively recent phenomenon. They coincide roughly with the rise of social regulation and the vast bodies of rules that came with that expansion of the federal government. Presidents came to realize that their grip on the course of domestic public policy hinged to a considerable extent on their ability to influence the thousands of rules that put programs into action. It should not be surprising that it was Jimmy Carter who initiated what was at that point the most far-reaching and diversified program of rulemaking management undertaken by an American president. Throughout his political career he was known to be intensely interested in the management of government programs. Like several of his predecessors and each of his successors, Carter was concerned with the role and effect of government regulation in American society. The program of management he devised had many elements, most of which survive either intact or in modified form more than three decades after the program's creation. Hence, a detailed review of his initiative is worthwhile.

Carter's rulemaking management program was embodied in Executive Order 12044, which created a "regulatory council," consisting of the heads of the agencies with the most substantial regulatory programs. The council was conceived of as a mechanism for the coordination of rulemaking activities across the entire government. It prepared a calendar of the most significant rules being developed in agencies and departments and attempted to identify areas of common interest or approach or potential overlap in these individual efforts. The council was also expected to conduct studies of the "cumulative effect of regulations on particularly vulnerable industries or sectors."[2]

Created along with the council was the Regulatory Analysis Review Group (RARG), headed by the Council of Economic Advisers. The mission of the RARG was to "improve the quality of analysis supporting proposed regulations, identify and attempt to resolve common analytic problems among the agencies and assure adequate consideration of least costly alternatives."[3] In addition, the group was used as a vehicle for all regulatory agencies to review and comment on the rules developed by a particular agency; the idea was that this participation would increase available expertise and promote consistency in rulemaking.

The Carter executive order also created a role for the Office of Management and Budget (OMB). It was to review rules to ensure that agencies were faithfully adhering to the recently enacted Paperwork Reduction Act and that rules embodied the general principles outlined in the order. Although it had no power to change rules that it reviewed, the OMB was to report to the president regularly on the performance of agencies in achieving the goals of the order.

Carter also established five principles to guide rulemaking management: policy oversight of rulemaking by agency heads, increased participation by the public in the development of rules, regulatory analysis, "sunset review" to eliminate rules no longer needed and to update or revise those that had become obsolete or ineffectual, and the use of "plain English" in rules to make them more accessible to those who must comply with their provisions.[4] Each of these principles was developed in response to a common problem in rulemaking. The active involvement of agency leadership in the planning and development of rules was designed to counteract the nearly total lack of central direction in rulemaking that the Carter administration found when it took office. Central oversight of rules in agencies was called "the most important element of the Order and the key to the success of [Carter's] regulatory reform program."[5] Increased participation by the public was seen as a way to improve the image of rulemaking while simultaneously enriching the pool of information that agencies had to work with when developing rules. Regulatory analysis was developed to inject a degree of self-conscious rationality into the process of rule development. When done correctly and seriously, such analysis forced attention to alternative ways of accomplishing public policy objectives. "Sunset reviews" by rulemaking agencies led to the demise of obsolete rules and the renovation of others that had developed, sometimes over many decades, in piecemeal fashion. Anyone who has read the *Federal Register* or the *Code of Federal Regulations* will immediately understand what the "plain English" initiative was all about.

Carter's rulemaking management program was in effect for fewer than three years, yet it stimulated change in each of the areas it targeted. In a 1979 report on the implementation of the executive order, the OMB noted that overall progress was mixed, with some reforms showing well and others relatively poorly. In answer to the call for more systematic and aggressive oversight of rulemaking by agency leaders, several agencies established their own regulatory councils or steering committees. The composition and functions of the councils and committees varied, but there were examples of agency leaders playing an active role in both the initiation and final approval of rules. Considerable progress was reported in the area of public participation, and the results of sunset reviews were truly dramatic. Several agencies' reviews led to major revisions of their body of regulations. The Occupational Safety and Health Administration (OSHA), for example, reduced its fire safety standards from 400 pages to 30. The Department of Health, Education and Welfare (HEW) reviewed more than 2,800 pages of rules. The result was that 719 pages were deleted outright and 500 pages were rewritten. Similar efforts were reported in the Department of Transportation (DOT). The campaign for plain English in most agencies focused on the preambles to rules, using them as a layman's guide for translating the technical and legal jargon found in actual regulations into words that nonspecialists could understand. Progress in the area of regulatory analysis was generally weak. The OMB report concluded that "some individual examples of good analyses are available, but no department can be commended for having a department-wide, continuously successful effort in place."[6]

The performance of Carter's management program cannot be fully appreciated until we consider the enduring influence of many of its basic principles and structures. One could easily argue that many of the elements of his program were hardly original. The Regulatory Council, for example, was a more focused version of the old Council on Wage and Price Stability. Regulatory analyses can be viewed as the next logical step after the impact analyses of the Nixon and Ford administrations. Nevertheless, the breadth, coherence, and specific focus of Carter's program were distinctive and influential. When Ronald Reagan, George H. W. Bush, Bill Clinton, and George W. Bush fashioned their own regulatory reforms, they retained many of Carter's tools while adding distinctive features of their own. Barack Obama is doing the same.

Reagan did not wait as long as his predecessor did to put his rulemaking management system in place. Shortly after taking office, he issued Executive Order 12291, which instituted a sixty-day moratorium on new rules, a mandatory cost-benefit analysis for all major regulations, a requirement that all such regulations meet a "net benefit" criterion, and a review of all proposed and final rules by the OMB. The order was part of a general policy of the Reagan administration to reduce the burden of regulations on the American economy by making it more difficult for agencies to issue them; the administration also wanted to ensure that those that were written could be justified. The moratorium was an effort to prevent "midnight" rules from being issued by holdovers from the Carter administration who might possess a more expansive view of regulation than that of the Reagan team. The mandatory cost-benefit analysis and the "net benefit" rule codified more strictly the regulatory analysis program that had been in effect under Executive Order 12044. The OMB review as Reagan designed it carried with it the power to delay issuance of proposed or final rules that did not comport with the philosophy of his administration. His decision to make the OMB review mandatory strengthened a review program that Carter had put in place. This single act had a more profound effect on the rulemaking process than the entire Carter program.

President Reagan also created the Vice President's Task Force on Regulatory Relief. In doing so he elevated to primary status a secondary function of Carter's Regulatory Council, consideration of the impact of regulations on particularly fragile sectors of the economy. The Reagan administration also incorporated the semiannual regulatory agenda, a compilation of major rules being developed by federal agencies, and an annual version of the regulatory calendar containing summaries of the work of the OMB in review of agency rules.

When George H. W. Bush took office in 1989, he kept virtually all of Reagan's rulemaking program intact but changed significantly the Task Force on Regulatory Relief he had chaired as vice president. Renamed the Council on Competitiveness in 1991, it reviewed individual rules that were likely to have an especially significant impact on the economy in general or on particular sectors of the economy. President Bush continued one tradition by putting the council under the chairmanship of his vice president, Dan Quayle. It selected rules with considerable potential impact or high visibility for special scrutiny. The council received staff assistance from the component of the OMB that normally conducted the analysis of regulations. Bush also instituted moratoria on rulemaking when conservatives began to complain that he had lost the will to resist regulation. The effects of instruments like the Council on Competitiveness and the moratoria will be covered in Chapter 6.

The rulemaking management program of Bill Clinton focused on familiar issues and review mechanisms. It is best viewed as part of the president's larger initiative to improve government effectiveness, the National Performance Review. As one would expect, the president chose to retain OMB review but open it to public scrutiny and limit it to "significant" rules. "Significant" is defined by economic impact, budget impact, inconsistency with other rules, or novel legal or policy issues. The order required each agency to name a "regulatory policy officer," a senior official who would "be involved in each stage of the regulatory process to foster the development of effective, innovative, and least burdensome regulations."[7] These officers comprised a "regulatory working group to assist in cross agency coordination."[8] The Clinton order emphasized planning and review of existing regulations. In Vice President Albert Gore, President Clinton vested the authority to set the government-wide rulemaking agenda.[9]

George W. Bush took rulemaking management to yet another level of sophistication. He made a conscious decision to operate largely under the provisions of Clinton's Executive Order 12866, opting for continuity and avoiding the controversy that would attend the issuance of a new executive order. In addition, the new director of the Office of Information and Regulatory Affairs (OIRA) launched an ambitious program, issuing directives to agencies. The new Bush programs included a requirement for more formal communication from the OMB to agencies with whom the OMB disagreed on rules, new guidelines on the documentation that must accompany proposals for significant rules, a requirement of "prompt letters" from OIRA to agencies recommending areas where new rules may be needed, information quality standards, larger staff in OIRA, a science advisory group, a system to allow the public to recommend review of existing rules, and reaffirmed commitment by the administration to openness and transparency throughout the management process.[10] Later in his administration Bush issued an executive order that extended OIRA review to "guidance" documents issued by agencies and required a presidential appointee in each agency, which he named a "regulatory policy officer," who would have authority to review proposed and final rules.[11]

At the time of this writing in 2010, there have been some mixed signals regarding President Obama's thoughts about the management of rulemaking. Like many of his predecessors, when he took office Obama prohibited the publication of any pending rules from the Bush II administration that were in the pipeline.[12] In addition, Obama repealed two Bush executive orders that had been criticized by groups and individuals critical of the Bush regulatory review program. Executive Order 13422, among other things, provided OIRA with the power to review agency guidance documents and allowed regulatory policy officers to stop regulations without input. Executive Order 13258 had eliminated the vice president's formal role in reviewing regulations and effectively removed him from resolving interagency conflicts.[13]

Within the first couple of weeks of the Obama presidency, a memorandum was sent to the agency heads asking them to work with the director of the OMB to develop recommendations for a new executive order on regulatory review.[14] A little over a month later, in an unprecedented action, the OMB director requested public comments "on the principles and procedures governing regulatory review."[15] The action was unprecedented in that previous administrations had not so openly asked for public input on such internal regulatory review issues, and this was even acknowledged in the *Federal Register* notice.

By mid-April 2009, over 180 comments had been received from the general public. It is interesting to note that many of the comments came from regulatory policy scholars as well as from individuals who had been in the past or were currently quite active in the regulatory review process. There were a range of comments, although many focused on issues of the positive or negative implications and the role of cost-benefit analysis, the transparency of the regulatory process, and the interrelationships among OIRA and the executive agencies.[16] By early 2010, there had yet to be any formal issuance of a new executive order to govern regulatory review. This could possibly be due to other priorities within the administration, such as the economy, health care, and the wars in Afghanistan and Iraq, or perhaps to some internal disagreements within the administration regarding what direction to take a new order. At this writing the Obama administration continues to use Executive Order 12866 as its basis for regulatory review and appears to be satisfied with how this is working.

Like presidents before him, Obama selected a prominent individual to head OIRA, tapping Cass Sunstein—a prolific and influential scholar—to lead that most important arm of presidential power. Sunstein, however, met with considerable opposition from both the right and the left. A hold was placed on his nomination by Republican senators ostensibly concerned about the nominee's writing on animal rights and alleged support for curbs on hunting. The left voiced concerns about Sunstein's long-standing advocacy for the use of cost-benefit analysis in the development of rules, seen by proponents of aggressive regulation as a device used by their opponents to block or delay new regulations. In the end the holds were dropped, his nomination proceeded to vote, and the president's choice prevailed by the relatively slim margin of 57–40. This may be a harbinger of greater congressional scrutiny of Sunstein's stewardship of Obama's management of rulemaking or merely another example of the partisanship that characterized the legislative branch's deliberations and actions on initiatives of the new administration.

President Obama reinforced his message of change in certain regulatory arenas by naming White House–based "czars" for various areas of domestic policy. For example, Carole Browner, former administrator of the Environmental Protection Agency (EPA) under Clinton, was named special advisor for energy, sparking speculation that she would be a major force in a wide range of regulatory decisions but essentially out of public view and account-ability. These too generated considerable commentary and criticism from a number of quarters with claims that they would be the real forces behind the administration's actions on new regulations. But, at this writing, it is simply too early to determine whether the so-called czars will emerge as formidable players in rulemaking and, as such, rivals to the director of OIRA.

Presidential efforts to manage rulemaking as an identifiable govern-ment-wide activity have been sophisticated and influential. More will be presented about the effects of these management efforts in Chapter 6. Presidents Carter, Reagan, George H. W. Bush, Clinton, and George W. Bush approached the management of rulemaking in a manner not unlike efforts to manage a diffuse and fragmented national security apparatus. Recent man-agement systems operating out of the White House reflect many of the struc-tures and procedures established by Carter. But it was Reagan who put real bite into presidential management of rulemaking. Clinton's program was a hybrid of rulemaking management under Carter and Reagan; George W. Bush sought to retain the selectivity of White House review and long-standing principles while ensuring that his OMB retained its independence from agencies. At the same time, Bush's continuation and intensification of the important innovation of selecting a smaller number of rules for intense scrutiny retained for the office of the president an active role in rulemaking. His effort to extend the reach of the White House to encompass guidance documents of various sorts and insert a regulating policy officer with White House ties in each agency also revealed both a seriousness of purpose and a sophisticated understanding of the behavior of government agencies. His program attempted to weed out the unnecessary and excessively burden-some rules, as did Reagan's program, but like Carter's it acknowledged that rulemaking is an important and permanent government function. As such, it should have clear direction and effective day-to-day management.

Management on the Agency Level

Individual agencies have many good reasons to manage rulemaking. Most are quite independent of the interest a president may take in one or another aspect of the process. As we have seen in previous chapters, rulemaking is the primary way agencies define the programs they implement and adminis-ter. They are under considerable pressure from sources other than the White House to produce rules. Congress, interest groups, other agencies, and their own staffs may be clamoring for new or revised regulations. An agency's ability to sort out these demands for rules and to be responsive depends to some extent on its management of the overall rulemaking process. There are other reasons for management. The political leadership of an agency will likely have a policy agenda to promote, whether it is the president's larger program or the agency administrator's own priorities. Good management can supply the vigilance and discipline to ensure that the rules that are issued are consistent with that agenda. Finally, rulemaking uses resources. Some agencies devote significant shares of the budgets provided them by Congress to rulemaking. Careful management of such an expensive government function as rulemaking is an obvious obligation to taxpayers.

The Elements of Management

Agency-level management of rulemaking goes well beyond the structures and procedures that have been included in various presidential programs. Whereas presidents have been concerned with policy and higher-level processes, agency management programs encompass administrative activities as well as policy considerations. To examine the management of rulemaking at the agency level, one must first determine what the elements of such a system might look like. Drawing on case studies of rulemaking and the general literature devoted to public administration, we are able to identify what the basic elements of a management system might include.

A word is in order here on how the information about rulemaking management practices in federal agencies was assembled for this chapter. In past editions two basic sources were used. The first was guidance documents and internal reports on rulemaking prepared by agencies themselves; internal studies and reports provided descriptions of some of the elements of rulemaking management in selected agencies. These documents were not available or current in all cases, and where they did exist they frequently addressed only a portion of the activities and structures of the agency in question. To obtain a more complete picture of rulemaking management, we surveyed experts in agencies of the federal government who had substantial rulemaking responsibilities. For the first edition of the book, Kerwin questioned people in thirty-five agencies. For the third edition, he conducted a new set of thirteen interviews to determine whether major changes had occurred in agencies that were, and still are, prominent sources of rules. This edition draws on a different source of information. Many of the observations and insights contained in this report are drawn from the authors' communications with government officials. Among the more important and recent were the discussions that occurred during a one-day symposium sponsored by the Center for the Study of Rulemaking at American University (AU). On June 5, 2005, a group of senior officials with varying but significant responsibilities for the management of rulemaking in their departments and agencies gathered in a "principals only" session to discuss current developments and issues related to the topics covered in this chapter. The results of this symposium were summarized in a report written by Kerwin and sponsored by the IBM Center for the Business of Government titled "The Management of Regulation Development: Out of the Shadows." In a number of sections that follow we quote extensively from that document.[17]

After more than twenty years of studying agency-level management of rulemaking, it is apparent to us that for the purposes of this edition it is more important to identify major functional categories and variations in management approaches and techniques than to attempt a comprehensive survey of all rulemaking agencies. This edition appears early in a new presidential administration, a time when changes in management of rulemaking have not yet fully formed. Consequently, the information from the 2005 AU symposium provides an adequate basis for understanding the key elements of rulemaking management and the ways it has been carried out. Change will occur in philosophy and methods, to be sure, but will be far less common in the major categories of rulemaking management functions.

A Process for Setting Priorities. By setting priorities throughout its domain, an agency can control the types and sequencing of the rules that it produces. Priority setting enables the agency's leadership to determine how it will respond to internal and external demands for rules and how the agency's resources available for rulemaking will be spent. Agencies vary considerably in their attention to setting priorities. At one extreme is a fully centralized system in which the priorities are set at the top of the agency; at the other is a fully decentralized system in which no overarching set of priorities is imposed on the operating units of the agency. Between these extremes one might find a system in which agency leadership designates some rules as high-priority projects, leaving the operating units to determine the rest of the rulemaking agenda. Still another is an essentially decentralized approach that allows for intervention by agency leadership when an emergency, political or otherwise, arises.

Seventy-four percent of the agencies in our original survey reported that they had systems to set priorities for rulemaking, and the numbers are at least that high today. These systems varied considerably, however. Some did little more than assemble the semiannual regulatory agenda required by executive order. Others were comprehensive and rigorous. This spectrum of variation was evident at the AU symposium, during which agency experts highlighted important nuances that add uncertainty and complexity to this basic design and provide the basis for an important observation about the stability of priorities.

The EPA, with a number of operating subunits dealing with different media and types of pollution, uses a "tiers" system that categorizes individual rulemaking projects according to their significance. Tier 1 consists of rules whose economic impact, controversy, or visibility make them the highest priority. These rules require careful attention from multiple offices at regular intervals and on strict schedules. They constitute only 5 percent of the agency's rulemaking projects at any given time, but they consume a disproportionate share of resources. Tier 2 consists of rules with less compelling policy, economic, or political issues but that still warrant serious attention from senior officials. These also have set deadlines. It is estimated that these make up about 15 percent of the EPA rulemaking workload. The remaining rules are in Tier 3 and receive no agency-wide attention; their production is entirely in the hands of the responsible program office.

The Animal and Plant Health Inspection Service (APHIS) in the Department of Agriculture also uses a tiering system, but one that more clearly delineates stages of planning. APHIS has four tiers. Tiers 1 and 2 consist of actions that are already at the rulemaking stage and are considered the highest by the administrator ("1") or a high priority ("2") by the deputy administrator. Tiers 3 and 4 consist of actions where rulemaking has not commenced but for which a risk assessment is authorized or under way ("3") or related to potential imports that have been slated for regulatory actions ("4"). The Department of Veterans Affairs places rulemaking projects in three categories: simple, complex, and "hot." Hot means very high priority and close monitoring.

In contrast, the Department of Transportation (DOT), another organization consisting of multiple agencies, has no unified priority-setting process, but its component agencies are active. For example, the Federal Aviation Administration (FAA) has a highly disciplined system. The FAA places its rulemaking projects on two lists, A and B, with the former consisting of the highest priority rules for its operating divisions and the latter composed of rules that are important but will be worked on only when time resources permit. The FAA's "A-list" rules are ones to which the agency has committed considerable staff expertise and that it is prepared to set and adhere to a fixed schedule for completion. The National Highway Transportation Safety Administration (NHTSA) uses risk assessments to determine the priority order of projects. In this respect, the NHTSA practice resembles the APHIS system.

The Nuclear Regulatory Commission (NRC), an independent body with fewer major operating units than the EPA or Transportation, also has a unified priority-setting system that may be the most disciplined in government. Points are assigned to each rulemaking project based on importance regarding a number of critical dimensions such as safety/security (awarded the highest number of points), effectiveness, and openness/transparency. Each rule is scored, and the resultant numerical ranking determines priority order.

The Departments of Labor, Treasury, Commerce, and Homeland Security demonstrate additional nuances in setting priorities. The Department of Labor relies on the Regulatory Plan and Regulatory Agenda, established decades ago by executive order, for this purpose. It is the only department that reported using either of these familiar government-wide instruments for serious priority setting. At Treasury, the operating units enjoy nearly complete discretion in determining the order and importance of rulemaking projects, but the department also reported strong influences from external groups in at least two of their organizations with significant rulemaking responsibilities. The Department of Commerce asserts that external influence in priority setting is effectively institutionalized for its National Marine Fisheries Service (NMFS) and its international trade agencies. NMFS rulemaking is heavily influenced by input from fisheries management councils, powerful advisory committees established decades ago in its foundation-authorizing legislation. The international trade rulemaking agenda at the Department of Commerce is affected by any changes in treaties, protocols, and other instruments of international trade law.

A classic example of an agency in need of a capability to alter its priorities on very short notice is the Department of Homeland Security (DHS). The United States Coast Guard, a major DHS operating unit, manages its priorities through a system that scores rulemaking projects based on the type and amount of external and internal interest (for example, congressional, judicial, White House, or DHS). The Coast Guard's system is reportedly less formal and determinative than that in place at the NRC and is used as a device to assist the organization in keeping track of projects with high political and public salience.

Categories of priority-setting systems are useful heuristic devices, but are by their nature crude and cannot convey the richness and variety of priority setting found in operating systems in federal agencies. Some of this variation depends on the "issue networks" (consisting of interested groups, institutions, and individuals) that surround the department or its subordinate unit and how the agency's staff and leaders are positioned within them. This highlights another management function—participation. It also leads to an important finding.

Priority-setting systems are susceptible to external disturbance as the concerns of external "principals" and their "agents" inside the agency or department change with shifting events and circumstances. This also means that the departments and agencies with broad regulatory responsibilities that touch the health, safety, or economic well-being of large or powerful interests will struggle with inherently fragile, unstable priority-setting systems. Very recent work undertaken by Professor William West also sheds light on the difficulties in priority setting by highlighting the multiple forces that can come into play. He notes that whether a given regulation development effort is mandatory (i.e., ordered by Congress in a court) or discretionary (i.e., under agency initiative) is an additional and important factor in priority setting.[18]

Participants in the 2005 symposium at American University were virtually uniform in their assessment of the effects that changing priorities have on the overall rulemaking management system. Changes in priorities divert resources for months or more, making them difficult if not impossible to reassemble. Diversions of resources are momentum killers that also threaten the often tenuous internal and external coalitions that the writers of significant rules rely on to produce the consensus their superiors usually seek to achieve.

The optimal priority-setting system is one that balances the conflicting pressures that put careful planning and the ability to adapt at odds. The priority of rulemaking projects must reflect legal obligations but should also consider the relative importance of a given rule to the accomplishment of the agency's mission and its ability to advance the general welfare. There is no question that solid systems are in place, but instability in priority setting is also common. Hence, chief among the skills needed for priority setting is the ability to scan and predict—or at least react quickly to—perturbations in the external environment. It is not unreasonable to expect that agencies with substantial rulemaking responsibilities develop plans to buffer high-priority projects that may be at risk if the external environment dictates diversion of resources and effort. This requires, among other things, management of participation by internal and external actors.

A Process for Initiating Rules and Securing Early Input. Virtually all agencies require some form of approval, even if it is nothing more than inclusion in the agency's priorities or a semiannual agenda. In the original survey, a substantial majority of agencies (63 percent) reported that those wishing to initiate rulemaking must obtain separate prior authorization from senior agency management. Permission nearly always has to be requested in writing. The most recent update indicates that approval prior to initiation is still the norm.

Several agencies rely on a formal structure, such as a committee or board, to approve the start of rules. The start of each rulemaking project at the NRC requires an affirmative vote of a majority of the five commissioners. The Department of Veterans Affairs requires initiation authorization by the secretary's Office of Policy, and for some organizations in the Department of Agriculture, such as APHIS, approval by the undersecretary is the norm. Other departments, including Commerce, Treasury, Homeland Security, and Transportation, have no routine department-level initiation requirements, but this does not mean their operating units do not commonly have elaborate processes. For example, within DHS, the Coast Guard requires all proposed projects to be reviewed by its Regulations Coordinating Committee. If this group deems them to be significant, they are forwarded directly to the commandant for approval. In a virtually identical procedure, the FAA's Rulemaking Council screens all rulemaking projects and sends those considered significant to the associate administrator.

Since at least the Carter administration there has been concern that individual rulemaking may be disconnected from policies or principles adopted by a new administration. A mechanism that allows senior officials to provide early technical or policy guidance is a natural complement to priority setting and rule initiation systems. Assuming a degree of consistency in the senior leadership, this management device can ensure that all rules, or at least the most significant ones, reflect a common substantive or procedural philosophy. At a more practical level, it can also minimize the problems caused when senior officials find unacceptable a fully developed rule that finally reaches them for review. The costs of conflict, delay, and wasted resources that accompany these "late hits" by senior managers can be substantial. Involvement of senior officials in the rulemaking process early enough for them to influence the direction of a rule can avoid these problems.

The results of the original survey yielded four categories of agencies: those that require guidance by senior officials for all rules; those that require guidance only on rules deemed important enough for all rules; those that require guidance only on rules deemed important enough for senior management's attention; and those that have no system of this sort. Today, virtually all agencies have systems that fall into the first two categories.

For example, the EPA's tiering procedures contain explicit provisions for varying levels of guidance and subsequent reviews by senior agency officials. Other agencies employ similar arrangements. The critical question with regard to initiation and guidance is how well both work in practice. Be it in the context of a sophisticated priority-setting system like those at the NRC, APHIS, and the EPA, or one with less departmental-level discipline, obtaining early guidance is a significant challenge. The senior officials whose views on regulation are needed are hard to reach through normal bureaucratic channels, are busy, and are less than omniscient on policy matters. Even when the attention of senior officials is secured, the time they spend on the matter will be brief and the preferences they articulate may be superficial or poorly informed. When the technical and policy issues related to the rule are also not fully developed or known, which is frequently the case, serious early involvement by senior officials is compromised. Whatever the difficulties, early involvement of senior officials is indispensable for rules of high salience.

The Preparation of Planning Documents. The significance of planning documents may not be immediately apparent, but they can be effective management tools. A detailed work plan forces those responsible for writing rules to make their intentions clear and known to all who read them. Combined with a system for approving the initiation of rules, a work plan can give senior management officials sufficient information to intervene at the early stages of a rulemaking if it appears that the rule writers are pursuing an unacceptable or infeasible course of action. Even when work plans do not serve as an instrument for oversight, they can still be useful. Depending on their content, they can force those writing the rule to consider the full range of policy, technical, operational, and resource issues that will arise and must be resolved during the rulemaking. Work plans are thus a mechanism for anticipating the types of problems for which rulemaking is often criticized.

In the survey first conducted for the inception of this book 66 percent of the agencies reported using planning documents to chart the course of all rulemakings, and a substantial portion of the rest used them selectively. More recent interviews indicated that the same basic pattern still holds. The documents vary from agency to agency in content and purpose. Some planning documents also serve as a mechanism for an agency to initiate a rulemaking. They generally include background on the need for the rule, the type of information required to complete it, the availability and sources of information, the policy issues involved, public interest and involvement in the rule, and needed resources and schedules. The documents frequently provide the information needed for the semiannual regulatory agenda mandated by the executive order.

For years the EPA required a lengthy planning document for its many important rulemakings. Staff members complained that the document was a waste of effort, redundant, and of little practical use. Thus they frequently ignored the requirement or reduced the document to a boilerplate. The EPA has since abandoned the requirement, replacing it with an "analytical blueprint," comparable to the old planning document but required for only the most important, potentially controversial, or organizationally complex rules.[19]

Two agencies of the Department of Agriculture have used work plans prior to commencement of effort on rules. The Food Safety and Inspection Service actually uses two documents—a preliminary report and a work plan—to set out all aspects of a rule to be developed. The Animal and Plant Health Inspection Service, too, employs what it calls a regulatory work plan. Among the topics addressed in these and other planning documents are the purpose of the rule being developed, the intent of the legislation that the rule will implement, the effects of existing rules on the one being developed (and vice versa), the information and resources needed to complete the rule, the impact of the rule on the affected population, deadlines that must be met, the forms of public participation appropriate for the rulemaking, and the likely points of controversy. Agencies use work plans to determine the significance of actions, a determination that affects the degree of scrutiny the action will get from senior officials and external parties such as the OMB.

Schedules. Experienced and thoughtful observers of the rulemaking process contend that setting a firm schedule can reduce or eliminate delay.[20] A schedule provides a benchmark to measure the performance of those writing the rule, and if linked to a staff performance appraisal process, it can provide strong incentives to complete the rulemaking on time. Those setting a schedule cannot avoid the substantive and procedural issues whose resolution consumes the bulk of time in any rulemaking. Like a planning document, a schedule requires attention to key issues and how they might be resolved. For that reason one would expect to find schedules incorporated into planning documents.

Agencies continue to report that they set schedules for all of their rulemakings. An example of a very elaborate schedule format used by the Federal Aviation Administration is shown in Figure 4-1. It identifies key milestones. The FAA also has targets for the time to be spent on each stage. The FAA leadership reviews schedules for individual rulemaking projects twice a week, and the FAA system feeds into a department-wide tracking system maintained in the Office of the Assistant General Counsel for Regulation at DOT. The Nuclear Regulatory Commission also reports close attention to schedules. Virtually all agencies set schedules on a rule-by-rule basis, but the FAA also emphasized at the 2005 symposium a goal of writing rules to allow use of new aviation technologies by the industry and public in one year or less.

Agencies reported that schedules were routinely adjusted. In other words, in many agencies schedules slip. Some note that schedules are of little use because of the frequency of shifts in priorities and externally imposed deadlines. This is by no means an indictment of scheduling. The

FIGURE 4-1 Rulemaking Process Flowcharts, Federal Aviation Administration

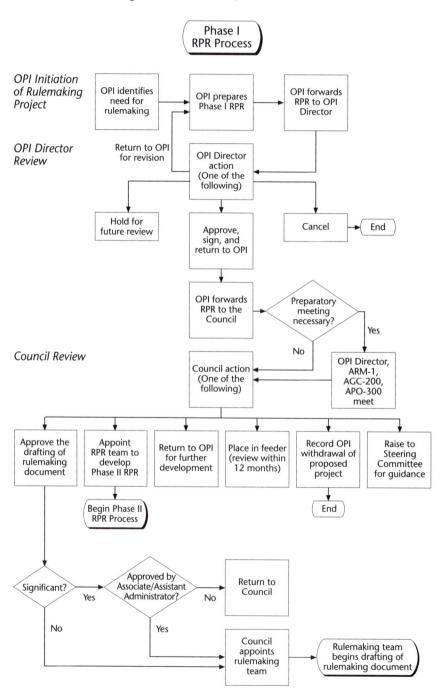

FIGURE 4-1 *(continued)*

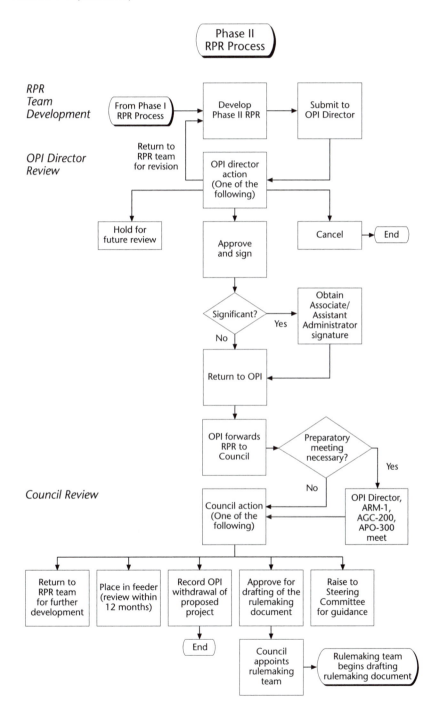

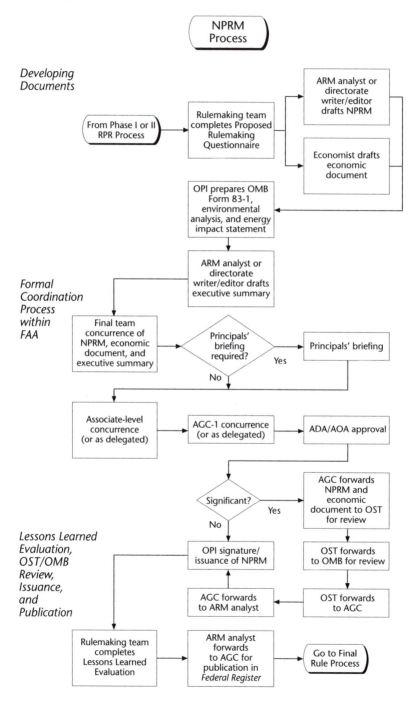

FIGURE 4-1 *(continued)*

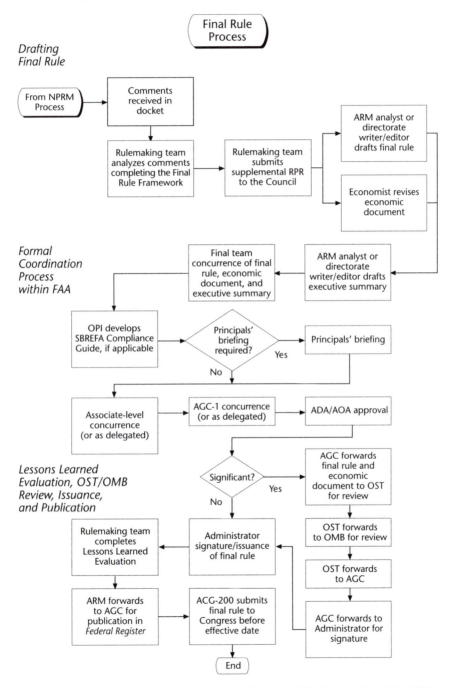

Final Rule Process

Drafting Final Rule

From NPRM Process → Comments received in docket

Rulemaking team analyzes comments completing the Final Rule Framework

Rulemaking team submits supplemental RPR to the Council

ARM analyst or directorate writer/editor drafts final rule

Economist revises economic document

Formal Coordination Process within FAA

ARM analyst or directorate writer/editor drafts executive summary

Final team concurrence of final rule, economic document, and executive summary

OPI develops SBREFA Compliance Guide, if applicable

Principals' briefing required?

No

Yes → Principals' briefing

Associate-level concurrence (or as delegated)

AGC-1 concurrence (or as delegated)

ADA/AOA approval

Lessons Learned Evaluation, OST/OMB Review, Issuance, and Publication

Significant?

No

Yes

AGC forwards final rule and economic document to OST for review

OST forwards to OMB for review

OST forwards to AGC

AGC forwards to Administrator for signature

Rulemaking team completes Lessons Learned Evaluation

Administrator signature/issuance of final rule

ARM forwards to AGC for publication in *Federal Register*

ACG-200 submits final rule to Congress before effective date

End

Source: Federal Aviation Administration, *FAA Rulemaking Manual* (Washington, D.C.: FAA, 1998).

value of a schedule, as Neil Eisner, the assistant general counsel for regulation at DOT, has argued, does not lie primarily in whether it is adhered to religiously. On the contrary, a schedule is an objective. If it is not met, it requires another to be set and the assumptions that led to the first to be reexamined.[21] That so many agencies set schedules and monitor progress in meeting self-imposed deadlines is significant for this reason alone.

The results of the 2005 American University symposium were supplemented and generally supported by a recent Government Accountability Office (GAO) report. In a 2009 study of related aspects of federal rulemaking it found:

- DOT officials at the FAA and the NHTSA identified common milestones, including development of a draft concept, management reviews within administrations, review by the secretary's office, and external review.
- The EPA identified fourteen milestones for nonroutine rulemakings from initiation to publication of the proposed rule, including assigning a working group, development and approval of an analytic blueprint, and management reviews. After the proposed rule is published, the EPA tracks an additional four to five milestones to develop the final rule.
- Food and Drug Administration officials emphasized that regulatory development is similar throughout the FDA. The Center for Food Safety and Applied Nutrition and the Center for Drug Evaluation and Research used milestones such as assigning a working group, and drafting and conducting analyses and management clearances.
- Securities and Exchange Commission officials stated that Corporate Finance and Investment Management identified as common milestones generation (typically including public input), drafting, and approval by the commissioners.[22]

Budgets. Writing rules costs money, sometimes a hefty share of an agency's budget. It is not clear, however, how agencies allocate and manage the resources devoted to developing rules. They could budget for an entire rulemaking program or for specific rules. Budgeting, like scheduling, demands attention to the process and substance of writing rules; the necessary funds cannot be estimated if the tasks that must be performed are not understood. In addition to combating delay by ensuring that needed funds and personnel are available, budgeting can make a positive contribution to the quality of rules.

Of the thirty-five agencies in the original survey, only four reported that they budgeted for rulemaking, and only one of these did so on an overall programmatic basis. Interviews for the third edition of this book indicated that this situation had changed somewhat but that elaborate line-item budgets for individual rules were not the norm. Agencies reported giving consideration to the costs of developing rules. Most of the agencies interviewed reported that the statement about the resources that were likely to be required was expected either during the process of securing permission to start rules or in planning documents. The EPA indicates it prepares budgets for higher-priority rules, and the FAA requires an estimate of labor hours in its rulemaking project record. The FAA also notes in its guidance that initiation of a new rulemaking project amounts to a commitment from all involved to provide the resources needed to complete the work. Budgeting reminds us that whatever else it is, rulemaking is a major drain on agency resources. Most agencies that reported no formal budget process for rulemaking when questioned, such as the Federal Communications Commission (FCC), the Food Safety and Inspection Service (FSIS), and the Federal Motor Carrier Safety Administration (FMCSA), also reported either special circumstances, such as recent changes in workload or the relative youth of the agency, or acknowledged that rulemaking costs were considered in large, more generic budgetary systems.

At the symposium in June 2005, a larger number of officials reported on efforts to budget prospectively for rulemaking, notably those from the NRC and, within the Department of Homeland Security, the Coast Guard. In addition, DHS as a department reported the ability to track the person hours needed to complete the most important rulemakings for the year. It reported that this capability not only ensures adequate progress on key projects but also provides information critical to efforts to approach Congress for additional funding for projects that might otherwise slip. DOT reported on its ability to engage in a modest amount of resource reallocation for high-priority projects. But among the agency experts who assembled at American University in 2005, there was a healthy dose of skepticism regarding the value of classical budgeting for rulemaking.

In some cases, budgeting difficulties are a function of technical complexity, such as the inability to assign portions of the cost of large-scale research efforts that support entire regulatory programs to a particular rulemaking proposal. Fish stock analyses done by the National Marine Fisheries Service in the Department of Commerce, undertaken for a variety of reasons, are good examples of such complexity. Others opined that budgeting is even more difficult when the cost of securing information for a regulation is a complex mix of original research, institutional information, staff expertise, and insights from the public.

The timing of budget preparation and submission requirements is often not in sync with the dynamic elements of regulation development. Agency budgets are submitted far in advance and according to a firm schedule. The need for rules, prompted by new legislation, court decisions, or emergencies, and the drivers of rulemaking costs, such as the nature and amount of information required or the amount of public participation involved, present themselves without concern for budget schedules. The ability of an agency to correctly predict these dynamics in a time frame consistent with budget submission schedules and to convince Congress to provide the funding needed is, to understate it, very limited. Classical budgeting is undone by the churning of departmental or agency priorities for regulation development referred to earlier. It makes little sense to attempt to estimate costs with precision when resources are routinely diverted to either other rulemaking projects or completely unrelated agency activities.[23]

It is also important to note that rulemaking budgets usually consist entirely of the cost of personnel and information, and these are highly interrelated. Agency personnel costs are generally expressed in terms of full-time equivalents (FTEs). Work that cannot be completed using agency personnel, because of its volume or the lack of internal expertise, is done by consultants and contractors.

The general conclusion of the 2009 GAO study of sixteen selected rules was that little systematic information was available within agencies on the time, staffing, and contracting costs associated with the development of individual rules.[24]

Responsibility for Developing Rules

As in all complex and important public functions, selecting the right people to accomplish the task is crucial to the eventual success of the enterprise. Agencies that issue relatively simple rules and that place a premium on speed and accountability may make a single individual responsible for rule development. When the rulemakings require complex and varied information and affect multiple interests, and when consensus in decisions is important, this function may be given to a work group or task force. Either of these general models of staffing for rulemaking, and each of the numerous variations on them, raises significant issues.

When a single person is responsible for a rule, it is always possible that he or she lacks a crucial element of expertise or skill. How individual rulemakers compensate for their shortcomings is not clear. Nor is it immediately obvious how offices with a legitimate interest in the rule get access to the single rulemaker and a response from that person. Work groups or task forces, in contrast, can be used to assemble the necessary expertise and to provide a forum for the airing of all significant points of view. But questions arise as to how members of work groups are chosen and how the work group itself is managed. Leadership and participation in work groups are key variables. Whether the work group functions as a mechanism for collective rulemaking with all members responsible for drafting sections of the rule or merely as an advise-and-consent body is also significant. We would expect these models to behave quite differently and bring about different results.

In the original survey a majority of agencies reported that they used work groups or task forces to write all or some of their rules. Those that used work groups on a selective basis reserved them for major or especially complex rules. The use of work groups or teams has become even more common. Agencies use a variety of devices to determine the composition of work groups. They always include the program office that is responsible for the statute to be implemented by the new or revised rule. The Office of the General Counsel is usually a regular participant in work groups because questions of legal sufficiency—both substantive and procedural—are the most common in rulemaking. In most agencies the general compositions of work groups show little variation. It appears quite common that, in addition to the responsible program office and the general counsel, the offices charged with policy analysis and management of the rulemaking process, overall, have regular seats at the table. Agencies that vary the composition of their work groups do so for many reasons and build them in a variety of ways. The EPA, for example, uses work groups only when the cross-agency issues are so significant that sustained involvement from other program areas are needed. In the FSIS a central rulemaking office has used a "call memo" to agency leadership, who can then appoint team members.

Where responsibility for writing rules is delegated to a single office or individual, it is still rare for the work to be done in truly splendid isolation. For its lower-priority rules, and those with confined impact, the EPA still requires the use of "side agreements" with offices that have an interest insufficient to elevate the rulemaking to a higher level. At APHIS, where the formal responsibility rests with a single rule writer, the informal reality is that he or she consults with a wide range of people to get his or her job done.

Concurrence Systems

Securing the approvals of those with influence or authority is a potentially powerful aspect of rulemaking management. It means that all significant issues have been dealt with to the satisfaction of those in the agency who hold primary responsibility for them. It can, however, be a source of conflict and delay, especially if there are no mechanisms through which these actors can be informed and consulted while the rule is being drafted. Conflict at late stages in the rulemaking, the already noted "late hit," is a particularly devastating obstacle to timely and efficient rulemaking.

Two types of concurrence are identified in the literature devoted to rulemaking. Horizontal, or lateral, concurrence involves offices other than the one with the primary interest in the rule being developed. Vertical concurrence involves senior managers and political appointees.[25] The overwhelming majority of agencies included in previous studies reported systems to ensure both types of concurrence. While the names of offices have changed in some cases, all have the frequency of rulemaking and concerns of political leadership. The state of concurrence systems in the early years of this decade, however, highlight the most important dynamics of obtaining approval for a proposed or final rule. Work groups are mechanisms for horizontal concurrence. Theoretically, if the work group is properly constituted and performs effectively, additional horizontal concurrence will not be necessary. Theory notwithstanding, most of the agencies that use work groups to write rules have separate, and sometimes elaborate, mechanisms for horizontal concurrence.

With some exceptions, agencies reported some form of horizontal concurrence that reaches beyond the expectation that work group members are fully empowered by their management superiors. The National Highway Transportation Safety Administration (NHTSA) and the Federal Motor Carrier Safety Administration (FMCSA), both units of the Department of Transportation, have used standard sets of horizontal sign-offs. The offices of Rulemaking, Enforcement, Policy and Operations, Research, and Chief Counsel were prominent at the NHTSA. The FMCSA involves all associate administrative offices, including legal. Tailored to the particular functional organizations of individual agencies, systems similar to these could be found in agencies as varied as OSHA, the Mine Safety and Health Administration (MSHA) in the Department of Labor, and the Animal and Plant Health Inspection Service.

The key to vertical concurrence is the number of steps in the management chain that a rule must climb before leaving the agency. This in turn depends on the formal status of the rule—significant or not—and its visibility to senior managers or political leaders. In OSHA, for example, most of the rules were either significant or otherwise viewed as important. There, when the rule was approved by the senior executive it had been reviewed, in sequence, by the assistant secretary, the Policy Planning Board, the solicitor, and the secretary of labor. APHIS reports an elaborate system for significant rules that combines elements of horizontal concurrence and vertical concurrence, with contingent feedback loops. There, the proposal goes from the deputy administrator of APHIS to the administrator, who consults the heads of the Office of the General Counsel, the Budget and Program Analysis Office, and the chief economist in the Office of Cost-Benefit and Risk Analysis. It then goes to the Office of Civil Rights. It is then returned to the chief information officer at APHIS, who forwards it to the Department of Agriculture's undersecretary for marketing and regulatory programs and then to the secretary of agriculture. Other agencies, most notably the independent regulatory commissions, have flatter vertical chains, even for significant rules. For example, following horizontal concurrence, a rule at FERC and the Nuclear Regulatory Commission, goes from the responsible office director directly to the executive director, who has delegated authority to issue some rules, and then to the full commission, when needed.

Public Participation

The management of public participation in rulemaking involves two important actions: deciding on the mechanisms that will be used to solicit input from the public and evaluating the comments and criticisms that result. Agencies generally enjoy discretion in organizing both functions, but statutes that mandate or authorize rulemaking contain provisions that require agencies to do more than give "notice and comment," as provided under the Administrative Procedure Act. Responsibility for dealing with public comment, which can be voluminous, is significant, because the agency is obliged to take such comment into account when finalizing the rule. In short, participation affects the substantive content of the rule and the response of the public to what is finally decided. So the mechanisms to ensure that the results of participation are incorporated or otherwise accounted for in the final rule are important management devices.

In the original survey half of the agencies reported that the program office developing the rule had authority to determine the form of public participation, although many of these agencies reported that they consulted with others before making this decision. The Office of the General Counsel was most frequently mentioned in this regard. In other agencies, programs for public participation were reported to be determined by statute or long-standing agency policy.

Evaluation of the results of public participation, whether written comments or transcripts from informal or formal hearings, can be handled in two ways: by the staff that develops the rule or a split of responsibility between the staff and other offices.

Information from more recent interviews indicates that management of participation follows the same general pattern but with greater variation in details. At the NRC, the FCC, APHIS, and the EPA, for example, the lead office determined the mode or form of public participation that would be used, but most of these indicated that higher-level officials could influence these decisions or preempt them altogether. The MSHA and the NHTSA reported that the decisions about the mode of public participation were made by offices other than the program office developing the rule, or at higher levels. OSHA noted that it relied heavily on the parameters set in established policy, and the FAA noted an assumption in favor of written comment, be it electronic or hard copy.

There is considerable variation in agencies' approaches to the evaluations of public comments. The FCC, the NRC, FERC, OSHA, the EPA, and the FAA report that the lead program office or the work group evaluates the content of input from the public. At the MSHA, the rulemaking work group reviews the content of comments, but only after they are screened by a "regulatory specialist." At the FMCSA, selected members of the rulemaking team decide which comments are influential after they are reviewed by the whole group. At APHIS, the rule writer determines what material from comments will be incorporated. The NHTSA routinely requires separate analysis and recommendations from several of its offices because of differing perspectives. The content of a rule, including that influenced by public comment, is subject to the effects of vertical concurrence. It is important to note that in the most recent interviews a significant number of agencies reported the use of contractors in the review of public input, with most indicating that the role of these outsiders included reading, summarizing, and categorizing comments. It is inevitable, however, that in carrying out these functions contractors have some influence on the agencies' responses to the content of public participation.

Interviews and symposium discussions underscore the growing importance of proactive management of public participation. Agency representatives repeatedly emphasized the importance of this issue. Presidential initiatives and legislation written since that call for closer relations with the public, combined with the dominance electronic communication that is discussed in Chapter 5, have made agencies' management of public participation more diversified than ever before.

Liaison with the OMB and Congress

Writing significant rules requires frequent and extensive contacts with the OMB, which was granted multiple authorities under the Paperwork Reduction Act and various executive orders. Agencies and the OMB come in contact with one another in the latter's overall review of proposed and final rules, regulatory impact analyses, and requests to collect information. These contacts, which can influence the review process, may be managed by those responsible for writing the rule, by a central office in the agency, or by senior officers. Similarly, Congress may take an interest in a rule under development, creating, at minimum, a liaison function and, at maximum, a political dimension that could influence profoundly the content of the rule. The arrival of legislation mandating review by the GAO and the possibility of full congressional review created new management challenges.

Agencies manage liaison with the OMB during its review of rules in a variety of ways. At the EPA it is handled by the Office of Regulatory Policy and Management, but the EPA also reports constant contact with work groups for the same purpose. At some agencies, the liaison function depends on the level of issue involved, with higher-level matters being handled by the administrator. In the agencies of the Department of Transportation the primary liaison is through the Office of the Assistant General Counsel for Regulation, but individual agencies maintain routine contacts as well. The Regulatory Ombudsman at the FMCSA maintains the relationship with the OMB.

Somewhat surprising are recent reports from agencies regarding management of communications with Congress. Agencies reported more active communication with Congress during the course of individual rulemaking than was the case in the first survey for this book. Not emerging as a major management chore is the liaison needed to meet the requirements of the Congressional Review Act. Most agencies described it as a routine transfer of information from a designated agency office to the GAO. It was not characterized in terms that would suggest that the GAO was as influential in the process as the OMB. The reasons for this apparent nonchalance are discussed in Chapter 6.

Drafting the Rule

Responsibility for drafting the language of the rule cannot be taken for granted. It was noted in the preceding chapter that poorly crafted rules can lead to problems. Some of these problems relate to sloppy drafting or the inability to capture in words exactly what the rule seeks to accomplish. The choice of drafter is important.

Research for the first edition revealed that no agency relied exclusively on technical staff to put rules in the format and language that will ultimately appear in the *Federal Register*. In half of the agencies, the language and format of proposed and final rules were developed jointly by the staff and some other office, usually the Office of the General Counsel; OSHA reports such a system currently. The other half of the agencies established offices with specialists in regulation drafting. The FAA, for example, employs a corps of "writer-editors." A writer-editor is assigned to each rulemaking. More than mere writers of drafts, the FAA writer-editors serve as "assistant managers" of the rulemaking. They get involved in all phases of the rulemaking, including preparing summaries of public comments and responses to them. They are senior civil servants with training in group facilitation and team building. In the original survey the Social Security Administration and the Health Care Financing Administration reported similar arrangements. Rule-writing specialists were reported at the FAA and at APHIS, the EPA, the MSHA, and the FSIS as well.

Summary

It is safe to conclude that most federal agencies with significant rulemaking responsibilities have well-developed rulemaking management systems. To varying degrees, such systems set priorities, control the initiation of new rules, provide early guidance on important policy matters to the rule writers, ensure horizontal and vertical concurrence, and maintain a degree of discipline in the rule writers' dealings with the OMB and Congress on proposed and final rules. Nevertheless, it would be incorrect to assert that rulemaking is given a level of management attention comparable to other major bureaucratic functions, such as budgeting, finance, procurement, and personnel.

The creation and institutionalization of "rulemaking offices" marked an important milestone in the management of rulemaking. Exemplified by the work of the assistant general counsel for regulation at DOT, these offices may shepherd working groups, monitor schedules, and expedite concurrence and required analysis. They generally serve as visible, organizational reminders of the importance of rulemaking management. But there is little consistency across the government in structure, function, and importance.

Today, one would have significant difficulty identifying a central locus of rulemaking management authority in many agencies by reference to a staff directory or organization chart. The titles of the senior rulemaking managers who assembled at American University in 2005 reflect this diversity of approach to whatever management aspects of regulation are centralized:

> Acting Director of the Regulatory Management Division, Office of Policy, Economics, and Innovation
> Chief Counsel of Regulations, Office of the General Counsel
> Assistant General Counsel for Regulation Enforcement, Office of the General Counsel
> Attorney and Regulation Development Coordinator
> Chief of Staff
> Senior Policy Strategist
> Director of Rulemaking
> Director of Regulatory Policy

Marine Biologist and Ecologist
Head, Regulatory Staff
Assistant General Counsel
Attorney, General Counsel
Chief for Regulatory and Administrative Law
Deputy Associate General Counsel for Regulations

Despite the general failure to identify rulemaking management by name, it is clear that most agencies recognize the function and staff it. These offices or clusters of responsibility have not been studied in any systematic manner. What is known about the functions they house is largely anecdotal. They include stewardship of the priority-setting process, scheduling monitoring of deadlines, working group support (and occasional facilitation), management of the concurrence processes and clearance, liaison with the OMB, oversight of compliance with ancillary legal requirements, drafting services and communication with the Office of the Federal Register, and development/delivery of staff training. In most agencies, these offices have limited authority and staffing. But such offices carry the potential to elevate the regulation management function: They have the potential to extend and enhance key aspects of regulation management such as staff development.

Agency-level management systems can be sources of, and solutions to, certain problems. If procedures for setting priorities and initiating rules work well, they should reduce the number of unnecessary rules. Early policy guidance, concurrence systems, and effective liaison with the OMB and Congress can increase the quality of rules and decrease the conflict in the rulemaking process. Scheduling and monitoring can expedite rulemaking, and thus reduce delay in the issuance of important rules.

If they work poorly, however, management systems at the agency level can delay rules. Volatility in priorities can be particularly costly. Frequent changes in the priority of rules lead to erratic application of resources to individual projects, delaying those that are suddenly downgraded. Similarly, initiation procedures and concurrence systems can lengthen the rulemaking process. Rulemaking management systems must be able to adapt to changing circumstances. Several forces have converged in recent years to threaten the ability of agencies to keep their management systems current. As we noted earlier, although the management tasks of agencies have increased dramatically, their resources have not kept the pace.

We know the pace of change has been rapid, and the management systems described here can change quickly, as can senior political appointees. We cannot render a comprehensive judgment on the effectiveness of rulemaking management systems in agencies. We can, however, state that rulemaking management at the agency level has not yet attracted scholarly or practitioner attention commensurate with its importance. The same is true for management at the level of the individual rule.

Managing Individual Rules

Work groups and concurrence systems were created to ensure that all vital information and perspectives on a rule could be captured and represented during the course of its development. The other side of this important function of participation is conflict. When the net is cast broadly across an agency during rulemaking, the likelihood of conflict increases. The issue is not the occurrence of conflict; all agencies that write rules house multiple interests that are bound to clash when something as important as rulemaking is undertaken. The real issue is how well this conflict is managed and resolved during the development of individual rules. Two key variables affect management of the process: information and people.

Managing Essential Information

At its most basic, rulemaking is the transformation of information into authoritative statements of law or policy. For regulations whose development requires significant management effort, the necessary information is only infrequently completely available at the outset of the work and almost never completely in the possession of the person responsible for the project. Every rule, be it major or minor, has seven dimensions that determine the types of information that may have to be collected and analyzed:

1. Legal information includes what is required or allowed by statutes, executive orders, and court decisions.
2. Policy information includes guidance on the priorities and approaches preferred by the current administration.
3. Content information consists of the technical or scientific requirements or guidance being established or revised in the rule.
4. Impact information provides insights to the effects of the regulation on both regulated parties and intended beneficiaries.
5. Political information contains the views and positions of the internal and external interests affected by the rule under development. In many instances political information may not be easily distinguishable from policy impact or technical information, and is frequently presented as critiques of a particular approach or of certain supporting data, or with regard to the negative effect the rule could have on existing programs or conditions.

Consequently, what is essentially a political reaction to a proposed rule is couched in policy or technical terms.

6. Implementation and compliance information details how new requirements will be communicated and enforced.

7. Management information is knowledge of the agency's internal management system and the requirements it imposes on their particular rulemaking.

A critical task in the early stages of regulation development is an assessment of the state of information in each of these categories and the formulation of a strategy for how any gaps in information will be filled.

There are few, if any, systematic studies of the sources of information used by agencies in rulemaking and, certainly, there is nothing approaching a comprehensive analysis. Yet the categories of sources available to agencies for this purpose are well known. Legal information is invariably provided by the agency's office of general counsel or its functional equivalent, working in closer proximity to the program with primary responsibility for development of the regulation.

Information about procedural requirements based in law is also obtained from the general counsel, and it is quite common for agencies to develop guidance documents on common obligations—for example, those associated with the various executive orders and general legislation, such as the Paperwork Reduction Act. Rulemakers use these sources to determine which of many possible requirements apply and how to comply with them. When an agency program involves the writing of multiple versions of the same general rule, substantive and procedural legal requirements are widely understood. Rules such as the FAA's airworthiness directives, the Department of Agriculture's marketing orders, and even the EPA's new source performance standards for air and water pollution require relatively little original legal information. When an agency undertakes to write rules for a new statute or amendment to an existing law, or when it moves into a new area covered by established legislation, the amount of legal information it requires will increase. With the increase the influence of agency attorneys in the rulemaking will grow, at least in the early stages. Policy information in the form of guidance on the preferred content or approach is provided by political appointees or, in the case of independent agencies, commissioners or their surrogates.

Policy information is obtained through the management systems outlined above. White House guidelines are published and distributed broadly across all agencies. These primary documents are usually accompanied by agency supplements that provide further explanation of the requirements and how they apply. Agencies have similar documents covering their own policy priorities and initiatives. In addition, many agencies appear to have procedures that require or allow senior officials to review rulemaking projects at some stage in their development. It is during this review that the policy priorities of both the White House and the particular agency are reinforced.

Content or technical information may be provided by a variety of sources either internal or external to the agency. The internal, or established, sources of these analyses and data include the resident expertise and institutional memory of agency staff, independent academic research, studies previously commissioned by the agency and conducted by a wide range of outside experts, studies conducted by other government agencies or the agency's own personnel, and data collected during the course of the agency's implementation and enforcement activities. External sources of information are also varied. Agencies support programs of extramural research whose results may support regulation development efforts, such as the fish stock analyses mentioned previously, or they may commission data collection and analyses that focus specifically on a particular rule by the agency. External parties affected by or otherwise interested in a given rule may supply information or opinion before, during, or after the public comment phase or rule development. Existing in a status somewhere between purely disinterested, objective research and the input of interested parties is the information provided by formal consultative bodies created under the strict guidelines of the Federal Advisory Committee Act. These too may be launched to provide assistance in the development of a specific rule or cover a much broader area of concern that may affect an entire suite of new regulations. Technical information is tied inextricably to the substantive legal information mentioned above. The technical content of the rule commonly includes information on various alternatives that can be considered and the impacts of each. When the best alternative is selected, the focus then shifts to what is allowed or required, who is affected and who must comply, the means by which the provisions will be implemented and enforced, and the consequences of failing to comply.

Impact information may come from the same sources, albeit in a different mix, that provided information for the content information. However, two internal sources loom large in this area: policy analysis offices within the agency and, for the regulations they have selected for review, the Office of Information and Regulatory Affairs in the OMB.

The sources of political information are many of the same ones that supply technical information. The political positions of those inside the agency are made known through concurrence systems and work group participants. The political positions of external parties are made known through public comments, during public hearings, and through the numerous informal contacts that occur between representatives of external interests and agency personnel.

Implementation and compliance information, an area too often ignored in discussions of regulation development, will be supplied by a given agency's central enforcement and public communications offices that specialize, respectively, in monitoring of and outreach to regulated entities; by field personnel in regional offices who have the day-to-day responsibilities to manage regulatory programs; and by external interest groups who represent those affected by the new regulations.

Finally, rulemakers can obtain information about the agency's management system from two sources: internal guidance documents and procedural regulations. In addition, many agencies at which rulemaking is a major function have training programs for staff. For example, the Environmental Protection Agency and the Federal Aviation Administration have instituted large-scale training programs for those involved in rulemaking. The EPA program focuses heavily on its internal management system. The program was started in 1988, and by the end of 2008 several thousand staff members had been through it. Other agencies have different methods of training their personnel. The FAA offers training twice a year, and APHIS has an annual session for its staff officers.

Whether a given regulation development effort will rely heavily on internal sources of information, external sources, or some combination of the two, experience and skill are needed to identify and obtain what is needed. As an element in the management of regulation development, the acquisition and use of information should also be understood to include the ability to share what is learned, regardless of the source, with all other stakeholders. Sharing information avoids duplication of effort, misunderstanding, and unnecessary conflict. Information dissemination is a necessary but not sufficient condition for the development of consensus that eases the path of a proposed regulation.

While these categories of information are well known, what we do not know is how often, in what combinations, and to what effect agencies actually rely on them during the course of regulation development.

Officials of the Federal Trade Commission, when asked in 1991 about where they obtain the information needed for the content of the rules they write, responded simply, "Wherever we can get it."[26] This may fail some tests of precision and sophistication, but it is blunt and accurate, and could have been uttered by anyone with significant rulemaking responsibilities.

The Role of Work Groups

As noted earlier, work groups are likely to be found in all agencies that have significant rulemaking responsibilities. Their composition and size, however, are functions of the programs the agency administers and its internal organizational culture.[27] In agencies that have limited statutory responsibilities, a work group might consist of a representative from the program office, an attorney from the Office of the General Counsel, and, perhaps, an economist or other type of policy analyst. The work group will be small; management of the work group will not likely be a serious problem.

In larger, more complex agencies that administer multiple, overlapping statutes, work groups tend to be larger and have a more diverse membership.[28] In these cases many program offices may be represented. In addition to attorneys from the Office of the General Counsel, lawyers concerned with the enforcement dimension of the rule may also participate. Attorneys from the Office of the General Counsel will be concerned with the congruence between the rule and what the statute it will implement requires or allows. Attorneys from the offices concerned with enforcement will want to ensure that the rule avoids some of the common problems that promote noncompliance or make enforcement actions difficult to defend in court when they are challenged.

Representatives from offices concerned with research and policy analysis are likely to be members of the work group. The research office will be concerned that information they have developed and maintained is used in the development of the rule. The policy analysts will push for full consideration of all reasonable alternatives and for a complete assessment of their economic effects.[29] The field personnel who are responsible for implementing the rule once it is complete may wish to be involved to ensure that what is written is feasible and easy to administer. They too will be concerned with enforceability and with the effects that the new rule will have on others they implement and on their resources.

The experiences of the EPA, the FAA, and other rulemaking agencies during the past thirty-five years indicate that the management of work groups hinges on three key variables: leadership, membership, and integration with senior management of the agency.[30]

Leadership. The leaders of work groups are usually selected because of their expertise in the subject matter of the new rule. But technical expertise is only part of the job. These individuals must perform many important and difficult functions, often in the face of strong and conflicting pressures from others in and out of the agency. In addition to possessing technical expertise, the work group leader must be a careful planner, a skillful manager of resources and group processes, a shrewd politician, a diplomat, and, at times, a scavenger. He or she must locate, bring together, and accommodate the information and views that will define the content of the rule and ultimately determine the success of the rulemaking.

Once selected, the work group leader must determine the goals of the rule, the substantive and procedural legal provisions that apply, and what information is needed to achieve these goals. Senior officials must be consulted on policy matters and agency attorneys on the legal issues. The leader is then in a position to assemble or influence the membership of the work group.

It is in the work group leader's best interests to ensure that membership is determined carefully. Leaving an important office off the work group can deprive the rulemaking of valuable information and insights. It can also lead to serious problems later in the process, when the group attempts to obtain concurrence from an office that has a real interest in the rule but was not at the table during its development. Although membership should be open to those with a significant interest in the rule, gratuitous participation is to be avoided. Large work groups are more difficult to manage than smaller ones. Communication, the logistics and conduct of meetings, development of consensus, and the concurrence process grow more complicated with each new office that joins the group. So the leader has an interest in ensuring that the work group includes everyone with a legitimate concern but excludes the merely curious. This said, it is difficult to exclude those who make a claim that their program or responsibility is affected unless senior officials enforce a degree of discipline.

Once the work group is constituted, the leader must brief it on the purpose of the rule, its legal dimensions, any decisions that have already been made regarding policy or actual content, and the schedule for its completion. Then the leader should discuss with the members how the work group will function and what each individual will be asked to produce. Work groups may meet frequently or infrequently, depending on what is needed from the members and the nature of the issues that arise. Frequent meetings may be needed when there are multiple issues on which consensus must be reached and when the members are expected to make substantive contributions to the content of the rule. Infrequent meetings may be more appropriate when there are few issues and the membership is expected to serve only as a means of securing the approval of the offices they represent for draft materials that the work group leader develops. Whatever the style of the group and the role of the members, they should be made clear at the outset so that there is agreement on how the group will function and the members can plan accordingly. If there is disagreement on either of these elements, the leader must act promptly to resolve it.

After the rulemaking has begun, the leader must maintain full communication with the work group in accordance with the operating principles established at the beginning. In addition to scheduling meetings and circulating drafts of the rule, the leader must set agendas, conduct the meetings effectively, and ensure that drafts are accurate and complete. During the process of rule development, the leader should monitor the work group closely and be aware of members who are not performing as expected or who show signs of disagreement and conflict. When members are not responding promptly or substantively to drafts, or when they are missing meetings or presenting personal views rather than the position of their office, the work group leader must intervene. Poor performance may be a sign of inexperience or overextension. Whatever the cause, it means the member is not delivering what is needed.

The member who pursues an agenda not authorized by his or her office is of particular concern. The work group leader needs to know how much authority a given member enjoys and the extent of the member's bargaining power for his or her office in negotiations over the rule. If members do not faithfully represent the management of their offices, there is a risk that a draft rule, when it is finally reviewed at these higher levels, will not be acceptable. This again is the "late hit." In extreme cases the rule will need to be completely reworked, with all the wasted resources and toll on internal working relationships that such a circumstance generates. At the very least, delay will occur. It is, of course, the responsibility of each member to represent his or her office, but it is in the best interest of the work group leader to confirm that the member actually does so. Such confirmation may require a direct confrontation with the member in question or a discrete inquiry through the respective management chains, but whatever the form, it is usually worth the temporary discomfort it might cause.

While the rule is being developed, the work group leader must assemble the information needed to complete it and any required analysis. Information not provided directly by the work group members must be obtained from other sources. The leader's responsibility for ancillary analyses (for example, paperwork, regulatory impact, and regulatory flexibility analyses) will be determined by the system followed in the agency. In some agencies the work group leader must do some or all of these analyses; in others they are conducted by one or more central offices. We can find this same variation in the management of internal concurrence, public participation, and the relationship with the OMB for the mandatory reviews of proposed and final rules. The work group leader must also draft the rule in language and format acceptable to the *Federal Register* or work closely with those who perform this function.

As the work group leader performs these many and varied functions, he or she must contend with the strong pressures mentioned earlier. The nature and strength of these pressures are determined by the controversy that attends a given rule and the manner in which the work group leader is evaluated. If the leader is thought to be successful because the rule is completed on schedule and within budget, any controversy that may occur, especially within the agency, will threaten the leader's ability to perform to expectations. Similarly, if the criterion for success is qualitative, such as the production of a rule that represents internal consensus, proves to be easy to implement and enforce, or survives court challenge, controversy may be a sign that one or more of these objectives is in danger.

Based on anecdotal evidence from work group leaders in the EPA and other agencies, Kerwin reported in a previous edition that meeting a preordained deadline was a more common criterion for success than meeting qualitative standards. But in more recent interviews agency officials mentioned quality as frequently as timeliness when asked how agency personnel responsible for rulemaking were evaluated. The emphasis on deadlines makes intuitive sense if we consider the nature of rulemaking and bureaucracies in general. Performance in relation to a schedule can be measured easily. Producing a consensus may or may not be valued by the leadership of a given office. More important are the preferences of the agency's senior political officials. If they want rules that reflect a consensus, the proclivities of a given office may not matter. But if individual offices are given considerable decision-making discretion, they may view other organizations within the same agency as rivals, adversaries, or both. They may be indifferent to consensus or directly opposed to it. Complaints that a rule is difficult to implement or enforce can be dismissed as efforts by field staff to avoid work and responsibility or as the whines of chronically cautious or dissatisfied lawyers. In some agencies compliance may be seen as someone else's problem. A legal challenge to the rule may be of even less concern to the rulemaker. Litigation happens after the rule is published, and the case may not be resolved for a very long time, usually well after the rulemaker expects to have left his or her current position.

Time pressures make it harder for leaders to meet any standards that might be used to measure performance. Tight deadlines can limit efforts to collect the best possible information, to involve work group members fully, to stimulate serious discussion of alternatives, to expose potential flaws in the rule as it is developing, and to resolve conflicts to everyone's satisfaction. Of course, not all rulemaking is done under time pressures of this sort. Nevertheless, the frequency with which quality was mentioned in relation to rulemakers' performance indicates that this dimension deserves greater attention from scholars. At the very least, we need to understand better than we do now how "quality" in rulemaking is being defined *and* measured.

Membership. Work group members also have many functions that they must perform if this collective type of rulemaking is to be successful. Most of these functions are suggested by the foregoing discussion of the role of the work group leader. Ideally, we might expect that the work group members function as true intermediaries between their offices and the work group leader, balancing their interests with the goals of the rule. But this is not a realistic expectation. Members are there to represent an office and its particular concerns. This means they must be fully conversant with the goals of the rule and the statutory provisions it will implement. They need not concern themselves with procedural requirements, whether imposed by law or by the agency's internal management system, unless these requirements somehow bear on the interests of their office. Members must understand the policies of their own office and what their superiors wish to accomplish in the rulemaking. To that end they must be clear about the limits of their own authority and the room they have to negotiate on substantive issues in the name of their office.

Beyond this, members must be alert to developments in the rulemaking that threaten the interests they are there to protect. This means faithful and attentive participation in work group meetings and careful reading of draft materials. They must be able and willing to seek advice and counsel from others in the office when they are unclear about the implications of a particular approach or wording and when office policy on a given matter is not apparent. They must make every effort to recognize potential or real problems as early as possible and move immediately to get them acknowledged and resolved. In this they must be willing and able to negotiate, drafting alternative language when they object to that proposed by the work group leader or another member. Whenever possible the alternative language should accomplish the objective embodied in the original language while ameliorating the problem that offends the member's office. While maintaining a flexible and cooperative stance, the member must also recognize intractable conflict or a situation in which the concerns of his or her office are not being addressed. Then the only answer is to elevate the issue to superiors, who will deal with their counterparts in the other office or offices involved.

Members, like the work group leader, face certain pressures when performing their functions. In this case, however, the pressures are most likely to be related to their own workloads. Membership in work groups is often an "add-on" responsibility that competes for their time. Frequently, members are not rewarded or punished for how well or how poorly they participate. Their professionalism may be the only incentive to read draft materials promptly, to attend and participate actively in work group meetings, to be sensitive to potential problems, and to seek out the type of help they might require.

Workload pressure and the lack of potential sanction for poor performance, however, are not the only obstacles to effective participation. Those selected as members of work groups, especially in agencies that produce a large volume of rules, may lack the experience and expertise to represent their offices adequately. Unable to spare more senior staff, the offices may be forced to place newer employees in work groups, particularly in those groups whose rules do not enjoy high priority. Furthermore, a member may not have access to the additional resources or expertise that he or she needs to participate effectively. Sometimes a member is taken off a work group for assignment to a rule with a higher priority or to a completely different set of responsibilities, and a new member must act as a substitute. This type of turnover, especially at the middle and late stages in a rule, can be particularly problematic, because the new member must struggle with a steep learning curve in a compressed period of time. Finally, a member may not be given clear authority to represent the office. This is a tolerable situation if the member is astute enough to recognize a serious issue when he or she sees one and has ready access to those in the office with the authority to make decisions.

Integration with Senior Management. The last major element in the management of work groups is their integration with senior managers across the agency. Senior managers and political leaders should be involved at the beginning of work group operations, throughout the rule development process, and at the point of completion. At the outset they need to set the overall direction of the rule, making the agency's policy clear regarding the rulemaking in question. Once this is done, they are able to set the limits of discretion that their representatives in the work group can exercise. As the rulemaking progresses, they should provide guidance to the work group on issues that were not anticipated at the beginning. To ensure expeditious rulemaking, they must be able to respond promptly to such requests for guidance or independently intervene if the work group has reached an impasse. In the latter case they must have open lines of communication to their counterparts in other offices so that the conflict can be discussed and resolved and the rulemaking can move forward. Finally, once the rule has been written, the senior officials must complete the concurrence process promptly and in a manner consistent with the positions they have taken at earlier stages in the development of the rule.

Like leaders and members of work groups, these officials in the management chain are working under pressure, the sources of which, at this level, are time and politics. Senior managers often track many rules, and rulemaking is far from their sole concern. They are working at the level at which external political pressure on the agency or office is expressed most directly and intensely. This political pressure can cause their priorities in rulemaking to shift and their positions on individual rules to change. For these reasons, work group leaders or members may have difficulty getting the attention of senior managers. Inaccessibility, delay in responding to requests for guidance, and shifting priorities and policy positions create problems for work groups and for rulemaking generally.

Evolution of the Work Group Model. Developments in recent years at the Environmental Protection Agency suggest one way the work group model of individual rule management will evolve. It has moved away from its practice of appointing a work group for all rules. This move was prompted by the gradual realization that a full work group approach was not needed for many rules. Facing significant resource constraints and criticisms of long delays in issuing rules, the agency fashioned a new, more sophisticated tier system.

The first tier contains a few rules that are classified as Administrator's Priority Actions because of unusually serious concerns over crossmedia effects and the general impact on the public. These rules are developed in work groups composed of high-level EPA staff, with early involvement and close monitoring by the administrator or deputy administrator. The second tier, larger than the first, contains rules with major crossmedia or crossagency concerns and high levels of interest from external groups. These rules are developed by work groups as well, but generally with lower-level staff; the involvement of senior officials is determined on a case-by-case basis. Most rules belong in the third tier, which consists of regulations that can safely be developed by a single EPA office because of the nature of the issues and the relative lack of controversy that attends them. The lead office need not convene a work group; it can determine independently the types of guidance and consultation with other offices that are needed to produce a rule of acceptable quality. Such consultations will most often take the form of "side agreements" with interested or affected offices reached early in the regulation development process. When nearing completion of the rulemaking, the lead office must certify that all side agreements have in fact been honored.

The EPA and the FAA both have had long experience with work groups, and both manage rulemaking systems that are under intense pressure and receive considerable external scrutiny. For example, the FAA was the subject of a review by what was then the General Accounting Office, mandated by a congressional subcommittee concerned with the pace of rulemaking. An internal survey of personnel resulted in equivocal findings, but many work group operations, including team leaders, and team collaboration and cooperation received high marks. Less successful, in the eyes of those surveyed, were standards of quality for the work group product and some aspects of the role of senior managers.[31] The EPA and the FAA clearly have shared a deep respect and concern for the role of work groups, evidenced in part by the highly detailed and directive guidance both issued regarding the responsibilities of both work group leaders and work group members.[32] Other agencies might not be as explicit in their policies, but they are no less reliant on work group performance in meeting rulemaking obligations.

Given the wide variations in rulemaking across government agencies and the different political conditions under which they currently labor, it is certainly plausible that many will gravitate toward the new EPA paradigm. In effect, it tailors the management of individual rules to the degree of exposure and conflict agency leaders anticipate from them, based on the magnitude and complexity of the issues involved. In this regard the tiering approach is consistent with general approaches to regulation; small entities have been regulated less stringently than large ones because their behavior poses less significant threats to health and safety and because they are less able to absorb compliance costs. The tiering model also allows agencies facing the twin pressures of tight resources and even tighter schedules to invest their people power in rational ways.

Conclusion

Rulemaking is intensively managed at all three levels examined in this chapter: the presidential level, the agency level, and the level of the individual rule. Although there is considerable overlap, each level of management focuses on distinctive concerns and objectives. Presidential management seeks to ensure that the substantive policies and political agenda of the administration are reflected in the rules issued by federal agencies. Agency-level management is concerned with the president's program, but it may have its own agenda and distinctive policies and procedures. Management at this level seeks coherence, consistency, legal resilience, quality, timeliness, and a disciplined use of the resources available for rulemaking. At the individual level these general concerns are present, but a stronger focus is likely to be placed on completing required tasks, managing bureaucratic relationships, meeting deadlines, producing a quality product, however defined, and advancing or protecting the rule writer's career.

Although we have evidence of an enormous amount of management activity, we have yet to see authoritative treatises or handbooks on effective rulemaking management. We have little evidence of the effects of management on the rules that are finally issued. Does management make a difference? Do different management systems yield systematically different results?

Answers to these key questions remain woefully incomplete. The problems start at the most fundamental level of analysis. We simply lack most of the basic information needed to evaluate various levels and systems of managing rules. We can measure how long it takes to complete a rule, but we rarely ask, in a disciplined manner, how well it works. To understand fully the quality of rules, we must ultimately link their content to the performance of the public program that they define. The content and performance of rules is bound inextricably to the public those rules affect, and how they influence results. We turn now to public participation in rulemaking to explore how this influence is expressed.

Notes

1. The history of presidential management of rulemaking presented in this chapter is necessarily brief and draws on many extensive studies. See Howard Ball, *Controlling Regulatory Sprawl: Presidential Strategies from Nixon to Reagan* (Westport, Conn.: Greenwood Press, 1984), and National Academy of Public Administration, *Presidential Management of Rulemaking in Regulatory Agencies* (Washington, D.C.: National Academy of Public Administration, 1987).

2. Office of Management and Budget, *Improving Government Regulations: A Progress Report* (Washington, D.C.: Executive Office of the President, 1979), p. 6; James Blumstein, "Regulatory Review by the Executive Office of the President: An Overview and Policy Analysis," *Duke Law Journal* 51, no. 3 (December 2001): 851; Steven Croley "White House Review of Agency Rulemaking: An Empirical Investigation," *University of Chicago Law Review* 70 (2003): 821.

3. Ibid., p. 7.

4. Ibid., pp. 8–27.

5. Ibid., p. 9.

6. Ibid., p. 19.

7. Office of Management and Budget, "Report on Executive Order No. 12866, Regulatory Planning and Review," *Federal Register,* May 10, 1994, p. 24276.

8. Ibid.

9. "White House Shifts Role in Rulemaking Process," *Washington Post,* October 1, 1993, p. 1.

10. Office of Management and Budget, "Draft and Report to Congress on Costs and Benefits of Regulation," *Federal Register,* March 28, 2002, pp. 15017–15023.

11. Office of the President, Executive Order 13422, *Federal Register,* January 17, 2007, pp. 2763–2765.

12. For a discussion of this phenomenon of stopping these "midnight" regulations see Anne Joseph O'Connell, "Political Cycles of Rulemaking: An Empirical Portrait of the Modern Administrative State," *Virginia Law Review* 94, no. 4 (June 2008).

13. Office of the President, Executive Order 13497, *Federal Register,* January 30, 2009.

14. "Memorandum of January 30, 2009—Regulatory Review," *Federal Register,* February 3, 2009, pp. 5977–5978.

15. "Federal Regulatory Review," *Federal Register,* February 26, 2009, p. 8819.

16. Readers can see the full accounting of comments at the following site: www.reginfo .gov/public/jsp/EO/fedRegReview/publicComments.jsp.

17. The following is a list of the agencies represented at the session. Where noted, with the exception of the Department of Agriculture, representatives from both department-level and subordinate unit offices attended.

- Department of Agriculture
  - o Animal and Plant Health Inspection Service
  - o Food Safety Inspection Service
- Department of Commerce
  - o National Marine Fisheries Service
- Department of Homeland Security
  - o United States Coast Guard
- Department of Labor
  - o Occupational Safety and Health Administration
- Department of Transportation
  - o Federal Aviation Administration
- Department of Veterans Affairs
- Environmental Protection Agency
- Federal Energy Regulatory Commission
- Nuclear Regulatory Commission

The findings of this symposium were first published in a report prepared for the IBM Center for the Business of Government in 2007. Sections of that report are reproduced in their entirety or partially in what follows. Each of these agencies maintains a Web site with information about its rulemaking management system. See also Cornelius Kerwin's monograph "Out of the Shadows" (Washington, D.C.: IBM Center for the Business of Government, 2008), which quotes heavily from this publication, including sections devoted to information acquisition, priority setting, initiating rules, and securing early input and budgeting.

18. William West, unpublished manuscript, 2009.

19. For another description of the EPA's analytic blueprint, see Environmental Protection Agency, Office of Policy, Economics and Innovation, "EPA's Action Development Process" (Washington, D.C.: October 26, 2006), p. 13.

20. Neil Eisner, "Agency Delay in Informal Rulemaking," *Administrative Law Journal* 3 (1989): 7–52.

21. Ibid.

22. U.S. Government Accountability Office, "Improvements Needed to Monitoring and Evaluation of Rules Development as Well as to the Transparency of OMB Regulatory Reviews" (Washington, D.C.: GAO, April 2009), pp. 14–15.

23. Kerwin, "Out of the Shadows."

24. Ibid., p. 20; U.S. Government Accountability Office, "Improvements Needed to Monitoring and Evaluation of Rules Development."

25. Fred Emery, *Rulemaking as an Organizational Process* (Washington, D.C.: Administrative Conference of the United States, 1982).

26. Personal interview with professional staff member, Federal Communications Commission, February 1991.

27. Thomas McGarrity, "The Internal Structure of EPA Rulemaking," *Law and Contemporary Problems* 54 (1991): 54–110; and William F. West, "The Growth of Internal Conflict in Administrative Rulemaking," *Public Administration Review* 48 (July/August 1988): 773–782.

28. McGarrity, "Internal Structure of EPA Rulemaking."
29. West, "Growth of Internal Conflict."
30. Information on the various elements of work groups comes from a variety of sources. See Wesley Magat, Alan Krupnick, and Winston Harrington, *Rules in the Making* (Washington, D.C.: Resources for the Future, 1986); McGarrity, "Internal Structure of EPA Rulemaking"; West, "Growth of Internal Conflict"; Emery, *Rulemaking as an Organizational Process.*
31. U.S. General Accounting Office, "Aviation Rulemaking: Further Reform Is Needed to Address Long-Standing Problems" (Washington, D.C.: GAO, 2001), app. 2, pp. 88–95.
32. See Federal Aviation Administration, *FAA Rulemaking Manual* (Washington, D.C.: FAA, 1998), chaps. 3–5; and Environmental Protection Agency, "EPA's Action Development Process," pp. 12–17, 51–55.

CHAPTER 5

Participation in Rulemaking

Because we are a representative democracy and because lawmaking is the ultimate power granted our government under the Constitution, rulemaking presents us with a profound dilemma. On the one hand, we have established that in order for government to be truly responsive to the incessant demands of the American people for public programs to solve private problems, rulemaking by government agencies is essential. It frees Congress to attend to many more problems than it would otherwise have time to deal with. It relieves Congress of the burden of maintaining and managing enormous staffs who possess the expertise essential to refining the operating standards and procedures for myriad programs. Finally, it is the best means yet found to break legislative deadlocks and to avoid difficult political decisions, while still taking serious actions. On the other hand, as an indispensable surrogate to the legislative process, rulemaking has a fundamental flaw that violates basic democratic principles. Those who write the law embodied in rules are not elected; they are accountable to the American people only through indirect means. Our elected representatives have confronted this dilemma on numerous occasions and decided that one answer is direct participation by the public in rulemaking.

Implicit in the various discussions of participation in rulemaking is a fundamental debate analogous to the trustee/delegate dialectic in the political science literature regarding the proper role of elected officials. With rulemaking, however, the arguments for each archetype are actually more pointed. Those who would dismiss either the value or constitutional need for public participation point to the fact that a statute is written by duly elected representatives. Furthermore, the legislature's decision to entrust subsequent lawmaking needed to implement the goals of the statute contains a delegation of authority to agency-based experts who are fully capable of developing the information they need for a given rule without the input of the public, who are less well-informed, technically competent, and objective. And, given the grave implications of decisions made during the development of rules, do we truly wish to have the opinions and demands of an interested but inept public delay or, worse, color the decisions of those charged with protecting our health, safety, wealth, and general quality of life?

The opposing argument notes that lawmaking is the seminal power granted in our Constitution, and whether it is written by elected representatives or unelected bureaucratic experts, the voice of the people must be heard to confer legitimacy on the mandates the resultant laws contain. Why, they would ask, should the will of the people be confined to the enactment of legislation when it is widely accepted that the most specific statements of Americans' rights and responsibilities are to be found in rules and regulations? Advocates for participation would note that whatever the levels of expertise extant in government agencies, none are omniscient, and all face profound challenges in the face of growing responsibilities and expectations arising from new statutes or simply changing conditions. The "people" have access to vast expertise in the form of interest groups they comprise and support. Public participation is not, in their eyes, a trivial symbolic exercise but one often essential if agencies are going to function with the best and most current information when writing rules.

We will see in the pages that follow that the extreme versions of both arguments have little to commend them, and the truth, while lying somewhere in the middle, also varies dramatically from case to case. We begin with a review of the development of public participation over time and then turn to a review of actual patterns of involvement.

The legitimacy of the rulemaking process is clearly linked to public participation. Phillip Harter, a prominent observer of rulemaking, noted, "To the extent that rulemaking has political legitimacy, it derives from the right of affected interests to present facts and arguments to an agency under procedures designed to ensure the rationality of the agency's decision." Harter is also a staunch advocate for using more consensual techniques for developing rules, arguing that their most important benefit is enhancement of public participation and "the added legitimacy a rule would acquire if all parties viewed [it] as reasonable and endorsed it without a fight."[1]

The Purposes of Participation

Harter's remarks imply, correctly, that participation contributes more than legitimacy to the rulemaking process. By referring to "rationality," he is suggesting that participation can also enhance the authority of the rule. The credibility and standing a rule enjoys with those who will be regulated by it or enjoy the benefits it bestows depend heavily on the accuracy and completeness of the information on which it is based.[2] Agencies rely on the public for much of the information they need to formulate rules. Therefore, if participation is hampered by hostility, intransigence, secrecy, or incompetence on the part of the agency, the rule will be deprived of information that is crucial in establishing its authority with the affected community. Put another way, stupid rules do not beget respect.

Another reason for participation is less frequently cited but potentially important nonetheless. The content and tone of expressions from the public can help rulemaking agencies plan for the circumstances they will confront when the rule is written, and the next phase, implementation, begins. If one remembers that rulemaking is not an end in itself but the critical bridge between the aspirations articulated in law and the reality expressed in program operations, one can comprehend the special significance of participation.

The contribution of public participation to the content of a rule is easy enough to understand. Agencies are not omniscient, and they are not sufficiently endowed to conduct the research needed for all the rules they are expected to write. Comments from the public alert agencies to gaps in their knowledge and provide them with an understanding of the conditions in the private sector they are attempting to ameliorate or regulate. Such comments are especially useful if the agency is dealing with a sector of the population it has not dealt with in the past or with an otherwise unfamiliar activity. Agencies can also begin to understand how much learning will be required of regulated and benefiting parties and how much teaching will be required of implementing officials.

Public comments help agencies determine the degrees of acceptance and resistance in the affected communities to the rule under development. This information can be crucial in many ways. In regulatory programs the results of public participation help agencies design monitoring and enforcement systems. If the affected parties appear from comments to be generally in favor of the new rules, the enforcement program might rely on self-reporting or some other nonintrusive, low-key means of guaranteeing compliance. If, however, the response of the affected public suggests significant opposition to the rule, hostility, and evidence that compliance will be difficult, a more aggressive and expensive enforcement program may be unavoidable. Comments from the public also help the agency gauge the likelihood of a lawsuit challenging the rule before its implementation. Litigation of this sort has a profound effect on the rulemaking programs of many agencies. Because of public participation, a lawsuit need not come as a surprise.

William West, a prominent scholar of rulemaking and administrative procedures, summarizes the major rationales for rulemaking participation a bit differently. One that mirrors the above is that the participation provides meaningful opportunities for interested parties to influence administrative policy. Furthermore, these procedures "promote responsiveness" and aid political actors in overseeing the bureaucracy.[3] This argument flows from the writings of Mathew D. McCubbins and Thomas Schwartz and of McCubbins, Roger Noll, and Barry Weingast, which state that procedures are used by political principals to guard against policy that may vary from legislative intent.[4] Finally, some have argued that these procedures are little more than symbolic efforts that hide the fact that public participation rarely has any major effect on administrative rules.[5]

In this chapter we will examine the efforts by government agencies to broaden and diversify the mechanisms for public participation in rulemaking. Then we will turn to the actual patterns of public participation that occur in rulemaking to determine how those interested in rules under development take advantage of the opportunities to contribute afforded by the agencies.

Although public participation can contribute much to the quality, acceptability, and ultimate success of the rule, it can also complicate rule-making and place the agency squarely between powerful contending forces. It is therefore important to get some historical perspective on how the current mechanisms and practices of public participation in rulemaking came into being.

The Origins and History of Participation

It stands to reason that there was some kind of participation by persons outside of agencies from the very start of rulemaking. The number of areas in which rulemaking occurred was initially quite small, but those who wrote rules were no more omniscient than they are now. Often, as now, those who knew the most about the subject of the rulemaking were those it would affect. It is likely that the public did participate in these early years, but we have no record that they did so. With the coming of the twentieth century, scholars started to focus on rulemaking more systematically. The record of participation by the public in the development of rules then began to change.

Early Inattention

The Attorney General's Committee on Administrative Procedure noted in 1941 that until the early years of the twentieth century Congress paid virtually no attention to how rulemaking was being conducted by officials of the executive branch. Participation by the public in the act of creating law was effectively ignored. When Congress began to take an interest in rulemaking, it was more because of the growing prominence of groups representing business and professional interests than any sense of concern for the constitutional ramifications of lawmaking by unelected surrogates in administrative agencies. Interest groups are deeply and aggressively involved in the development of rules, and their impact is great. But success begins with opportunity, and it is the opportunities for participation in rulemaking and the ways they developed over time that must first be considered.

Participation at the Turn of the Twentieth Century

The earliest systematic research into the process of rulemaking was concerned in part with what, if any, legal status Congress conferred on those affected by rules. Thanks again to the work of the Attorney General's Committee, we know of statutes at the turn of the twentieth century that encouraged or required executive branch officials to consult with various groups before issuing rules. These laws are quite important because they begin to form the basis for patterns of public participation that persist to this very day. For example, the committee discovered an appropriation statute enacted in 1902 that provided funds "to enable the Secretary of Agriculture, in collaboration with the Association of Official Agricultural Chemists, and such other experts as he may deem necessary, to establish standards of purity for food products."[6] Although often not required by law, this type of interaction occurred between rulemakers and interested groups at a variety of agencies, including the Federal Reserve Board (now called the Federal Reserve System), the Federal Communications Commission, the Maritime Commission, and the Children's Bureau. From these informal communications between agencies and their clients, participation grew and diversified.

The Situation at the End of the New Deal

After its survey of agency practices, the Attorney General's Committee concluded that five basic forms of participation were in wide use by the close of the 1930s: oral or written communication and consultation; investigations; specially summoned conferences; advisory committees; and hearings, of which there were two general types.

An investigation was any systematic collection of information to determine whether a rulemaking was necessary and the general content that such a rule might contain. Many agencies worked closely with outside groups and individuals at this crucial early stage in rulemaking. The committee noted, for example, that the Bureau of Biological Survey in the Department of the Interior "has always been in close touch with state officials, conservationists and sportsmen."[7] This precursor to the Fish and Wildlife Agency used these contacts as the basis for all its rulemaking. The interaction was formalized to some extent when the bureau submitted its findings and conclusions relevant to the new rules to the International Association of State Game, Fish and Conservation Commissioners. A similar approach was used by the Food and Drug Administration (FDA). According to the Attorney General's Committee, it "employs a Food Standards Committee which collects information on products for which standards are to be proposed."[8] The Food Standards Committee consisted of members from industry. A similar arrangement was in place at the Interstate Commerce Commission for certain rules governing dangerous cargo, but the ICC took the approach one step further by delegating this exploratory work entirely to the Bureau of Explosives of the American Railway Association.[9] We see that at these earliest stages of rulemaking, the decision to act and the initial consideration of options, the public was actively involved.

Oral and written communications and consultations need little further elaboration. They were the oldest and perhaps most common form of participation at the time the committee conducted its research, and in all likelihood they remain so today. Even when statutes, then and now, require other forms of participation, informal contacts of this type will occur. They may be the most preferred and effective mode of participation for both the public and private sectors. Examples of this type of consultation were numerous by the late 1930s. The Attorney General's Committee noted, for example, that the "Securities and Exchange Commission ... has rarely failed to submit its proposals to those regulated before promulgating rules." Similarly, "the Federal Communications Commission ... has found it possible to dispose of a large portion of its rulemaking problems by consultation with the industry it regulates."[10]

Conferences were a more structured and focused form of participation and, in the opinion of the Attorney General's Committee, "[introduce] an element of give and take on the part of those present."[11] This type of interaction is not possible when consultation is essentially a set of bilateral contacts between an agency and an interested or affected party. The Federal Reserve Board's practices were "particularly noteworthy because of the Board's virtually complete reliance on conferences ... as a means of enabling affected parties to participate in the rulemaking process." The Federal Reserve Board conducted conferences "with the public directly and through the American Bankers' Association."[12]

Advisory committees were as common as conferences and proved to be a more resilient and popular mode of participation. The Attorney General's Committee found advisory committees at work in a wide variety of agencies, and in some instances these bodies were far more than a resource from which the agency could draw information, expertise, and opinion based on experience. Several examples demonstrate the degree of influence exerted by advisory committees during the course of rulemaking. The Bureau of Marine Inspection and Navigation used an advisory committee composed of "consultants drawn from the industries affected who met continuously with the Bureau's officers and participated in the drafting of particular sets of regulations governing the construction of vessels."[13] The most extraordinary influence of any of the advisory committee arrangements was exerted under the mandates of the Fair Labor Standards Act: "[W]age orders of the Administrator varying the statutory minimum wage rates in particular industries shall originate with committees of the employers, employees and public representatives."[14] This is remarkable in several ways. First, the law effectively transforms the agency into a ratifier of decisions made by a group of external parties. Second, it includes on the advisory committee a "public" member, a feature notably absent in other advisory committee schemes of the time.[15] Third, it establishes a structure for rules to be developed through negotiation by parties with contending interests. This form of participation, called for in the Fair Labor Standards Act, was a precursor of negotiated rulemaking, an important reform that is discussed in more detail later in the chapter.

Hearings, as a form of participation, come in two types: informal and formal. Informal hearings are patterned after the familiar legislative sessions. Witnesses are summoned, sworn in, asked to present testimony, and questioned by the representatives of the agencies who are presiding. Informal hearings are decidedly one-sided. Their clear purpose is the collection of information that the agency will use in developing the rule. It is not to answer questions or challenges from those who are testifying. In this sense informal hearings would appear to offer little substantive or procedural advantage to potential participants over the even less formal conferences mentioned earlier. In fact, it is easy to see how the limited formalities of legislative hearings might significantly reduce the give-and-take that is so important if public participation is to provide all it can to rulemakers. Nevertheless, these types of hearings were popular when the committee conducted its study and remain so today.

Legislative hearings can be mandatory or voluntary. For example, the Interstate Commerce Commission was required to conduct hearings as a condition of its rulemaking authority. Hearing requirements can be found in statutes written as early as 1903. The Attorney General's Committee found mandatory hearings common in transportation statutes generally and in agencies dealing with certain types of wages, trade and tariffs, prices, and marketing. Voluntary use of hearings was adopted by many business-related regulatory agencies, including the Federal Power Commission, the Federal Communications Commission, and the Department of Agriculture.[16]

Formal hearings are adversarial proceedings based on the model of a civil trial conducted in a court of law. At the time the Attorney General's Committee conducted its research, this type of hearing was required for certain rules or rulemaking situations, usually when there were disputes over matters of material fact. The Fair Labor Standards Act, the Bituminous Coal Act, and the Food, Drug, and Cosmetic Act all carried provisions for what has come to be called formal rulemaking. Many other agencies voluntarily used this type of proceeding for individual rules.[17]

Then, as now, formal rulemaking was a cumbersome, difficult, time-consuming, and expensive process. For example, a coal price order by the Bituminous Coal Board was issued only after generating "a record and exhibits ... total[ing] over 50,000 pages; the trial examiner's report of approximately 2,800 pages in addition to exhibits and a Director's report of 545 single-spaced legal sized pages."[18] Although formal rulemaking was more common in the 1930s than it is today, when formal procedures are undertaken in contemporary rulemaking, the supporting paper and elapsed time dwarf those of the former years.

Today we live with a persistent concern that agencies will be captured by those they regulate or who serve as beneficiaries. The apparent coziness between rulemaking agencies and the industries or groups they regulate that emerges from the work of the Attorney General's Committee is striking. Contacts between public officials and representatives or consultants from industry were the norm. In several instances the influence of the latter over the decisions of the former was substantial. Involvement of members of the general public, if it occurred at all, was certainly not prominent in the report of the committee. In no small part the system of participation, so skewed in favor of regulated or benefiting interests, was due to the nature of the programs being managed by federal agencies at that time and the fact that professional and industrial interests were comparatively well organized. Their counterparts, representing broader social interests, were not. Read in a contemporary context, public participation in the 1930s had all the earmarks of capture by powerful private interests. Indeed, this became a common criticism of government programs in later years.

Aside from the imbalance in the population of participants, what may be most striking about the findings of the Attorney General's Committee is the rich diversity of participatory forms and practices in place more than sixty-five years ago. One would be hard-pressed to find a mechanism of participation in rulemaking currently in force that cannot be traced back to this period.

The Attorney General's Committee conducted its work at a time when rulemaking and the behavior of administrative entities were receiving considerable attention from Congress, the courts, and the White House. The Walter-Logan bill, vetoed by President Franklin Delano Roosevelt, would have required much of the administrative process to adopt the adversary model mentioned earlier.[19] And New Deal programs and activities, including rulemaking, were being challenged in the courts. Shortly after the completion of the committee's work, the nation was thrust into a war effort that put consideration of administrative reform on hold. But soon after the Second World War, Congress returned to the subject and enacted a landmark statute, the Administrative Procedure Act of 1946.

The Administrative Procedure Act

The rulemaking provisions of the Administrative Procedure Act may seem curious in light of the information about participation that was available to Congress. The Attorney General's Committee found many different forms and models of participation in its study of agency procedures, but Congress chose to adopt a minimalist approach to public involvement embodied in Section 553 of the act. These "notice and comment" provisions codify a limited form of what the committee termed "consultation" as the basic mode of participation the public could expect from rulemaking agencies. Congress also provided for formal rulemaking but restricted it to situations in which an individual statute mandated its use. At the same time the act ignored the other forms of participation uncovered by the committee. Furthermore, it allowed agencies to write rules without benefit of any participation in emergency situations or when it was deemed, by the agency, to be in the public interest.

It would be wrong, however, to view the Administrative Procedure Act as a repudiation of the diverse forms of public participation already operating in most agencies. The act is a general framework, bounded by notice-and-comment provisions at one end and trial-type procedures at the other. Within those boundaries, existing statutes, future legislation, and the exercise of agency discretion define administrative procedures more specifically, allowing systems of participation to develop that make the most sense for particular programs. By establishing notice and written comment as the minimum, Congress rationalized the rulemaking procedure that critics had found so badly lacking during the New Deal era. In retrospect, this action appears to be of greater symbolic than substantive importance. Unless the Attorney General's Committee conducted woefully inadequate research, by the late 1930s most agencies with any appreciable program of rulemaking were reaching out and interacting with the public, albeit the well-organized public. The real significance of the Administrative Procedure Act was its statement that participation in rulemaking would henceforth be open to anyone who wished to become involved. It gave those who were interested the minimum information and access needed to get involved.[20] Effective participation, however, still would require organization, resources, and political sophistication. Not until the 1960s and 1970s would the voices heard by the rulemaking agencies become more numerous and diverse.

Converging Forces: The "Participation Revolution" and the Rise of Social Regulation

Although their origins are difficult to date with precision, two developments in the 1960s and 1970s altered dramatically the status and process of rule-making. The first was a movement to involve citizens in government decision making in ways that were more direct, and intended to be more effective, than the ballot. The second, discussed in detail in Chapter 1, was the vast expansion of social regulation that extended the reach of government in such a way that previously unorganized interests now had more than ample incentive to come together for collective action. The convergence of these two forces, once in motion, was both inevitable and important.

The revolution in participation was not a single, coherent movement. It included many disparate initiatives with widely variable effects. The driving force of the revolution, however, was a lack of faith in the ability of established government institutions to understand the popular will and respond appropriately. In the 1960s and 1970s the American people witnessed a violent struggle for civil rights, unsatisfactorily explained assassinations of revered public figures, an unpopular war, shocking political scandals, and a growing disaffection with government, which appeared unable to accomplish ambitious social objectives. The motives of those seeking to expand public participation ranged from a near-paranoid mistrust of the government's own motives to a simple belief that direct input from citizens would improve the quality of the government's decisions. Also prominent was a faith in participation as a means of empowering and involving the disenfranchised and unrepresented among the population.

Congressional Action to Promote Participation

To open government decision making, Congress passed a variety of laws. The Freedom of Information Act allowed private citizens to review the way agency officials made their decisions. The Privacy Act allowed individuals to gain access to the information the government might have about them, to learn the uses to which the information was being put, and to correct errors in those records while requiring the responsible agency to take steps to prevent unauthorized disclosures. The Government in the Sunshine Act opened many agency meetings and deliberations to the public. The Federal Advisory Committee Act required that membership on those potentially powerful groups be balanced with regard to affected interests, and it opened their deliberations to public scrutiny as well.

Other efforts sought to provide for more direct participation of the public in government decision making. The Great Society programs of Lyndon Johnson adopted this approach, and the movement for direct citizen action continued through the 1970s. By one estimate, hundreds of programs required "some form of citizen participation" by the end of that decade.[21] In some instances there was a displacement of existing government institutions and processes. The Model Cities Program, a crown jewel of the Great Society, mandated a governance structure consisting of separately elected citizen boards that completely bypassed local executive and legislative officials. Alternative governments, often competing with establishment officials for power and influence, were rapidly becoming the order of the day.

Expansion of Scope, Diversification of Forms

The citizen participation movement was in full flower when the era of social regulation dawned. The National Environmental Policy Act of 1969 (NEPA), which many see as the symbolic start of that era, embraced fully the participation ethic of the time. Both elements of the movement, full disclosure of the information on which government bases its decisions and direct public involvement, provide the cornerstones of NEPA. Government agencies were required to develop detailed statements on the environmental impact of their contemplated actions. The statements were to be prepared only after a public "scoping session" at which citizens could voice their concerns and opinions about likely environmental effects. Once completed, the statement was subjected to another round of public participation before it could be declared final. Although opinions concerning the effects of the NEPA provisions vary considerably, there is evidence that the act contributed to significant changes in many federal agencies.[22]

The hundreds of statutes establishing and amending programs of social regulation embraced the concept of expanded public participation as well. But in each instance Congress tailored participation provisions to the program in question. Some statutes expanded on the basic provisions of the Administrative Procedure Act (APA). For example, laws establishing programs of social regulation called for extended periods of public comment. The 1977 amendments to the Clean Water Act allowed sixty days for public comment on effluent guidelines for toxic water pollutants.[23] One motive for this type of provision was to give organizations, groups, and individuals new to the rulemaking process additional time to analyze and respond to the frequently complex proposed regulations needed to implement programs of social regulation. But other motives may have been at work as well. The extended periods delay the issuance of rules and give opponents more time to alert congressional, administration, and private sector allies who might help in blocking or altering the new rules.

Other statutes expanded the APA's notice requirements by calling on agencies to release to the public analyses on which they were relying for the content of their proposed rules. Such disclosure requirements can be found in the Federal Trade Commission Improvements Act of 1980 and the Consumer Product Safety Act amendments of 1981.[24] Again, the motives behind these provisions were mixed. Certainly, additional information can assist members of the public in determining whether to participate and help them focus their comments or stated opinions. It also can delay the issuance of the proposal. More important, it exposes the agency to challenge. The studies and reports disclosed in this manner may be criticized from many different perspectives, and if their reliability or validity is called into question, the entire rule may be in jeopardy.

Several of the general models of participation that were observed by the Attorney General's Committee in the 1930s reappeared in statutes of social regulation in the 1970s. Especially popular were provisions requiring agencies to go beyond the written comments called for in the APA and allow interested parties to present information and views orally. These legislative-type hearings were included in the Occupational Safety and Health Act, the Consumer Product Safety Act, the Safe Drinking Water Act, the 1977 amendments to the Clean Water Act, and the 1978 revisions of the Endangered Species Act.[25] A few statutes, notably the Magnuson-Moss Warranty–Federal Trade Commission Improvements Act and the Toxic Substances Control Act, went well beyond the legislative model by allowing for cross-examination of witnesses by participating interests.[26] It is thought that hearings provide a compelling form of participation because they put agency personnel in direct contact with those members of the public who will be affected by their rules. But hearings are also time consuming and expensive to manage. Although hearings can generate a wealth of information and views, this is not an unequivocal benefit to those writing the rules. The agency must subsequently take this information into consideration when finalizing the rule. In addition, because the transcripts of hearings become part of this material "record" of the rulemaking, they can be used to mobilize political support or opposition and thus may figure prominently in subsequent litigation attacking the rule.

Innovations in participation were not confined to the latter stages of the rulemaking process. Some legislation, like the Federal Trade Commission Improvements Act and the Energy Policy and Conservation Act, required advance notices of proposed rulemaking.[27] At least two statutes—the Consumer Product Safety Act and the Medical Device amendments to the Food, Drug and Cosmetic Act—contained "offerer provisions."[28] These provisions authorized nongovernment groups and organizations to develop and propose rules to agencies, which would then decide whether to issue the rule in the form proposed.

Overall, Congress was a major force in promoting greater participation in rulemaking proceedings. Legislation was an important element in the "participation revolution" that swept government in general and in the larger "procedural revolution" that has altered rulemaking in recent decades. Other institutions also were heavily involved in opening rulemaking to direct influence by the public.

Throughout the 1980s Congress continued to tinker with participation provisions in new authorizing statutes as well as in amendments to existing legislation. These provisions added few new vehicles for expression of the public will. During the 1990s, however, two notable legislative innovations occurred. In the Negotiated Rulemaking Act of 1990, Congress authorized direct bargaining with affected and interested parties as an approved means for developing regulations, and it established operating principles for these negotiations.[29] The theory and performance of some of the techniques endorsed by the act will be discussed later. Congress made an equally dramatic statement about public participation with the passage of the Small Business Regulatory Enforcement Fairness Act of 1996, an amendment to the Regulatory Flexibility Act.[30]

This legislation reflected Congress's long-standing concern about how small businesses were affected by new rules, in particular those issued by the Occupational Safety and Health Administration and the Environmental Protection Agency. If a regulation under development has substantial implications for a significant number of small businesses, OSHA or the EPA are now required to convene a panel whose task is to develop information and secure recommendations from affected interests. The panel then reports these findings to the officials responsible for the rule in question; they are expected to incorporate the information in the regulation or its supporting analyses. The first panel convened at the EPA developed information on a rule concerning air pollution by nonroad diesel engines. In 1997 the panel issued a report that clearly indicates the potential effectiveness of this new form of participation.[31] The report offered five recommendations for reducing the rule's impact on small businesses, and it charged the EPA with giving them serious consideration.

The current decade brought the Information Quality Act, discussed in an earlier chapter. While its purpose was ostensibly framed in its title, the legislation opened yet another door for participation by allowing the public to challenge the "quality, objectivity, utility and integrity" of information used in rulemaking.[32]

Presidents and Participation

Carter's Reforms. President Jimmy Carter assumed office in 1977 determined to improve the operation of regulatory programs. Enhanced public involvement, he firmly believed, would produce the desired change. While Carter's presidency was more than thirty years ago, we linger here on it because it was a renewal period for participation in rulemaking. Much of what has since occurred has its roots in this brief period.

The means of increasing public participation took many forms in the Carter administration. One simple means was to increase the period for public comment on proposed rules from the usual thirty days to sixty days or longer. Better and earlier information on agencies' plans for rulemaking was to be supplied through the publication of a regulatory agenda and calendars. These would provide early warning to the public of rulemaking projects being contemplated or in the beginning stages of development. A more ambitious approach to achieving the same objectives is the *advance notice of proposed rulemaking,* also instituted during Carter's presidency under Executive Order 12044. This is a device that involves the public in the development of individual rules at a very early stage. The advance notice announces the agency's intent to write a regulation or its concern that an issue or problem may require a rule. The agency solicits the views of the public on the need for the regulation or its ideas on how the issue or problem that will be addressed in the rule might be resolved. In effect, the advance notice is an invitation to join the agency at the start of the rulemaking process.

President Carter charged the Office of Management and Budget (OMB) with evaluating agencies' progress in implementing the provisions of the executive order. In this task the OMB relied on the agencies' own reports, its independent inquiries, and responses from a survey of interest groups who were asked to comment on the performance of the agencies they dealt with in the area of participation. The summary assessment in 1979, roughly one year after the executive order was promulgated, was "mixed" in most areas.[33]

Semiannual agendas were being produced by most agencies and were generally viewed as a positive development by the external groups that were surveyed. In some instances the agendas were produced on something less than a semiannual schedule. In others the descriptions of problems, and the rules that were being developed to deal with them, were skimpy or vague. Groups complained that the schedules announced in the agendas were frequently inaccurate, tending to be overly optimistic about how quickly the work would be completed.[34]

Since its inception during the Carter administration, the regulatory agenda program has continued to develop, and the quality of agency submissions is more uniform. The descriptions are now quite clear and sufficiently informative that external parties can easily understand why an action is being undertaken and how the agency is thinking about the problem. The program has been retained by the presidents who followed Carter, but its primary focus has shifted from rulemaking participation by the public to agency accountability to the White House.

Carter's OMB evaluators found that several agencies that had not used advance notices of proposed rulemaking in the past were experimenting with them. The response from the public was generally positive but not unanimous. Surprisingly, some groups appeared to resent agencies' reliance on advance notices, viewing it as "a 'cop-out' to have the public do the [agencies'] work for them."[35]

The sixty-day period for comments was usually observed by agencies, but the effect on the public was marginal. The sixty-day period afforded only a modest amount of additional time. Sometimes the agencies were more generous, allowing as much as a half a year or more for comments. The OMB found these extensive periods of public comment to be particularly useful.[36]

The OMB study did report on agencies' innovative approaches to outreach during rulemaking. These initiatives fall into two general categories. The first includes efforts to diversify the ways agencies communicate with the public on actions they are planning to take. However improved, notices that appear only in the *Federal Register* or in a semiannual agenda will have limited circulation. Agencies experimented with a variety of techniques and media more familiar, accessible, and understandable to the general public (for example, notices in newspapers, television and radio announcements, and mass mailings). The second category includes efforts to make public involvement in rulemaking more personal and less antiseptic than the submission of written comments. To give citizens a sense that rulemaking agencies cared about their views, various forms of public hearings were conducted around the country.[37]

Case studies done in conjunction with the OMB evaluation provide important insights into public participation in individual departments and agencies during the late 1970s. These studies review participation in five departments—Agriculture; Health, Education and Welfare; Labor; Interior; and the EPA.

The Department of Agriculture's rulemaking program that established agricultural marketing orders for commodities provides a particularly interesting case study. The program came into being as part of the New Deal. Its intent was to stabilize the markets for agricultural products through many different means, the primary device being rules that established quality standards and limited the amounts of various commodities that could be shipped to market. For most of its history it was a classic example of a "captured" regulatory program. The hearings associated with the marketing order rulemakings were rarely attended by consumer interests, nor did those interests actively oppose the program, which, it would appear, was not designed to benefit them.[38] The inactivity of consumers is explained by conventional theories of regulation that underscore the advantage that a highly specialized and small group, producers in this case, enjoys over a group that is large, diverse, and difficult to organize, such as consumers.[39]

The Department of Agriculture "discovered a significant amount of outside interest in the marketing order programs that was not being accommodated through the formal hearing process" during the Carter years.[40] In response, the department established a "prenotice public participation requirement." In effect, this was a preliminary investigation of public attitudes and views on a planned marketing order through a solicitation of comments mailed directly to affected groups.

Participation in rulemaking was an area of major change for the Department of Health, Education and Welfare (HEW), now the Department of Health and Human Services. The issues facing the department involved reaching and listening to enormous numbers of potential participants. The initiative undertaken in response to the Carter program suggests the magnitude of the task. In an effort to bring the rulemaking process to the people, HEW conducted a series of public meetings outside of Washington and sent out special mailings about rules that were under way. In 1978 alone the department reported that more than 3,100 persons attended the public meetings and that it had sent more than 110,000 individual letters.

To get the public to participate in the development of rules concerning food labels, the FDA sent out more than "40,000 letters," distributed "500,000 pieces of literature," and did an "experimental television survey" in Columbus, Ohio. These efforts were both successful and sobering. The good news was that more than 10,000 public comments were received on the labeling regulations.[41] The sobering fact was that each one had to be read and a response prepared; decisions then had to be made about possible changes in the final regulations. The experience of the FDA and HEW reminds us that the price of public participation in terms of staff time, delay, and opportunity costs can be high.

The efforts of the Department of the Interior to implement Carter's executive order demonstrate some of the benefits and costs of early participation by the public in rulemaking. Among other things, it appeared to be particularly useful in weeding out unnecessary provisions in regulations. In one case the number of eligibility criteria for a grant program was reduced from 100 to just 6, and the number of items included in an application for right of way on public lands went from 20 to 5.[42]

As was noted earlier, strategies to involve the public early on are not without their critics. In the case of the Department of the Interior, the unhappiness centered on advance notices of "technical or complex" rules. The OMB evaluation concluded that these did not result in "substantive, useful comments." According to one industry interest group, "Notices of intent give a phony appearance of public participation—technical rules need specifics. If they don't ... you can't comment."[43] The comment suggests that the people in this group may not have realized that they were being asked to help design a rule from the ground up. Alternatively, they did understand the request but were loath to invest substantial resources in an effort that might provide them no benefits whatsoever.

The Department of Labor's most important and controversial rulemaking organization is the Occupational Safety and Health Administration. Given its history and adversarial environment, one would predict that new opportunities for participation would be enthusiastically received, but in fact OSHA had an experience similar to that of the Department of the Interior when it attempted to introduce early public input into its rulemaking process.

The OMB evaluators found that the various agencies in the Department of Labor tailored their methods of outreach to the public to fit their particular constituencies. OSHA officials concluded that "constituent groups apparently believe they can have the most impact by addressing issues raised in a specific proposal" and are "reluctant to use their limited resources on relatively undeveloped concepts identified early in the process."[44]

According to the OMB report, the EPA "had a tradition of effective public participation."[45] For years the agency had used advance notices and distributed supplemental information to the public on rules under development. But these notices and supplements were frequently not as informative as they might have been. New regulations required the EPA to use various forms of public participation when developing rules for its solid and hazardous waste, drinking water, and clean water programs. It received more than five hundred comments on these procedural regulations, a significant percentage of which were received over a special toll-free long-distance telephone system. The new regulations established public meetings, hearings, and advisory groups as the major means for obtaining the public's input on these three important programs.[46]

Some groups accused the EPA of circumventing requirements for public participation by using devices other than rules and regulations for setting regulatory policy. The devices took numerous forms, including "policy circulars," "guidelines," and "technical corrections." They were issued by the agency without any of the procedural steps normally associated with rulemaking. Confusion arose as to the status of these devices. Were they equal in legal terms to an actual rule or regulation? If so, should not normal rulemaking procedures, including public participation, apply to their development? One who criticized their use reflected a widely held view: "Where these … have major effects the public should have an opportunity for comment."[47] As it happens, the EPA was not the only department that may have been avoiding public participation requirements.

Use of these instruments of public policy as alternatives to rules has increased, and so has the controversy associated with them. The courts have insisted that when agencies take actions that create or alter obligations borne by the public, they must use appropriate procedures. Yet in 1992, thirteen years after the OMB study, use of guidelines, advisories, and the like were still very popular with rulemaking agencies, according to a study conducted by the Administrative Conference of the United States. This study, drawing on prevailing cases, called on agencies to engage in rulemaking whenever there is a question about the actions they are taking. The study concluded that agencies are likely to continue using these devices in marginal cases, and the evidence accumulated since confirm this prediction.[48] First, there are always going to be instances when agencies do not perceive the action they are taking as any more than a clarification of existing rules or policy. Of course, any clarification will have the effect of transforming a gray area into one that is black and white, and this change alone may be enough to trigger a protest. Second, as noted in Chapter 1, what Thomas McGarrity called the "ossification" of rulemaking under the weight of multiple, complex procedures creates incentives for agencies to find quicker, easier ways to manage their programs. While the effects of ossification have been disputed in one study,[49] it is also true that the use of devices other than rules to set or elaborate on policy became widespread. As noted in a previous chapter, it became sufficiently prominent that George W. Bush issued an executive order to rein in the practice.[50]

The last years of the Carter administration represent a high-water mark for participation in rulemaking as a public policy concern. Although there was not enough time for the program to be fully implemented, Carter's public participation initiative was taken seriously by government agencies and produced results because it had the force of the presidency behind it. By the end of his presidency, most of the major avenues for public involvement in rulemaking had been explored. The strengths and weaknesses of each were well understood. Ultimately, programs of public participation in rulemaking must be tailored to the subject matter and constituencies of the programs for which the rules are being written. In many of the departments and agencies such a tailoring process had been in use for more than fifty years and would reappear twenty years later.

Reagan's Changes: Participation of a Different Sort. The transition from Carter to Reagan brought dramatic change. The new administration took a very different view of public participation. Jeffrey Berry, Kent Portney, and Ken Thomson, experts in the field of citizen participation in government, summarize President Reagan's position in the following way:

> In rather sweeping fashion, the Reagan administration pursued its policies under the belief that federally mandated citizen participation caused the bureaucracy to become unresponsive to officials elected by the people and that citizen participation therefore actually became antidemocratic. In a call for the return to the orthodox view of administrative responsiveness, the Reagan administration suggested that agencies had become responsive to clients and special interests in a way that was inconsistent with what the general citizenry wanted. In contrast, advocates of citizen participation argued that there is nothing antidemocratic about citizens working with agencies to fulfill the spirit and intent of the programs enacted by Congress. The debate continues today.[51]

The Reagan administration did not disdain all participation, only that which sought expansion of certain government benefits and most regulations. The Reaganites viewed most of the initiatives of the 1960s and 1970s as empowering those very organizations and groups that had a strong vested interest in big government. They were correct. Reagan succeeded in rolling back a few of the mechanisms for public participation in rulemaking, notably public funding. But his major accomplishments were halting further expansion of participation opportunities and installing counterweights to the influence exerted by advocates of big government.

The main offsetting mechanism was review of all proposed and final rules by the Office of Management and Budget. What is significant here is the new form of participation that the OMB review program stimulated. The

OMB staff members who reviewed proposed regulations became another point of decision making for organizations and groups to influence. Again, if it is true, as Theodore Lowi has stated, that politics flows to the point of discretion, the Reagan program created just such a point.[52] Certainly, the various review programs instituted by previous presidents created similar opportunities, but none was so sweeping as the charge given the OMB under Executive Order 12291. The authority of OMB officials was not confined to particular types of rules, or rules with particular types of potential effects, or rules already on the books. Here, for the first time, was a comprehensive program to review all rules with the implicit charge to alter those whose content contradicted, or failed to promote, the policy goals that President Reagan took as his mandate. In short, the president known as a skeptic of public participation had created one of the most inviting opportunities for involvement in rulemaking in American history. But in the opinion of many, the invitation was extended only to a privileged few.

Theoretically, important changes in a rule, valuable delay, and even complete defeat of a proposed regulation could be achieved through effective lobbying of the right officials in the OMB. If a given interest group was confident about securing a sympathetic ear, it could pursue a strategy of nominal involvement during the agency phase of rulemaking while putting heavy pressure on the OMB staff and officials responsible for the review of the rule. In this way the interest group could attain its goal at a comparatively low cost.

Given the general policies of the Reagan administration, the willingness of the OMB staff to listen to those with concerns about proposed and final regulations depended very heavily on who was speaking. Critics of the OMB program accused the Reagan administration of creating a backdoor through which influence peddlers representing big business and antiregulation forces could slip; once inside they could change or block outright those rules they failed to influence satisfactorily by dealing directly with the responsible agencies. In addition, critics charged that contacts between lobbyists and OMB staff members constituted an illegal violation of the long-standing principle that all information used to determine the content of a rule be known and subject to review by the courts and the public in general.

The charges were vehemently denied by those in the administration, but their protestations were not sufficient to silence the critics. Several years after the OMB program was instituted, the head of the Office of Information and Regulatory Affairs, the office that conducted the reviews, issued a set of binding guidelines that established standards for contact with the public and for recording the results of meetings or other forms of communication. Restrictions were placed on the communication between the staff and external interests, and that which occurred was to be consistent with the principle of a rulemaking record; that is, it had to be open to public review and, during litigation, to judicial scrutiny.[53]

President George H. W. Bush, having headed the Task Force on Regulatory Relief in the Reagan administration, continued this forum for those critical of proposed and existing rules. Its new name was the Council on Competitiveness, chaired by Vice President Dan Quayle. The council had authority to review any rule it deemed sufficiently important to the operation of the American economy. Its review criteria were vague, and the council operated without benefit of the procedural restrictions that were imposed on the OMB. Provided with ample staff support from the same unit in the OMB that conducted reviews of rules, the council aggressively altered regulations it considered unnecessarily burdensome on the economy. The same, albeit more intense, criticism was leveled at the council as had greeted OMB review a decade earlier. Now, however, there were direct claims that preferential treatment was being given to those who supported the president's 1988 campaign and to those whose support the administration coveted for 1992. It became common to refer to the operation of the council as a form of regulatory pork barrel politics in which the White House doled out economic benefits in the form of reduced compliance costs. Nonetheless, the council won major battles with intransigent agencies that persisted in their views.

The effect of the council on important rules was sometimes dramatic. In a highly publicized struggle with the leadership of the Environmental Protection Agency, the council succeeded in rolling back proposed notification requirements in rules developed under the 1990 Clean Air Act. The action meant that polluting firms would not have to notify the public when incidents of excess emissions occurred, and thus it relieved affected businesses from potentially high costs and public scrutiny. Critics issued withering assessments of these council practices and the secrecy with which it conducted its business. In a joint report on the council, two organizations frequently critical of the approach of both Reagan and Bush to regulation stated:

> By directly meddling in ongoing regulatory actions, the Quayle Council undermines the entire system of federal regulation. Over the years, Congress has charged expert agencies such as the Environmental Protection Agency (EPA), the Food and Drug Administration (FDA), and the Occupational Safety and Health Administration (OSHA) with the task of safeguarding the public's health and safety. These agencies, in turn, are governed by an elaborate legal structure designed to ensure that they are open to the public, that they hear from all sides, and that they base their

decisions on complex scientific or technical matters only on substantive merits.... By contrast, the Quayle Council invites regulated corporations unhappy about the results of regulation to quietly turn to the White House for relief.... Because it acts in utter secrecy, the Quayle Council has set itself up as a channel for improper industry influence in regulatory decision-making. If it continues to expand its operations, the nation's health and safety standards will be in tatters.[54]

Clinton and George W. Bush's Approaches. President Bill Clinton elevated public participation in rulemaking to the level of a major theme in his National Performance Review (NPR). The creation of partnerships between the public and private sectors became the preferred method of decision making, characterized by negotiation rather than adversarial relations and dictates from Washington. In some instances these collaborative relationships generated projects and programs that displaced conventional rulemaking altogether. One example was the Common Sense Initiative of the Environmental Protection Agency, which focuses on six industries—automobile manufacturing, iron and steel, metal finishing, electronics and computers, petroleum refining, and printing—in an effort to bring together representatives of business, government, community organizations, labor, and environmental groups. These groups were charged with finding ways to "change complicated, inconsistent and costly regulations"; new rules were to replace those found to be dysfunctional.[55]

The Bush II administration confined its efforts to broad statements and initiatives regarding participation sensitive to criticisms of the earlier Bush administration. Its approach stressed an openness that "responds to past complaints that OMB decision making was secretive and more rooted in interest group politics than professional analysis."[56] It focused on the OMB and its Office of Information and Regulatory Affairs by ensuring transparency in all its rulemaking-related interactions with the public and by inviting widespread public participation in decisions to review existing rules.[57] Still, there are a few participation tools that this administration used as it relates to participation efforts. As noted in Chapter 3, the Information Quality Act, passed in 2000, allows interest groups to challenge the quality of information used in the development of rules. In 2004 the OMB published a notice in the *Federal Register* soliciting nominations for regulatory reforms that may affect the manufacturing industry.[58] A January 2007 amendment to Executive Order 12866 brought guidance documents into the purview of OMB review and generally ensured they be treated more like regulations.

As noted in Chapter 4, President Barack Obama has signaled that public participation will be an important feature in his rulemaking management program. Indeed, unlike his predecessors, he invited the public to offer its views on how his rulemaking management program should be structured. Several hundred groups and individuals responded to his invitation.[59] Nearly two hundred comments were received on how to structure the rulemaking management program and the role of cost-benefit analysis in regulatory review. As of mid-2010, the Obama administration had not issued a new executive order on regulatory management.

Actual Patterns of Participation

Opportunities to participate do not ensure that participation will actually occur, and the act of participation does not guarantee the participant success. Therefore, it is important to discover who participates in rulemaking, why they do it, the devices they employ, and the successes they achieve.

Participation in rulemaking has prerequisites. A participant must be aware that a rule is being developed, understand how it will affect particular interests, be familiar with the opportunities for participation, possess the resources and technical expertise needed to respond, and, when necessary, have the ability to mobilize others in the effort to influence agency decision makers. These requirements suggest that in most instances participants in rulemaking will be groups, organizations, firms, and other governments. Single individuals will become involved, but they will be less prominent than institutional participants, although we do note that there has been an increase in individual participation with the growth of e-rulemaking. Nevertheless, we focus on interest groups, broadly defined, in this examination of the participants in rulemaking. For our purposes, interest groups are defined as organizations that attempt to influence public policy. They include companies, business and trade associations, unions, other levels of government, and public interest groups.

Most of what is known about participation in rulemaking comes from three sources: case studies of individual rulemakings and rulemaking programs, analyses of official records of government agencies, and surveys of interest groups. There are numerous case studies of rulemaking. Analyses of official rulemaking records and surveys of interest groups pertaining specifically to their involvement in the development of rules were as rare as hens' teeth when the book was first written in the early 1990s. The situation has improved significantly in recent years.

Earlier editions of this book relied extensively on our own research regarding rulemaking participation because very little empirical work in this area had been done. Our surveys were administered nearly ten years apart. Although we employed somewhat different sampling methodologies in the two efforts, for both surveys the number of respondents and their characteristics indicated that the information we collected is representative and provides an accurate view of interest groups participating in federal agency rulemaking at those times.[60] They also provide a view of rulemaking's importance over time, as well as the salience of related issues and the perceived effectiveness of tactics, techniques, and devices. Importantly, rulemaking research has taken on greater prominence in recent years as more and more scholars recognize this critical policy arena and the role participation plays in developing rules. As such, while we will still reference our own survey research in this area, we now also have a variety of other studies to help us draw conclusions regarding participation in rulemaking.

Does Participation Actually Happen?

If we were to rely solely on case studies, we would immediately conclude that participation by interest groups is a prominent part of all rulemaking. In his classic study of the rule that mandated warning labels on cigarette packages, *Smoking and Politics,* A. Lee Fritschler recounts the efforts of the tobacco industry, the advertising industry, health groups, and consumer groups to influence the Federal Trade Commission. Ross Cheit's case studies of four separate rulemakings that established safety standards found participation to be common, as has research into the development of agricultural marketing orders and the setting of health-related workplace rules. William West analyzed rulemaking at the Federal Trade Commission and also found participation by groups, albeit those who were well organized and had ample resources.[61]

However, according to other scholars and the Government Accountability Office (GAO), agencies failed with some regularity to comply with the notice requirements (see Figure 5-1).[62] One GAO study found that half of the final rules in 1997 were published without prior notice. But many rules are exempted from prior notice requirements under one of the APA provisions mentioned in Chapter 2, and agencies may simply neglect to mention the prior notice in the final rule. There is insufficient information to determine whether the apparent infrequency of notices of proposed rulemaking results from evasion, legitimate exemptions, or a simple failure to mention the notice in the final rule.

If it does not appear from these data that participation is as frequent as the available case studies would lead us to believe, there are reasons. One is the type of rules and rulemaking programs that scholars study. In all the case studies cited earlier, the rules or rulemaking programs are prominent; the potential effects are large and the issues frequently controversial. For these

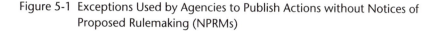

Figure 5-1 Exceptions Used by Agencies to Publish Actions without Notices of Proposed Rulemaking (NPRMs)

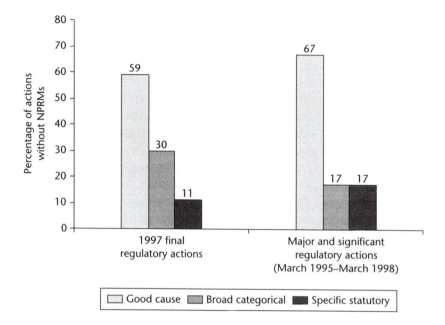

Source: GAO analysis of *Federal Register* notices for final regulatory actions. U.S. General Accounting Office, "Federal Rulemaking: Agencies Often Published Final Actions Without Proposed Rules," GAO/GGD-98-126, August 1998, p. 20, www.gao.gov/archive/1998/gg98126.pdf.

Note: The data on all 1997 final actions without NPRMs show percentages estimated on the basis of GAO's sample results. The data on major and significant actions show the percentages for final actions without NPRMs that were identified during previous assignments. These actions were published between March 1995 and March 1998.

reasons they were highly likely to attract serious attention from interest groups. The *Federal Register* sample contains all rules, many of which are quite minor, routine, and noncontroversial. These kinds of rules are not likely to attract much notice from interest groups because their individual effects are small. For rules that are issued routinely or in serial fashion, groups try to influence the general standards and procedures that structure the entire program rather than each individual rule. There is another possible explanation for these data that indicate low participation rates: Other means by which groups can affect rules do not appear in the preambles of rules. The responses to formal notices of proposed rulemaking provide an incomplete picture of the forms and frequency of interest group participation.

Table 5-1 Comparative Importance to Interest Groups of Involvement in Rulemaking (percentages from surveys 1 and 2)

Degree of importance	Lobbying Congress		Grassroots work		Political contributions		Litigation	
	1	2	1	2	1	2	1	2
Far less	9.8	4.3	12.2	7.0	16.3	20.6	13.5	14.4
Somewhat less	23.3	20.0	20.6	27.2	13.8	15.9	7.9	10.8
About the same	34.6	44.3	20.6	27.2	6.5	21.5	17.5	18.9
Somewhat more	17.3	20.9	29.0	20.2	18.7	16.8	16.7	23.4
Far more	15.0	10.4	17.6	18.4	44.7	25.2	44.4	32.4
As important or more important	66.9	75.6	67.2	65.8	69.9	63.5	78.6	74.7

Empirical research by Marissa Golden suggests wide variation in participation. The number of comments filed on eleven rules she studied ranged from 1 (income eligibility for Department of Housing and Urban Development programs) to 268 (elderly and disabled programs).[63] This is almost certainly true of rulemaking in general. It is characterized by large numbers of rules that generate little interest and a substantial number in which interest is very high. But there is little question that as a function of government, rulemaking commands the attention of interest groups.

Of the groups that responded to our surveys, roughly 80 percent reported that they participate in rulemaking. The first and second surveys show little variation in this figure. The importance the groups attach to this activity compared with other activities is shown in Table 5-1. A large majority of the groups in the more recent survey (75.6 percent) rate involvement in rulemaking on a par with, or of greater importance than, lobbying Congress. This number has increased by nearly nine percentage points between the first and second survey. The data in Table 5-1 indicate that when stalking the corridors, interest groups are in search of rules.[64]

Furlong's research has examined the differences that occur between legislative and executive branch lobbying. Drawing on compliance data required by the Lobbying Disclosure Act of 1995, he found efforts to influence Congress far more numerous than efforts to influence executive branch agencies in their development of rules.[65] Although his research focuses only on written comments—just one form of lobbying—the magnitude of the difference is nearly 5 to 1 in favor of congressional contacts. These results provide a contrast that is not easily explained, but it is possible that some portions of the congressional contacts are intended to activate legislators about a rule under development. We present some evidence supporting this proposition in Chapter 6.

Overall, evidence from case studies, the *Federal Register,* and the survey provide support for the notion that active public participation in rulemaking is real. Although it is not universal and its occurrence depends on the characteristics of the rule being developed, participation is taken seriously by the interest group community. Opportunities to participate that have been developing for nearly one hundred years are being exploited, but by whom?

Who Participates?

The conventional wisdom and some scholarship would lead one to hypothesize that groups representing business interests participate in rulemaking more often than other types of groups. There are at least two reasons why this imbalance in participation is a reasonable expectation. First, business organizations have long been thought to have superior political resources and skills and are thus better positioned to influence a process that requires sophistication and staying power. Second, in an era of big government, the business community has more to lose than other groups—the poor, the elderly, environmentalists, consumers—who are often perceived to be the primary clients of the agencies writing rules. As James Q. Wilson has noted, people are more likely to get involved in politics and government decision making to save something that is threatened than to gain something new.[66] Rules and regulations often restrict the discretion businesses enjoy and impose costs for compliance. Business often has something real at stake when rulemaking is undertaken.

There are, however, reasons to doubt both of these propositions and to take an alternative view. Progress was made in the 1960s and 1970s to facilitate participation by groups that might otherwise lack the money or resources to get involved. In this way Congress, the White House, and the courts moved to offset the traditional advantages enjoyed by business in the rulemaking process. Then, during the Reagan-Bush years, pro-business policies hostile to the traditional clients of many rulemaking agencies gained presidential support, giving nonbusiness groups plenty of good, defensive reasons to participate in rulemaking. Suddenly, they too had a lot at stake. The available evidence, once again, presents a mixed view on who participates.

As noted earlier, Fritschler's study of smoking and politics found evidence of involvement by many types of groups. Business was active in rulemaking, but so too were health and consumer interests. Another study, one that examined effluent guidelines by the EPA, found rulemaking participation by regulated industries far more common than participation by environmental groups. The authors of this study attribute the apparent imbalance to a combination of ingrained bias and tactics. They note that environmental groups perceived the rulemakers in the EPA as kindred spirits who could be trusted to protect their interests. In effect, a different form of "capture" occurred that ensured environmental groups the results they wanted without the burdens of direct participation. Or environmental groups may have concluded that their lack of comment and involvement would expedite the rulemaking process and ultimately lead to more and quicker pollution control than if the EPA had to respond to both industry and environmentalists.[67]

Golden's research lends support to the argument that business interests dominate rulemaking participation. Her study of comments filed in eleven rules in three agencies finds businesses the most frequent participants by far in rules developed by the EPA and the National Highway Traffic Safety Administration, and a mixed pattern in the Department of Housing and Urban Development.[68] Furlong's studies also find that businesses and trade associations are more frequent participants in rulemaking.[69] Sheldon Kamieniecki finds that business interests are more active by percentage in EPA rulemaking compared to natural resource rulemaking, which has more input from citizen organizations.[70] Jason Webb Yackee and Susan Webb Yackee, in a study examining over thirty regulations from four different agencies, find that over 57 percent of the public comments came from business interests.[71]

The *Federal Register* reports on participation in such a way that patterns in participation by certain groups are difficult to discern, and many of the studies above had to rely on docket information in order to determine what types of groups are participating. Frequently, the agencies publishing the final rules focus on the substance of comments rather than the type of group submitting them. When groups are identified, it is often a single, generic reference. Our survey of interest groups provides evidence that participation in rulemaking is not the sole province of business interests, but they are heavily represented.

Data we have collected in our previous surveys suggest that businesses, and the trade associations that represent businesses and professions, are involved in rulemaking more often than are other groups, and they devote to it greater slices of their likely larger budgets and staffs. A strong case can be made that their superior resources and experience lead to a degree of influence in rulemaking that others cannot match. But the data from our surveys are not sufficient to establish such a case. It could be that fewer citizen organizations, a category that includes environmental and consumer groups, are involved in rulemaking because these types of groups specialize more than business groups. But, again, the participation gap appears to have narrowed. Perhaps business and trade associations are so frequently threatened by rulemaking that comparatively few can afford to devote their attention elsewhere. Other data from our survey do indicate that businesses and trade associations are more likely than citizens' groups to rank rulemaking ahead of other forms of political action. Still, is this evidence of their "defensive" posture, or simply greater sophistication? The responses to our surveys do not answer this question.

In his study of safety standards, Cheit also found more frequent and more intense involvement by the regulated industries than by workers and consumers. But he, too, cautions against drawing conclusions from his observations. In several instances consumers were represented in rulemaking proceedings by those acting effectively as surrogates, such as the National Academy of Sciences. Cheit's work also makes it plain that business interests were not monolithic and sometimes disagreed with each other.[72] Golden found the same phenomenon in her study. She notes, "I did not find undue business influence in rules ... in part because businesses did not present a united front."[73] The study of the agricultural marketing order program found substantial participation by producers and handlers of the affected commodities. These groups did not always see eye to eye, either. However, the involvement of the ultimate consumers of the products regulated by the program was nominal at best.[74]

In short, business and nonbusiness organizations have good reasons to invest their time and energy in rulemaking.

Monitoring Rulemaking, Influencing Rules

To succeed in the rulemaking process, interest groups must know what the agency is preparing to do and use the mechanisms at their disposal to influence it. Neither the case study literature nor material found in the *Federal Register* is particularly instructive on the question of how interest groups monitor rulemaking agencies. In the case study literature, authors are generally concerned with the substance of the rulemaking in question rather than the details of how interest groups go about their work. And one would not expect to read about the monitoring behavior of interest groups in the preambles of final rules published in the *Federal Register.*

In our surveys we asked respondents how frequently they used various devices for monitoring rulemaking. It is evident that interest groups use a host of different devices, some more than others. The *Federal Register,* professional newsletters, and networks of colleagues are used often; consultants are relied on infrequently. Of course, it is also important to note that changes and improvements in technology and the ease of access to documents such as the *Federal Register* make it easier for all to monitor rulemaking activity. In her study of sources of information for participants in rulemaking, Golden also found that the most often used sources were the *Federal Register,* trade and professional associations, and informal networks.[75]

Another potential way to monitor agency activities is through the use of the Unified Regulatory Agenda, which tends to focus on significant regulatory actions. The Obama administration is examining ways to make the rulemaking process more transparent and open, and, as stated in a recent report by the Congressional Research Service, the Unified Agenda provides such an opportunity. Importantly, it could alert the public of potential regulatory action prior to the publication of a proposed rule.[76]

Of course, a key issue in participation is the ability of groups to influence rulemaking and how they go about it. Our survey results on these issues (see Table 5-2) are quite interesting for a number of reasons. It is evident that interest groups do not rely on a single method of monitoring; they employ several devices on a regular basis. The same is true of tactics used to influence rulemaking, and, as with monitoring devices, some techniques are more popular than others. Written comments, coalition formation, and contact with the agency both before and after the notice of proposed rulemaking appear to be used most often. More interesting, and potentially significant, are the interest groups' ratings of the effectiveness of the various tactics (see Table 5-3). Here the results are somewhat different from the results on the techniques the groups actually use.

Coalition formation and informal contacts before the notice of proposed rulemaking is issued are perceived to be the most effective, as they were in the first survey. This is also confirmed by William West in his study of forty-two regulations where only six did not have some informal gathering of information.[77] On reflection, these results should not be surprising. Contact with an agency before it has committed itself to a particular proposal allows the interest group to influence the earliest thinking about the content of the rule.[78] Coalition formation increases the number of groups that will communicate a consistent message to an agency. Comments in the *Federal Register* and grassroots mobilization are also viewed as effective. However effective informal contacts may be, groups can ill afford not to put their views on the public record by providing written comments. In the first survey, filing petitions, serving on advisory committees, and participating in public hearings emerged as the least effective, although not entirely useless. In the new survey, attendance at hearings was ranked nearly as high as providing written comments and more effective than grassroots mobilization and informal contact with agencies after notice of proposed rulemaking.

Table 5-2 Devices Employed by Interest Groups to Influence Rules, by Frequency of Use (percentages from surveys 1 and 2)

Frequency	Written comments		Attendance at hearings		Formation of coalitions		Mobilization of grassroots support		Informal contact with agency before notice		Informal contact with agency after notice	
	1	2	1	2	1	2	1	2	1	2	1	2
Never	1.5	5.3	7.0	1.7	3.1	0.9	11.5	10.8	8.4	2.7	4.6	3.6
Sometimes	21.4	39.9	54.3	60.2	35.9	21.2	42.8	55.8	40.4	50.2	40.0	53.8
Frequently	23.7	25.7	23.3	29.2	40.5	50.4	25.2	23.4	21.4	36.6	26.2	25.9
Always	53.4	29.2	15.5	8.8	20.6	27.4	20.6	9.9	29.8	10.7	29.2	17.0

Table 5-3 Ratings by Interest Groups of the Effectiveness of Techniques (percentages from surveys 1 and 2)

Effectiveness	Written comments		Attendance at hearings		Formation of coalitions		Mobilization of grassroots support		Informal contact with agency before notice		Informal contact with agency after notice	
	1	2	1	2	1	2	1	2	1	2	1	2
Least effective	4.6	1.9	12.5	0.9	0.8	0.9	7.8	4.8	6.8	1.9	10.9	4.8
Somewhat effective	11.5	12.4	24.2	16.0	8.5	2.8	17.8	24.0	8.3	8.5	21.1	18.1
Effective	29.8	31.4	30.5	33.0	21.5	15.7	24.8	25.0	13.6	21.7	18.8	35.2
Very effective	38.2	42.9	21.1	31.1	38.5	48.1	34.1	33.7	37.9	42.5	32.8	29.5
Most effective	16.0	11.4	11.7	18.9	30.8	32.4	15.5	12.5	33.3	25.5	16.4	12.4

Nothing in the literature, scholarly or professional, provides an explanation, or even a solid clue, for this change. In the new survey, we probed about techniques that have achieved recent prominence. The respondents reported frequent involvement in policy dialogues and advance notices of proposed rulemaking and rated them effective but not on a par with coalition formation, informal contact with agencies, or written comments on proposed rules. The respondents also rated informal contacts after the notice of proposed rulemaking as effective in both surveys. This may point to situations in which agencies are surprised by the results of public comment and work informally with interest groups to fix the proposed rule.

Recent research by Susan Webb Yackee suggests influence occurs through the traditional notice-and-comment process. Using content analysis to examine what changes occurred between the proposed and final rules, she examines the types of changes requested by different forms of interest groups and whether comments caused the rule changes. The studies find strong support that comments on proposed rules lead to changes in the final rule. She finds comments lead to the degree of government regulation embodied in a rule, and the agencies adopt specific recommendations made by commenters. Yackee notes that agencies are sensitive to the degree of consensus in public comments and are willing to make significant changes in the final rules to respond to interest group comments. In a separate study, Susan and Jason Webb Yackee find evidence to suggest the type of interest matters. Business commenters appear to have more sway over rule content, and as the proportion of their comments increases, so too does their influence.[79] This second study specifically examines more "typical" rules, not highly visible or controversial ones. Examining prominent rules may show more participation from nonbusiness interests.

But there is another, different theme in participation research. Kamieniecki finds that group input has a minimal influence on shaping a final rule regardless of the organizational type. He comments that the content of the proposed rule is "probably a better indicator of the amount of influence business has in the rulemaking process."[80] By this he means the different policy postures of presidential administrations and Congresses (e.g., pro-business, pro-environmental, etc.) drive the content of rules and both the opportunities and challenges of interest groups. Success is easier when a group is supporting an existing agency proposal than when it is attempting to secure change in a proposal that has emerged after months or years of work. This raises important questions about access to the executive branch and in particular the issue of informal communication that occurs between groups and regulatory agencies.[81] A study conducted by William West focuses specifically on the role of pre-proposal participation in rulemaking.

The results of interviews conducted for this study suggest that communication between interest groups and agencies prior to the proposed rulemaking is quite common. Consistent with other research findings, the West study suggests that business interests participate more actively and effectively during the important early stage of rule development. There is substantial variation among agencies West studied in terms of how this participation happens and who it may include, but it is clear that it can have an important effect on rule development.[82] Similarly, in recent case study research Sara Rinfret also finds pre-proposal participation to be an important aspect of interest group participation and potential influence. As she notes from respondents in her interviews, "We have less wiggle room after an NPRM [notice of proposed rulemaking] and we make influence when talking to the agency during rule development."[83]

The West findings, and the others noted earlier, lend additional support and substance to our survey findings regarding the frequency and importance of informal contacts during the proposal development stage of rulemaking. And these informal communications between interest groups and the agencies do not flow in only one direction. Consequently, in our survey when respondents were asked how often, if ever, agencies contacted them during the course of rulemaking, 59 percent (in the 2002 survey) stated that agencies initiated contact with the interest groups. The East West Research Group study cited earlier also finds that agencies will often initiate such contacts in order to collect information and improve their rule development.[84] These results suggest that public participation occurs on a regular basis in rulemaking even when interest groups do not initiate the involvement. It is not surprising that a common reason for these contacts is to get information for the rule under development. Agencies need this kind of help, especially when dealing, as they often do, with production processes and technology or business practices. Some legislation contains specific provisions empowering agencies to collect this type of information. But the data collected in both surveys suggest that agencies are attentive to politics, possible legal challenges, and the conditions they are likely to confront when they attempt to implement and enforce the rule under development. In fact, our data showed substantial increases in the reported frequencies of agencies trying to obtain guidance on rules, a group's reaction to rules, and support. Getting a group's reaction enables an agency to predict the degree of difficulty it will confront if it chooses to move forward with its proposals. Interest groups are not shy about telling agencies when they are unhappy, nor are they loath to threaten political and legal action should the agency proceed on an unacceptable course.

Seeking a group's support is grounded in obvious motives. The later survey also contains evidence of simple outreach by agencies; 54 percent of the respondents indicated that they are at least contacted sometimes by an agency requesting that they participate. But what do agencies think of methods used by interest groups to monitor and influence them? In separate research, Furlong tested the same techniques explored in the surveys done for the book, as well as others, with a sample of officials from federal agencies. He found that the techniques common to all studies ranked in the following ways, in identical descending orders for frequency of use and perceived effectiveness: written comments, public meetings/hearings, informal communication, and grassroots activity.[85]

There are differences in the rank ordering of frequency and effectiveness for those methods and techniques studied by Furlong alone and in our joint work. In his, informal contacts do not rank as high; hearings and written comments rate a bit higher. In general, however, the differences in the results of the two studies with regard to these dimensions are not great. It is important to note that Furlong did find that one means of influence not studied in our two surveys—communicating with congressional committees or staff— rated highly on both frequency of use and effectiveness with agency respondents. Furlong's respondents considered the use of Congress more frequently used than all techniques other than written comments, participation in public meetings, and informal contacts with agency officials. And they found it more influential than all techniques other than written comments and public meetings. We will note in the next chapter how Congress exercises oversight of rulemaking, but the subject of Congress as a direct participant in rulemaking and its ability to exert political influence is a ripe territory for future research.

The multidimensional nature of groups' monitoring and influencing behaviors is striking. Although the frequency of use and perceived effectiveness vary widely, no source of information or technique of influence has been abandoned entirely by interest groups, or dismissed by agencies. The overall approach appears to be both sophisticated and broadly based. The data on the relative effectiveness of influence mechanisms in our studies are especially compelling. They show that informal mechanisms and difficult-to-observe mechanisms for communicating views to agencies are used a great deal and are thought to be as or more effective than the traditional means—such as written comment—that figure so prominently in the procedural law and academic literature on rulemaking. But recent research also suggests that written comments play an important role in influencing rulemakings. It is evident that existing research is not of one voice on the frequency and efficiency of participation, though there is no question it is a force in rulemaking and a major priority of those seeking to influence law and policy. Whatever else, participation is a method for those seeking to influence the rulemaking process, and it can be exercised to full advantage using available technology.

Electronic Rulemaking: Participation Most Modern

President Clinton's National Performance Review supported, and in some instances stimulated, increased use of information technology in all appropriate facets of government activity. It was a cornerstone of his management reform program. In its 1996 report on implementation of the NPR, the White House noted specifically the increasing use of information technology in regulatory programs and processes.[86]

A significant example of early electronic rulemaking (or e-rulemaking) can be found in the work of the Nuclear Regulatory Commission. The NRC began using electronic bulletin boards to collect and supply information on proposed rules to the public in the mid-1990s. Its goal was to make all rulemaking documents, including relevant studies and the text of written comments, available to anyone with access to the database.[87]

Other agencies conducted similar experiments using information technology. Also beginning in the mid-1990s the EPA began accepting public comments on rules using e-mail. It also developed listservs, similar to the interest and expertise caucuses at the NRC, to distribute proposed and final rules and to solicit comments. In another example, the Bureau of Land Management focused its energy on managing rules that prompted voluminous public comments. The bureau used scanning and network database capabilities "to manage the receipt, distribution, and analysis of some 30,000 comments on a rangelands proposed rule and [environmental impact statement]."[88]

With electronic communications spreading so rapidly, controversy over electronic rulemaking is inevitable. Responding to both the pace of change and substantive issues, the Administrative Conference of the United States published a study in 1995 on the use of information technology that focused, in part, on rulemaking. The author, Harry Perritt, concluded that "running a … rulemaking proceeding electronically" would not violate "the basic requirements of the Administrative Procedure Act." If "electronic notices and opportunities to comment electronically … enhance the opportunity for broader segments of the public to know about agency rulemaking proposals and submit their views," Perritt believed, "the purpose of Section 553 will be enhanced by automation."[89] He also recommended that steps be taken to assist those who were not currently able to participate electronically, that care be taken with copyrighted materials that "are provided and shared electronically," and that the equivalents of a rulemaking "chat room" be free of the requirements of the Federal Advisory Committee Act.[90] His overall assessment was positive, and he urged agencies to accelerate the use of the Internet and the World Wide Web in rulemaking.

Agency-based efforts to establish electronic dimensions to rulemaking continued through the later 1990s, but the launch of a broader e-government initiative by President George W. Bush accelerated matters considerably. Contained in the Office of Management and Budget's "E-Government Strategy," published in the *Federal Register* on February 27, 2002, Bush's vision emphasized that "government needs to reform its operations—how it goes about its business and how it treats the people it serves."[91] The Bush administration viewed e-government as a means to make the business of government more "citizen-centered" and efficient. It also led inexorably to a new and more centralized phase for e-rulemaking efforts.

The current state of e-rulemaking was summarized in a report to the president and Congress prepared by the Committee on the Status and Future of e-Rulemaking that operated under the auspices of the American Bar Association. It was endorsed by a wide variety of groups concerned in one way or another with rulemaking. The committee noted that by 2008 e-rulemaking at the federal level consisted of three interrelated elements:

1. The FDMS (Federal Docket Management System) e-docket, an electronic repository for digitized versions of rulemaking documents organized in electronic dockets, with associated document management capabilities;
2. FDMS.gov, a password-protected interface through which agencies access the repository; and
3. Regulations.gov, the public interface through which those outside the federal government access publicly available materials in FDMS and can submit comments on proposed rules.

The committee concluded that "The federal government's eRulemaking Initiative has had significant success. More than 170 different rulemaking entities in 15 Cabinet Departments and some independent regulatory commissions are now using a common database for rulemaking documents, a universal docket management interface, and a single public website for viewing proposed rules and accepting on-line comments."[92]

But the committee also cautioned: "At the same time, much work remains to be done. So far, the Initiative's focus has been largely limited to putting existing notice-and-comment processes online. Even this has not been entirely successful. A number of significant structural and policy issues must be addressed before the full potential of federal e-rulemaking can be realized."[93]

The committee issued recommendations in a number of key areas, including the architecture of the system, funding, decision-making authority, the ability of the public to use the system, and the capacity for diversification and innovation. Among the more notable were calls for a multileveled system of governance committee that included representatives of the various users, a number of actions that could improve the quality and accessibility of information in the system, steps to improve ease and frequency of use by the public, and ideas for promoting the development and use of best practices while exploring promising innovative techniques. The value of deeper involvement with the issues involved in a given rulemaking concerned the committee as well, and it endorsed exploration of a variety of interactive techniques that would promote for extensive give-and-take between and among agencies and participants.[94] The recommendations of the report, if fully implemented, would require a major and long-term commitment by both the new Obama administration and a wide range of external parties, including existing and potential participants in rulemaking, scholars of the process, and practitioners. But skepticism lingers on a very fundamental point. To paraphrase a very familiar line, if they build it, will the public come?

The committee's strong endorsement of the potential of e-rulemaking notwithstanding, at least one of its members has cautioned against excessive exuberance. In 2006 University of Pennsylvania professor Cary Coglianese wrote that the fundamental obstacles in the path of a robust and heavily used e-rulemaking system have little to do with the system itself. Reflecting on the body of scholarship reviewed earlier in this chapter, he finds little evidence that the common man or woman is anything other than a rare participant in rulemaking. He makes the important point that what stands in the way of broader and deeper participation is not so much inadequate technology or opportunity, but knowledge of the importance, content, and process of rulemaking, and a strong motivation to get involved. He notes that while participation may increase due to e-rulemaking, it will be selective.[95] This, again, underscores the role of organized interests and the inevitability that whatever else e-rulemaking does, it will strengthen the already influential players.

We would be remiss if we did not note that there is also a strain in literature that views e-rulemaking as a threat to the ability of agencies to do their work effectively. E-rulemaking raises the specter of vast expansion of the electronic equivalents of form letters and postcard comment campaigns by savvy interest groups. Scholars have cautioned that electronic participation in rulemaking, taken to extremes by groups with narrow agendas, can immobilize rulemakers with huge volumes of comment.[96] Agencies are bound by law to read and respond to the comments they receive. But the advocates for e-rulemaking see hope even here in the development of pattern recognition software that will enable agencies to scan, organize, and respond to large numbers of public comments in an effective and efficient manner.

E-rulemaking is a reality, and there is no question that it will be a very prominent, if not dominant, force in the mechanics of public participation. But, as Coglianese and others have noted, e-rulemaking in itself will not bring people and interests to the table who should be present but are not when agencies write rules. Another innovation in rulemaking seeks to do just those things.

Negotiated Rulemaking: Participation at Its Most Intense

Negotiated rulemaking, or *reg neg,* as it has come to be called, offers the public the most direct and influential role in rulemaking of any reform of the process ever devised. Its origins can be traced back more than seventy years to the Fair Labor Standards Act, which established committees of management, labor, and other interested parties to work cooperatively to make rules that affected wages and other important conditions of work in a variety of sectors and industries. John Dunlop, a Harvard professor of economics and later secretary of labor, proposed in 1975 that rules and regulations affecting the workplace be determined by a consensual process that involved in a direct and substantial way those interested parties that held a stake in their content. Long a prominent theoretician and practitioner of mediation, Dunlop believed that the same general principles that guided collective bargaining for wages and other conditions of employment could be profitably applied to the process of rulemaking.

This fundamental idea began to take more specific shape in the early 1980s as scholars and practitioners began to write about the topic. They set out the rationale for regulatory negotiation, its likely benefits, the conditions for success, and the obstacles to its implementation. The most influential of these writers was Phillip Harter, whose article "Negotiating Regulations," which appeared in the *Georgetown Law Journal* in 1982, is perhaps the most frequently cited and influential exposition of the case for regulatory negotiation.

Harter's argument proceeds from a withering critique of the methods of rulemaking that it would supplant. His survey of contemporary rulemaking found it to be a fundamentally adversarial process in which affected parties jockeyed with each other and with the agency for influence and advantage. The process of developing the information for the content of the rule had become a ritual dance in which the participants staked out extreme positions and offered what they knew selectively to bolster their particular position. Information became distorted, and some participants used the comment process simply as a means of establishing in the rulemaking record a basis for a subsequent lawsuit. A profound "malaise" had settled over this most crucial instrument of government. Much of the blame, Harter believed, could be attributed to a design that separated the interested parties in a rulemaking from each other and the agency through an antiseptic process of written comment or the limited exchanges of a legislative-type hearing or the stylized adversariness of formal rulemaking. Issuance of rules was frequently delayed, their quality often poor. Rules enjoyed little support from key constituencies, implementation was difficult, and compliance was anything but automatic. Involved only remotely in the development of rules, affected parties and interest groups had no stake in their success. Put simply, the legitimacy and authority of rules were undermined because the process used to develop them was flawed.

Harter offered an alternative process, one in which conflict was acknowledged but resolved through face-to-face negotiations. As he put it, "the parties participate directly and immediately in the decision. They share in its development and concur with it rather than 'participate' by submitting information."[97] This approach explicitly altered the role of agency officials by reducing them to the status of participants in the group that would negotiate the content of the regulation.

Harter and other advocates of regulatory negotiation were quick to point out that it was neither feasible nor necessary for many rules. It is unnecessary when there is little controversy associated with the development of a rule. When the course of action is clear and undisputed, or when there is little interest in the result, investment in regulatory negotiation would be frivolous. But, even when the rule and the conflict surrounding it are substantial, there are criteria by which to determine whether regulatory negotiation has a reasonable chance to succeed.

The criteria were drawn from well-developed principles of mediation and bargaining, and from Harter's own experience with the technique. Rules that present conflict over deeply held values are not candidates for negotiation. Sufficient information about the likely effects of a rule is needed so that those who might participate in the negotiation can be identified. Potential parties to the negotiation must be able to perceive gain from the process and must be sure that, with or without their participation, a decision on the rule will be made. The success of negotiated rulemaking depends in large part on the ability to identify and invite to the table all the substantially affected interests. Leaving a critical actor behind exposes the negotiation to legal challenges, undercuts its legitimacy, and reduces the likelihood that the result will be of high quality. Conversely, the list of invited parties should not be too long. As Harter puts it, "Negotiations will clearly not work among an auditorium full of people."[98] The give-and-take of issues and positions can occur only with a limited number of people.

Negotiations must have deadlines. Without them they are subject to manipulation by parties more interested in delay than in results. The parties must agree on what constitutes consensus and, when it occurs, accept the results. Here the role of the agency is critical. In a negotiated rulemaking the agency must maintain a delicate balance. On the one hand, the agency cannot accept a consensus agreement that is illegal, bad public policy, or simply infeasible. On the other hand, the agency cannot walk away from such an agreement solely because it did not achieve all of its preferences. Doing so would alter the negotiation, transforming it into a glorified public hearing or policy dialogue. Finally, negotiated rulemaking requires ground rules that the group will observe during the bargaining session and a neutral, competent convener, preferably skilled in the techniques of mediation. These are essential if the process is to move smoothly and fairly.

What would an agency gain by using negotiated rulemaking instead of conventional rulemaking? In negotiated rulemaking, according to Harter and others, the freer flow of information in the possession of the parties leads to higher-quality results produced in less time than is possible with conventional rulemaking. Even when negotiations do not proceed to a complete and full agreement, the information developed during the bargaining sessions can be put to good use should the rulemaking revert to a more conventional process. The parties, because they have become stakeholders in the rule, will not litigate after the rule is completed, and the perceived legitimacy of the regulation will increase in the eyes of those affected by it. This increase in legitimacy and the understanding of the rule's requirements engendered during the negotiations will speed implementation of its provisions and ostensibly the flow of benefits. The public sector will save money on enforcement costs because the participants in the negotiations will comply with the rule voluntarily and knowledgeably.

These arguments were sufficiently convincing that Congress, prodded by the Administrative Conference of the United States, enacted legislation that endorsed the technique and established principles for its use. It stopped short of mandating the process, but subsequent, more narrowly focused statutes did require agencies to employ it. Several programs in the Department of Education and Nuclear Regulatory Commission rules dealing with use of radioactive isotopes in health care contained such provisions.[99] Whole programs that mimic key features have been adopted. Significant variations on the technique were enacted in the Federal Aviation Administration (FAA) authorizing legislation for creating the Aviation Rulemaking Advisory Committee (ARAC). Composed and convened in the traditional way, the committee would have responsibility for developing FAA regulations in many different areas using the same principles of consensual decision making that form the basis for regulatory negotiation. The plan was that "ARAC ultimately will be the primary source of the FAA's rulemaking program."[100]

The Clinton administration also boosted the program. Bargaining is implicit in the partnerships that President Clinton hoped would drive or replace rulemaking. The administration promoted bargaining between the public and private sectors by means other than general admonitions in the NPR. In 1993, before many of the NPR projects got under way, the president issued a memorandum to all agency heads expressing his support for negotiated rulemaking.[101] More than an expression of support, the memorandum required each agency to select at least one rule scheduled for development that could be written using this device. It also required a detailed explanation if the agency could not come up with such a rule. By the beginning of Clinton's second term, most cabinet-level departments and several independent regulatory commissions had launched one or more negotiated rulemakings.

The theory of negotiated rulemaking is clear, but what has been the actual practice? The Administrative Conference of the United States issued a report in 1990 that described the subject matter of the negotiated rules in eight agencies and summarized how the proceedings were concluded. Of the nineteen negotiations discussed, ten reached final consensus and two did not conclude with an agreement.[102] The remaining were still in process at that time. The agencies reported that despite the lack of consensus, the information developed during negotiations contributed substantially to the rule that was ultimately produced, providing some supporting evidence for at least one claim of the advocates.

Cary Coglianese, writing in the *Duke Law Journal* in 1997, examined the timeliness and litigation experience of rules developed using negotiation. He found that negotiated rulemaking fared poorly on both counts. His data did not support the arguments of proponents that negotiated rules are produced more quickly than are rules developed using conventional procedures.[103] His results challenge those of an earlier and more limited study of four negotiated rulemakings at the EPA by Kerwin and Furlong.[104] He has also questioned the soundness of a process that may compromise the constitutional functions of government and that elevates consensus above other, more fundamental values. He continues to raise these and related concerns, and others continue to express varying degrees of support for the technique.

The most rigorous study of negotiated rulemaking was sponsored by the Administrative Conference of the United States. Laura Langbein and Kerwin examined rules developed using reg neg and compared them with roughly equivalent rules developed using conventional techniques.[105] Negotiated rulemaking fared quite well. Compared with participants in conventional rulemaking, negotiated rulemaking participants gave the process higher marks for the quality of information it generated and the amount they learned. Participants in negotiated rulemaking also reported that their influence on the final rule was greater than that of those who engaged in conventional rulemaking. On a wide range of criteria (economic efficiency, cost effectiveness, compliance, legality, the quality of the overall process, net benefits for the participants' organization, and the participants' personal experience with the rulemaking), negotiated rulemaking received higher ratings than did conventional proceedings. Langbein, in a follow-up to this study, also found that negotiated rules tended to be more responsive than conventional rulemaking. Of course, the question of responsiveness to which interest group must also be addressed. [106]

In another study Langbein and Jody Freeman argue that negotiated rulemaking may also yield what they call a "legitimacy benefit."[107] Interviewees for the Administrative Conference study did note that they had developed a deeper appreciation for the complexities of government decision making and a better understanding of positions taken by persons with different interests. There is no dispute about costs. Negotiated rulemaking is expensive, and the time and resource costs are disproportionately high for small businesses.

Although the Langbein-Kerwin study is based on a survey technique that asked respondents for obviously subjective judgments, it is the most compelling evidence to date that negotiated rulemaking produces, on many fronts, results that are superior to conventional rulemaking and consistent with the theory outlined earlier. While the later Langbein study raises possible concerns of inequity of results between small and big businesses, it is unclear if inequities that occur in negotiated rules are any greater than conventional rulemaking. The arguments for and against negotiated rulemaking are both important and interesting, but the compelling fact is that the actual use of the technique has fallen on very hard times. Even its most ardent supporters must admit that in recent years it has been used far less often than they would have predicted or preferred. Writing recently, Jeffrey Lubbers, a prominent expert on rulemaking, notes its decline in use, which he attributes to a confluence of powerful forces. He cites the demise of the Administrative Conference of the United States (an early and strong institutional supporter), tight agency budgets, opposition or indifference by the leaders of the Office of Information and Regulatory Affairs, the use of somewhat similar but less burdensome methods known collectively as "reg neg lite," skepticism by some scholars, and the constraints of the Federal Advisory Committee Act as combining for what amounts to a perfect storm. Lubbers concludes that without reversal on several of these fronts and a strong boost from Congress, whatever its potential, negotiated rulemaking will have a limited role at best.[108]

Few important rules in the future will be developed without the use of one or more of the features of formal negotiations. Although Harter cautions against undisciplined and uninformed uses of negotiation and mediation in rulemaking, he remains, after twenty-five years, convinced of its value. He views it as an important form of deliberative democracy that transforms but does not diminish the role of agencies. This form of rulemaking is, to Harter and others, a middle course between a system dominated by political power and one that relies ultimately on agencies to make the right decision, even when conditions of great uncertainty prevail.

Does Participation Matter?

In his influential *Harvard Law Review* article titled "The Reformation of American Administrative Law," Richard Stewart argued that "interest representation" was the primary function of our contemporary bureaucracy and the administrative procedures it uses to make decisions.[109] If his analysis is correct, we would expect participation to be the single most important element in rulemaking, for it is through this device that bureaucrats learn what these varied interests want. It is important, then, to learn how agencies act when the preferences of interest groups are revealed. When interests are at odds, some must win and some must lose.

Determining whether interest groups that participate get what they want is an analytical task as difficult as it is important. Much must be known about the law that established the boundaries of the rulemaking, the true preferences of the groups affected, the accuracy of the communication of those preferences to the agency decision makers, and the benefits the rule bestows and the costs it imposes. For each of these dimensions, questions arise: How does the authorizing statute increase or limit the prospects for those who want to participate in the rulemaking? If the law requires agencies to base their rules on rigorous assessments of risk to human health and safety, some of the information needed to conduct such studies will be in the possession of the regulated community. How does this affect interest groups' ability to participate? Harter has argued that the current rulemaking process often leads interests to distort their true positions for strategic purposes.[110]

At the most basic level it is important to learn whether agencies take public participation as seriously as interest groups do. Evidence from all sources, including the research already reviewed earlier in this chapter, indicates clearly that agencies take public comments very seriously indeed. As noted earlier, interest groups believe that their comments, whether in writing or delivered less formally, are effective and that agencies frequently seek out their views and change rules in response to comments. An examination of the *Federal Register* confirms that comments are carefully recorded and agencies respond to their contents in the preambles of final rules. While a review of the *Federal Register* will not answer questions such as the importance of a particular comment to an interest group, or even who is making the comment, it does show that agencies take the comments seriously.

Case studies provide yet another view on the matter. Most case studies deal with rules that have substantial consequences for businesses of one kind or another. Thus, the question they are most likely to address is whether business interests dominate or succeed disproportionately in their efforts to influence rulemaking. The case study literature is instructive, not because it yields an unequivocal answer to this important question but because it demonstrates the complexity of the issue. There are examples of programs that are seemingly dominated by what we would call business interests. One example is the agricultural marketing order program. The analysis of that rulemaking program made it quite clear that the producers and handlers of the regulated agricultural commodities dominated the committees from which the rules originated. But, at the same time, a degree of conflict between these two business interests effectively prevented either of them from dominating the process. Although representatives of consumers were rather few and far between, the Department of Agriculture, which holds the ultimate authority for issuing the marketing orders, served, at least on occasion, as an effective check on those business interests. The dominance of decision-making processes and rulemaking outcomes by business is not apparent in other studies, however. The cigarette labeling case is a prominent example of strong opposition by a powerful industry that was ultimately unsuccessful. Cheit's case studies provide additional examples of business interests faring poorly at the hands of rulemakers. He found that the safety standards that OSHA set for grain elevators were opposed by operators "with vigor."[111] Three different trade associations became involved with the Consumer Product Safety Commission's rule relating to woodstoves, but Cheit found that collectively "they were barely more effective than no association at all."[112] When that same commission issued a rule related to ventilation for gas-fired space heaters, the Gas Appliance Manufacturers' Association immediately petitioned to have it revoked.[113] When the Federal Aviation Administration, reacting to a fire that killed passengers on an Air Canada flight, issued regulations governing fire extinguishers, congressional pressure for action completely eclipsed any influence of the industry.[114] In their study of water pollution rules by the Environmental Protection Agency, Wesley Magat and his colleagues at Resources for the Future found that affected industries commented on the standards far more often than did environmental and other nonbusiness groups. Their comments were usually critical of the rules, but Magat and his colleagues found that they had, at best, limited success in obtaining the changes they desired.[115] In nine of the eleven rules Golden studied, changes occurred between draft and final rules, presumably because of comments.[116] But only one rule "changed a great deal," whereas others had "some" or "minimal" change. Finally, Rinfret's more recent case research did not find significant differences between how industry groups framed issues in their attempt to influence rules pre-proposal compared to other organization types.[117]

Should we conclude from these cases that business lacks influence in the rulemaking process? Certainly not. No easy generalizations about the overall influence of business interests can be drawn from this handful of cases. Case studies, as noted earlier, are often done on rules selected because of their prominence and the controversy that attended their development. In more recent studies discussed earlier, a number of scholars do find not only an increased level of participation at all levels by business but also a bias toward business influence. Business interests may be powerful, but they are not politically omnipotent. More important, the case studies demonstrate that business interests do gain important concessions in rulemaking even when they are not able to achieve all they wanted. The cigarette labeling rule did not, at least when it was first issued, make the warning to consumers as strong as it might have been. The grain elevator rule contained a standard that, although opposed by industry, was eight times less stringent than the most demanding alternative that OSHA had considered. In the matters of the unvented gas space heaters, the trade association representing the manufacturers was ultimately successful in getting the commission's rule revoked, but the manufacturers then faced the uncertainty of regulation at the state and local levels. The gas space heater rule is also interesting because industry itself was split on it. Although the trade association clearly opposed it, "some major retailers saw a clear advantage in federal regulation."[118] What prompted this unexpected support was the fear of what might happen if state or local governments began acting on the issue. Finally, in the case of water quality regulations, the analysts found evidence of success for a portion of the companies studied. It appears from their data that companies represented by large trade associations with plentiful resources obtain somewhat less stringent standards than do other types of firms.[119]

The relationship between rulemaking agencies and business groups differs from program to program and from rule to rule. The variable factors include the discretion the statute being implemented allows; the pressure on the agency from Congress, the White House, and the courts; the quality of information at the agency's disposal and who controls it; the degree to which business groups perceive benefits or costs; the ability of the business community to organize a response to the agency's initiative; and the opposition to the business position from other organized interests.

Before leaving the matter of influence through participation, we should review survey data. Groups who participate in rulemaking do so to get what they want. Success, or the lack of it, will certainly affect future participation. Accordingly, it should be interesting to determine what groups think about their ability to influence the content of rules when they get involved in rulemaking. Respondents were asked how often they achieved what they had set out to achieve. Virtually no group characterized itself as completely successful or unsuccessful. More than 80 percent in the first survey and slightly more in the second considered themselves able to influence rulemaking on a regular basis. This is a very optimistic assessment, and there are several reasons to question these self-evaluations that point to high levels of success. Organizations that represent the interests of their members before the government have clear incentives to present themselves as successful in their efforts. If an organization reported that it lost consistently, the members might wonder about the shrewdness and influence of their Washington representative. If an organization presented itself as the winner in all cases, the members might begin to question the difficulty of the task they were paying to support. Therefore, another perspective on the effectiveness of interest groups is needed. Research by Furlong provides an alternative set of views on the effectiveness of interest group participation in rulemaking.

Instead of asking the groups, Furlong directed the question to the rulemaking agencies. He asked agency respondents to estimate on a scale of 0 (never) to 10 (always) the frequency with which they made changes in rules under development as a result of comments from various types of groups.[120] The results were averaged for each type of organization and are summarized in Table 5-4.

The rulemakers are somewhat less sanguine about the ability of interest groups to influence their decisions than are the groups themselves. The various groups (with the exception of labor unions) differed little with regard to the influence they believed they had with the rulemakers. Of course, the rulemakers' numbers must be considered in light of another kind of potential bias. Agency rulemakers are by now quite sensitive to charges of "unresponsiveness" and "capture" by special interests. Very low or very high scores on Furlong's question could be interpreted as unwillingness to listen to the public or, alternatively, as willingness to serve as a doormat. Curiously, the

Table 5-4 Frequency of Changes by Agencies to Rulemakings Based on
Participation by Interest Groups, by Type of Organization

Type of organization	Average number of changes
Trade association	4.6
Business	4.0
Labor union	2.1
Citizens' group	4.1
Other government agencies	4.7

Source: Scott Furlong, "Interest Group Influence on Regulatory Policy," Ph.D. diss., School of
Public Affairs, American University, 1992.

responses cluster around a midpoint of behavior by agencies, somewhere
between turning a deaf ear to regulated entities and doing whatever it is
that they are told. The evenhandedness suggested in the survey has been
observed in other studies of regulatory decision making as well.[121] Examining
agency responsiveness from another perspective, it is clear that agencies are
definitely interested in what the public has to say prior to the proposal, as
discussed earlier. We also see a level of responsiveness in the reg neg studies.
So is there any reason to believe that agencies would not also take public
comments seriously when crafting a regulation?

The evidence on participation in rulemaking lends support to Stewart's
concept of "interest representation." During the past several decades, the
opportunities to participate have grown and diversified, creating a rulemaking process in which interest groups are major forces. Interest groups are
aware of the importance of rulemaking. They devote resources to it and use
a variety of devices to monitor what rulemakers are doing. Groups employ
numerous tactics to influence the course and outcomes of rulemaking. They
consider themselves quite successful in achieving their objectives. The rulemakers acknowledge their presence, listen attentively to what they have to
say, and are convinced by their arguments with some degree of regularity.
The outcome of each rulemaking is influenced by many variables. Participation
by the public is clearly one of those variables.[122]

Other influences have not yet been discussed. Each of the major
branches of government—Congress, the president, and the judiciary—has
compelling reasons to take an interest in the development of rules. Their
review of rules both during and after they are developed by agencies constitutes another major influence on the rulemaking process. It is to the review
of these three branches that we now turn.

Notes

1. Phillip Harter, "Negotiating Regulations: A Cure for the Malaise," *Georgetown Law Journal* 71 (1982): 17, 31.

2. Ibid., p. 14. See also Glen O. Robinson, *American Bureaucracy* (Ann Arbor: University of Michigan Press, 1991), pp. 128–129.

3. William F. West, "Formal Procedures, Informal Process, Accountability, and Responsiveness in Bureaucratic Policy Making: An Institutional Policy Analysis," *Public Administration Review* 64, no. 1 (2004): 66–88.

4. Mathew D. McCubbins and Thomas Schwartz, "Congressional Oversight Overlooked," *American Political Science Review* 78 (1987): 165; Mathew D. McCubbins, Roger G. Noll, and Barry R. Weingast, "Administrative Procedures as Instruments of Political Control," *Journal of Law, Economics, and Organization* 3 (1987): 243.

5. West, op. cit.

6. Attorney General's Committee on Administrative Procedure, *Administrative Procedure in Government Agencies,* S. Doc. 8, 77th Cong., 1st sess., 1941, p. 103 (hereafter cited as Attorney General's Committee).

7. Ibid., pt. 7, Department of the Interior, p. 66.

8. Ibid., p. 114.

9. Ibid.

10. Ibid., p. 104.

11. Ibid.

12. Ibid.

13. Ibid., p. 105.

14. Ibid., p. 104.

15. Ibid.

16. Ibid., pp. 105–108.

17. Ibid., pp. 108–111.

18. Ibid., p. 110.

19. David Rosenbloom, "Public Law and Regulation," in *Handbook of Public Administration,* ed. Jack Rubin, W. Bartley Hildreth, and Gerald Miller (New York: Marcel Dekker, 1989), p. 556.

20. For interesting perspectives on the notice-and-comment provisions of the Administrative Procedure Act by two men who were deeply involved in the Attorney General's Committee, see Kenneth Culp Davis and Walter Gellhorn, "Present at the Creation: Regulatory Reform before 1946," *Administrative Law Review* 38 (1986): 511–533.

21. Jeffrey Berry, Kent Portney, and Ken Thomson, "Empowering and Involving Citizens," in *Handbook of Public Administration,* ed. James Perry (San Francisco: Jossey-Bass, 1989), p. 209.

22. See, for example, David Mazmanian and Jeanne Neubauer, *Can Organizations Change? Environmental Protection, Citizen Participation, and the Corps of Engineers* (Washington, D.C.: Brookings Institution, 1979).

23. Benjamin Mintz and Nancy Miller, *A Guide to Federal Agency Rulemaking,* 2nd ed. (Washington, D.C.: Administrative Conference of the United States, 1991), pp. 172–173, n. 12.

24. Office of the Chairman, *A Guide to Federal Agency Rulemaking* (Washington, D.C.: Administrative Conference of the United States, 1983), pp. 67–70.

25. Ibid.

26. Ibid.

27. Ibid.

28. Ibid.

29. 5 United States Code 561–670 (hereafter cited as U.S.C.).

30. Public Law 104–121.

31. Thomas Kelly et al., *Final Report of the SBREFA Small Business Advocacy Review Panel for Control of Emissions from Non-Road Diesel Engines* (Washington, D.C.: Environmental Protection Agency, 1997).

32. Jeffrey Lubbers, *A Guide to Federal Agency Rulemaking,* 4th ed. (Chicago: American Bar Association, 2006), p. 181.

33. Office of Management and Budget, *Improving Government Regulations: A Progress Report* (Washington, D.C.: Executive Office of the President, 1979), p. 9.

34. Ibid., pp. 13–15.

35. Ibid., p. 15.

36. Ibid., pp. 15–16.

37. Ibid., p. 16.

38. James Anderson, "Agricultural Marketing Orders and the Process and Politics of Self-Regulation," *Policy Studies Review* 2 (1982): 97–111.

39. Mancur Olson, *The Logic of Collective Action* (New York: Schocken Books, 1965); James Q. Wilson, "The Politics of Regulation," in *The Political Economy,* ed. Thomas Ferguson and Joel Rogers (New York: Sharpe, 1987), pp. 84–88.

40. Office of Management and Budget, *Improving Government Regulations,* p. A6.

41. Ibid., pp. A29–A30.

42. Ibid., p. A45.

43. Ibid.

44. Ibid., p. A55.

45. Ibid., p. A78.

46. Ibid., pp. A78–A79.

47. Ibid., p. A79.

48. Robert Anthony, "Interpretive Rules, Policy Statements, Guidelines, Manuals and the Like—Should Agencies Use Them to Bind the Public?" *Duke Law Journal* 41 (1992): 1131–1384. See also Jeffrey Lubbers, *A Guide to Federal Agency Rulemaking,* 3rd ed. (Chicago: American Bar Association, 1998), pp. 69–74.

49. Jason Webb Yackee and Susan Webb Yackee, "Administrative Procedures and Bureaucratic Performance: Is Federal Rule-making 'Ossified'?" *Journal of Public Administration Research and Theory Advance Access,* June 10, 2009.

50. See U.S. Government, Executive Order 13422, *Federal Register,* January 23, 2007.

51. Berry, Portney, and Thomson, "Empowering and Involving Citizens," pp. 209–210.

52. Theodore Lowi, "Two Roads to Serfdom: Liberalism, Conservatism, and Administrative Power," *American University Law Review* 36 (1987): 295–322.

53. Executive Office of the President, *Regulatory Program of the United States Government* (Washington, D.C.: Government Printing Office, 1991), app. 3.

54. Christine Triano and Nancy Watzman, *All the Vice President's Men: How the Quayle Council on Competitiveness Secretly Undermines Health, Safety, and Environmental Programs* (Washington, D.C.: OMB Watch/Public Citizen, 1991), p. i.

55. Al Gore, *Common Sense Government Works Better and Costs Less: Third Report of the National Performance Review* (Washington, D.C.: National Performance Review, 1996), p. 45.

56. Office of Management and Budget, "Draft Report to Congress on the Costs and Benefits of Regulation," *Federal Register,* March 20, 2002, p. 15017.

57. Ibid., p. 15022.

58. Scott Furlong, "Businesses and the Environment: Influencing Agency Policymaking," in *Business and Environmental Policy,* ed. Michael E. Kraft and Sheldon Kamieniecki (Cambridge, Mass.: MIT Press, 2007).

59. "Federal Regulatory Review" Request for Comments, *Federal Register,* February 26, 2009, p. 8819.

60. In the second survey, we employed a random selection process and achieved a response rate of over 25 percent. In the first survey, the response rate was lower, attributable in part to our attempt to secure responses from the entire interest group population. The distributions in both samples compare favorably with the following study, which remains the benchmark in this type of work: Kay Scholzman and John Tierney, *Organized Interests and American Democracy* (New York: Harper and Row, 1986). The composition of the respondent pool for our survey is similar to that found by these researchers. The studies compare as follows:

Organization type	Study 1 (%)	Study 2 (%)	Scholzman and Tierney study (%)
Trade association	54	46.2	45
Business	11	25.5	21
Labor union	3	0.7	3
Citizens' group	13	5.5	14
Government	2	11.0	3
Research, think tank	3	2.0	NA
Religious	1	NA	NA
Other	13	5.5	13

61. A. Lee Fritschler, *Smoking and Politics,* 4th ed. (Englewood Cliffs, N.J.: Prentice Hall, 1989); Wesley Magat, Alan Krupnick, and Winston Harrington, *Rules in the Making* (Washington, D.C.: Resources for the Future, 1986); Ross Cheit, *Setting Safety Standards: Regulation in the Private and Public Sectors* (Berkeley: University of California Press, 1990); Anderson, "Agricultural Marketing Orders"; Mark Rothstein, "Substantive and Procedural Obstacles to OSHA Rulemaking: Reproductive Hazards as an Example," *Boston College Environmental Affairs Law Review* 12 (1985): 627; William F. West, *Administrative Rulemaking: Politics and Processes* (New York: Greenwood Press, 1985).

62. Juan Lavilla, "The Good Cause Exemption to Notice and Comment Rulemaking Requirements under the Administrative Procedure Act," *Administrative Law Review* 3 (1989): 317; Christopher Mihm, "Regulatory Reform: Prior Reviews of Federal Regulatory Process Initiative Reveal Opportunities for Improvements," GAO-05-939T (Washington, D.C.: July 2005), p. 5; "Federal Rulemaking Agencies Often Published Final Actions Without Proposed Rules," GAO-GGD-98-126 (Washington, D.C.: August 1998).

63. Marissa Golden, "Interest Groups in the Rule-making Process: Who Participates? Whose Voices Get Heard?" *Journal of Public Administration Research and Theory* 8 (April 1998): 252–253.
64. Lowi, "Two Roads to Serfdom," p. 307.
65. Scott Furlong, "Lobbying the Executive Branch: Exploring Interest Group Participation in Executive Policymaking," in *The Interest Group Connection,* 2nd ed., ed. Paul Herrnson, Clyde Wilcox, and Ron Shaiko (Washington, D.C.: CQ Press, 2004).
66. Wilson, "Politics of Regulation," p. 85.
67. Magat, Krupnick, and Harrington, *Rules in the Making,* p. 40.
68. Golden, "Interest Groups in the Rule-making Process," pp. 252–253.
69. Furlong, "Lobbying the Executive Branch," and "Businesses and the Environment: Influencing Agency Policymaking," in *Business and Environmental Policy,* ed. Michael E. Kraft and Sheldon Kamieniecki (Boston: MIT Press, 2007).
70. Sheldon Kamieniecki, *Corporate America and Environmental Policy: How Often Does Business Get Its Way?* (Palo Alto, Calif.: Stanford University Press, 2006).
71. Jason Webb Yackee and Susan Webb Yackee, "A Bias toward Business? Assessing Interest Group Influence on the Bureaucracy," *Journal of Politics* 68, no. 1 (2006): 128–139.
72. Cheit, *Setting Safety Standards,* p. 141.
73. Golden, "Interest Groups in the Rule-making Process," p. 262.
74. Anderson, "Agricultural Marketing Orders."
75. Golden, "Interest Groups in the Rule-making Process," pp. 245–270.
76. Curtis W. Copeland, "Using the Regulatory Agenda to Improve Rulemaking Transparency and Participation," Congressional Research Service (June 29, 2009).
77. West, "Formal Procedures, Informal Process, Accountability, and Responsiveness in Bureaucratic Policy Making."
78. Stephen Breyer, *Regulation and Its Reform* (Cambridge: Harvard University Press, 1982), p. 107.
79. Susan Webb Yackee, "Sweet-Talking the Fourth Branch: The Influence of Interest Group Comments on Federal Agency Rulemaking," *Journal of Public Administration Research and Theory* 16 (January 2006): 103; Yackee and Yackee, "A Bias toward Business," p. 128. For the second study, it is important to note that the authors select rules to study that are purposely considered "everyday business." Rules with a large number of comments that may signify increased levels of controversy or prominence were excluded.
80. Kamieniecki, *Corporate America and Environmental Policy,* p. 133.
81. Ibid.
82. The East West Research Group, George Bush School of Government and Public Service, Texas A&M University, *Outside Participation in the Development of Proposed Rules,* September 26, 2006.
83. Sara Rinfret, "Changing the Rules: Interest Groups and Federal Environmental Rulemaking," Ph.D. diss., Northern Arizona University, August 2009.
84. The East West Research Group, *Outside Participation in the Development of Proposed Rules.*
85. Scott Furlong, "Political Influence on the Bureaucracy: The Bureaucracy Speaks," *Journal of Public Administration Research and Theory* 8 (January 1998): 55.
86. Office of Information and Regulatory Affairs, *More Benefits, Fewer Burdens: Creating a Regulatory System That Works for the American People* (Washington, D.C.: Office of Management and Budget, 1996), pp. 35–38.

87. Office of Nuclear Regulatory Research, *Improvement of the Rulemaking Process* (Rockville, Md.: Nuclear Regulatory Commission, 1998).

88. R. Kelly, "Electronic Rulemaking at Several Agencies," e-mail, December 9, 1994.

89. Harry H. Perritt, *Electronic Dockets: The Use of Information Technology in Rulemaking and Adjudication* (Washington, D.C.: Administrative Conference of the United States, 1995), p. 1.

90. Ibid., p. 2.

91. Executive Office of the President, *E-Government Strategy: Simplified Delivery of Services to Citizens* (Washington, D.C.: Executive Office of the President, 2002), pp. 1–37, www.whitehouse.gov/omb/inforeg/egovstrategy.

92. Committee on the Status and Future of Federal e-Rulemaking, "Achieving the Potential: The Future of Federal e-Rulemaking" (Washington, D.C.: Section of Administrative Law and Regulatory Practice, American Bar Association, 2008), p. 3.

93. Ibid.

94. Ibid., pp. 33–61.

95. Cary Coglianese, "The Internet and Citizen Participation in Rulemaking," *I/S: A Journal of Law and Policy for the Information Society* 1, no. 1 (2004/2005).

96. Jim Rossi, "Participation Run Amok: The Cost of Mass Participation for Deliberative Agency Decision-Making," *Northwestern University Law Review* 92 (1997): 173.

97. Harter, "Negotiating Regulations," p. 28.

98. Ibid., p. 30.

99. David Pritzker and Deborah Dalton, eds., *Negotiated Rulemaking Sourcebook* (Washington, D.C.: Administrative Conference of the United States, 1990), p. 346.

100. Federal Aviation Administration, *Regulatory Course: ARM Presentation* (San Antonio, Texas: FAA, 1992), p. 21.

101. *Public Papers of the Presidents of the United States: William J. Clinton, 1993–2001,* vol. 1 (Washington, D.C.: Government Printing Office, 1995).

102. David Pritzer and Deborah Dalton, eds., "Agency Experience with Negotiated Rulemaking," in *Negotiated Rulemaking Sourcebook* (Washington, D.C.: Administrative Conference of the United States, 1990), pp. 327–344.

103. Cary Coglianese, "Assessing Consensus: The Pressure and Performance of Negotiated Rulemaking," *Duke Law Journal* 6 (1997): 1255–1349.

104. Cornelius M. Kerwin and Scott Furlong, "Time and Rulemaking: An Empirical Test of Theory," *Journal of Public Administration Research and Theory* 2 (1992): 118.

105. Laura Langbein and Cornelius Kerwin, "Regulatory Negotiation: Claims, Counter Claims, and Empirical Evidence," *Journal of Public Administration Research and Theory* 10 (July 2000): 599–632.

106. This study uses the same data as Kerwin and Langbein (1997) and Langbein and Kerwin (2000) and attempts to address some methodological issues of these studies and also examine the issue of inequity that may occur in conventional and negotiated rulemaking process: Laura Langbein, "Responsive Bureaus, Equity, and Regulatory Negotiation: An Empirical View," *Journal of Policy Analysis and Management* 21 (summer 2002): 449.

107. Laura Langbein and Jody Freeman, "Regulatory Negotiation and the Legitimacy Benefit," *New York University Environmental Law Journal* 9 (2000): 60–151.

108. Jeffrey Lubbers, "Achieving Policymaking Consensus: The Unfortunate Waning of Negotiated Rulemaking," *South Texas Law Review* 49 (2008): 987.

109. Richard Stewart, "The Reformation of American Administrative Law," *Harvard Law Review* 88 (1975): 1667–1711.

110. Harter, "Negotiating Regulations," pp. 449–450.

111. Cheit, *Setting Safety Standards,* p. 58.

112. Ibid., p. 110.

113. Ibid., p. 141.

114. Ibid., pp. 71–72.

115. Magat, Krupnick, and Harrington, *Rules in the Making,* pp. 39, 147–148, 157.

116. Golden, "Interest Groups in the Rule-making Process," pp. 259, 260.

117. Rinfret, "Changing the Rules."

118. Cheit, *Setting Safety Standards,* p. 141.

119. Magat, Krupnick, and Harrington, *Rules in the Making,* p. 157.

120. Scott Furlong, "Interest Group Influence on Regulatory Policy," Ph.D. diss., School of Public Affairs, American University, 1992.

121. Terry Moe, "Control and Feedback in Economic Regulation: The Case of the NLRB," *American Political Science Review* 79 (1985): 1094–1116.

122. The East West Research Group, *Outside Participation in the Development of Proposed Rules*; Langbein, "Responsive Bureaus, Equity, and Regulatory Negotiation: An Empirical View."

CHAPTER 6

Oversight of Rulemaking

Holding those who write rules accountable for the decisions they make and the manner in which they make them is critical to the maintenance of our democracy. Earlier we discussed the shaky constitutional status of a governmental process in which unelected public officials formulate law. But the legitimacy of rulemaking is bolstered considerably when the people are secure in the knowledge that rulemaking is being conducted under the close scrutiny of elected officials and judges sworn to uphold the Constitution and laws of the nation. Mechanisms of accountability can ensure that the original intent of congressional statutes is truly reflected in implementing regulations. The will of national majorities, expressed every four years in presidential elections, can be translated into rules if presidents can find means to hold the rulemakers accountable. The judiciary, with whom we entrust the structure and operation of a constitutional democracy, can preserve basic legal principles if given the opportunity to examine the content of rules and the processes by which they are formulated.

This chapter deals with the mechanisms of accountability that the constitutionally established branches of government—Congress, the president, and the judiciary—have developed to keep rulemaking in check. Some of these are quite direct and are familiar even to casual students of government. Others, as recent studies have argued, are more subtle, indirect, implicit, and perhaps more effective. A harder question, which will be explored but not fully answered, is how well these various mechanisms actually function in directing the work of rulemakers. Each of the three branches of government has different objectives when it attempts to influence the course of rulemaking. These differences in perspective and priorities lead to a struggle for control of rulemaking. This contest for supremacy has occasionally erupted in confrontation and conflict between the branches, most often between the president and Congress. But the courts have joined the fray as well, sending messages to rulemakers that at times make it difficult for them to act as the obedient agents of the legislature or executive.

There is more to learn in this interbranch struggle for the hearts and minds of rulemakers than another lesson in petty politics or institutional hubris. This competition has had a profound effect on the rulemaking process and the contents of the rules it produces. More significant, perhaps, is what these conflicts tell us about the status of rulemaking and its importance to the three constitutional branches of government. The resources and ingenuity each branch devotes to the battle for supremacy testify to the centrality of rulemaking in our public policy process. Each branch has acknowledged that its relationship with the rulemaking process can easily slip into one of dominance and dependence. In a very real sense these institutions act to prevent the servant from becoming the master, to prevent what is supposed to be a secondary function from becoming one that overwhelms its constitutionally established powers and authority. Each branch's activities will be considered separately, and a brief section at the end of the chapter will highlight the rivalries, and occasional cooperation, that characterize efforts to hold rulemaking agencies accountable to Congress, the president, and the courts. We begin with the institution in which all rulemaking originates: Congress.

Accountability and Congress

Political scientists who are concerned about the relationship between Congress and the bureaucracy have debated which party in that crucial relationship really exercises control. On one side are scholars like Theodore Lowi and William Niskanen, who view the bureaucracy as dominant, partially because of the authority it has been delegated and partially because bureaucrats are thought to have certain strategic advantages in the relationship. Information about what public programs cost and how they actually work was considered one of the most important of these advantages.[1] It has been a common assertion that oversight of the bureaucracy by Congress is flimsy, nonsystematic, and easily frustrated by canny bureaucrats.

A different perspective is principal-agent theory of legislative-bureaucratic relations.[2] In this model the principals are the elected officials in Congress and the White House; their agents are the public officials and employees who are supposed to be carrying out their wishes—and, by that, ostensibly, the will of the people. Principal-agent theory acknowledges that each side of the relationship has distinctive goals and objectives, responds to different incentives, and has different tools at its disposal. Elected representatives try to stay in office by providing for their constituents, or avoiding blame when they fail to do so. Bureaucrats may be operating from a more complex set of objectives, ranging from the avoidance of work to the pursuit of their own policy agendas. The fundamental issue in principal-agent theory is if and how the former can effectively control the latter.

Scholars have argued that carefully structured administrative procedures and informal oversight are influential and that they are frequently ignored or denigrated by those who have not looked into the matter closely enough.[3] Some would argue that subtle forces are at work in the relationship between Congress and the agencies when the latter perform their most important functions, including rulemaking.[4] These studies admonish scholars to avoid the error that occurs when they assume that because bureaucrats are observed making decisions without any direct input by Congress they enjoy complete or extensive discretion.[5] On the contrary, these scholars focus on a network of subtle but powerful influences emanating from Congress that effectively curtails the exercise of bureaucratic discretion. As Randall Calvert, Mathew McCubbins, and Barry Weingast concluded in a frequently cited article:

> The analyst of agency policymaking must ask why the agency has the particular structure, procedures, jurisdiction, and personnel that it does; why particular leaders are in office at any given time; and what unspoken expectations agency personnel have about the conditions under which their elected overseers might invoke sanctions.[6]

Limiting Delegation

Critics of Congress assail it for not being more specific in the substance of its delegations of authority to implementing departments and agencies. It could, according to these critics, avoid the disingenuousness of complex procedure and exorcise the demons of bureaucratic discretion by simply writing the laws so specifically that no important decisions are left in the hands of rulemakers. David Schoenbrod has taken a view that delegation of responsibility to write rules is an unacceptable perversion of basic democratic principles. He views rulemaking by agencies as a shirking of elected representatives' obligations in a republican form of government.[7] Theodore Lowi, a political scientist and long-standing skeptic of administrative discretion, has expressed preference for legislation that evolves from the general to the increasingly specific.[8] This is, to a large extent, what has happened in many statutes that undergird contemporary social regulation. Many environmental programs, first enacted in the early 1970s, have by now been reauthorized and amended on several different occasions. The statutory bases for clean air and water programs are considerably more detailed today than they were twenty-five years ago, because Congress has specified more fully the substances to be regulated and the techniques by which pollution control is to be achieved.

Despite this constant legislative activity, Congress has not achieved the type of prospective control over the content of rules that would satisfy these critics. The reasons are many: demands from the public for action on an ever-increasing list of problems, the technical and scientific complexity and uncertainty of rules, conflict over rulemaking goals, and the political timidity of elected officials. If Congress is to hold rulemakers in the bureaucracy accountable, it will have to find ways in addition to the "black letter" of its statutes.

Procedural Approaches. As we have seen in earlier chapters, Congress has clearly moved in this direction. Chapter 2 documented the ever-increasing strictures that Congress has placed on the process of rulemaking. These obligations to employ certain procedures for public participation, particular types of analyses as prerequisites for decisions, and specific criteria for establishing standards have grown numerous and influential. There is no question that each additional procedure a rulemaking agency is required to use restricts its freedom of action and causes it to produce information that it must then take into account in formulating the substance of the rule. Social scientists have argued persuasively that these additional procedures are anything but neutral. They assert that in imposing them on rulemakers Congress is not simply seeking some scientifically objective means for establishing a regulation or providing freer access to rulemakers for the general public; the procedural tinkerers in Congress may also be seeking to use process to benefit political interests they are unable or unwilling to identify in the clear language of the statute. As the team of Mathew McCubbins, Roger Noll, and Barry Weingast put it: "Together, the legal constraints imposed by procedures and the incentives created by threat of sanction establish a decision-making environment that stacks the deck in agency policy in favor of constituencies important to political overseers."[9]

Still, we must acknowledge that precious little empirical evidence exists to indicate whether these additional procedures truly restrict rulemaking agencies on a regular basis. Evidence presented or cited in Chapters 3 and 5 call into question the extent to which these additional procedural requirements, including the basic provisions of the Administrative Procedure Act, are actually observed by agencies in many rulemakings. Determining whether procedures that might be intended to rig rules to favor certain interests actually yield such results is an exceedingly difficult task. Given the fact that Congress often hides its intentions behind the twin veils of substantive vagueness and procedural complexity, it may be very hard to determine exactly which interests it was seeking to benefit in the first place. And if and when this detective job is accomplished, the analyst then faces the daunting task of determining which interest(s) won or lost, and to what extent.

Money. The power of the purse as a mechanism of accountability is formidable. Budgets can be used to endow those rulemaking projects that members of Congress want completed and to penalize those agencies that have failed to provide them with the types of rules they prefer. At first blush, it appears that all rulemaking projects are treated with equal amounts of budgeting neglect. Whatever additional funds agencies need to meet new rulemaking obligations in authorizing statutes must be drawn from regular appropriations for program operations. In recent years there has been what amounts to an inverse relationship between the rulemaking responsibilities established in authorizing legislation and the funding provided in appropriations. With record deficits looming, it is unlikely that this general situation will change soon.

Although there is little evidence that Congress uses the budget process in a truly systematic way, disciplined to reward or punish agencies, recent research makes it plain that Congress does use appropriations bills to influence rulemaking.[10] A study conducted by Curtis Copeland of the Congressional Research Service (CRS) found that appropriations bills have been used frequently, over a considerable period of time and in a variety of ways, to both support and suppress rulemaking activities. As noted earlier, these actions by Congress do not qualify as being systematic, or even program-wide, but their collective impact is likely far greater than has been previously noted in the literature. Among the actions found in appropriations bills that are supportive of rulemaking activities are those ordering the initiation of a specific rule or rules and limitations on the use of funding that would delay or otherwise interfere with the development of rules. The use of appropriations language to restrict rulemaking appears more common. Examples include prohibitions on the use of funding for particular classes of rules, such as corporate average fuel economy (CAFE) standards by the Department of Transportation, and for finalization of rules that have reached the proposal stage. The CRS report notes that such restrictions may be single legislative events or be repeated in appropriations for a number of fiscal years. It is interesting to note that in taking action of this sort, Congress appears to be heavily influenced by entreaties from interested parties who question the need or basis for rules, voice a variety of economic concerns, or express worries about "midnight" rules being issued by a lame-duck administration. While this practice remains obscure in the academic literature, it has not escaped the notice of the practitioner and think tank communities who line up for or against the appropriations bill according to their oxen's susceptibility to goring.[11] We can only speculate on the extent to which this powerful and tempting appropriations tool will be used to influence rulemaking in the future. In the appropriations process, Congress may have found a device that will prove more resilient or practical than others that have been tried and abandoned.

Deadlines and Hammers. Another prospective device to limit the discretion of those writing rules is the use of *deadlines* and *hammers*. The term *deadlines* is self-explanatory; *hammers* are provisions in statutes that will take effect on a certain date should the agency fail to issue an alternative regulation. Hammer provisions usually embody regulatory requirements that no one, including Congress, truly prefers. They are used to put pressure on agencies to expedite the rulemaking process. The Resource Conservation and Recovery Act, for example, called for a total ban on land disposal of wastes if the Environmental Protection Agency (EPA) did not produce alternative policies in the form of rules.[12] One can see why the various players involved—the agency, the affected parties, and Congress—might endeavor to make the completion of rules with hammer provisions a high priority.

Threat or not, and with or without accompanying hammer provisions, deadlines have been a popular accountability tool of Congress. As early as twenty years ago it was estimated that Congress had enacted hundreds of statutory deadlines for the EPA alone.[13] The intent and effectiveness of such deadlines have been a matter of considerable discussion. In one very important sense a deadline may be the classic example of Congress's use of an indirect method to achieve a substantive result.

Many have noted that congressional deadlines for rulemaking are often hopelessly unrealistic. One reason is the inertia that attends any function of a large bureaucracy. In addition, rulemaking is an activity that Congress rarely funds at levels commensurate with the magnitude and complexity of the tasks involved. Congress imposes deadlines fully cognizant of the fact that agencies will be unable to meet them or in so doing will almost certainly produce an incomplete or flawed product. If Congress is seeking tactical advantage for a particular set of interests, a missed deadline or a bad rule is a fine outcome indeed. Why? Because these failures of the rulemaking process are subject to nearly immediate and searching judicial review. The current dynamics of such review can lead to situations in which the litigating party, presumably a representative of the group that Congress seeks to benefit, may achieve a highly favorable judicial ruling. Such decisions may effectively position the party bringing the lawsuit to exert a dominating influence over the content of the rule at issue.[14] The looming presence of the judiciary, combined with the unmistakable legislative intent of a fixed deadline, make this device the most powerful, and arguably the most predictable, indirect mechanism of accountability at the disposal of Congress.

Overseeing Rulemaking Performance

The intriguing debate about the extent to which bureaucratic discretion in rulemaking is limited by Congress requires consideration of traditional forms of oversight. "Keeping a watchful eye" is something Congress must do.[15] It has been fashionable to dismiss congressional oversight of administrative agencies as erratic, superficial, politically motivated, and largely ineffective. There is another view of oversight that challenges the implicit assumption that the function must be comprehensive and systematic in order to be meaningful. If we think about it for a moment, comprehensiveness in oversight is a mind-boggling prospect. Congress could do nothing else and still not cover the vast federal establishment in depth and on a regular basis. Expecting a systematic approach, however, is not unreasonable. In fact, there may be a method to what appears unsystematic, if not random.

Mathew McCubbins and Thomas Schwartz distinguish between two types of oversight—*police patrol* and the *fire alarm* variety.[16] *Police patrol* oversight is proactive, with Congress setting its own agenda for programs to review. As such, it would have the characteristics that the earlier critics found so lacking in oversight. *Fire alarm* oversight is a congressional response to a complaint filed by a constituent or other politically significant actor. When the alarm is sounded, Congress responds with one of many possible actions, ranging from a simple inquiry about the issue to a full-blown investigation, replete with hearings preceded by reports by the Government Accountability Office (GAO). Mixed metaphors notwithstanding, appropriations to influence rulemaking as reviewed earlier are excellent examples of the type of rifle shot one would expect in fire alarm oversight. The authors argue that fire alarm oversight is likely to be the most prevalent form because it is the most efficient and effective for individual members of Congress. There are several reasons. First, the mere fact of a complaint provides reason for inquiry, whereas a general police patrol may turn up nothing of concern. Second, the fire alarm type is really a hybrid of oversight and constituency service, an activity of compelling and enduring attractiveness to elected representatives. Finally, fire alarms can accumulate and provide Congress with good reasons to initiate oversight that more closely resembles the police patrol model; whole programs of rulemaking, rather than a single rule, then become the focus of the inquiry.

Case studies and general assessments of oversight suggest both the fire alarm and police patrol models of oversight are at work in rulemaking. In his book *Signals from the Hill,* an award-winning analysis of congressional oversight of regulatory programs, Christopher Foreman lists these activities of the committees overseeing the Food and Drug Administration:

- examine and pursue an "orphan-drug" program;
- take more effective action against pesticide residues on imported foods;
- delay action to ban the sugar substitute saccharin, "notwithstanding any other provision of law";
- study ways to expedite the approval of veterinary drugs for use in minor species;
- exercise caution in changing food labeling regulations;
- require the baby food industry "to monitor and report heavy metal content—with particular emphasis on lead—of the food as it is received and after it is packaged."[17]

In his book *Keeping a Watchful Eye: The Politics of Congressional Oversight,* Joel Aberbach surveyed congressional staff and, among other things, asked them to identify and rank in order of frequency and effectiveness various oversight mechanisms (see Table 6-1).

Striking in these data was the fact that the oversight of regulations ranks relatively low in both frequency and oversight effectiveness. It is also quite possible, if not probable, that the issue that triggers many of the other forms of oversight is a rule or a rulemaking. No systematic analysis of these potential interactions is available, however.

Legislative Veto

The legislative veto was once the most aggressive, intrusive, and potentially effective means of holding rulemakers accountable. Beginning in the 1930s, statutory provisions required government agencies to submit proposed rules to Congress for review and approval. At the peak of use of the legislative veto, some 350 separate statutory provisions allowed for this oversight mechanism.[18] Like the overall incidence of oversight, the use of legislative veto provisions increased the most during the period in which we experienced major increases in rulemaking: the New Deal and the subsequent years up through the 1970s, with the attendant explosion of social regulation (see Table 6-2).

Legislative veto provisions were richly varied in their form. Some called for congressional approval, others disapproval. Some vested power for action with both houses of Congress, others in just one, and still others granted authority to committees. The legislative veto combined elements of the police patrol and fire alarm models of oversight. Because legislative veto

TABLE 6-1 Frequency and Effectiveness of Oversight Techniques, Ninety-fifth Congress

Technique	Mean		Number of cases		Rank	
	Freq.	Effec.	Freq.	Effec.	Freq.	Effec.
Staff communication with agency personnel	1.274	1.430	91	86	1	1
Member communication with agency personnel	2.802	1.626	86	83	9	2
Oversight hearings	2.561	1.714	89	84	3	4
Program reauthorization hearings	2.685	1.688	73	61	5	3
Hearings on bills to amend ongoing programs	2.756	1.750	70	60	7	5
Review of casework	3.551	2.694	87	72	13	14
Staff investigations and field studies (other than for preparation of hearings)	2.644	1.780	90	82	4	6
Analysis of proposed agency rules and regulations	2.800	2.279	90	86	8	10
Agency reports required by Congress	2.813	2.534	91	86	10	12
Program evaluations done by congressional support agencies	2.382	2.000	89	88	2	8
Program evaluations done by the agencies	2.954	2.541	87	85	11	13
Program evaluations done by "outsiders" (nongovernmental personnel)	3.227	2.523	88	84	12	11
Program evaluations done by committee staff personnel	2.696	1.891	89	83	6	7
Legislative veto	4.304	2.085	82	35	14	9

Source: Adapted from Joel Aberbach, *Keeping a Watchful Eye: The Politics of Congressional Oversight* (Washington, D.C.: Brookings Institution, 1990), pp. 132, 135.

provisions were directed at whole programs of rulemaking and were generally comprehensive in their scope, the police patrol model applied. But the mere existence of legislative veto provisions does not mean they were used. A fire alarm pulled by an interest group or a constituent could focus the power of the veto on a single rulemaking and stimulate members of Congress to invoke its authority.

TABLE 6-2 Legislative Vetoes Passed by Congress, by Decade

Decade	Number of acts	Number of provisions	Percentage increase in provisions over preceding decade
1932–1939	5	6	—
1940–1949	19	20	230
1950–1959	34	36	80
1960–1969	49	70	94
1970–1980	248	423	507

Source: Barbara Craig, *The Legislative Veto: Congressional Control of Regulation* (Boulder, Colo.: Westview Press, 1983), p. 27.

Christopher Foreman's case studies provided insights into the dynamics of the legislative veto. He examined two separate rules issued by the National Highway Transportation Safety Administration dealing with automobile passenger safety, two considered by the Federal Trade Commission covering used cars and the funeral industry, and the so-called saccharin ban considered by the Food and Drug Administration. In these cases Foreman concluded that the political salience of the issue and the relative power of affected interests were more influential than any general element in the relationship between rulemaking agencies and Congress.[19] Foreman also observed: "A fundamental point to remember in all the legislative veto cases considered is that such cases are rare."[20] We might be distressed by such a finding, but we should not be surprised.

It is curious that a mechanism so popular with Congress in the abstract would be practiced so infrequently. But that was the pattern with the congressional veto until it was invalidated by the Supreme Court in the landmark case of *Immigration and Naturalization Service v. Chadha* in 1983.[21] More than a decade later Congress revised the concept of rule invalidation, but with even less impressive results. Like many other forms of oversight, the threat of sanction is more efficient and likely to be as effective as the sanction itself.

Congress revived the legislative veto concept in 1995 when it instituted "Corrections Day." Using expedited procedures, Congress can enact legislation to correct a clear error in existing law or regulation with a statute that must be signed into law by the president. This innovation has been used sparingly, but largely successfully. Between 1995 and early 1997, Congress had enacted two dozen proposals, and only one was vetoed by the president. In the majority of cases, the action deemed needed under the

Corrections Calendar was not a repeal or revision of a rule but of a statutory provision.[22]

In 1996 Congress passed another bill to hold those who write rules accountable. Under the Small Business Regulatory Enforcement Fairness Act, all new final rules must be submitted to both houses of Congress and to the GAO. The Office of Information and Regulatory Affairs (OIRA) in the Office of Management and Budget (OMB) determines whether the new rule is "major." If it is, the rule cannot take effect for at least sixty days. This gives Congress time to take expedited action, not unlike the Corrections Day procedure, to disapprove the rule. The GAO provides Congress an analysis that establishes whether the process used to develop the rule met all applicable procedural standards. Under the Congressional Review Act (CRA) Congress is empowered to disapprove any rule using an expedited legislative process. This was, in effect, the revival of the legislative veto without the constitutional disabilities that led to the *Chadha* decision more than a decade before. But now, more than a decade later, Congress has been less than aggressive in using the powers of the CRA. According to a report issued by the Congressional Research Service in 2008, since enactment of the statute there have been 47,560 major and nonmajor rules referred to the GAO by government agencies. Of these, only 47 have stimulated the introduction of joint resolutions of disapproval in Congress, and of those 47 only one has actually been enacted and resulted in the elimination of a regulation[23] The one example where the CRA was used successfully is telling as to why there has only been one case. The OSHA Ergonomic Rule was passed as a midnight regulation in the final month of the Clinton administration. Upon George W. Bush taking office, the Republican-controlled Congress passed a joint resolution rescinding the rule, and President Bush signed it. Unless an agency acted truly independently or new information became available, this is likely one of the only reasons why such a rescission could occur. It would be unlikely for an agency to go forward with such a major and controversial rule unless the sitting president approved. A successful situation would almost have to call for a change in party control in the White House, as well as for unified party control in Congress. Again, one cannot judge the deterrent effects of the statute, but given the virtual absence of credible threat, they would not appear to be great.

In sum, there are many tools at the disposal of a Congress that seeks to influence the results of rulemaking. Of those reviewed, the "rifle shots" of appropriations riders and informal contact with agency rulemakers would appear to merit additional research.

Also revealing about the extent of concern by Congress is the large inventory of reports on rulemaking provided to Congress by the Government

Accountability Office. The GAO has occasionally supported congressional oversight investigations of rulemaking across the government. Among the concerns of Congress when taking on systemic issues are delay in the issuance of rules, implementation of broad reforms, and general requirements such as the Paperwork Reduction Act or Regulatory Flexibility Act.[24] There are also hundreds of reports focusing narrowly on particular agencies and on individual rulemaking programs or rules.[25]

Of all the levers of influence at the disposal of Congress, one of the most obvious is direct communication with an agency about a rule under development. Given the fact that Congress clearly pays attention to rulemaking during the appropriations process—or at least receives regular reports from the GAO on various rulemaking activities, and conducts oversight—it is reasonable to assume that contacts with agencies during the development of individual rules is common. There is fragmentary evidence in the rulemaking literature that supports this proposition, but nothing approaching definitive research has yet been done. Nevertheless, such contact is a natural extension of the casework responsibilities of individual members of Congress or the interactions with interest groups that occur at the subcommittee or committee levels. And it is reasonable to assume that when individual members of Congress speak on pending rules, particularly those who sit on a given agency's authorizing or appropriating bodies, they are heard. A sweeping conclusion as to their influence awaits more substantial scholarship.

Accountability to the President

Chapter 4 introduced presidential review of proposed and final rules. Although management of rulemaking out of the White House was discussed as a direct means of ensuring accountability, we did not explore many of the nuances of the president's involvement or the actual effects of such intervention. Those are the foci of this section.

Objectives

There is more than ample justification for the president to be involved in overseeing those who write rules. Presidents are elected by all the people and can boast a mandate different from that of members of Congress. A president's perspective is broader than that of the subcommittees and committees where legislation originates and develops. If public policy is to be truly managed, the president is the most likely candidate for the job. But this "coordination ... on a grand scale" is severely limited by the paucity and poor quality of information about the effects of policy on society as a whole.[26] What can and now does occur is a much less ambitious but still important form of oversight based on clearly articulated principles and fixed procedures.

Just as congressional influence begins with the act of writing authorizing legislation, the president has a seminal moment in exercising executive control of the rulemaking process. Presidential signing statements are, as the name suggests, documents issued when the chief executive signs legislation and thus makes it law. They contain the president's interpretation of his obligations under the new statute and have been a part of the lawmaking process for a long time. Lately, however, their use has increased and become highly controversial; presidents have used the statements to, in effect, direct their administrations to ignore key provisions of new laws or approach their implementation in ways viewed as contrary to congressional intent.[27]

Obviously, signing statements that order such actions have a profound effect on rulemaking since they may prevent the development of some rules that might otherwise be undertaken and send others in a direction acceptable to the White House but not Congress. The purpose here is not to review the interesting and important debate about signing statements. Since no systematic research currently exists on the actual effects of signing statements on rulemaking, we simply note that they are a potentially important element of the president's oversight program.

Presidents since Richard Nixon have become increasingly involved with the rulemaking process. Through evolutionary steps, presidents have come to focus their attention on rulemaking as the most promising way to channel or curtail regulation. Since the Carter administration, each president has articulated a set of principles, often in the form of an executive order, that has become the basis for review of individual rules by White House staff. Two general purposes have been articulated for the review of individual rules. The first is to link individual acts of rulemaking to the broader mandate a given president perceives for himself. Another is to resolve conflicts and inconsistencies in rules written by different agencies.

A now classic example of conflict between the rules issued by the Occupational Safety and Health Administration (OSHA) and the Department of Agriculture dealt with the condition of floors in meatpacking houses. The former called for floors to be dry at all times to protect the safety of workers; the latter called for floors to be hosed regularly to protect the purity of the meat. The Department of Agriculture and the Federal Trade Commission were once locked in a protracted dispute over the contents of labels on foods. And there is the already noted problem of varying the levels of acceptable risk that are allowed under different environmental, health, and safety laws. Some agencies fix the acceptable level at one death per hundred thousand people, whereas others fix it at one death per million. Clearly, the president can play a role in the resolution of such conflicts, but their origins frequently can be traced to statutes that provide inconsistent guidance on the same general topic to different agencies. The president can force a resolution of these situations when agencies have the discretion to interpret the statutory provisions that are causing the conflict. But when the statutes are explicit or appear strongly to support different interpretations, the president's prerogatives will be more limited or more controversial.

Accountability through Review: The Reagan/Bush Program

The review of rules based on policy principles outlined in executive orders has proven considerably more controversial than presidential involvement to eliminate conflict and inconsistency. It has also proven far more common. For example, President Jimmy Carter articulated principles that emphasized rational decision making, sound management practices, and involvement of the public during the course of rulemaking. Ronald Reagan and George H. W. Bush's principles also stressed rational decision making in the form of cost-benefit analysis, and Reagan's program emphasized reducing the burden of regulation on business. Critics viewed this latter criterion as simply an attempt to reward an important constituency, which led to charges that the review of individual rules was being carried out solely to cut back programs of social regulation. The debate about the Republican president's program continues on several levels to this day, so it is useful to review its actual results.

Table 6-3 shows the number of reviews and types of actions taken by the OMB on agency rules from the inception of the program in 1981 through 2009. The data from the Reagan and Bush years provide insights into their oversight process, yet they also raise intriguing questions. During the 1980s the percentage of rules approved without change declined. With this information in hand, we should not find it surprising that the frequency of changes in rules as a result of OMB review increased by approximately the same amount. We can also see that the numbers for rules returned for reconsideration or withdrawn by the agency, which are the most extreme results of presidential review, are stable throughout the 1980s and quite small.

These data can be interpreted in several ways. By and large, the White House agrees with the results of agencies' rulemaking efforts. At their least successful, agencies were still obtaining approval of rules without change in more than 70 percent of the cases until 1991. But this also means that in the best years—during the early 1980s, when Reagan's review program was still relatively new—several hundred rules submitted to the OMB required change. It is also interesting to note the steady decline in the performance of

Table 6-3 Types of Actions Taken by the OMB on Agency Rules, 1981–2009

Percentage of rules reviewed by the OMB

OMB Action	1981	1982	1983	1984	1985	1986	1987	1988	1989	1990	1991
Approved without change	87.3	84.1	82.3	78.0	70.7	68.3	70.5	70.9	73.8	71.8	63.2
Approved with change	4.9	10.3	12.7	15.1	23.1	22.9	23.7	21.9	19.4	19.3	27.1
Withdrawn by agency	1.8	1.2	1.6	2.4	3.1	2.8	2.5	2.4	2.7	2.5	2.8
Returned to agency for reconsideration	1.6	2.1	1.3	2.7	1.5	1.4	0.4	1.2	1.3	1.0	1.1
Total*	95.6	97.9	97.9	98.2	98.4	95.4	97.1	96.4	97.2	94.6	94.2

	1992	1993	1994	1995	1996	1997	1998	1999	2000	2001	2002
Approved without change	64.7	67.4	53.4	53.2	41.4	37.5	36.1	31.5	34.3	28.1	31.7
Approved with change	25.8	23.4	37.3	39.1	51.5	56.0	59.3	62.2	60.4	45.6	54.2
Withdrawn by agency	4.6	6.0	4.3	4.9	5.1	5.2	3.1	3.1	3.9	22.0	7.6
Returned to agency for reconsideration	0.4	0.4	0.0	0.5	0.0	0.8	0.0	0.0	0.0	2.6	0.8
Total*	95.5	97.2	95.0	97.7	98.0	99.5	98.5	96.8	98.6	98.3	94.3

	2003	2004	2005	2006	2007	2008	2009
Approved without change	30.3	29.8	27.0	26.5	21.0	23.4	17.1
Approved with change	60.3	62.7	65.5	69.1	72.3	69.8	71.6
Withdrawn by agency	6.8	6.5	6.5	3.6	6.3	5.6	10.4
Returned to agency for reconsideration	0.3	0.2	0.2	0.0	0.2	0.3	0.5
Total*	97.7	99.2	99.2	99.2	99.8	99.1	99.6

Source: Executive Office of the President, Office of Management and Budget, www.whitehouse.gov/omb/inforeg/concluded_executive_orders.html.

*Percentages may not add up to 100.0 percent due to rounding.

agencies in relation to OMB standards during the first six years of the program and its stabilization at about 70 percent.

The results of White House review for individual rulemaking agencies vary considerably. The rules that were changed by the agencies in question or that were subject to more serious actions by the OMB cover an enormous range of subject matter. These aggregate data do not allow us to probe the type of change that OMB review induced. There is certainly some evidence that the White House review programs focused more heavily on agencies with programs that an administration views with considerable suspicion.

In 1988 and 1989, for example, the EPA and the Departments of Housing and Urban Development, Education, Labor, and Health and Human Services all experienced comparatively high rates of changes in the rules they submitted for OMB review. Each of these departments housed programs that the Reagan administration criticized and, in one instance (a program in the Department of Education), vowed to abolish. Some critics have charged that the OMB review singled out important forms of social regulation for especially harsh treatment. Harold Bruff, professor of law at the University of Texas, analyzed in detail two cases, one at the EPA and the other at OSHA.[28] Under heavy pressure from the OMB, the EPA withdrew two proposed regulations in the mid-1980s that would have imposed stringent controls on the production and use of asbestos. OMB officials took the position that the EPA should defer to other agencies for the regulation of asbestos. Ironically, when another agency did regulate asbestos, the resultant rule was stricter than the EPA proposal.

The OMB also thwarted efforts by OSHA to regulate workers' exposure to ethylene oxide, a chemical used to sterilize hospital equipment. In this case a proposed rule that fixed short-term exposure limits was forwarded to the OMB for review. The office responded the next day with a detailed analysis of the regulation, stating that in its current form it did not meet the cost-effectiveness criteria established by President Reagan. One day after receiving the OMB response, OSHA forwarded an amended rule to the *Federal Register* simply deleting the sections related to short-term exposure limits. OSHA admitted in a subsequent lawsuit that it had changed the rule primarily because of the OMB's response to the draft. Others point out that the speed of the OMB critique and its detail make it plain that the office had been in contact with the agency well before the date that the proposed rule was forwarded for White House review.

A highly visible instance of White House intervention involved the Council on Competitiveness, chaired by Vice President Dan Quayle. The council effectively vetoed an EPA regulation that would require polluting firms to inform the public whenever their discharges exceeded the limits established in clean air regulations. Unlike the previous examples of White

House intervention, this was not a case in which the agency's leadership openly cooperated with the White House or tacitly accepted its position. The EPA leadership fought and lost.[29] These examples should not be viewed as definitive but are intended to demonstrate how the power of regulatory review can be exercised.

Selectivity in Review: The Clinton Program

The changes President Clinton ordered in the OMB review program were dramatic. Compared with the Reagan/Bush approach to OMB review of agency rulemaking, the Clinton administration's approach was more selective. Under Executive Order 12866 agencies submitted to OMB rules under development that they considered "significant," and after discussions with the OMB some or all would be reviewed. The criteria for determining whether a rule was significant were broad, but the number of rules reviewed by the OMB declined considerably. The OMB devoted more time to the rules it did review than it had during the presidencies of Reagan and Bush.

In 1994, the first year of Clinton's program, the number of rules reviewed declined more than 50 percent from the level established in 1992, and in 1997 the number was less than one quarter of that figure. More time per rule increased the impact by the president on rulemaking. During the last year of the George H. W. Bush administration, some 64.7 percent of the rules reviewed were approved without change, and the figure remained at roughly that level in the first year of the Clinton administration. During 1994, however, the percentage of rules approved without change dropped to 53.4 percent and in 1997 declined to only 37.5 percent.

Care must be taken when making direct comparisons of the approval statistics in two so dissimilar programs. For example, many of the rules approved during the Reagan and Bush years might not have been considered "significant" under Clinton's OMB. Nevertheless, in 1997 considerably fewer than half of the rules escaped without a change presumably induced by OMB staff. At the very least, this suggests that the screening process predicted with considerable accuracy those rules that required modification in order to be consistent with President Clinton's stated policies. It suggests further that OMB review evolved into a more refined tool for ensuring accountability to the president.

Presidential Review Broadened and Deepened: George W. Bush

The Clinton administration celebrated the election of George W. Bush with an ethusiastic acceleration of rulemaking designed to push still-incomplete policies into law. The action was hardly novel, but the response of the new president was distinctive. The Bush II administration responded with a directive, since known as the Card memorandum, in which the White House chief of staff, Andrew H. Card Jr., directed agency leaders to delay the effective dates of rules that had already been published in the *Federal Register* and to withdraw any that had been forwarded to the OMB for review. The purpose was as obvious as the reaction of loyal Democrats was predictable. The Bush appointees sought to ensure that the "midnight" actions of the Clinton administration did not limit their prerogatives or options. Bush's directive affected a large number of Clinton's late-term rules.

Moving beyond this initial action, in a relatively short period of time the new Bush administration proved to be the most sophisticated yet in the approach to presidential management of rulemaking. Rather than trigger more controversy and possible lawsuits, Bush initially decided against a new executive order and chose to continue to operate under the general provisions of Clinton's Executive Order 12866. The Bush team did issue various sorts of directives to agencies that guided their submissions to the OMB. Among them were information requirements that agencies were to meet when submitting rules for OMB consideration and a general set of policies designed to improve the quality of information used in government decision making that was actually prompted by congressional actions described earlier in this chapter. The question of information quality emerged quietly and strongly; agencies were expected to develop subject-specific standards in response to the OMB's general policies. It was also evident that the OMB and its OIRA were concerned with the validity and reliability of regulatory impact analyses that were to accompany rules determined to be economically significant. OIRA officials cautioned, however, that it would be a mistake to presume that the sole or even chief concerns of the Bush administration's analytical programs were economic. They noted an increased emphasis on risk analysis, particularly as it informs the rulemaking that affects vulnerable subpopulations, and on using the tools of political and decision sciences that assist in making determinations under conditions of uncertainty. These are indications that during the preceding twenty years presidential management of rulemaking through OIRA review had become far more sophisticated and diversified, and there are others.

The Bush administration demonstrated early that it would be more proactive and perhaps less informal and conciliatory with rulemaking agencies. It revived the "return letter," a device established in the Clinton executive order but little used. Return letters were devices that both rejected agency submissions and did so in a way that asserted the independent authority of OIRA. In addition to transmitting a given rule back to the agency or origin, the letters also specified what agencies needed to do to win OMB approval.

We can see in Table 6-3 that the first year of George W. Bush's administration saw a higher percentage of rules returned to agencies than any since the earliest and most aggressive Reagan years.

An innovation of the Bush team was the "prompt letter," a device that allowed the OMB to assume a role different from "Dr. No." The prompt letters identified areas where rulemaking could produce beneficial regulatory results. Of the first five prompt letters sent to agencies the issues ranged from the risks of trans-fats to the benefits of defibrillators in the workplace and the harm caused by types of frontal collisions in cars and light trucks.[30] OIRA also noted that its experience with prompt letters suggests that preliminary consultations with agencies prior to their issuance could be of value, suggesting that a rigid attitude toward informal agreements with agencies is not likely.

The administration also invited the public to recommend existing rules for review, change, or elimination. Following a notice in the *Federal Register,* the OMB received seventy-one nominations for rules to be reviewed and roughly half received active attention from the agencies affected. It is also interesting to note that the seventy-one recommendations came from thirty-three separate commentators. The administration conducted studies on roughly one third of the recommended rules. More than half of the recommendations came from the Mercatus Center at George Mason University, a conservative research organization that has long been active in regulatory analysis and advocacy for less burdensome and intrusive means to accomplish public policy objectives. The concentration of comments from a single source, combined with the administration's avowed commitment to broad participation in such initiatives, prompted efforts to bring groups with other points of view to the table. This reaction to the first call for review of existing regulations prompted several strong public pronouncements on the question of transparency in decision making at the OMB and OIRA. In addition to adhering to the principles and practices adopted by previous administrations, the OMB took other steps. It made available on the OIRA Web site all directives and policies; information on meetings; written correspondence; and prompt, return, and post-clearance letters.

Obama's Program

Like a number of presidents before him, Barack Obama assumed office with a different regulatory perspective than his predecessor. As noted earlier, it has become common for agencies to attempt to push through regulations before the new president comes on board. President Obama, like President Bush before him, also asked the regulatory agencies to put a freeze on all regulations that were in the pipeline and to consider regulations finalized in the final days of the Bush administration but not yet implemented. The moratorium came in the form of a January 20, 2009, letter from Chief of Staff Rahm Emanuel to all agency heads stating that the new president's appointees should have the ability to review these actions.[31] The political rationale for this is clear. A new Democratic administration may have very different perspectives regarding these regulations than the outgoing Republican administration, and the president was using his executive authority to take the opportunity to evaluate, change, or cancel these policies.

The first year of the Obama administration saw the lowest level of approval without change in the history of presidential review of rules. This should not be particularly surprising in light of the sharp policy differences between President Obama and his predecessor. It would be reasonable to expect this number to increase somewhat as the White House tightens its grip on its departments and agencies.

The OMB and Delay

Another dimension of White House review is the time it takes. Courts have insisted that White House review be conducted so that statutory deadlines for issuing rules are met. Beyond this, the Reagan executive order establishing OMB review set time periods for review of proposed and final rules at sixty and thirty days, respectively. Clinton's Executive Order 12866 set a ninety-day limit for all rules unless the action had already been reviewed by the OMB, and there had been no subsequent changes. For these rules the review time dropped to forty-five days.

Table 6-4 summarizes the review-time performance of the presidents from Reagan through Obama. While there were some notable exceptions during the Bush II administration, the OMB has, on average, complied with the review-time provisions of the executive orders. Nevertheless, these average figures obscure a large number of cases in which the OMB held proposed or final rules for long periods of time. During the Reagan administration, the average review time for Department of Labor rules was nearly twice that called for in Executive Order 12291. And there have been persistent complaints that rules of other agencies of social regulation, notably the EPA, have been stalled at the OMB.[32] The Obama administration has gotten off to a strong overall start on review times.

Long-delayed rules usually impose substantial compliance costs on the private sector. Obviously, the longer the delay in the issuance of the rule, the longer the period of relief from compliance costs for the affected sector or industry. Also, the passage of time brings a change in agency priorities or

Table 6-4 Average Review Times by the Office of Information and
Regulatory Affairs (in days)

President	Economically significant	Other
Reagan	34	18
Bush I	51	29
Clinton	45	43
Bush II	43	57
Obama	33	40

Source: Office of Management and Budget, Office of Information and Regulatory Affairs, www
.reginfo.gov/do/eoCountsSearchInit?action=init.

in external pressure for the issuance of the regulation, leading to abandon-
ment or formal postponement of the rulemaking. Hence, review time is an
apparently passive but actually potent dimension of the White House review
program.

The OMB and the Agencies

The relationship between the White House and rulemaking agencies is complex and variable. Even more than Congress, the agencies have what appear
to be significant advantages in their relationship with White House overseers.
The agencies have greater expertise and vastly superior numbers of staff
when compared with OIRA, the arm of the OMB that conducts rulemaking
reviews. The OIRA staff members who are actively engaged in the review
process number no more than a few dozen, and have educational backgrounds in general policy analysis rather than the scientific and technical
subjects that lie at the base of so much contemporary rulemaking.[33] But as a
counterweight to this mismatch of resources and expertise, the OMB possesses many advantages: some depend on the relationships between career
staff and political appointees in the agencies that write rules; others relate to
the position and powers of the OMB.

Harold Bruff, writing at a time when OMB and agency relations were
particularly contentious, noted four advantages that the OMB enjoys in the
review process. First, "the power of persuasion 'depends on' the cogency
of its positions and the power of those asserting them." Second, the power
created by the threat of delay is considerable. Third, the OMB can summon
allegiance to the administration on the part of senior political appointees
in agencies in which proposals developed by career staff conflict with
White House policy. Finally, by linking its recommendations on agencies'

budgets to the degree to which agencies produce rules that comply with the executive order, the OMB can increase its leverage over rule writers.[34]

What emerges from studies of OMB review is a relationship that operates at two levels. The staff-to-staff working relationships vary considerably. It is extremely difficult for OMB desk officers to develop close working relationships with all agency rulemakers because of their sheer numbers. Consequently, the degree of conflict between an agency and the OMB at this level is a function of the general attitudes about OMB review, the working style and negotiation skills of the two parties, and the bureaucratic incentives facing the rulemaker and the OMB analyst. Some agencies have developed a culture of hostility to OMB review, whereas others have accepted it as a legitimate and even valuable function. Some agencies dismiss OMB analysts as politically motivated dilettantes; others accept their role as generalists with concern for administration policy. Bureaucrats who place a high premium on autonomy and the technical content of rules may bristle at what they see as interference that is irrelevant or worse. Others, more concerned with bringing the rule to a successful conclusion, may compromise their professional values in order to expedite the review process. Of course, the analysts at the OMB have professional values and different incentives as well. By and large, however, the sheer numbers of rules and rulemakers and the differences in the perspectives of the two sides lead to frequent disagreements that require some form of resolution.

When agency staff and OMB analysts reach an impasse, the issues are elevated to superiors in both organizations. Because the organizations are bound by an apparent commitment to the same administration, a proclivity to negotiated agreements is likely to be the norm. As Bruff put it, "Because agency heads and OMB officials deal with each other on a multitude of issues, each has a strong incentive to reach compromise on controverted issues ... rather than spending limited institutional capital ... over a particular regulation."[35] In general, then, we can anticipate a White House review process with numerous incidences of conflict at the staff level that are ameliorated as issues move up the two organizations for resolution. But we should also anticipate periods of adjustment, especially when presidential administrations change and along with them the political leadership of the rulemaking agencies and the OMB, as was the case in President Clinton's appointment of Sally Katzen as head of OIRA, as well as President Bush's appointment of John Graham and President Obama's appointment of Cass Sunstein to the same position.

Few aspects of rulemaking have received more attention from students of public administration and policy than OMB review. Scholars have debated the constitutionality of the process. They have examined the motives of those conducting reviews, the effectiveness of the process, and the implications it has for the relationship between the White House and Congress. Courts have ruled that presidential management of rulemaking is constitutional as long as it does not interfere with explicit congressional or judicial mandates.[36] The motivations that drive White House review are, like any significant governmental function, complex and varied. Goals ranging from the perfection of the rulemaking process to the securing of short-term political or economic advantage have been articulated and pursued.[37] Scholars have offered a variety of constitutional theories to rationalize the respective roles of Congress and the president in rulemaking and its oversight.[38]

Throughout the 1980s and early 1990s clashes between the White House and Congress were frequent and occasionally intense. Cases like the asbestos, ethylene chloride, and public notice rules convinced many in Congress that OMB review and regulatory task forces were little more than backdoors for politically powerful interests intent on frustrating normal and statutorily authorized regulatory processes. Congress retaliated with hearings, investigations, cutoffs of funding for OIRA review functions, and refusals to confirm nominees to head that office. A temporary truce in the interbranch war was achieved in 1986 when OIRA issued guidelines governing staff communications with external parties and disclosure of such communications. A detailed version of an "administrative agreement" between Congress and the OMB on regulatory review procedures and information disclosure was entered into the *Congressional Record* in November 1989. In turn, Congress reauthorized the Paperwork Reduction Act, which provided OIRA with the power to review and approve collections of information attendant to new rules. In addition, Congress refrained from writing legislation that would drastically limit the ability of the OMB to review rules. But Congress did not authorize funding specifically for regulatory review, and it continued to consider proposals to exempt particular types of rules from the OMB process.

Although conflict over OMB review was far less prominent during the Clinton administration than it was during the presidencies of Reagan and George H. W. Bush, it occasionally erupted. Republican representative David McIntosh of Indiana, a longtime critic of regulation, called OIRA's performance during the Clinton years "dismal" and stated that he was considering legislation to abolish it outright.[39] The Congressional Research Service interpreted the Clinton program differently when it described the role of OIRA as that of a "counselor." Suggesting that the Clinton OIRA sought to accomplish its policy goals through dialogue and negotiation with agencies, it also contrasted it with the posture of the next administration.[40]

The Bush II administration's program of regulatory review was considered by the CRS as establishing a "gatekeeper" role, returning to the original mode established for OIRA during the Reagan years.[41] Indeed, when we examine the Bush II program it is notable in terms of the innovation employed to increase the reach and depth of White House involvement. We have noted a number of these new or refurbished tools of influence, including prompt and return letters, stronger emphasis on the use of cost-benefit analysis in decision making, stricter controls on the use of guidance documents to avoid the requirements of rulemaking, and the directive to agencies to make regulatory policy officers, accountable to the White House, who would review proposed and final rules. Whether or not the Clinton presence was as benign as the CRS report suggests may be disputed,[42] but there is no question that his successor, over time, established an aggressive, multifaceted program of regulatory review. As the data in Table 6-3 demonstrate (see page 235), the percentages of rules requiring change or withdrawn increased during the Bush II administration.

Table 6-5 summarizes the experiences of five prominent rulemaking agencies during each of five presidential administrations. Remembering the change in review protocols noted earlier, the most dramatic shift in these data is from the Clinton to the Bush II years. For these agencies as a group, outright approvals by the OMB were cut in half, and in individual instances even more. It supports the view that review by OIRA during Bush II was highly active. At the same time, it is interesting that for Labor and the EPA, all presidents since Bush I—including Obama during his first year—the scrutiny has been close. Speculation abounds at the outset of the Obama administration regarding the volume and direction of rulemaking and the role of OIRA. Both conservatives and liberals have expressed concerns, but most agree that Obama will respond to calls for more aggressive regulation on multiple fronts. This means additional rulemaking and, presumably, more work for OIRA. A test will be whether Obama's appointments in key agencies will be sufficiently true to the administration's goal to reduce the need for OIRA to change what it is asked to review.

At various times presidential oversight of rulemaking review has received at least the qualified support of many influential organizations and numerous scholars who have considered the issue. The National Academy of Public Administration, the American Bar Association, and the Administrative Conference of the United States have each acknowledged the legitimacy and potential value of presidential oversight. Each, however, has suggested reforms of the process that would lead to better working relationships and results. The list of recommendations is long and has included full public disclosure of OMB communications and actions, increased numbers and training for OMB review staff, enhanced communication and coordination between the OMB and rulemaking agencies, and a statute that specifically authorizes and sets the parameters of presidential review. Although we can expect further refinements of the process and inevitable disagreements about

Table 6-5 Percentage of Rules Approved by OIRA without Change

President	HHS	Interior	Transportation	Labor	EPA	All
Reagan	70	83	73	59	75	77
Bush I	62	80	81	45	43	69
Clinton	50	64	62	12.5	20	50
Bush II	21	30	25	23	9	27
Obama	22	13	19	4.5	7.2	17.5

the substance, OMB review of proposed and final rules is an accepted and effective method of presidential oversight.

The effectiveness of presidential oversight of rulemaking is disputed. Some have concluded from case studies that the actual influence OMB and related reviews provide the president is limited and that agencies have at their disposal means to resist that which they consider unwise or untoward.[43] For their part, former directors of the Office of Information and Regulatory Affairs have generally assumed a rather modest posture regarding the influence of their former positions. But their public comments also reveal important nuances with regard to the sources of power and roles of the office that provide important supplements to the research of Bruff and others. At a symposium held at the University of Pennsylvania Law School in late 2006, Wendy Gramm and Sally Katzen, leaders of the office in the Reagan and Clinton administrations respectively, stated that OIRA power was often overstated. They emphasized the role of the office in ensuring that all agencies with an interest have an opportunity to voice their positions so that the president or his representatives can determine where the best expression of the public interest might lie. John Splotila, director during the latter years of the Clinton presidency, focused on the ability of OIRA to ensure a minimum level of quality across the government in rulemaking. James Miller, who also served during the Reagan years, underscored the ability of OIRA to leverage the larger budget authority of the OMB when dealing with recalcitrant agencies. John Graham, director of OIRA during much of the Bush II presidency, noted that on occasion OIRA was an important ally for a rulemaking agency facing substantial opposition from elsewhere in the White House.[44] During the Bush years, due in part to the leadership and professional background of John Graham, the director of OIRA, greater emphasis was placed on the use of risk analysis and assessment. Most of those who examine White House review programs and the reaction to them in many quarters suggest that presidential oversight of rulemaking is effective. Existing research and the behavior of key institutions and organizations tend to support this conclusion.

Studies of the effects of OIRA review strongly indicate it is influential with at least some of the rules it chooses for special attention. For example, in a 2003 study, the Government Accountability Office found that OIRA influenced the content of twenty-five of eighty-five rules it examined in depth. There are many other references to the effects of OIRA review on individual rules, some with examples, in the scholarly literature. The report also makes it plain that OIRA communicates extensively with agencies on an informal basis, prior to the formal submission of proposed or final rules to them. The GAO study noted, "OIRA has said it can have its greatest influence on agencies' rules during this informal review period."[45]

Although there is no definitive empirical study of the rules that are affected, Table 6-3 (see page 235) demonstrates a process housed in the OMB resulting in changes, reconsiderations, or withdrawals of several hundred proposals from agencies per year. These numbers do not include the number of rules that were changed prior to submission because of informal communications with OMB staff mentioned earlier. Even more difficult to discern: change in the rulemaking agencies that has occurred as a result of the thirty years of looming presence that is presidential oversight. The threat of presidential oversight, like the CRA, may be sufficient in some instances to alter the course and content of rules. We also have the implicit acknowledgment of the potential power of presidential oversight in the actions of Congress, the National Academy of Public Administration, the Administrative Conference of the United States, and a host of interest groups. Organizations like OMB Watch and Public Citizen have issued reports replete with warnings about the threat that regulatory review poses to the integrity of the regulatory process. Other interest groups have challenged individual actions resulting from presidential oversight in court.

The overall conclusion one is compelled to reach is that the president is every bit as active a player as Congress in the rulemaking process. Harold Bruff writes about OMB review: "From the point of view of the administration ... the program enjoyed unprecedented success in imprinting regulation with the President's own principles."[46]

President Obama and future residents of 1600 Pennsylvania Avenue will seek to do the same. Presidential oversight is a permanent fixture in the rulemaking process. Whatever form it takes, it gives presidents their best hope for a broad and deep impact on public policy.

A Note about Cost-Benefit Analysis

Promoted in the policies and executive orders of numerous presidents, cost-benefit analysis has been a fixture in rulemaking for over twenty-five years. Its most ardent supporters think economic analysis is needed to point decision makers to the most rational content for rules. A substantial literature exists on cost-benefit analysis in general and its application to rulemaking.[47] Three themes in this literature are important. First, the information needed to do comprehensive cost-benefit studies is often as hard to obtain as the scientific and technical data on which many rules are based. Second, profound skepticism greets the use of cost-benefit analysis by those who view it as a device to prevent, delay, or reduce any form of government intervention. Third, the criteria for its use have allowed agencies to avoid conducting such studies for most rules. Cost-benefit analysis has been reserved for "major" rules, a threshold that is very high.

With regard to controversy, the experience of the Bush II administration's efforts to establish a set of operating principles for risk analysis is instructive. In 2006 the administration issued a "proposed risk assessment bulletin" and took the additional step of calling on the National Academy of Sciences to conduct a "peer review" of the document.[48] The bulletin adopted and built upon the five principles previously established by a working group during the Clinton administration. The National Academy's evaluation of the proposed bulletin was critical of the document and recommended a number of changes. The Bush administration responded with a memorandum issued in September 2007 titled "Updated Principles of Risk Analysis," which attempted to address a number of shortcomings by essentially withdrawing the bulletin and replacing it with the text of the Clinton administration statement of principles, with commentary.[49] Prominent critics of the Bush administration's overall posture toward regulation and rulemaking noted their relief that no new standards were being imposed. But they remained suspicious and concerned that OIRA was implying only those risk assessments consistent with its commentary on the 1995 principles would be considered influential.[50] The point is that the same difficulties in conceptualization, research design, data collection and analysis, and standard setting that afflict cost-benefit analysis beset risk analysis and assessment as well.

Accountability to the Courts

No institution of government has been as persistent in its oversight of rulemaking for a longer period of time than the federal judiciary. Before Congress concerned itself in any meaningful, systematic way with the rulemaking process it set in motion, the courts were reviewing its results and determining whether they were lawful instruments of governmental authority. Decades before any president sought to oversee the rulemaking that occurred in departments and agencies, judges were remaking the process of rulemaking and reformulating the substance of rules through decisions in individual cases. The courts remain extremely important, but decentralized, overseers of rulemaking.

Objectives

The objectives of the president and Congress when conducting oversight are political and, occasionally, institutional. Both the president and Congress attempt to make rulemaking produce results that promote their respective policy preferences, and, especially when controlled by different political parties or philosophies, these branches vie for control over the rulemakers. The primary concerns of the judiciary are more complex. At the very least, its role in relation to rulemaking is to ensure that the function is performed in accordance with basic constitutional principles and that the law, both substantive and procedural, is obeyed. Judges are not without legal and political philosophies, however, and when they review the rules, they do so through the prism of these beliefs. Although not linked to a constituency that votes them in or out of office, judges are embedded in the political system. This must be taken into account, along with other characteristics of the judicial system, if the role of judges as overseers of the rulemaking process is to be properly understood. In America we have few options when seeking an institution to protect the integrity of our constitutional system. Because the executive and legislative branches of government are inherently political, they have each demonstrated a frightening capacity to subjugate constitutional protections to the transient whims of a vocal electorate. We have placed the ultimate responsibility for protection of the Constitution with the federal judiciary and attempted to remove judges from the temporary and partisan motives that too often drive the other branches.

Federal judges hold lifetime appointments after they are nominated by the president and confirmed by the Senate. Politics plays an important role in the screening of candidates for the bench, but once they are confirmed, judges become the least constrained of our public officials. Because we vest in them the power to declare the acts of the other branches, including the making of law, null and void, it is vital that they be removed from the political arena. Tenure so long as their actions are unimpeachable, protection from reduction of their salaries, and removal from office only through an elaborate impeachment process insulate federal judges from the pressures that might be exerted by Congress, the president, interest groups, and the public. The courts are certainly not immune to criticism or attacks from external sources, but they are well equipped to withstand such attacks.

In many ways the most enduring legacy a president can leave is the federal judges he appoints during his term. Even the most dramatic and far-reaching programs of social or regulatory policy are altered almost from the moment they are enacted. Soon they barely resemble what was initially created. Appointments to the federal bench endure, however, changed only by the intellectual and professional development of the individuals holding these jobs. This creates in our system an inherent tension. Even when the White House and Congress are controlled by the same party and are working in concert, there is no guarantee that coherent policy will be the ultimate result. Litigation, being so common, ensures that the policy initiatives of a given administration or Congress will be subjected to the scrutiny of a federal judge, or federal judges, who were likely appointed by a previous president and confirmed by a previous Congress, sometimes with quite different ideas about what is legally permissible and constitutionally sound.[51] Therefore, if incumbent presidents screen their candidates for the bench carefully, with an eye to putting a distinctive philosophical stamp on the judicial branch, conflict in the next administration is bound to be the result. The diversity of views held by the more than one thousand federal judges, sitting in hundreds of courts geographically dispersed, militates against consistency and coherence in the outcomes of litigation. We can expect these characteristics of our judiciary to influence the ultimate content of rules.

The power of the judiciary is expressed in a multitude of ways, some so subtle that they are very difficult to observe. The mere existence of the judiciary and the threat of litigation exert a powerful deterrent effect on the behavior of rulemaking bureaucracies, as it does on Congress and the White House. Those writing rules have learned that when their work affects persons and groups with sufficient sophistication and resources to sue, litigation is a distinct possibility. They also know that judges are not reluctant to obliterate years of work if the court is convinced that the law has been violated in some way.[52] In Chapter 4 we noted that a representative of the office of general counsel is virtually always included in agency work groups assigned the task of writing important regulations. One reason is to advise those developing the content of the rule how to avoid litigation or how to survive it should it occur. The presence of courts not only fosters a healthy respect for the myriad of legal principles and issues that attach to rulemaking but may also be a powerful force pushing agencies to consider more seriously the views of those who might challenge the rule in court. This is because judges look at issues differently than do most rulemakers. Judges are preoccupied with constitutional principles, statutory intent, and procedural correctness and less concerned with the substance of policy and its effects.

When litigation does occur, judges frequently accept agreements reached by the parties. Settlements are a common means of ending a lawsuit. There is no empirical evidence that suggests that litigation involving rules is more or less likely to end in settlement than are other types of disputes. Hence, the power of the court may be in its role as a context for the resolution of a dispute between an agency and a private party and as a ratifier of the agreement the litigants have reached. When a lawsuit is not settled and it falls to the judge to make the decision, the power of the judiciary is most in evidence. A rule may be fully vindicated, partially invalidated, or totally rejected by a reviewing court.

The federal court system includes three levels: district courts, courts of appeal, and the Supreme Court of the United States.[53] The courts at each of these levels perform a distinctive role in the judicial system. District courts are trial courts; their primary mission is the resolution of the disputes that created the cases in the first place. Trials in district courts are presided over by a single judge, whose primary task is to move the cases from an active to terminated status. Courts of appeal, as their title suggests, usually review cases that have already been decided in another court. Their function is to review previous decisions when one of the parties believes that the result was incorrect. For some types of cases, including most of those involving rulemaking, the courts of appeal also function essentially as trial courts, being the first tribunal of the federal judicial system to hear the case. Therefore, in rulemaking, courts of appeal are hybrids because without a district court decision they are the first court to consider fully the legal issues presented. Cases in the courts of appeal are heard by groups of judges called panels. Most often three judges hear cases, but on some occasions the panel can be all the judges assigned to the court. Finally, there is the Supreme Court of the United States, composed of nine members. Almost all of its caseload is discretionary, and it grants full hearing to only about a hundred cases each year. Challenges to rules are not often heard by the Supreme Court.

Decision making in courts of appeal is collective. Variations in legal philosophy and political predilection are likely to be more pronounced at the trial court level, since judges there need not accommodate their views to others in order to reach a resolution of the dispute. At the appellate level judges do not hear witnesses directly; they work from the transcript of trials, written briefs, agency records, and oral arguments from attorneys. Their task is to ensure the correctness and quality of decisions reached in trial courts or administrative tribunals. They often return cases to trial courts for further litigation or reconsideration, and they express their decisions in written opinions that are frequently quite lengthy.

The effect of judicial oversight on rulemaking can vary quite dramatically, depending on the level of court that has issued the ruling. Decisions by trial courts apply to the individual cases in which they were rendered. If the decisions are used as precedent for future decisions, their effect is often confined to the federal judicial district in which the court operates. Some districts encompass entire states, but many cover only a portion of a state. Since the individual decisions of trial courts are not always accompanied by lengthy published opinions from which judges in future cases can take guidance, the effects of a trial court decision may be limited to the parties involved and the thinking of the judge who rendered the decision.

Decisions by appellate courts are quite different in their effect. Like district courts, courts of appeal and the Supreme Court pass judgment in cases that may raise issues about rulemaking in general or a statute that affects a broad spectrum of rules. The difference is that decisions by these higher courts apply to a much larger geographic area. The decisions of appellate courts become precedent for multistate regions, known as circuits, and the decisions of the Supreme Court apply to the nation as a whole. Some courts of appeal hear more rulemaking cases than others simply by virtue of their location. For example, the Court of Appeals for the District of Columbia Circuit has become a major force in the law of rulemaking, since its location in Washington makes it the court of choice for a large portion of the litigation challenging rules.[54] The decisions of courts of appeal and the Supreme Court are written and can be referred to by other courts and agencies. To the extent courts in future cases take guidance from these decisions and to the extent agencies pattern their behavior according to the principles outlined in written opinions, a single decision by one of these courts can be a powerful form of oversight of rulemaking.

Considerations in Judicial Oversight

There are four large categories of issues to consider when a rule is challenged.[55] The first is who has the right to challenge a rule in court. Second, we must consider the types of complaints those who dispute a rule may bring to the court. Third, the standards that the courts apply when they consider challenges to agency rulemaking are crucially important. Last, we must summarize the actual effects of judicial oversight on the conduct of rulemaking and its substantive results. We begin with the question of who may sue.

The qualifications a person, group, or organization must possess in order to bring a lawsuit in federal court are covered by the principle of *standing*. The principle of standing is crucial to the conduct of judicial oversight of rulemaking because courts lack the authority to initiate cases by themselves. The judicial power established by our Constitution extends only to cases and controversies in law or equity and does not encompass other types of disagreements and disputes. Unlike the oversight conducted by the other branches, the exercise by judges of any supervisory powers over rulemakers must await the arrival of a lawsuit. While standing tells us little about what a court will decide when reviewing the content of a rule or the process by which it was determined, it does establish how judicial oversight of rulemaking may begin. Until the 1940s it was exceedingly difficult for those unhappy with an action taken by a government agency to obtain a hearing in federal court. The judiciary had embraced a test for standing that came to be known as "legal interests."[56] Under this test a party was required to show that harm would result from the action the government had taken or was contemplating and that the damage would be done to an interest that had explicit legal protection in statute or the common law. Generally, the latter was confined to a rather narrow concept of real private property. Challenges to rulemaking occurred, as we noted in the famous cases that invalidated large portions of the New Deal. But the interests affected in these instances fell under the narrow version of real private property.

The limitations on litigation as a check against the abuses of arbitrary, misguided, or unrestrained executive or bureaucratic power, under the legal interests test, persuaded Congress to encourage the courts to adopt a more liberal test for the law of standing. The judiciary opened its doors a bit more in the 1930s and 1940s, when it noted that individuals who might otherwise not qualify for standing would qualify in certain instances if they were acting as "private attorneys general."[57] Such an individual might be able to bring to the courts a dispute with an agency that allowed the judges to consider the broader question of whether the government was carrying out its functions in a legally permissible, constitutional manner. Of course, this principle left it entirely to the judges to determine which circumstances would qualify an individual to serve as a private attorney general.

The most prominent example of congressional encouragement of a more liberal doctrine of standing came in the Administrative Procedure Act of 1946. In it Congress extended judicial review to "persons aggrieved" by a given agency decision.[58] It provided no further definition of the term, nor examples of what types of interests other than real private property might be included under it. In time, however, the courts moved in the direction of what Congress sought. In fact, some might argue that they went well beyond its goal. Along with the rise of interest groups and the explosion of social regulation, the decades of the 1960s and 1970s saw the eventual opening of the judicial system to virtually any person or organization who could articulate a complaint with an action taken by government. Congress was an active party to this movement and included "citizen lawsuit" provisions in many statutes that created programs of social regulation.[59]

A high-water mark in the liberalization of the law of standing can be observed in a case involving a rate decision by the Interstate Commerce Commission. A group of law school students, organized temporarily as something called "Students Challenging Regulatory Agency Procedures," otherwise known as SCRAP, took issue with the rate because it would, in their considered judgment, hamper the transport of recyclable materials. This, they argued, would damage their members in direct and indirect ways, including their recreational activities and their aesthetic enjoyment of the landscape. The Supreme Court in 1973 agreed that the members of SCRAP were in fact aggrieved. The Court accepted what it called the "attenuated line of causation" between the ICC's action and the alleged harm, such as the impairment of hiking on the C&O canal in Washington, D.C. The Court granted standing and allowed the group to try to convince a trial court that harm would occur and that the commission was acting illegally when inflicting it on them.[60]

Courts appeared to back off from this extremely permissive view of standing in other cases. In one, a rule issued by the Internal Revenue Service (IRS) reduced the amount of free services a hospital had to extend to poor persons in order to qualify for tax-exempt status. A welfare rights organization challenged the rule, arguing that it would have the effect of reducing available health care for its members. The Supreme Court denied standing and stated that the group's issue was with hospitals and not with the IRS.[61] This 1976 decision raised fundamental questions of whether indirect effects of the sort that were considered relevant in SCRAP could any longer be considered as a basis for granting standing. The Court answered that question in the affirmative in 1978 when it allowed an environmental group to challenge a law that limited the liability the operators of nuclear power plants could suffer as a result of an accident. The group claimed that this limit to liability was a form of subsidy without which nuclear plants would not be built. The Court agreed and granted standing. The difference between this and the earlier case involving indirect effects is that the Court was convinced that the action being challenged—the building of a nuclear plant—was causally linked to the limitation on liability.[62] It was not convinced that hospitals would deny care to the poor simply because of the IRS ruling. The Court has also made it clear that groups alleging harm must establish it clearly and relate it to the challenged government action.

The law of standing is complex, with numerous subtleties. These include distinctions between individuals and groups seeking standing, what it means to be injured by a rule, whether participation in the rulemaking that caused an alleged injury is prerequisite to standing to sue over the result, and whether the affected interest falls within the "zone" of interests contemplated in the statutes.[63] "Generalizations about standing to sue are largely worthless," wrote Supreme Court Justice William O. Douglas in a 1970 decision.[64] Forty years later that is at least somewhat extreme, but contradictions in judicial holdings in the area are still quite possible.[65] It is safe to say, however, that to have standing to challenge rules, a group, person, or organization must demonstrate either real or potential harm, be it minimal or hypothetical, that is attributable to decisions made during the course of rulemaking.

Establishing the standing to sue an agency that has issued a rule does not, in itself, establish the timing of the lawsuit. Although a court may challenge a rule, it is not permitted to do so at any stage in the rulemaking process. On the contrary, courts are careful not to be drawn into disputes between agencies and affected parties prematurely, preferring to wait until the rulemaking process has run its course. The principles at work here are "finality" and "ripeness for review." Together they forestall judicial review until the agency has completed its work and the rule is published in its final form in the *Federal Register* or, when available, petitions for reconsideration are exhausted. With some notable exceptions, like death row appeals and provisions for early review in certain statutes, courts should not intervene in a basic function of another branch of government until it has completed its work. As long as the rule remains under development, there is a chance that the issues of concern will be resolved. The principle of withholding judicial oversight until the agency is done prevents the usurpation of agency authority and allows the courts to devote their scarce resources to controversies for which no alternative means of resolution are available.[66]

The second large category of issues relates to what is known in administrative law as the *scope of review,* and an early authoritative statement on it is found in the Administrative Procedure Act. Section 706 of the act states:

> To the extent necessary to decision and when presented, the reviewing court shall decide all relevant questions of law, interpret constitutional and statutory provisions, and determine the meaning or applicability of the terms of an agency action. The reviewing court shall—
>
> (1) compel agency action unlawfully withheld or unreasonably delayed; and
>
> (2) hold unlawful and set aside agency action, findings, and conclusions found to be—
>
> (a) arbitrary, capricious, an abuse of discretion, or otherwise not in accordance with law;
>
> (b) contrary to constitutional right, power, privilege, or immunity;
>
> (c) in excess of statutory jurisdiction, authority, or limitations, or short of statutory right;
>
> (d) without observance of procedure required by law;
>
> (e) unsupported by substantial evidence in a case subject to sections 556 and 557 of this title or otherwise reviewed on the record of an agency hearing provided by statute; or
>
> (f) unwarranted by the facts to the extent that the facts are subject to trial de novo by the reviewing court.

In making the foregoing determinations, the court shall review the whole record of those parts of it cited by a party, and due account shall be taken of the rule of prejudicial error.[67]

Most of these provisions have continuing significance for contemporary rulemaking. The first provision relates to actions that are unreasonably delayed. The amount of time it takes agencies to issue rules is a persistent problem. Of course, what constitutes a delay that is "unreasonable" is a matter of judgment unless clear standards are set. With the increased use of deadlines in authorizing statutes that specify quite clearly when Congress expects particular rules to be issued, the question of reasonableness is rendered effectively moot. If Congress imposes a deadline and the rulemaking agency misses it, there is no doubt that the courts will entertain a lawsuit, and it is highly likely that those attempting to force the agency's hand will prevail. When no deadlines exist but legislation establishes a clear expectation that an agency will produce a rule in a given area, it will be at the discretion of the judge whether to hear the case and to determine if the rule in question has been unduly delayed.[68]

That a rule that allegedly violates the Constitution is a proper matter for judicial review needs little elaboration. No act of government that violates the requirements of that document can stand. Because the ultimate responsibility for protection of the Constitution resides with the judiciary, there is little question that it should extend to rules and how they are written. Issues of constitutionality are not common in challenges to rulemaking, but they do occur, as in cases noted earlier involving the legislative veto and OMB review of rules.

In section 706(2)(c) of the APA, Congress takes care to establish in the court system both a check against a runaway bureaucracy and a safeguard for its own lack of precision in delegations of authority. It is elemental that agencies cannot write law unless authorized to do so by the legislature. When the authority of an agency to write a rule is challenged, the courts must look to the legislation that delegated responsibility for the program in question. On rare occasion, agencies knowingly step beyond the bounds of the authority they have been granted. More common are situations in which the authority to write a given rule is unclear, but the agency, sometimes under pressure from external interests or the political leadership of the agency, writes it nevertheless. This provision of the act requires the courts to be the arbiter of congressional intent when rules are challenged on the grounds that their development is an illegitimate exercise of bureaucratic power.

Section 706(2)(d) of the act requires courts to consider the process by which a rule is developed. As we have seen, Congress has added much procedural complexity to the original design for rulemaking established in the Administrative Procedure Act. By adding new requirements to consider general issues (such as the environment, paperwork, and small businesses), by increasing the types of studies and analyses on which rules are based, and by affording greater opportunities for public participation, Congress has invited lawsuits under this provision of the APA. When such issues are raised in a lawsuit, the courts must consider them.

The avoidance of rulemaking in favor of other procedures is also an issue that might arise under this provision. We have already noted the use of different devices—such as guidelines, technical manuals, and policy statements—to establish new standards and expectations. Sometimes the motivation is to avoid the procedural rigor, participation, and openness that characterize rulemaking by using mechanisms that can be developed internally. Courts review such documents when litigants argue successfully that they are, in effect, rules. Courts will sometimes force agencies to conduct some form of rulemaking to replace the rejected document. But judicial attitudes in this area vary, as well, and courts are mindful of the contending and legitimate interests of both government and private parties.[69]

Finally, we come to section 706(2)(a), which grants federal courts the right to question the judgments of our rulemakers. The language of this provision does not appear to establish a particularly rigorous standard for those who write rules. The dictionary meanings of *arbitrary* and *capricious* would appear to give rulemakers considerable freedom to fashion rules without the fear of being repudiated by a judge.[70] The term *abuse of discretion* lacks any inherent meaning and is entirely dependent on the context provided by the statute that authorizes rulemaking in the first place. But, as we will see in a moment, these words and phrases have been given meanings by the courts—meanings that create criteria for rulemaking agencies to meet that are more exacting than the literal meanings might suggest.

The scope of judicial oversight is broad. It encompasses every significant aspect of rulemaking. Courts are free to determine whether an agency has the authority to write a rule in the first place, whether it has acted quickly enough with the authority it has, whether it has observed proper procedure when doing so, and whether the result is sound law and public policy. This final element of the courts' oversight power is far and away the most potent and controversial. When courts make decisions about the content of rules, they are inevitably substituting their judgment for that of administrative officials whom Congress charged with the development of rules. Such actions by unelected officials with long tenures cannot be taken lightly in a democracy. Hence, the standards that the courts employ when reviewing a challenge to agency rulemaking is crucially important.

The criteria that courts use to determine whether an agency has performed its rulemaking task in a legally permissible manner vary with the issues in dispute. All require judgments by reviewing judges. If the issue is the constitutionality of a given rule, the judges first have to be convinced that a constitutionally protected right or principle is at issue. If they decide that it is, they must then exercise judgment as to whether it has been violated. Constitutional issues do arise in rulemaking, and when they do the courts usually weigh the interests of the government against those of private parties. On occasion the courts are asked to resolve a constitutional issue that involves the balance of power between the branches of government or issues of constitutional integrity. This occurred in the successful challenge to the legislative veto and the largely unsuccessful challenges to presidential review of rules. The dispositions of these types of cases hinge on the judges' conception of the principle of the separation of powers. These types of cases are sufficiently uncommon and the circumstances are sufficiently diverse that outcomes are determined by the unique blend of facts and judicial philosophy that is present in each instance.

When litigation over rulemaking involves questions about the authority of an agency to write a rule, the court must go to the statute and, if it is unclear, to its legislative history to determine the intent of Congress. If the issue is the adequacy of the procedures used to develop a rule, the court must once again return to statutes, but in this case more than the authorizing law may be involved. At minimum the court refers to the Administrative Procedure Act, the authorizing statute the rule seeks to implement, and any general statute that might be relevant given the subject matter of the rule, such as the National Environmental Policy Act, the Paperwork Reduction Act, and the Regulatory Flexibility Act. If the issue is whether the substance of the rule is consistent with the statutory provisions it seeks to implement, the court must take cognizance of all the issues raised earlier, since they all bear on the substance of the rule. When appropriate, the courts are also attentive to the quality of information and analytical techniques that the agency drew upon when formulating the rule. In the instances when the substance of the rule is being challenged, the court, in its review, must inevitably question the judgment of the officials who wrote the rule. In these circumstances the general posture of the courts toward rulemakers becomes critically important. The extent to which judges defer to the many types of judgments an agency writing a rule must make often determines the outcome of court review.

There are strongly contrasting views of the role courts should assume when considering challenges to agency rulemaking. One, expressed in a series of Supreme Court decisions from the early 1970s to the mid-1980s, argues for a searching and skeptical review by the judges. Perhaps the most frequently cited opinion taking this view was issued in 1971 in *Citizens to Preserve Overton Park v. Volpe*. The Court ruled that the "arbitrary, capricious" standard of the APA required review that was "searching and careful."

The Court must determine "whether the [agency's] decision was based on a consideration of the relevant factors and whether there had been a clear error in judgement."[71] Although judges should not routinely substitute their judgment for that of agency experts, they need to scrutinize decisions closely. *Overton Park* set what came to be known as the "hard look" standard of review. It appeared to be reinforced in the Court's 1983 decision in *Motor Vehicle Manufacturers Association v. State Farm*. In that opinion the justices stated that a rule should be rejected

> if the agency has relied on factors Congress had not intended it to consider, entirely failed to consider an important aspect of the problem, offered an explanation for its decision that runs counter to the evidence before it or is so implausible that it could not be ascribed to a difference in view or a product of agency expertise.[72]

The opinion would insinuate courts deeply into the detailed substance of rulemaking and allow judges considerable freedom to find a rule defective. This general approach to review reveals strong doubts about the ability of agencies to carry out their rulemaking tasks competently and within the bounds set for them by Congress. Under the "hard look" doctrine, the remedy for these expected bureaucratic shortcomings is a vigilant and aggressive judiciary.

There is, however, another view of the proper relationship between courts and the agencies whose rules they review. It is best expressed in two Supreme Court decisions, one dealing with rulemaking procedures and the other with the substance of the decisions that agencies make. In *Vermont Yankee Nuclear Power Corp. v. Natural Resources Defense Council* the Supreme Court called for a halt to judicial tinkering with the elements of the informal rulemaking process.[73] In the late 1960s and through much of the 1970s judicial decisions were rendered that had the effect of altering rulemaking procedure. In the *Vermont Yankee* case in 1978, the issue was whether the Nuclear Regulatory Commission had acted properly when it used notice and comment rulemaking or whether a more formal type of process was required. The statute under which the NRC operated for the rulemaking in question did not mandate the use of formal, trial-type procedures. A lower court had agreed with the litigants and ordered the commission to use more elaborate procedures. The Supreme Court found this to be an unacceptable usurpation of agency discretion by the judiciary. The opinion admonished the lower courts to refrain from what it called "Monday morning quarterbacking" and allow agencies to fashion procedures they deemed appropriate to the rulemaking task at hand, within the confines of the statutory direction they had been given by Congress.

The Court took a similar tack in a 1984 case involving the exercise of substantive discretion by a rulemaking agency. The landmark *Chevron USA v. NRDC* decision appears to grant latitude to agencies as broad as that which the earlier *State Farm* case appeared to grant to the judiciary. *Chevron* involved challenges to EPA rules that define the sources of air pollution. In the case the Court stated:

> If the intent of Congress is clear, that is the end of the matter; for the court as well as the agency must give effect to the unambiguously expressed intent of the Congress. If, however, the court determines Congress has not directly addressed the precise question at issue the court does not simply impose its own construction on the statute as would be necessary in the absence of an administrative interpretation. Rather, if the statute is silent or ambiguous with respect to the specific issue, the question for the court is whether the agency's answer is based on a permissible construction of the statute.[74]

Under this model of judicial oversight, Congress is expected to be both "direct" and "precise," and when it is not, the agency need only convince a court that its actions are "permissible" or, as the justices state later in the opinion, "reasonable." Unlike *State Farm*, *Chevron* appeared to place much discretion in the hands of the agency writing rules under most statutes and restricted the ability of courts to exercise searching oversight of the rulemaking agencies. In these two cases the type of discretion the Court confronted was somewhat different. *State Farm* deals with the breadth of latitude agencies will be given with regard to the internal logic of a given discussion; *Chevron* deals with discretion in the interpretation of statute. In point of fact, the apparent dissonance between these two Supreme Court decisions, issued one year apart, is real. Legal scholars have attempted to demonstrate how these disparate judicial philosophies can be interpreted so as not to be hopelessly at odds with each other. But from the perspective of judicial oversight of rulemaking, it is more important to determine just how influential such doctrines are with the lower court judges who must apply them in individual cases.

Available evidence strongly suggests that any general policy articulated by the Supreme Court regarding review of rulemaking will be inconsistently interpreted by judges in the lower tribunals. Reaction to the *Chevron* case is instructive. Legal scholars examining its effects on the decisions of lower courts find two distinct patterns. One is consistent with the dominant interpretation of *Chevron*: some courts in some cases appear to defer to agency decisions when the judges determine that Congress was silent or obscure on the matter under review. Other courts have been no more deferential under *Chevron* than they had been when the "hard look" model of judicial oversight was in full force.[75] This continued aggressiveness is attributable to judges who either interpret *Chevron*'s statements about the substantive content of statutes loosely or interpret its standards for agency use of discretion—"permissible" and "reasonable"—quite rigorously. Like all general doctrines regarding the scope of judicial review, the standards in *Chevron* and *State Farm* are applied in a dizzying array of circumstances presented in thousands of cases before hundreds of different federal judges. Despite this volatility in the case law, a noted expert offers the following general principles and observations:

> 1. A reviewing court normally will not substitute its judgment for that of the agency in making factual conclusions, as long as the agency's conclusions have a substantial basis in the record; this is particularly true where the subject matter is technical, on the frontiers of science, or involves a considerable exercise of agency expertise.
>
> 2. A reviewing court generally will defer to agency policy judgments, as long as they are "rational" or "reasonable"—concededly vague terms—and they are the product of what has traditionally been called "reasoned decisionmaking." To demonstrate that reasoned decisionmaking has taken place, an agency must explain in its statement of basis and purpose why it has rejected significant alternative options, why it has departed from past policies, and how its conclusions are derived from the facts in the record.
>
> 3. A reviewing court will apply these same principles to agency deregulation, with emphasis placed on the need for the agency to fully explain why the deregulatory action is being taken, why prior policy is being revised, and whether less dramatic alternatives were considered and rejected.[76]

Judicial decisions are framed by the circumstances in each case and by the philosophy and experience of the judge. Ultimately, abstract discussions of the scope of review must give way to the practical implications of judges' decisions in individual cases. The critical issue that remains is the effect of judicial oversight on rulemaking.

The effect on rulemaking of judicial oversight, like presidential oversight, varies considerably across the agencies of the federal government. Certain agencies conduct many rulemakings each year that are rarely affected by adverse judicial decisions. Notable among these are the Federal Aviation Administration in the Department of Transportation and the Agricultural Marketing Service in the Department of Agriculture. There are many other agencies as well. The relative immunity of the rules they write is less attributable to the comparatively minor and routine nature of the rules than to the behavior of the constituencies affected by them.

The private sector that is affected is disinclined to sue agencies like these, and without litigious private parties the courts cannot take an active role in overseeing the rulemaking process. The reasons for the absence of numerous lawsuits are many. External constituencies that are most affected by the rules and best situated to litigate if they are unhappy may be intimately involved in the agency's rulemaking process and in general agreement with the overall results. This appears to be the case with both the Agricultural Marketing Service and the Federal Aviation Administration. Furthermore, a few agencies, such as the FAA, deal in highly technical areas, and the interaction between experts in the public and private sectors is both frequent and characterized by substantial agreement on what needs to be done.

The key variable that triggers the litigation that brings judicial oversight is the magnitude or perceived importance of the negative effects anticipated by parties with the resources and willingness to sue. One would be hard pressed to find a single rulemaking agency that can always avoid such circumstances. It is safe to say, however, that this type of situation is confronted most often by the major agencies of social regulation, and the reasons are clear enough. Their rules often have enormous effect on certain industries and sectors of the economy. These agencies, such as the EPA, OSHA, the Consumer Product Safety Commission, and the National Highway Transportation Safety Administration, confront multiple private—and sometimes public—constituencies that have opposing views on what rules should contain and whether they should be issued at all. Their work also spans whole sectors of the economy, affecting well-organized, well-resourced, and litigation-prone individuals, groups, and organizations. Litigation is inevitable. Consequently, judicial oversight is frequent and far-reaching in its effects.

The frequency of lawsuits that challenge rules in certain agencies is breathtaking. Virtually all health standards issued by OSHA have been litigated suit, and the rules have often been challenged by both labor and management. One routinely argues that the rules fail to meet the statutory obligation of protecting workers from risk of disease. The other complains that the rules demand levels of worker protection that are excessive and illegal. Agencies of social regulation provide the best opportunity to observe the full range of potential effects that judicial oversight can have on rulemaking. Fortunately, at least one, the EPA, has attracted sufficient scholarly interest that we now have a reasonably firm grip on the many ways judicial supervision can change rulemaking.

Rosemary O'Leary conducted an exhaustive assessment of the effects of federal court decisions on the EPA. Her work is valuable for many reasons, but one is especially pertinent to the topic of this chapter. She places the results of litigation challenging EPA action into categories based on the intensity of judicial oversight and the effects on the agency.[77] The categories and the examples she provides for each can easily be extended to other rulemaking agencies. For example, one category consisted of cases in which the decision of the EPA was reviewed and fully upheld by the court. This category held a high percentage of the cases she studied, which would support the agency's claim that, although it is frequently sued, it wins in court more often than not.

O'Leary found that sometimes the mere filing of the lawsuit appeared to trigger a change in EPA policy or practices. Examples of this type of situation include the agency's decision to study the chemical formaldehyde after a lawsuit was filed in an attempt to force the agency to do so and the agency's change in policy regarding substances that were disposed of in landfills.[78] Her findings confirm the power that courts exert in our system of government by their very presence. In these instances the availability of the courts to litigants persuaded the agency and the affected party to reach, in effect, an agreement on a matter in dispute.

Cases in which the courts took action to invalidate all or part of an agency action fell, according to O'Leary's ordering scheme, into three categories. The categories were based on the relative "activism" the judges displayed in their review of the EPA's performance. In the first category were decisions that reflected a relatively passive judicial presence. The courts were "reluctant to intervene ... but nonetheless issued decisions that affected EPA policy and/or administration." In this category one finds decisions that rejected agreements made between agencies and private companies on testing procedures for toxic substances, required the issuance of certain rules and accelerated the pace of others under the Resource Conservation and Recovery Act, and sent a set of Safe Drinking Water rules back for reconsideration because of "technical uncertainty." Other decisions in this group had the effect of increasing the power of the EPA over the environmental actions of other agencies and opened an entirely new area—the injection of waste into underground wells—for agency rulemaking.[79] Although these decisions cover a wide range of procedure and substance, they are distinguished by the fact that they required change but provided little additional direction.

The second category consisted of decisions in which the judges exercised normal "discretionary powers" to force the agency to make changes.[80] In this group the courts both required change and exercised what is now considered normal levels of supervision. A significant number of cases were in this group, and, again, they cover a wide range of substance and procedure. Examples include mandatory timetables for the completion of certain rules with mandatory semiannual progress reports to the court and mandatory meetings by the agency with all affected parties to develop plans for the completion of rules supervised by the judge. The characteristics that appear to set this group of cases apart from the previous groups are the degree of direction given by judges on the process the agency was to use to develop rules and the role of the judge in supervising the behavior of the agency after the decision was rendered.

The third category in this group included cases in which the judges involved had "gone beyond the normal patterns of judicial behavior" in their oversight of the agency. These cases were not uncommon. They, too, varied considerably in subject matter. One distinguishing factor in these cases was that the judges went beyond process considerations and rejected scientific and technical judgments by EPA experts. Among the rules affected were those dealing with PCB contamination, radionuclides, and a variety of substances covered by pesticide statutes. Also in this category of decisions were those in which procedural guidance that can only be termed extraordinary was given to the agency. In one case the judge ordered a private interest group, in effect, to oversee the agency's compliance with his decision by filing another lawsuit should compliance lag. In another, the judge doubled the statutorily established notice requirements. One remarkable decision found that a judge, clearly impatient with the pace of agency rulemaking, ordered the EPA to report on "all internal and external agency actions taken to minimize or eliminate all funding and personnel constraints that may serve as barriers to compliance" with his order.[81] In this case the judge was behaving very much like an irate supervisor building a case to terminate an employee with serious performance problems.

For the EPA, at least, this level of judicial interest and activity is not new. In his study of the early years of the EPA, R. Shep Melnick found that, soon after the passage of landmark environmental statutes, the agency was in court defending, often unsuccessfully, its performance in several areas of rulemaking. Melnick found judicial decisions that created and completely reoriented whole programs of rulemaking, altered time frames for the production of rules, and altered the process, both by changing patterns of public participation and by rejecting the scientific and technical analyses and judgments underlying regulations.[82]

Although the combination of frequency and intrusiveness of judicial supervision of EPA rulemaking may be unmatched, examples like those in each of O'Leary's categories can be found for most rulemaking agencies. Extrapolating from the experience of this one agency, we can see that no area of rulemaking is beyond the reach of the federal judiciary. Judges are full and active players in the rulemaking process and, in some instances, exert a degree of control that exceeds the reach and grasp of either Congress or the president. It is ironic, perhaps, that our most passive and least responsive branch of government will, in many instances, be the most aggressive and influential overseer of the rulemaking process.

The enormous volume of rulemaking and its central importance to our system of government have not rendered the constitutionally established branches powerless or irrelevant. Instead, the increase in rulemaking activity has caused a redirection of effort by members of Congress, occupants of the White House, and judges. They expend considerable time and effort attempting to learn about the rulemaking activities of the agencies and then to influence the content of the rules that are produced. The powers at the disposal of the three branches are quite different, but each is in its own way formidable. Some mechanisms are preemptive and direct; others are indirect and subtle. As we have seen in other dimensions of rulemaking, these mechanisms are not used in all cases. Oversight, like the many legal requirements of rulemaking procedure, becomes a factor most often for rules that are likely to have major effects on the public and generate opposition.

Between the branches in their struggle for control of rulemaking, there is competition and occasional cooperation. The competition is evident in the sometimes intense conflict between Congress and the White House over presidential review of proposed and final rules. But Congress has increased the scope of presidential oversight by passing the Paperwork Reduction Act with provisions for OMB review and clearance. The White House has returned the favor with its agreements on disclosure of rulemaking-related communications by OMB staff and its quiet acceptance of rulings of the lower courts on the importance of releasing rules by congressional deadlines. The courts have umpired this contest for institutional advantage. The results for the legislative and executive branches have been mixed, whereas the judiciary's oversight capacity has been carefully preserved. The courts eliminated the legislative veto, but they have consistently upheld the supremacy of legislative intent in the rulemaking process and enforced congressional deadlines. Judges have consistently upheld the legitimacy of presidential management of the rulemaking process, but they have made it plain that neither congressional nor judicial mandates can be ignored or subverted. For itself, pronouncements to the contrary notwithstanding, the judiciary has issued decisions that not only influence the process and content of rulemaking in profound ways but also invite lawsuits in the future. This is a way of ensuring that its inherent passivity will not be an obstacle to effective oversight.

Notes

1. William Niskanen, *Bureaucracy and Representative Government* (Chicago: Aldine, 1971), pp. 29–30; Theodore Lowi, "Two Roads to Serfdom: Liberalism, Conservatism, and Administrative Power," *American University Law Review* 36 (1987): 295–322.
2. Barry Mitnick, *The Political Economy of Regulation* (New York: Columbia University Press, 1980).
3. Mathew D. McCubbins, "Legislative Design of Regulatory Structure," *American Journal of Political Science* 29 (1985): 721–748.
4. Randall Calvert, Mathew McCubbins, and Barry Weingast, "A Theory of Political Control of Agency Discretion," *American Journal of Political Science* 33 (1989): 588–611.
5. Gary Bryner has argued that bureaucrats exercise little or no discretion during rulemaking. See Gary Bryner, *Bureaucratic Discretion: Law and Policy in Federal Regulatory Agencies* (Boston: Little, Brown, 1987).
6. Calvert, McCubbins, and Weingast, "A Theory of Political Control," p. 606.
7. David Schoenbrod, *Power without Responsibility: How Congress Abuses People through Delegation* (New Haven: Yale University Press, 1993).
8. Lowi, "Two Roads to Serfdom," p. 317.
9. Mathew D. McCubbins, Roger G. Noll, and Barry R. Weingast, "Administrative Procedures as Instruments of Political Control" (paper delivered to the annual meeting of the Midwest Political Science Association, Chicago, March 1987), p. 53.
10. Christopher Foreman, *Signals from the Hill: Congressional Oversight and the Challenge of Social Regulation* (New Haven: Yale University Press, 1988), pp. 93–94.
11. Curtis W. Copeland, "Congressional Influence on Rulemaking and Regulation through Appropriations Restrictions" (Washington, D.C.: Congressional Research Service, 2008).
12. 42 U.S.C. 6924(d)(1)(2).
13. Benjamin Mintz and Nancy Miller, *A Guide to Federal Agency Rulemaking*, 2nd ed. (Washington, D.C.: Administrative Conference of the United States, 1991), p. 15 at n. 54; Jacob E. Gersen and Ann Joseph O'Connell, "Deadlines in Administrative Law," *University of Pennsylvania Law Review* 156, no. 923 (2008).
14. Rosemary O'Leary, *Environmental Change: Federal Courts and the EPA* (Philadelphia: Temple University Press, 1993), p. 171.
15. Joel Aberbach, *Keeping a Watchful Eye: The Politics of Congressional Oversight* (Washington, D.C.: Brookings Institution, 1990).
16. Mathew McCubbins and Thomas Schwartz, "Congressional Oversight Overlooked: Police Patrols versus Fire Alarms," *American Journal of Political Science* 28 (1987): 165–179.
17. Foreman, *Signals from the Hill*, pp. 100–101. This list includes examples that fit in each of the categories established by McCubbins and Schwartz. Foreman notes that the examples include both "public spirited values and narrower constituency interests." Ibid., p. 100.
18. Barbara Craig, *The Legislative Veto: Congressional Control of Regulation* (Boulder, Colo.: Westview Press, 1983), p. 27.
19. Foreman, *Signals from the Hill*, pp. 139–140.
20. Ibid., p. 141.
21. *Immigration and Naturalization Service v. Chadha*, 462 U.S. 919 (1983).
22. Walter Oleszek, *The House Corrections Calendar*, Congressional Research Service, February 28, 1997.

23. Congressional Research Service, "Congressional Review of Agency Rulemaking: An Update and Assessment of the Congressional Review after a Decade" (Washington, D.C.: U.S. Library of Congress, R.L. 30116), p. 6 and et seq.

24. Sally Katzen, Statement to the Subcommittee on Commercial and Administrative Law, Committee on the Judiciary of the United States, September 12, 1997.

25. For example, see General Accounting Office, *The Consumer Product Safety Commission Needs to Issue Safety Standards Faster* (Washington, D.C.: General Accounting Office, 1977).

26. Harold Bruff, "Presidential Management of Agency Rulemaking," *George Washington Law Review* 57 (1989): 540.

27. See James Pfiffner, "Presidential Signing Statements and Their Implications for Public Administration," *Public Administration Review* 69, no. 2 (March/April 2009): 249–255.

28. Bruff, "Presidential Management," pp. 568–572.

29. Richard Weyman, "A Better Way to Conduct Regulatory Review," *Washington Lawyer* (November/December 1992): 17.

30. See Jeffrey Lubbers, *A Guide to Federal Agency Rulemaking*, 4th ed. (Chicago: American Bar Association, 2006), p. 204; Office of Management and Budget, Office of Information and Regulatory Affairs, www.reginfo.gov/public/jsp/EO/promptletters/jsp.

31. Rahm Emanuel, "Memorandum to Heads of Executive Departments and Agencies: Regulatory Review," January 20, 2009.

32. Robert Percival, "Checks without Balance: Executive Office Oversight of the Environmental Protection Agency," *Law and Contemporary Problems* 54 (1991): 156–161.

33. Bruff, "Presidential Management," pp. 557–558. See also Steven Croley, "White House Review of Agency Rulemaking: An Empirical Investigation," *University of Chicago Law Review* 70, no. 3 (summer 2003): 821–885; and William F. West, "The Institutionalization of Regulatory Review: Organizational Stability and Responsive Competence at OIRA," *Presidential Studies Quarterly* 35, no. 1 (2003): 76–93.

34. Bruff, "Presidential Management," pp. 560–562.

35. Ibid., p. 561.

36. See *National Grain and Feed Association v. Occupational Safety and Health Administration*, 866 F.2d 717 (5th Cir. 1989) and *Environmental Defense Fund v. Thomas*, 627 F. Supp. 566 (D.D.C. 1986), discussed in Mintz and Miller, *A Guide to Federal Agency Rulemaking*, p. 33.

37. National Academy of Public Administration, *Presidential Management of Rulemaking in Regulatory Agencies* (Washington, D.C.: National Academy of Public Administration, 1987); see also Bruff, "Presidential Management"; Croley, "White House Review"; and West, "The Institutionalization of Regulatory Review."

38. The controversy over the OMB's role triggered a considerable amount of theorizing about the proper roles of Congress and the president in rulemaking. For a review of these theoretical arguments, see James Bowers, "Looking at OMB's Regulatory Review through a Shared Powers Perspective," *Presidential Studies Quarterly* 23 (spring 1993): 331–345; and Joseph Cooper and William West, "The Theory and Practice of OMB Review of Agency Rules," *Journal of Politics* 50 (1988): 864–895.

39. "For McIntosh, No Middle Road," *National Journal: Congress Daily*, April 2, 1998, p. 7.

40. Curtis W. Copeland, "Federal Rulemaking: The Role of the Office of Information and Regulatory Affairs" (Washington, D.C.: Congressional Research Service, 2009), summary.

41. Ibid.

42. Elena Kagan, "Presidential Administration," *Harvard Law Review* 114, no. 8 (June 2001): 2245–2385.

43. George Eads and Michael Fix, *Relief or Reform? Reagan's Regulatory Dilemma* (Washington, D.C.: Urban Institute Press, 1984).

44. "Presidential Oversight: A Panel with Regulatory 'Czars' from Reagan to Bush" (Philadelphia: University of Pennsylvania Law School), December 6, 2006.

45. "Rulemaking: OMB's Role in Reviews of Agencies' Draft Rules and the Transparency of Those Reviews" (Washington, D.C.: U.S. GAO, 2003), GAO-03-929.

46. Bruff, "Presidential Management," p. 595.

47. For a good review of literature and an in-depth discussion of the use of cost-benefit analysis in rulemaking, see Thomas McGarrity, *Reinventing Rationality: Regulatory Analysis in the Federal Government* (Cambridge: Cambridge University Press, 1991).

48. Committee to Review the OMB Risk Assessment Bulletin, Board on Environmental Studies and Toxicology, National Research Council of the National Academies, *Scientific Review of the Proposed Risk Assessment Bulletin from the Office of Management and Budget* (Washington, D.C.: National Academies Press, 2007).

49. Susan Dudley and Sharon Hays, "Updated Principles for Risk Analysis," Office of Management and Budget and Office of Science and Technology Policy, September 19, 2007.

50. For examples of criticisms, see Public Citizen, "OMB Subjects Science to Politics, Continues to Push Agencies in Risk Assessment," September 19, 2007, www.citizen .org/autosafety/regs/whitehouse/articles.cfm?ID=17124.

51. Howard Ball, *Courts and Politics* (Englewood Cliffs, N.J.: Prentice Hall, 1980), chap. 8.

52. R. Shep Melnick, *Regulation and the Courts* (Washington, D.C.: Brookings Institution, 1983).

53. The discussion that follows draws on the analyses found in Lawrence Baum, *American Courts: Process and Policy* (Boston: Houghton Mifflin, 1988), chaps. 2, 7, and 8; and Ball, *Courts and Politics,* chaps. 3, 6, and 7.

54. Mintz and Miller, *A Guide to Federal Agency Rulemaking,* pp. 304–307.

55. The outline of issues and the selection of cases related to judicial review closely adhere to analyses that can be found in many administrative law texts. See, for example, Stephen Breyer and Richard Stewart, *Administrative Law and Regulatory Policy* (Boston: Little, Brown, 1985); or Walter Gellhorn, Clark Byre, and Peter Strauss, *Administrative Law: Cases and Comments,* 7th ed. (Mineola, N.Y.: Foundation Press, 1979). For this section we have also relied heavily on part IV of *A Guide to Federal Agency Rulemaking.* It is both authoritative and accessible to nonlawyers.

56. *Perkins v. Lukens Steel,* 310 U.S. 113 (1940).

57. *Associated Industries v. Ickes,* 134 F.2d 694 (1943).

58. 5 U.S.C. 702.

59. For example, see 42 U.S.C. A-7604.

60. *U.S. v. SCRAP,* 412 U.S. 669 (1973).

61. *Senior v. Eastern Kentucky Welfare Rights Organization,* 426 U.S. 26 (1976).

62. *Duke Power v. North Carolina Environmental Group,* 438 U.S. 59 (1978).

63. Lubbers, *A Guide to Federal Agency Rulemaking,* pp. 410–421.

64. *Association of Data Processing Service Organizations v. Camp,* 397 U.S. 150, 151 (1970).

65. Lubbers, *A Guide to Federal Agency Rulemaking,* pp. 410–431.

66. Ibid., pp. 440–468.

67. 5 U.S.C. 706.

68. Lubbers, *A Guide to Federal Agency Rulemaking,* pp. 471–472.

69. Stephen M. Johnson, "Good Guidance, Good Grief," *University of Missouri Law Review* 72, no. 3 (summer 2007): 695.

70. See Martin Shapiro, "APA: Past, Present, Future," *Virginia Law Review* 72 (1986): 454. He notes that the plain meaning of these terms would allow agencies to issue rules with any content as long as judges did not find they had "acted like a lunatic."

71. 401 U.S. 402 (1971).

72. 463 U.S. 29 (1983).

73. 435 U.S. 519 (1978).

74. 467 U.S. 637 (1984).

75. Lubbers, *A Guide to Federal Agency Rulemaking,* pp. 480–488.

76. Ibid., p. 489.

77. O'Leary, *Environmental Change,* chap. 7.

78. Ibid., p. 154.

79. Ibid., p. 155.

80. Ibid., pp. 155–156.

81. Ibid., p. 37.

82. R. Shep Melnick, *Regulation and the Courts.*

CHAPTER 7

Rulemaking: Theories and Reform Proposals

Practical, pragmatic readers are no doubt casting a wary eye on the title of this final chapter. They likely value facts, cold-eyed realism, and a problem-solving attitude. For many, "theory" connotes a painfully abstract or irrelevant academic exercise too removed from the problems of the real world to help those who must live with them, or try to solve them. Theorizing, like anything else, can be done badly. But it is folly to dismiss it out of hand. The simple fact is that the construction of a theory of rulemaking is not a luxury; it is an indispensable tool for all students of rulemaking, whether their interests lie in scholarship or practice.

The Value of Theory

Theory promises to bring order and simplicity to a large and otherwise fragmented body of knowledge about rulemaking. It highlights the general features of rulemaking and the most important variations in each. Theory explicitly and clearly defines the relationships between those different characteristics of rulemaking and reveals how such interactions affect its process and results. By positioning what is understood about rulemaking, theory provides the essential foundation for the creation of new knowledge. Theory enables the development of predictions, or hypotheses, about rulemaking, which can then be tested through empirical research. The new knowledge that is created during the course of this research contributes, in turn, to the further development and refinement of theory.

The identification of theory with scholars, however, can divert attention from the important contributions it can make to actual practice. Theory is a tool for both research and practice. It helps those engaged in any aspect of rulemaking to understand how their particular work contributes to the larger whole and how their contributions are affected by others working on other aspects of the process. At any given moment, someone is at work attempting to change rulemaking in order to achieve a higher purpose, fix a recognized problem, or advance interests. These changes are promoted by members of Congress, the president and his staff, judges, the many bureaucracies of the federal government, or interest groups. Whatever the motivation of those who would change the rulemaking process, be it lofty or base, they proceed on the belief that the actions they contemplate will produce desired results. Theory, properly tested by solid research on actual rulemaking practice, can give these change agents confidence that the reform they are supporting will be successful, or at least not make matters worse.

The Elements of Rulemaking Theory

To be of value, a theory of rulemaking must provide the answers to at least three fundamental questions. First, why does rulemaking occur? The reasons why rulemaking has come to play so crucial a role in making law and establishing policy are many and reveal much about our institutions of government and the nature of our politics. Second, what determines the results of rulemaking? The conduct of rulemaking and the content of rules are influenced by many different forces. Identifying these forces and the means by which they influence rulemaking is critical to understanding how the process works and the factors to be considered when contemplating reform. Third, and most important, what are the implications of rulemaking for our constitutional system? Each of these questions has been raised and addressed in various ways in the previous chapters. A review of what we know about each of these questions strongly suggests that a comprehensive theory of rulemaking is well within our grasp.

Why Does Rulemaking Occur?

In Chapter 1 we briefly reviewed the reasons institutions and groups gravitate to rulemaking. Given the fact that rulemaking has been occurring since the dawn of the Republic, its age and prominence must be owed to something quite fundamental in our political system. At the most naive level, some have argued that rulemaking happens because the legislature always turns to the executive branch or independent administrative entities to provide the minor details of programs set in motion by statutes. In this view, while technically a legislative function, rulemaking is not to be confused with the real powers of Congress. The subject matters of rules are too innocuous, trivial, or routine to be considered on a par with statutes. Congress is simply handing off work that is not worthy of its attention to subordinates who act on its behalf. This type of argument was embraced by the federal judiciary early in the twentieth century when it rejected arguments that Congress was unconstitutionally delegating important powers to agencies. However reassuring this quaint view of rulemaking might be, material presented in earlier chapters makes it plain that it is an unsatisfactory explanation for the occurrence of rulemaking. Many rules are inconsequential or minor, but others, by any measure, are quite consequential, and their cumulative weight most certainly is not trivial. The roots of rulemaking are found in the relative capacities of governmental institutions and the preferences of the various actors who together comprise our political system.

The growth of the federal government, particularly, is both the cause and the consequence of rulemaking. As members of Congress create ever-greater responsibilities for the federal government, they repeatedly confront and acknowledge the limitations of their own institution. Unable to provide all the essential elements of every public program they formulate, they turned to agencies for help. Whether the growth of government since the onset of the Great Depression is a result of Congress's responsiveness to unprompted constituency demands or its discovery of the electoral bullet-proofing provided by "pork," the effects on rulemaking are indisputable. Congress has always chosen to cede crucial elements of the design and virtually all implementation of thousands of programs to rulemaking. Overwhelmed by demands from the public or by their own ambition, members of every Congress since the first realized that they could not provide in statutes all that was needed to define and guide public policy.

To argue, in effect, that rulemaking is both a cause and consequence defies logic. Perhaps it is more accurate to say that a symbiotic relationship exists between the growth of government and the role of rulemaking. Government could not have grown as rapidly as it did unless rulemaking had supplied the specifics of law, policy, and procedure. Rulemaking would not be so prominent if the reach of public policy and law was less ambitious. The habit of relying on rulemaking, once established, has proven impossible to break as successive waves of statutes have created ever-larger agendas for rulemaking by agencies. Although it is conceivable that Congress could provide all the necessary operating principles and procedures of every public program it creates, the time taken in assembling the requisite information and resolving the inevitable disputes over these minute details would ensure there would be far fewer programs than there are today. In addition, the enormous technical complexity would stymie the current Congress. An alternative is a vastly larger Congress and attendant staff, a development that would require massive institutional change and raise constitutional issues related to separation of powers. Of course, there is always the option of turning general and vague statutes over to agencies without the authority to write rules. Then, agencies could function entirely free of the channeling and constraining effects of rules and deal with all clients, regulated parties, and applications according to their own discretion. Under our Constitution this would obviously be unacceptable. Some critics argue that even under our present system bureaucratic discretion is too great. Congress sees rulemaking as a tool for maintaining accountability.

The institutional limitations on Congress and the huge legislative capacity that rulemaking adds to our governmental system are important factors in explaining the occurrence of rulemaking. But at an even more fundamental level the incidence of rulemaking can be explained by an examination of the preferences of the actors who make up our political system. It was argued in Chapter 1 that rulemaking served the interests of Congress, the president, the courts, agencies, and organized interests. It is useful to review at somewhat greater depth the reasons these actors prefer rulemaking to other means of specifying law and policy.

Any attempt to explain the occurrence of rulemaking must begin with Congress. Fortunately, there is considerable literature devoted to the general question of delegation of legislative authority and even more to questions related to Congress's apparent preference for transferring powers like rulemaking to administrative agencies. Some years ago Morris Fiorina developed the "shift responsibility" model of legislative behavior.[1] In it, members of Congress delegate functions like rulemaking to administrative agencies whenever they suspect that the decisions made during the course of these types of actions could stimulate controversy, criticism, and adverse political consequences. Since many, if not most, of the programs initiated since the start of the New Deal carried with them the possibility of alienating one or more powerful interests, Fiorina's model, now accepted by many political scientists, would explain the great profusion of rulemaking. By shifting responsibility and deferring difficult or dangerous decisions to rulemaking, Congress does not necessarily cede control over the content of rules. Congress remains concerned and active with regard to rulemaking through a variety of oversight devices. Kenneth Culp Davis argued nearly forty years ago that by insisting on rulemaking Congress increases its capacity to oversee the administrative process.[2] Rulemaking is easier to track, observe, and intervene in than other forms of bureaucratic action, particularly those involving formal enforcement actions or hearings and their attendant legal strictures.

Presidents and judges, to the extent that they prefer rulemaking, do so for reasons different from those of Congress. Administrative agencies present both the executive and judicial branches of government with formidable challenges to their constitutional responsibilities and prerogatives. For the president, this vast bureaucracy is a threat to his ability to obtain the policies promised during campaigns. For the judges, administrative agencies are the source of millions of decisions with quite direct and sometimes profound effects on the law and the lives of individuals. The actions that cause these effects must be grounded in the law that judges interpret and apply. The observation and supervision of rulemaking are distinctly advantageous to both the president and the judiciary.

The clearing of rules through the Office of Management and Budget could have been initiated by any president. Presidents may prefer minimal rulemaking whatsoever and move to frustrate it, as recent presidents have. But rulemaking is inevitable, so presidents must choose an alternative route to influence it. Rules are a form of administrative action that is peculiarly susceptible to presidential scrutiny. In addition, rules establish general policies and procedures that form the basis of the countless actions taken in individual cases by thousands of bureaucrats. This makes rulemaking a tempting target for intervention. Any effort to control other types of administrative actions, such as the granting or denial of government benefits, enforcement actions in regulatory programs, or the direct delivery of services, would simply not be feasible because of the sheer volume and variability of these types of actions. Review of rulemaking allows the president to put a policy stamp on significant agency decisions that in turn affect all pertinent aspects of a program's implementation.

The judiciary faces a problem similar to that of the president, with the obvious difference that our judges are not proactively pursuing a partisan political or policy agenda. Davis argued strongly that courts should insist that agencies write rules in order to assert their authority over administrators.[3] The enormous number and variety of interactions between agencies and people, all of which are supposed to be based on law, far exceed the limited capacity of the courts to hear cases or the ability of those aggrieved by illegal agency actions to bring them in the first place. Rulemaking alters both of these conditions. While quite numerous, to be sure, significant rules are far fewer than other forms of administrative action. More important, rules often affect a large number of people, and when these effects are adverse, such groups have the incentive and may have the organization and resources to challenge the legality of the proposed governmental action. Their authority thus invoked through litigation, the judges are presented with the opportunity to review and influence rules in a manner analogous to that used by the White House, albeit for very different reasons. In this instance judges who are so inclined are able to impose their view of the law on the development of rules, thus having a broad effect on the programs for which rules provide the architecture. Rulemaking provides both the president and the courts, institutions with limited capacities, something that no other common form of administrative action provides: an opportunity to observe and supervise the bureaucracy. We would expect the chief executive and the judiciary, whatever their attitudes, at least grudgingly to encourage rulemaking because it broadens their oversight powers.

To put it mildly, rulemaking is congenial to interest groups. During the past several decades interest groups have grown in number, diversified, and narrowed their focus. Interest groups are sufficiently sophisticated to understand the benefits and costs that may arise from rules. They have also developed the means for monitoring rulemaking processes and for communicating their views to the rulemakers. They prefer the relative calm and predictability of a process that operates according to fixed procedures; participation requires at least a modicum of technical expertise and a certain understanding of bureaucratic decision making. Much congressional decision making hinges less often on arcane technical considerations than on broader policy and political considerations. While rulemaking may affect large numbers of people, it also tends to deal with narrower or highly specific issues. As rules become increasingly detailed, more specific to an industry or product, and more technical, the rulemaking process grows more susceptible to the strengths of interest groups. In such situations agencies frequently lack some or all of the essential information to formulate the rule and must turn to interest groups or their individual members for the data or analyses that are required. Information becomes influence.

Finally, there are the personnel in the agencies that write the rules. Much has been written about those who populate our federal agencies. The most persistent distinction drawn in the literature is between political appointees and the career civil servants. Of the two, it can be argued that the political appointees—unless they are staunch advocates for free market approaches—are more likely to welcome rulemaking unequivocally. The ability to review rules written in the offices and bureaus under their discretion allows appointees, like presidents, to influence policy. It also enables these officials to express themselves in the content of rules and in the way they are written. Involvement in rulemaking provides political appointees one of the best ways to leave a mark on an agency that they will probably be with for only a short time.

The posture of career civil servants toward rulemaking is not as clear, because these individuals may be motivated by many different goals. In his classic work *Inside Bureaucracy,* Anthony Downs posits that there are five types of bureaucrats: climbers, conservers, advocates, zealots, and statespersons. Climbers are personally ambitious. Conservers are cautious, even fearful, of any action that might expose them to criticism or disturb the status quo to which they have grown accustomed. Advocates are more pragmatic bureaucratic politicians; they act to protect their particular office's programs.

Zealots are true believers, ideologues who are convinced that theirs is the sole legitimate vision for the program in which they work. Statespersons are concerned with the health of their agency and its programs, seeking consensus based on reasoned discourse and fair consideration of all positions. Some may consider these caricatures, rather than true archetypes. Motives and behavior vary with situations. The literatures of bureaucratic behavior are viewed by the vast contemporary reader as somewhat antique. However, whether we consider them archetypes, traits, or tendencies, Downs's general models are valuable. His types do capture important tendencies that can still be observed in real-world federal employees. Each of these tendencies can find the opportunities for expression in rulemaking.[4]

The climber can enhance his or her reputation by leading a work group responsible for a significant, highly visible rule. The conserver, while generally preferring a low profile, finds solace in those agencies and situations in which rulemaking is a collective decision-making process with many participants and multiple layers of review and approval. Then, rulemaking is a process in which the individual participant can easily avoid the sometimes harsh light of recognition. The advocate can participate in rulemaking work groups and protect his or her program. The zealot regards rulemaking as a marvelous opportunity to impose his or her world view on a program, comparable to rewriting the statute. Finally, the statesperson views the collective nature of the most significant rulemaking quite differently from the conserver. Work groups and task forces are seen by the statesperson as vehicles for forging consensus. Therefore, rulemaking holds the potential to serve the additional organizational purpose of strengthening the agency and its programs.

The occurrence of rulemaking is thus explained by the convergence of four factors:

- the volume of demands presented to Congress by the American people;
- the tendency of Congress to respond positively to those demands;
- the limitations that prevent Congress from writing laws specific enough to be administered;
- the confluence of interests among the most important actors in our political system.

The first cornerstone of a theory of rulemaking is in place.

What Determines the Content of Rules?

Of the fundamental questions that a theory of rulemaking must address, this one is clearly the most complex and difficult. It is also one that is the most intriguing to scholars and practitioners alike. For scholars, the answer to this question reveals much about the underlying dynamics and distribution of power in our contemporary political system. Practitioners should be anxious to learn about the forces that impinge on them and affect what they produce when they function as rulemakers. Those who have read to this point have some appreciation for why the answer to this question is neither simple nor easy to construct. As we have seen, rules are enormously varied in content and effect. This ensures significant variation in the basic forces that are present to a greater or lesser extent in all rulemaking efforts.

General Influences. The results of rulemaking, including the content of rules, are determined by four large and interrelated forces. Some combination of law, information, politics, and management ultimately determines every rulemaking effort. We are hardly the first scholars to identify these factors as important and note their interaction.

Keith Hawkins and John Thomas have argued that rulemaking is "a complex activity subject to a variety of legal, political and bureaucratic constraints."[5] The effects of each of these factors on rulemaking should now be apparent. Law establishes the substantive goals and procedural requirements for rulemaking; it directs agency efforts and provides the standards against which the agency's final product can be judged. Information is the raw material from which rules are formulated in accordance with law. The availability and quality of information largely determine the quality of the rule and its timeliness. Politics permeates the rulemaking process, bringing strong pressures to bear on those developing rules. Management can influence both the content and pace of rulemaking. Internal concurrence systems, for example, ensure that the political leaders of agencies have their say during the process, and various kinds of administrative devices can either expedite or impede the flow of rules.

We have treated each of these categories of influence in earlier sections of the book. We must acknowledge, however, that it is a serious mistake to consider these forces as mutually exclusive categories, or in some instances even easily distinguishable from one another. These dimensions overlap; each exerts some influence over the others. Through the interactions of these dimensions, rules are formed. Law sets the goals and objectives of rulemaking. In so doing it determines the type of information agencies must consider, provides parameters within which political forces will contend for influence, and provides management structures in agencies with their rulemaking mission. Information influences the content of law insofar as its availability and quality allows Congress to be specific in the goals and objectives it sets for agencies. Information is the currency of politics as it is practiced in rulemaking. The various parties use technical, scientific, economic, administrative, and attitudinal information strategically and tactically to influence the content of rules. The collection and analysis of information dominate rulemaking management systems, from the setting of priorities to the publication of a final rule in the *Federal Register.* Politics determines the content of law in the first instance. It heavily influences the interpretation and significance afforded information developed during the course of rulemaking. Politics affects both the internal and external environments that impinge on agency rulemaking management systems. The management of the rulemaking, including both culture and operating systems, determines the personnel who interpret the law and the means by which information is collected, analyzed, and used. The culture of agencies, consisting of widely held values and customary procedures, determines how internal politics play out and how rulemakers interact with the external forces attempting to influence their work.

Across the range of governmental rulemaking the variation within each of these dimensions is considerable. Law varies in the specificity and scope of goals it sets for agency rulemaking and in the type of information that must be considered during the rulemaking process. There are dramatic differences in the quality and availability of information in individual rulemakings. Political conflict can be widespread and intense or nonexistent. Management of rulemaking in agencies varies as well. In addition to the findings on management systems presented in Chapter 4, there is solid evidence that the rulemaking cultures of agencies can vary widely.

Every major player in the American political system—Congress, the president, the courts, interest groups, and the bureaucracy—is deeply involved in rulemaking and in each of its dimensions. They influence the formation and interpretation of law. Each generates or evaluates information used in the formation of rules. Most are politically active or must deal with the fallout from political conflict. Each is either actively involved in or trying to influence the management of the rulemaking process. But like the dimensions of rulemaking, there is considerable variation within each of these categories of major institutional players. None is monolithic. Congress is highly decentralized, speaking with many voices on any issue of substance. The courts, populated by judges who have varying legal philosophies, have been known to send conflicting messages to agencies. Interest groups come in all sizes, beliefs, policy concerns, and capacities to influence government decision making. The bureaucracy is populated by political and career officials. The political appointees may be faithfully following the president or pursuing their own agendas. There is tremendous variation in the educational backgrounds, professional orientations, and experience of career staff members. Furthermore, they bring to their work different motivations.

It is also important to note that each of these players may focus his or her attention on different dimensions of rulemaking in order to influence the result. Congress is preoccupied with setting goals and objectives through law, but doing so requires attention to information requirements. Congress—individual members and their staffs—also exerts political pressure during the rulemaking process and involves itself in management to the extent that statutes or oversight activities set rulemaking priorities, provide budgets for programs requiring rulemaking, and set deadlines for the completion of work. Presidents to date have focused on management, notably the review analyses, and on the political dimension. Interest groups try to influence the content of law, including information requirements. They use the information they have in hand to affect the agency's thinking about the content of rules. They too mobilize political pressure—both in and out of government—and bring it to bear on agencies. The courts focus on the law, leading them inexorably to the information on which rules are based. Decisions of courts can bear on management insofar as priorities, budgets, and deadlines are affected. Agencies must focus on all four dimensions. They interact with Congress on the formation of statutes. Once rulemaking is under way, they become preoccupied with management and information. And individual bureaucratic participants may attempt to mobilize political pressure to achieve their objectives.

Every one of these actors is important, but one, the bureaucracy, deserves special attention. Ultimately, the personnel in the rulemaking agencies are the ones who transmit the final rule to the *Federal Register* for publication. Each dimension of rulemaking is evident in the work of rulemaking agencies. If they hope to influence the content of rules or the process by which they are written, all of the other actors must focus their attention on the agencies. What, then, can existing theory tell us about the factors that determine how personnel in agencies reach decisions on the content of the rules they write? There are, in fact, two theories of agency behavior that offer contrasting ways to structure a study of rulemaking. Neither is adequate definitively, but one provides a point of departure for a more acceptable, albeit complex, theory of how rules are formulated.

The "Bureau Dominance" School. Law, information, politics, or management must structure, channel, or otherwise affect the behavior of bureaucrats if it is to influence rulemaking. Who or what controls bureaucracy is one of the central questions in contemporary scholarship devoted to public affairs. In this literature there are pronounced differences between those who have concluded that bureaucracy is the dominant force in the public policy process and others, who view bureaucrats as the servants of external masters. The bureau dominance school has included scholars as disparate as the political scientist Theodore Lowi and the economist William Niskanen. As evidence of bureau autonomy they pointed to massive delegations of authority; the near monopoly that bureaus enjoy with regard to critical information related to program operations; and the lack, in the other constitutional branches of government, of resources, power, or incentives to monitor and control agencies. Lowi has referred to the bureaucrats who write rules as "patrons" who dole out benefits to the American people, who have been reduced to "serfs." Niskanen focused on the behavior of bureaucrats in attempting to obtain budgets and argued that the congressional committees that reviewed such requests would frequently accede to their "budget maximizing" proposals.[6] According to the bureau dominance perspective, if law, information, or politics play a role in rulemaking, it is largely to the extent that bureaucrats allow.

Let's assume, for the sake of argument, that the bureau dominance school of thought is correct and that agencies are largely free to fashion rules to their liking. What implications does this hold for the content of rules? Existing scholarship on the composition and behavior of bureaucracies indicates that the results of rulemaking are influenced by personal, professional, and structural-cultural factors. The personal level has already been introduced through Downs's admittedly stylized bureaucratic types. Just as each type may adopt a different posture toward rulemaking per se, each seeks to achieve different results in rulemaking. The goal of conservers is likely to be a rule that represents the least threat to their comfortable status quo or, alternatively, the least potential disruption to their careers. Climbers actively pursue any rulemaking result that might advance their careers. This may mean acting to establish themselves as experts in a new area of law and public policy, thus enhancing career options in the private sector, or simply currying favor with a superior in the agency capable of recommending or granting promotion, a salary increase, or a bonus. Zealots seek content in the rule that mirrors their vision for the program, whatever that may be. Advocates promote the views of their particular corner of the bureaucracy and may be every bit as strident as zealots, albeit for different reasons and perhaps with less energy. Statespersons seek results and behave as conciliating versions of zealots.

Thus, bureaucracies that write rules are populated with people with different motivations and personal goals. As Downs notes, pure forms of these types are probably not as common as what he calls "mixed motive" bureaucrats who vacillate between behaviors of the various types, depending on the circumstances surrounding the rule and the stage of their careers.[7] What is clear, however, is that when these motivations and behaviors manifest themselves in rulemaking agencies, the results of rulemakings are affected.

William West, as we have seen, has identified professional differences among bureaucrats that affect the content of rules, focusing on the importance of training and viewpoint. He properly conceives of rulemaking as a bureaucratic task that routinely requires the involvement of lawyers, scientific and technical experts, policy analysts, and senior agency officials serving as political appointees. He hypothesizes that each of these professional groups brings different perspectives and objectives to the rulemaking enterprise. These arise from their education, training, and allegiance. Attorneys seek rules that are true to the statutes they implement, that are enforceable and capable of surviving judicial review. Scientific and technical personnel seek rules that reflect the state of knowledge in their respective disciplines, whereas policy analysts, at least those trained in cost-benefit analysis, want rules that maximize net benefits. Through a survey of agency personnel, West confirmed that the hypothesized differences can be observed in the responses of the professional groups to questions about various aspects of rulemaking.[8] Like Downs, West established that conflict is likely when different types of bureaucrats are engaged in rulemaking.

Thomas McGarrity has provided important insights into the variations in rulemaking structure and cultures. Based on his observations of the Environmental Protection Agency (EPA), the National Highway Transportation Safety Administration, and other agencies, he has developed five "structural models for the internal decisionmaking process" for rulemaking. Each emphasizes different agency values and different management approaches to the rulemaking task. The "team model" conducts rulemaking in work groups comprised of representatives from all agency offices "that have an interest in the outcome of the rulemaking process" and are "co-equal partners in pursuit of the common goals of promulgating a rule that will survive internal and external review."[9] We noted that many agencies use teams of some sort. McGarrity notes that team members share a commitment to reaching consensus on important issues. Under the "hierarchical model" of rulemaking "a single office is responsible for all aspects ... except the final determination of whether the rule is consistent with the particular statute involved."[10] The hierarchical model is most often used in highly technical issues and in agencies in which the essential expertise is confined to a single office, but it also may be used in other situations when the agency "is under great pressure to accomplish something in a hurry."[11]

Another model, the "outside advisor," combines features of the team and hierarchical models by vesting authority in a single office; the experts in that office reach out selectively to others in the agency on an as-needed basis.[12] Obviously, this model seeks to combine the virtues of speed and economy while preserving access to others across the agency, whose expertise or acquiescence may be needed. The "adversary model" is quite different in its approach. It actually sets up an internal, usually bilateral, trial in which interested officers develop and defend their own positions while challenging those of their adversaries; final decisions are made by senior decision makers.[13] Finally, McGarrity notes a "hybrid model" that was used for a time at the EPA. This model combines, improbably, elements of the team approach with certain features of the adversary model. The agency used an "options selection" process to consider different approaches that might be taken in selected rulemakings.[14] The process at that stage was adversarial, but when an approach was selected, the team model was then followed to develop the rule.

McGarrity's and more recent similar works are noteworthy because they describe bureaucratic settings in which these differences in motivation and professional orientation play themselves out. In rulemaking agencies that adopt the hierarchical model, the professional training of the individual(s) in whom decision-making authority is vested is quite important, although, as McGarrity points out, attorneys—due in part to concerns regarding the proper interpretation of statutes or fear of litigation—also have some say over the final product. Of Downs's types, the climber, zealot, or advocate could be relevant as well. In the team model all professional categories and bureaucratic types could be present. For team or work-group operations, the statesperson and the zealot are potentially important. The statesperson is likely to smooth differences and seek consensus and thus may serve as a mediator between advocates from various program and nonprogram offices. If the statesperson emerges as a team leader, a result that has widespread support becomes more likely. The presence of one or more zealots, on the other hand, makes the consensus-building process more difficult, because zealots are unlikely to yield much if they believe their vision for the program in question is threatened. In the outside-advisor model any professional may be consulted by the office with primary responsibility. Since policy analysts with training in cost-benefit methodologies are often assigned to specialized units, they are likely candidates for consultation. Because the adversary model places a clear premium on advocacy skills, one might assume that the passion Downs's zealots bring to the preparation of their case would make them particularly effective. From West's perspective, attorneys educated in the art of advocacy would appear well positioned to take on a central role.

So, if we accept the bureau dominance theory, it is evident that there are multiple influences and often internal spirited competition for control over the results of rulemaking. The literature devoted to bureaucratic motivation, professional training, and organizational culture and structure indicates clearly that some level of conflict is likely in significant rulemakings involving multiple personnel or offices in an agency. Even in the hierarchical model, the agency attorney, in making final determinations about the legality of the rule in question, introduces the potential for conflict. In the other models conflict is either explicitly sought, as in the adversary approach, or an almost certain by-product of throwing together diverse professional perspectives and personal ambitions. These factors have no intrinsic political bias from which one can hypothesize the emergence of a particular type of policy.

Although the bureau dominance theory is sufficiently complex to keep interested students of rulemaking busy for some time, it fails to encompass the true complexity of rulemaking. The most important test of the bureau dominance model is how well it explains how rulemaking really works. If the bureau dominance school is correct, we would expect to see those who work in agencies enjoying substantial, although not unbridled, discretion in the writing of rules. This is not what Gary Bryner found more than two decades ago in his study of the rulemaking processes in four major agencies: the Occupational Safety and Health Administration, the EPA, the Consumer Product Safety Commission, and the Food and Drug Administration. He summarized his finding this way: "If we mean by discretion that agencies are free to do as they choose, are free to allocate their resources and can exercise their power unencumbered by external checks then agencies clearly have little discretion."[15] The author went on to cite the "oversupply" of "overseers" as the major influence on rulemakers. During these intervening twenty years the number of overseers has not grown smaller, and they are much better armed. Attention must shift from inside the agency to these outside forces.

The "Principal-Agent" School. Those working in agencies are aware of and responsive to institutions and actors outside their walls. Even the literature whose focus is the internal workings of bureaus and bureaucrats acknowledges strong links to powerful external forces. We need not spend time teasing relationships between agencies and the outside world from this literature because there is now a large alternative body of scholarship that explores the powerful forces in the external environment that influence the course of rulemaking.

The alternative to the bureau dominance model, now a more widely accepted school of thought, was aptly described by Wesley Magat, Alan Krupnick, and Winston Harrington as the "external signals model" of rulemaking, which they attribute to the work of economist Roger Noll.[16] This general view of bureaucratic decision making has several variations, including the "interest representation" model of Richard Stewart, and the principal-agent model, identified first by Barry Mitnick.[17]

The principal-agent model posits an ongoing relationship between the bureaucratic "agent" and "principals," in this case the constitutional branches of government. The relationship is characterized by goals that motivate each of the parties but may not be compatible, and by bureaucratic operations that lead to results other than what the principal prefers. The principal sets its goals, establishing an agenda that it expects the agent to pursue. The agent, however, may be tempted to "shirk," preferring pursuit of other substitute or supplemental goals. Even when the agent's goals coincide with those of the principal, bureaus may employ decision-making procedures that lead to perverse results or manage programs in such a way that the desired results are much delayed. The principal-agent model thus explicitly seeks to account for the sometimes fierce competition among multiple principals, including the president and the courts, for influence.

Interest groups may never be considered direct principals, but they certainly influence the institutions that are. Their actions stimulate and sometimes motivate those of Congress, the White House, and the courts. When threatened by action or inaction by bureaucrats, interest groups petition Congress and the White House for help.[18] Of course, agencies with strong links to certain interests may respond directly to their entreaties. It is reasonable to suspect this to be especially true of political appointees in agencies.

Consider the information dimension of rulemaking mentioned earlier in the chapter. Early in the process agencies may rely on their own resources for the development of a proposed rule; or, as we saw in Chapter 5, agencies may reach out immediately to interest groups for necessary information. Whether they provide it early or not, interest groups have ample opportunity to share the information they do have during comment periods or other forums for public participation. Information from the White House during its review may alter the content of rules, and it is always possible that no matter where the information used by the agency comes from, a reviewing court will find it the wrong type or of insufficient quality.

The sources and channels of the political dimension are also richly varied. An agency's internal politics may profoundly influence the priority given a rule and determine which office in the agency and which personnel are assigned the task of writing it. But if internal political activity surrounding the rule is intense, external parties are likely to take an interest as well. Congress, the White House, and interest groups may be involved at any stage in the process, and communication is quite common among these actors and between them and the agency personnel writing the rules. The importance of the political dimension and the role of political pressure are influenced by other dimensions, notably law and information. Where the law is subject to alternative interpretations and where information is hard to get, of poor quality, or difficult to interpret, politics—both internal and external—is very important. Where law and information are precise and thus highly directive, politics holds less significance. When politics is important in rulemaking, we can also expect to find principals and agents joining in temporary and evershifting coalitions to leverage their individual capacities to influence rules. There are as many possible combinations as there are permutations of the players. It is possible to play out many plausible scenarios to demonstrate the conditions under which one or more of the actors will influence, or even dominate, the results of rulemaking.

As we explore a few scenarios, we would do well to consider the recent admonitions of two prominent students of bureaucratic decision making, Richard Waterman and Kenneth Meier. On the value of principal-agent theory, they write:

> Principal-agent models are supposed to be dynamic, not static. They characterize relationships that develop and evolve.... Political actors, whether politicians or bureaucrats, learn over time about both policy and politics; all institutions develop some capacity over time.[19]

The dynamism that Waterman and Meier believe characterizes principal-agent relations is quite evident in rulemaking. Rulemaking offers both participants and nonparticipating external parties opportunities to learn, change positions, and interact with one another while information is enhanced and goals shift. Complexity is the ultimate challenge to rulemaking theory and thus is worthy of further exploration.

Alternative Rulemaking Situations. When one attempts to sort out the factors that determine the content of rules, theory confronts enormous complexity. The range of the effects of rules created for the public leads to considerable variation in the viewpoints of external groups and institutions that participate in the rulemaking. Exploring a few alternative situations will establish this point more clearly.

One common situation is a rulemaking that is initiated in accordance with an unambiguous and clear statutory mandate. Authority for development of the rule has been vested within a single program office in the responsible agency. The expertise and information needed to complete the rule are in ample supply in the program office. Those outside the agency who will be affected by the rule have discussed the subject matter with the agency for many years. The agency and external interests have developed a close working relationship, with frequent informal consultations. The agency in question writes this particular type of rule so often that nothing other than the most routine check-in with the Office of General Counsel is required. The involvement by other offices in the agency is rare or nonexistent. The rule is formally or informally exempted from White House scrutiny because of its routine or noncontroversial nature. Congress takes little interest in the rule because no constituent has pulled a "fire alarm." The entire affair is handled with relatively little effort, internal tension, and external conflict. Hence, no litigation occurs.

Previous chapters have reviewed rulemaking programs not unlike the one described here. Many agricultural marketing orders, airworthiness directives, and airspace management rules and regulations that restrict or coordinate traffic on rivers display some if not most of these characteristics. The results of these types of rulemakings are dictated by technical considerations, be they accepted maintenance practices, characteristics of the physical space near airports, known relationships between the supply of a given commodity and its market price, or judgments regarding the allocation or principles of safe waterway use.

A dizzying variety of alternative situations arises when we consider how each of the general elements in any of the above examples could change. Consider the case of an agency that undertakes to write a rule to deal with a developing or newly discovered problem or situation that it believes to be within its statutory jurisdiction. The congressional delegation of authority to write rules in this particular area, however, may be ambiguous, or the statute is altogether silent. The agency may undertake a rulemaking that under authority it infers from the statutory language, but the agency's interpretation is subject to dispute. A struggle will ensue over the legal dimension of rulemaking. Alternatively, consider the situation when the authority to write rules is unambiguous, but the statute is unclear on the information or factors it expects the agency to consider when writing the rule. The parties will then contend over what information is relevant, making this dimension highly influential, at least temporarily. Responsibility within the agency for writing the rule may not be fixed, or there may be multiple offices with a legitimate claim of leadership or participation in its development. The rule may affect the jurisdiction of more than one program office, and since it represents a new area of activity, numerous policy options may be open. If the statutory authority is unsettled, the Office of General Counsel will take a keen interest. Visible and potentially controversial, it catches the attention of the political leadership of the agency as well. The management dimension of rulemaking emerges in these circumstances and takes on a special significance.

Because the rule is breaking new ground, it is likely that working relationships with affected interests will not be as well established. Some of these interactions may be hostile, at least initially, because government is viewed as once again extending its reach. Of course, there may be interests that support this new public initiative. Still, the securing of reliable and complete information is more difficult. There may be a number of affected interests with distinctly different views on what the rule should contain. They may have substantial resources, or be sophisticated about the importance of rulemaking; they may have strong links to Congress, the White House, or both. They bombard the agency with position papers, requests for meetings, and long written comments when the draft rule is issued. The information dimension again becomes important. The political dimension begins to loom large. The interested parties activate their allies on Capitol Hill or in the White House to exert pressure on the agency. They form coalitions to leverage information and political resources.

The bureaucratic types offered by Downs provide a point of departure for considering how the rulemakers in agencies perceive and interact with external principals. "Conservers" may seek to sidestep what they perceive to be dangerous levels of conflict in the external environment by finding a way to avoid involvement in the rulemaking, leaving the decision to more ambitious and less risk-averse officials. Among these are the "zealots," who are likely to join in an explicit or implicit coalition with those external principals whose views most closely match their own. They will use available information to bolster this position, perhaps on a selective basis. "Climbers" will champion the cause of those who can do them the most personal good. This may mean affiliating themselves with the White House, joining in a quiet coalition with principals in Congress, colluding with an external group, or undertaking some combination or all of these activities. Affiliation and joint action depend on whom the climbers wish to impress. "Statespersons" may express their concern for the agency's overall program by serving as brokers and mediators between the contending external principals. Those at odds with each other may or may not be receptive to agents' playing this type of role.

When the rule is issued, those interests that are unhappy sue in federal court. The legal dimension once again emerges and dominates. This complex scenario may not be as common as the first example, but neither can it be characterized as extreme or rare.

These two situations have many, many variants. Congress might be unambiguous about the delegation of authority to write rules but still unclear about the direction the agency might take in the rule or the criteria the agency is to employ when determining its contents. Within the agency an outside-advisor model might be used, or the agency might rely on a formal advisory committee to assist it with some aspect of rule development, or it might pursue full-blown regulatory negotiation. Information may be available but contradictory. The agency may have to conduct extensive original research to resolve the contradictions or, lacking the time or money to do so, attempt to reach a compromise position or delay that part of the rule affected by the conflicting or absent data. External interests may be numerous but unequal in their awareness of the subtleties of rulemaking and the resources at their disposal to influence the process. Consequently, the agency may find itself compensating for this imbalance by fashioning means of outreach in order to ensure that all points of view are represented before a rule is finalized. Or, alternatively, the golden rule applies—to those with the gold rule.

The mere bleat from a stuck constituent will not guarantee intervention by Congress or the president, but neither can it be ignored. Members of Congress may receive mixed signals from different groups. And, when they act, rulemakers do not treat all inquiries by Congress equally. Similarly, the White House must weigh the source of the complaint about a rule under development, and it must husband its resources by picking its spots.

In activating Congress or the president, interest groups must think strategically, because a victory from this type of intervention might be short-lived if it incurs the wrath of the others. Studies of presidential management of rulemaking emphasize the great power the president or those acting on his behalf can exert when choosing to become involved in rulemaking. But the notion that the White House will confront easy decisions regarding the positions it might take in a controversial rulemaking is certainly open to challenge. Although some recent presidential administrations have clearly tended to favor business in their review activities, one can hardly argue, given the volume of new rules that were produced during these years, that other interests enjoyed a monopoly of influence. Like Congress, the White House often faces powerful contending interests, and choosing between them is not always an attractive prospect. In such circumstances the presidential staff may take a hands-off attitude, preferring, perhaps insisting, that the agency find a way to accommodate the diverse positions that have been taken.

Groups possess an incomplete understanding about the positions adopted by their competitors and, more important, the relative quality of competing information. This is a potentially dangerous situation, especially when competitors are litigious and some in the agency are unhappy with the content of the emerging rule. Even with the backing of the White House, groups may choose to settle for a rule that is less than fully satisfactory but forestalls challenge by the competition. The main consideration here is litigation. The groups may reason that while they could initially have their way in the rulemaking, they might ultimately lose everything gained in the rule if a lawsuit were successful. We need only refer back to the preceding chapter to note the variation in the results of rulemaking brought about by judicial review. Agencies do not always simply win or lose; they often win or lose more or less. There are a number of possible results, ranging from a finding that a rule is utterly without merit because it is not authorized by the statute it claims to implement, to complete endorsement of the rule by the judge or judges hearing the case. In between these extremes are outcomes that require the agency to undertake revisions of varying degrees and types. The court might find misinterpretation of statutory intent, inadequate or inappropriate rulemaking procedures, insufficient information, or faulty analysis supporting a rule. In effect, the court can order the partial or full repeal of a rulemaking.

A Special Note on the Earliest Stages of Rulemaking. Evidence and theorizing from multiple sources indicate that the time at which information is supplied or pressure applied is a significant factor in determining the content of a rule. Signing statements issued by presidents to accompany newly enacted legislation to agencies for implementation provide the early direction to rulemakers. In Chapter 4 we detailed the importance of guidance provided at the initial stages by senior agency officials to those writing rules. Respondents to our surveys described in Chapter 5 rated communication with agency officials prior to issuance of a notice of proposed rulemaking highly among the tactics they employ and consider influential when attempting to influence the course of a rule development process. Research by various scholars on participation in rulemaking clearly indicates that public comments received by agencies from affected interests and the public are taken very seriously, but a fair reading of that literature leads to a conclusion that by the time comment is solicited, the agency has determined and committed itself to a course of action. Drawing on theory from the field of psychology, Stephanie Stern notes: "Consistency theory offers new insight into the familiar complaint that rulemaking is unresponsive to public input.... After agency members have devoted months, even years, to preparing a proposed rule the *attitude maintenance bias* [emphasis added] suggests suboptimal processing later inputs.... The effects of cognitive consistency is to decrease the frequency of ... position changes."[20] Put another way, once established, agency positions on a developing rule become a thing of value that, according to James Q. Wilson's work cited earlier in the book, will be aggressively protected in a regulatory setting. Major changes between the notices of proposed and final rulemaking stages are clearly very hard. Given the strong pressures on the agency, it would not be surprising to find change limited largely to matters somehow overlooked by the rulemakers or to minor changes.

Seminal work by William West in a series of interviews with agency personnel confirms the importance of early participation by interest groups. His research finds that communication during this important pre-proposal stage is very common. In addition, the research suggests that business interests, in particular, participate more actively and effectively during this time period of rule development.[21] Organizations that can be heard prior to the proposal may have some particular advantage in influencing the direction of a rule before an agency has determined a specific path. The perception that guidance documents, direct final rules, and interim final rules are now in greater use adds weight to the argument that for many, if not most, rules the critical work is done early and with input from those who have both the access and means to provide agency personnel what they need at the crucial formative stages of a given rulemaking.

The challenges this emerging "theory of early influence" (for want of a better term) presents to scholars, reformers, and participants are formidable indeed. For scholars, our ability to test hypotheses is challenged by the relative obscurity of a given rule's earliest stages, such as the initial transfers of responsibility and guidance from senior management or other influentials within the implementing agency. Our ability to conduct rigorous inquiry will also be affected by the extent to which documentary records of relevant internal and external communications are both complete and accessible. Moves by reformers to make the earliest stages more transparent or less susceptible to powerful external interests must be attentive to the law of unintended consequences. Greater transparency may chill the very frank and pointed exchanges of views that, internally, ultimately contribute to a stronger and more effective rule. Adding more notice and disclosure requirements about early communications with external sources of information will likely slow the process and further discourage the free flow of information to data-challenged agencies with similar effects on quality. These may be costs we are willing to bear, however, for the benefits of openness and objectivity that such reforms might bring. But for participants in rulemaking, when all is said and done, the key issue remains the imbalance of power we have noted elsewhere in this book. Placing more emphasis on early participation exacerbates the information and resource differentials that separate the powerful from the powerless in rulemaking.

As we consider agenda items for future research, it is vital to consider the formative influences that emerge of rulemaking's earliest stages. The world already has far too many tortured extensions and variations of the "big bang" theory that now dominates cosmology. That will not deter us, however, from piling on with one of our own. Indeed, it could be that much of what ultimately lands in the pages of the *Code of Federal Regulations* originates in the earliest days of rule development.

The Central Importance of Negotiation and Compromise. Across the dimensions and among the major players in rulemaking, negotiation and compromise are constants. This is especially true for major rules in which the issues are numerous, stakes are high, and conflict is intense. Whether they are mediations of a statesperson between a zealot and an advocate in an agency; discussions that occur in agency work groups and teams; informal consultations between responsible officials and external interest groups; full-blown regulatory negotiations; or give-and-take between agency personnel, congressional staff or members, and White House staff, negotiation and compromise—explicit or implicit—are ubiquitous elements of the process. In this crucial respect, rulemaking resembles the larger political system.

However deeply felt a personal ambition or deeply held a belief, and however strong a desire to gain or not to lose, many in the rulemaking process have powerful reasons to negotiate and compromise. The players in rulemaking have incentives to maintain good working relationships with one another. They may have to deal with one another again, whatever the outcome of the rulemaking at hand. McGarrity has shown us that within bureaucracies there are structures to promote consensus. Even structures other than the team model of rulemaking ultimately force contending parties to compromise. Several of Downs's traits will move toward compromise and negotiation. The statesperson does it for the public interest, the advocate to protect the interests of his or her office, the climber to curry favor, and the conserver to minimize disruption. Stewart's interest representation model is one way to look at the agency's role in negotiations. The agency may serve as an explicit or implicit broker among contending interests. Alternatively, it may be one party in a negotiation. Or it could be merely a ratifier of compromises reached by other parties.

External to the agency, the White House maintains an active dialogue with agencies during the course of rulemaking review. Congress, at the staff level especially, does the same. Chapter 5 discussed close communication among interest groups and between interest groups and rulemaking agencies that might not be called negotiation in a formal sense but certainly suggests a common if not pervasive tendency to seek accommodation.

Willingness to bargain is not universal, of course, but even when conflict persists and is unresolved during the entire rulemaking process, a compromise result is still possible. Litigation is always an option when affected parties are unhappy with the results of a rulemaking. It is not uncommon for a court to issue a decision that forces agencies to rewrite rules to correct errors or other shortcomings first identified by the persons bringing the lawsuit. In some instances the court requires the agency to negotiate and reach agreement with the plaintiffs. In this manner a result based on forced compromise and negotiation can occur after the rulemaking is completed.[22] Again, the foregoing does not suggest any consistent bias in the content of rules, and we can be reasonably certain that negotiation and compromise, within and between the major institutional players, are common if not ubiquitous elements of the process by which the most important rules are created.

Prospects for Rigorous Analysis. It is not unreasonable to state that we have identified the great forces that determine the content of rules. The dimensions—law, information, politics, and management—and the players—Congress, the president, the courts, interest groups, and agencies—are known, and a vast body of literature provides insights into their interests, tendencies, and behavior that can be mined for use in rulemaking research.

The great challenge for future scholarship is to examine these forces at work at the level of individual rules. These dimensions and players must be examined in a large number of case studies to determine the conditions under which each becomes particularly important. The research that is needed is enormous in scope, but we have at least one example that suggests the potential value of rigorous empirical research of this sort in explaining the content of rules.

Magat and his colleagues, using a rigorous research design and sophisticated statistical analysis, attempted to explain the varying levels of pollution control mandated in effluent guidelines issued by the EPA under the provision of the Clean Water Act.[23] These rules determined how much of specified pollutants would be allowed in the waste-water discharges from a large number of industries. They found that the quality of the information had a positive effect on the stringency of standards. Politics, measured by trade association budgets and firm profitability, had negative effects on standards. Written comments filed by affected parties were found to be not very persuasive to the EPA. The authors acknowledge, however, that other types of communication could be occurring, a proposition consistent with yet another set of case studies of effluent guidelines done by the Environmental Law Institute and with findings from the interest group survey reported in Chapter 5 of this book. Although it is not a comprehensive study of all dimensions and players in rulemaking—for example, the possibly important matter of early, less formal participation is not explored—the study by Magat and his coauthors provides encouragement to those seeking rigorous tests of existing theories. They were able to study the qualitative dimension of a particular type of rule, and they developed and measured many variables, each drawn from existing theory, to explain the level at which a given type of rule regulated the private sector. Magat and his colleagues have shown that rigorous empirical research is feasible and can be repeated in a large number of other rulemaking programs. Their work is now twenty-five years old, however, and we still have very few studies employing so rich a mix of independent variables or as precise a measure of the dependent variable. It is important that such research is conducted, because the last question a theory of rulemaking must answer makes it plain that the stakes are quite high for our democracy.

How Does Rulemaking Affect Our System of Government?

Rulemaking affects every institution and process of government, every participant in policy deliberations, and every person affected by rules. Rulemaking frees Congress from the drudgery and political perils of determining the essential details of every program it sets in motion through statute, and the endless task of updating provisions when conditions change. The legislature must, however, remain vigilant so that its bureaucratic agents remain true to statutory intent. Rulemaking also increases the opportunities for members of Congress to intervene on behalf of constituents, thus enhancing their prospects for reelection. Presidents are given an unparalleled opportunity to affect the course of public policy through the review of rules. But time and the rush of events severely limit the number of rules they personally can consider. So presidents must establish elaborate monitoring and review procedures, set criteria for staff intervention, and maintain the political will to withstand the inevitable criticism when their involvement benefits one group to the detriment of another. And the American voter should now be concerned when casting a vote for president how the candidate intends to become involved in rulemaking.

The judicial branch is also given the opportunity to shape law and public policy when presented with a lawsuit by a party aggrieved by a rulemaking. Again, the opportunity for influence is purchased at a cost. Rulemaking litigation represents a workload that competes with a wide variety of disputes for the judiciary's time and attention. It is often complex, hinging on arcane technical and scientific evidence or the nuances of procedure. And it frequently requires supervision after the fact, especially when judges impose deadlines for the completion of a rulemaking, or mandate that agencies and successful litigants work together to produce an acceptable rule and present their handiwork for judicial approval. Interest groups and others who seek to achieve public policy objectives must monitor rulemaking closely, determine how best to influence its course, and plan for those occasions when it does not go their way. If the groups surveyed in Chapter 5 are at all correct in their assessments, we have in rulemaking a governmental process that rivals in importance the legislative process in Congress for the production of law and public policy. And interest groups are responding by devoting resources to the task of influencing rulemaking and by developing sophisticated strategies to get what they want.

No history or explanation of the democratic form of government as it has evolved in this country is complete without the story of rulemaking being fully and accurately told. The will of the people, the concept from which all democratic principles arise, can never be precisely articulated without rules. So the democratic process is never completed until the close of rulemaking. Dislike it as we might, the health of our democracy now hinges in no small part on how well rulemaking works.

The Reform of Rulemaking

In Chapter 3 we explored issues associated with rulemaking that have been identified by academic and professional observers. Each of these observers suggested a condition for rulemaking that would be preferable to its current state. If rules are a poor reflection of congressional intent, we want them to be truer to the statutory promises they are supposed to be making a reality. If they are technically inept or otherwise poorly written, we want them instead to incorporate the best quality and most complete information. If there are too many rules, we want fewer. Of course, those of us who think there are too few want more. If it takes too long to issue rules, we want the process to move faster. But if compliance is going to cost us money, we may want to slow it down to a crawl. If we think that the public is not sufficiently involved in the development of rules, the process should encourage more participation. But we may also want participation of a certain type because we wish to make the process more equitable between the rich and the poor, the powerful and the not so powerful. To do this we will have to spend effort and money motivating and empowering those who do not currently participate. If the rulemaking process is fraught with conflict, as it most certainly will be if we ensure that all interests are represented, we must find, or at least seek, ways to make it more consensual.

Achieving any significant improvements will be a formidable task, because every reformer faces another whose interest would be damaged by a change. The conflict that attends the rulemaking process is merely an extension of the differences that divide persons and groups throughout the rest of the political system. Again, we are dealing with something quite fundamental, namely the pursuit of self-interest. The specificity of the subject matter dealt with in rules guarantees a very clear understanding of the implications of rulemaking for affected parties' needs, wants, and diverse values. It also guarantees that these will be presented clearly by those affected. To the extent that there are differences in needs, wants, and values, there will be conflict.

The shortcomings in public participation in rulemaking go deeper than the openness of the process and the resources available to those who are affected. If we are to avoid a "government by the interested" and a rulemaking process in which those not immediately and significantly affected have no role in the formulation of law, we must reverse the forces that have led to the issue networks and policy subsystems that dominate our political system. We must convince those with little or no direct stake in the outcome of a rulemaking that they too should be concerned with the result. This is a very tough sell when people are able to keep up with only a fraction of the issues that profoundly affect their lives and become involved in only a few of them. In a nation where so many fail to vote, is it reasonable to expect an outpouring of interest in rulemaking from average citizens with comparatively little to win or lose? Perhaps not, but lowering our expectations is a dangerous choice.

Rulemaking in all its aspects is a core governmental function that cannot be understood if considered in isolation or as a secondary or peripheral activity. Contemporary rulemaking is the product of a long evolution and now consists of complex institutional and political forces. To attempt fundamental reform of rulemaking without reform of these larger institutions and forces is futile. Rulemaking is inextricably bound to these forces; it cannot be separated from them. To fix what we think is broken in rulemaking, we must fix the core elements of our political system from which the problem truly arises.

Rulemaking now constitutes a layer of decision making so important that the constitutionally established branches of the national government compete, often consciously and aggressively, to control it. Furthermore, it has become a magnet for those interests sophisticated enough to understand where the policy that affects our lives most directly is made, and sufficiently well organized and in command of enough resources to be able to participate effectively in the development of rules. The Constitution's directive that the legislative power will be vested in Congress is not, and never has been, completely true. The functions performed by Congress and the other branches are central to the conduct of government, but no more so than the often obscure and homely rulemaking activities conducted in departments, agencies, commissions, and the like.

The twentieth century witnessed momentous events. Nations rose and fell while the great theories of government competed and warred for hegemony. One, democracy, survived and appears at this writing to be widely accepted as the government of choice for the twenty-first century. For this reason alone, rulemaking occupies a position of great importance. America is hardly alone among democratic nations in its inability to function without rulemaking. But rulemaking is especially central to the American democratic experience. Our popularly elected representatives have embraced an ever more expansive view of government. Never mind the incessant complaints issuing from Congress and the White House about government's stranglehold on our lives, its poor performance, mismanagement, and waste. The twentieth century is mute testimony to a faith, however misplaced, that no problem is beyond government's capacity to solve, no aspiration is beyond government's ability to realize. The growth in the scope and volume of rulemaking is a direct consequence of the growing and changing expectations of the American people. Change the political system—our expectations; the characteristics of Congress, the presidency, and the courts; the behavior of interest groups, bureaucrats, and bureaucracies—and rulemaking will inevitably follow.

Anyone concerned with the state of our democracy and the performance of our government must be concerned with the state of rulemaking.

We can be no less demanding about this process than we are about any other, and certainly no less aware. We should, for example, be as concerned with the frequency and quality of participation in rulemaking as we are with voter turnout in elections. Because we do not have the opportunity to determine through election who the rulemakers will be, participation in the actual process of developing rules is crucial to maintaining the link between democratic principles and lawmaking. The absence of elections is no small sacrifice of democratic principles, but we have virtually every other means of participating in the development of rules that is available to us when Congress is considering legislation. In fact, we may be in a better position to participate in rulemaking because the issues are usually more specific and their effects on our particular circumstances easier to predict. Rulemaking is a legislative process well designed for an era when both issues and interests are narrowly defined. We should be as demanding about the management of rulemaking by agencies of government as we are about any of the other functions they perform. Is rulemaking less important than personnel systems, budgeting, financial management, or procurement? Most agencies have acknowledged that it is important by establishing management structures that identify rulemaking as a significant function.

Today, nearly twenty years since the initial publication of this book, the importance of rulemaking cannot be easily discerned from the curricula of political science, public administration, and public policy programs that educate those who work in agencies. In these, rulemaking rarely, if ever, merits more than a portion of a single course. Clearly, this is an area in which the academic community lags behind practitioners. The best way for rulemaking to assume a more prominent place in our teaching is for it to become a more prominent topic for research. Yet we are encouraged by the increase in scholarly attention to rulemaking more recently triggered in part by a rush of interest in e-rulemaking and related technology. We are also encouraged by the revival of the Administrative Conference of the United States, a small but potentially important public agency that is charged with seeking better performance in the core legal functions of agencies, including rulemaking. It is a subject worthy of the attention of the finest minds in all disciplines. If it does nothing else, this book is worthwhile if it prods other scholars to examine some phase of rulemaking better than we have done here.

Through the rulemaking process pass the sum and substance of the hopes and fears of this democratic nation. We will understand it, our government, and ourselves better when we treat rulemaking as the most important source of law and policy for the conduct of our daily lives. It will occupy that status unless the improbable occurs and we find some very different way to govern ourselves.

Notes

1. Morris Fiorina, "Legislative Choice of Regulatory Forms: Legal Process or Administrative Process," *Public Choice* 39 (1982): 33–66.
2. Kenneth Culp Davis, *Discretionary Justice: A Preliminary Inquiry* (Urbana: University of Illinois Press, 1969), p. 15.
3. Ibid., pp. 220–221.
4. Anthony Downs, *Inside Bureaucracy* (Boston: Little, Brown, 1967), chap. 9.
5. Keith Hawkins and John Thomas, "Rulemaking and Discretion: Implications for Regulatory Policy," in *Making Regulatory Policy*, ed. Keith Hawkins and John Thomas (Pittsburgh: University of Pittsburgh Press, 1989), p. 265.
6. Theodore Lowi, "Two Roads to Serfdom: Liberalism, Conservatism, and Administrative Power," *American University Law Review* 36 (1987): 321–322; William A. Niskanen Jr., *Bureaucracy and Representative Government* (New York: Aldine Atherton, 1971).
7. Downs, *Inside Bureaucracy*, pp. 101–103.
8. William West, "The Growth of Internal Conflict in Administrative Regulation," *Public Administration Review* 48 (July/August 1988): 773–782.
9. Thomas McGarrity, "The Internal Structure of EPA Rulemaking," *Law and Contemporary Problems* 54 (1991): 90.
10. Ibid., p. 94.
11. Ibid., p. 95.
12. Ibid., pp. 97–98.
13. Ibid., pp. 99–100.
14. Ibid., pp. 102–103.
15. Gary Bryner, *Bureaucratic Discretion* (New York: Pergamon, 1987), p. 208.
16. Wesley Magat, Alan Krupnick, and Winston Harrington, *Rules in the Making: A Statistical Analysis of Regulatory Agency Behavior* (Washington, D.C.: Resources for the Future, 1986), p. 49.
17. Richard Stewart, "The Reformation of American Administrative Law," *Harvard Law Review* 80 (1975): 1667–1711; Barry Mitnick, *The Political Economy of Regulation* (New York: Columbia University Press, 1980).
18. Jeff Worsham and Jay Gatrell, "Multiple Principals, Multiple Signals: A Signaling Approach to Principal-Agent Relations," *Policy Studies Journal* 33, no. 3 (2005): 363.
19. Richard Waterman and Kenneth Meier, "Principal-Agent Models: An Expansion," *Journal of Public Administration Research and Theory* 8 (1998): 197.
20. Stephanie Stern, "Cognitive Consistency, Theory Maintenance, and Administrative Rulemaking," *University of Pittsburgh Law Review* 63, no. 589 (2002): 591.
21. William West, "Outside Participation in the Development of Proposed Rules," Bush School Capstone Report delivered to the Congressional Research Service, May 11, 2006 (with SangNam Ahn, Junlin Du, Ryan Garrett, Elia Martinez, Caitlyn Miller, Mark Needham, and Ge Song).
22. Rosemary O'Leary, *Environmental Change: Federal Courts and the EPA* (Philadelphia: Temple University Press, 1995).
23. Magat, Krupnick, and Harrington, *Rules in the Making*, chaps. 6 and 7.

APPENDIX

Titles and Chapters in the *Code of Federal Regulations*

Title 1—General Provisions
Title 2—[Reserved]
Title 3—The President
Title 4—Accounts
Title 5—Administrative Personnel
Title 6—Domestic Security
Title 7—Agriculture
   Subtitle A—Office of the Secretary of Agriculture (Parts 0–26)
   Subtitle B—Regulations of the Department of Agriculture
Title 8—Aliens and Nationality
Title 9—Animals and Animal Products
Title 10—Energy
Title 11—Federal Elections
Title 12—Banks and Banking
Title 13—Business Credit and Assistance
Title 14—Aeronautics and Space
Title 15—Commerce and Foreign Trade
Title 16—Commercial Practices
Title 17—Commodity and Securities Exchanges
Title 18—Conservation of Power and Water Resources
Title 19—Customs Duties
Title 20—Employees' Benefits
Title 21—Food and Drugs
Title 22—Foreign Relations
Title 23—Highways
Title 24—Housing and Urban Development
   Subtitle A—Office of the Secretary, Department of Housing and Urban Development (Parts 0–99)

Note: This list was revised January 1, 2010.

Subtitle B—Regulations Relating to the Department of Housing and Urban Development

Title 25—Indians

Title 26—Internal Revenue

Title 27—Alcohol, Tobacco Products, and Firearms

Title 28—Judicial Administration

Title 29—Labor

Subtitle A—Office of the Secretary of Labor (Parts 0–99)

Subtitle B—Regulations Relating to Labor

Title 30—Mineral Resources

Title 31—Money and Finance: Treasury

Subtitle A—Office of the Secretary of the Treasury (Parts 0–50)

Subtitle B—Regulations Relating to Money and Finance

Title 32—National Defense

Subtitle A—Department of Defense

Subtitle B—Other Regulations Relating to Defense

Title 33—Navigation and Navigable Waters

Title 34—Education

Subtitle A—Office of the Secretary, Department of Education (Parts 1–99)

Subtitle B—Regulations of the Offices of the Department of Education

Title 35—Vacated

Title 36—Parks, Forests, and Public Property

Title 37—Patents, Trademarks, and Copyrights

Title 38—Pensions, Bonuses, and Veterans' Relief

Title 39—Postal Service

Title 40—Protection of Environment

Title 41—Public Contracts and Property Management

Subtitle B—Other Provisions Relating to Public Contracts

Subtitle C—Federal Property Management Regulations System

Subtitle D—Other Provisions Relating to Property Management [Reserved]

Subtitle E—Federal Information Resources Management Regulations System

Subtitle F—Federal Travel Regulation System

Title 42—Public Health

Title 43—Public Lands: Interior

Subtitle A—Office of the Secretary of the Interior (Parts 1–199)

Subtitle B—Regulations Relating to Public Lands

Title 44—Emergency Management and Assistance

Title 45—Public Welfare

Subtitle A—Department of Health and Human Services, General Administration (Parts 1–199)

Subtitle B—Regulations Relating to Public Welfare

Title 46—Shipping
Title 47—Telecommunications
Title 48—Federal Acquisition Regulations System
Title 49—Transportation
   Subtitle A—Office of the Secretary of Transportation (Parts 1–99)
   Subtitle B—Other Regulations Relating to Transportation
Title 50—Wildlife and Fisheries

Index

Note: Page numbers followed by *f, t,* or *n (nn)* indicate figures, tables, or note(s), respectively.

Aberbach, Joel, 228, 265*n*15

Accountability. *See also* Courts under APA, 55–57
congressional budgetary approaches for, 225–226
congressional deadlines and hammers for, 226–227
congressional oversight of rulemaking performance, 227–228
congressional procedural approaches for, 224–225
legislative veto as means of, 228–232
limiting congressional delegation of authority and, 223–224
mechanisms of, 70–71
Obama's program for, 239–240
OMB's relationship with agencies and, 241–246
overview of, 221–222
perspectives on Congress and, 222–223
presidential, cost-benefit analysis as tool in, 246–247
presidential objectives for, 232–234
records of rulemaking documentation for, 65
regulatory agenda program and, 181
through broader and deeper presidential review, 237–239
through presidential review, 234, 236–237
through selective presidential review, 237
timeliness of rules and OMB/OIRA reviews for, 240–241, 241*t*

Adjudication. *See* Courts

Administration of rules. *See also* Enforcement; Implementation
consideration during draft rule stage for, 81–82

Administrations. *See also* Agencies
as type of agency, 4

Administrative Conference of the United States
acknowledgement of power of presidential oversight by, 246
on e-rulemaking, 202
on negotiated rulemaking, 207, 208–209
on presidential oversight, 244
on public policy instruments used in lieu of rulemaking, 184
revival of, 105, 295

Administrative discretion. *See also* Agencies; Congress; President
rulemaking as abuse of, APA on, 256
rulemaking as abuse of, litigation on, 258
rulemaking as means of containing, 32–33

Administrative law judges. *See also* Judges
for adjudicating rules under the APA, 55

Administrative Procedure Act (1946)
accountability as core element of, 55–57
agencies' observations of provisions of, 224
on alternate procedures avoiding rulemaking, 256
on authority of an agency to write a rule, 255
changes in rulemaking model in, 71–72

Administrative Procedure Act (1946) *(cont.)*
  constitutional questions on bureaucratic
    capacity and legislative limits under,
    29–31
  development of, 49–50
  e-rulemaking and, 202
  exceptions and exemptions in, 73
  general applicability rules in, 65
  information as core element of, 53–54
  judicial review for "persons aggrieved"
    under, 252
  participation in rulemaking and,
    54, 66–70, 175–176
  on process by which a rule is developed,
    255–256
  on public disclosure of information in
    rulemaking, 63–65
  rulemaking provisions in section 553 of,
    51–52
  on rules and rulemaking, 3
  rules classification by, 22
  rules classification prior to, 23
  on scope of judicial reviews, 254–255
Administrative Procedures in Government
    (Attorney General's Committee on
    Administrative Procedure), 50
Adversary model of rulemaking, 280,
    281–282
Advisory committees, 68, 75, 171, 172, 196
Advocates, bureaucratic, 274–275, 279,
    281, 290
Agencies. *See also* Bureaucracy; Career
    bureaucrats; Political appointees
  adversary process of rulemaking, 116
  APA's general applicability rules for, 65
  assigning responsibility for rulemaking
    by, 79–80
  captured by interest groups, public
    participation and, 174, 182
  conflicts among, due to rulemaking era of
    1970s, 15
  contacts with public prior to rule
    proposals by, 200
  culture and operating systems and
    rulemaking by, 277–278
  development of draft rules by, 81–82
  discretion by, rulemaking and, 116–117
  e-rulemaking used by, 202–203

information that must be considered in
    rulemaking by, 58–63
information that must be publicly
    disclosed by, 63–65
internal conflicts and timeliness of
    rulemaking in, 109–110
internal review of draft rules, 82
management deficiencies and timeliness
    of rulemaking by, 112–113
missions of, and substance and process of
    rulemaking by, 44–45
mixed record of business influence on
    rulemaking by, 211–212
need for government emergency response
    and, 30
OMB's relationship with, 241–246
originating, categorizing rules by,
    21–22
as origin of rulemaking activity, 78
participation importance to, 210–211
priority-setting processes of, 131–134
program implementation and volume of
    rules under, 94–96
public comments for Obama on
    interrelationships of OIRA with, 128
rarely affected by adverse judicial
    decisions, 260–261
rule initiation and early input processes
    of, 134–136
rulemaking and self-interest of, 272
rulemaking as strain on institutional
    capacity of, 91–96
rulemaking management. *See* Management
    by individual agencies
semiannual agendas under Carter of,
    180–181
shortage of resources and priorities of,
    112, 113
as sources of information for rules, 102
as sources of rules, 3–4, 91
on success of interest groups to influence
    rulemaking by, 213–214, 214*t*
timeliness of rules and rulemakings by
    other agencies and, 110–111
variable factors in relationship between
    business interests and, 212–213
work group integration with senior
    management of, 161–162

Agency officials. *See also* Career bureaucrats;
  Political appointees
  approval for rule initiation by, 134–136
  Carter on policy oversight of rulemaking
    by, 124, 125
  input for Obama on new executive order
    on rulemaking by, 127–128
  as originators of rulemaking activity, 78
  in principal-agent model, 222–223,
    282–283
  senior, guidance on rulemaking by, 80
  senior, work group integration with,
    161–162
  timeliness of rulemaking by agencies and,
    112
Aggrieved persons, APA on judicial standing
  for, 252–253
Agreements. *See* Rules
Agricultural marketing order program
  business interests and rulemaking
    on, 211
  consumer absence from hearings
    on, 182
  consumers affected by, 28
  legal information for, 153
  participation in rulemaking on, 195
  studies on development of, 190
  unambiguous and clear statutory mandate
    for, 285
Agricultural Marketing Service, 79, 260–261
Agriculture, Department of. *See also*
    Agricultural marketing order program;
    specific government entities reporting to
  Association of Official Agricultural
    Chemists and, 171
  comments on "organic" definition to, 115
  Marketing Service rule on handling and
    sale of specified commodities
    under, 44
  participation during Carter administration
    in, 182
  rule initiation in, 135
  rules conflict with other agencies, 233
  voluntary hearings of, 173
Ahn, SangNam, 296*n*21
Ahrens, Mike, 38*n*45
Airline pilots and crews, FAA rules on flight
  time for, 106, 107

Airspace management rules and regulations,
  44, 285
Airworthiness directives, of FAA
  information for, 101
  legal information for, 153
  timeline for issuing, 42
  unambiguous and clear statutory mandate
    for, 285
  unanticipated and changed conditions
    and, 30–31
American Bankers' Association, 172
American Bar Association (ABA)
  on delegated legislative authority of New
    Deal, 48–49
  on formal judicialization of
    rulemaking, 56
  on politics of rulemaking, 46–47
  on presidential oversight, 244
American Insurance Group (AIG), 1–2
American Railway Association, Bureau of
  Explosives, 172
American Recovery and Reinvestment Act
  (2009), 1
American University, 2005 symposium on
    rulemaking at
  on changing priorities and
    management, 134
  on elements of management, 130–131
  GAO report supporting results of, 142
  on management budgets, 143
  on schedules, 137
  titles of rulemaking managers at,
    150–151
Anderson, James, 86*n*3, 216*n*38, 217*n*61,
    218*n*74
Animal and Plant Health Inspection Service
    (APHIS)
  concurrence systems of, 146–147
  planning documents for rulemaking
    by, 137
  priority-setting process of, 132
  public participation management by, 147
  rule initiation in, 135
  rulemaking training programs of, 155
  rule-writing specialists at, 150
  timeliness of rules by, 107*f*
  volume of comments on ostrich
    importation to, 115

Anthony, Robert, 38*n*40, 38*n*43, 88*n*45,
216*n*48
Appeal, courts of, 250–251. *See also* Courts
Appropriations bills. *See* Budgets
Arbitrariness of rules, 55, 56, 256, 257–258
Association of Official Agricultural Chemists,
Department of Agriculture and, 171
Attitude maintenance bias, 288
Attorney(s) general
manual on public disclosure of
rulemaking information by, 64
private individuals as, 252
Attorney General's Committee on
Administrative Procedure
Administrative Procedures in Government
by, 49–50
on early inattention to participation in
rulemaking, 170–171
on fisheries' response to Interior Dept.'s
rules for, 46
on models of participation, 178
on participation at end of the 1930s,
171–175
on participation in rulemaking, 66
Roosevelt's purpose for, 11
Attorneys. *See also* American Bar
Association; General Counsel,
Office of
agency, rulemaking role of, 78, 109
in hierarchical model of
rulemaking, 281
Interior Dept. rulemaking and, 11
private sector compliance and need
for, 95
role in work groups, 156, 159
West on rulemaking role for, 279–280
Authority
of agencies to write a rule, APA on, 255
of agencies to write a rule, litigation
on, 257
information on proposed rules under type
of, 53
of rules, participation and, 168–169
for work group membership, 161
Authorization, for rulemaking, 79, 112
Authorizing statutes. *See also* Legislation
on information agencies must consider
when rulemaking, 58–60
on participation in rulemaking, 83

participation in rulemaking under, 110
public disclosure requirements in, 64
on public participation, 67
Aviation Rulemaking Advisory Committee
(ARAC), 79, 207–208

Ball, Howard, 164*n*1, 267*n*51
Banking rules, 21, 24, 26. *See also* Financial
institutions
Bardach, Peter, 120*n*32, 120*n*48
Basis of rulemaking. *See also* Purpose, for
rules
APA on accountability and, 55
proposed, information on, 53–54
public disclosure of information
on, 64
risk assessment as, 59
Baum, Lawrence, 267*n*53
Beneficiaries of rules
adjudication for procedural twilight zones
and, 51
administrative process in government
agencies and, 111
captured agencies and, 174
congressional self-interest and, 33
impact information for, 152
obscure or unclear rules and, 97
personnel adjustments to altered
requirements for, 95
on timeliness of rulemaking, 105
Benzene exposure, setting standards for
occupational exposure to, 26, 114
Bernstein, Marver, 38*n*47
Berry, Jeffrey, 185, 215*n*21, 216*n*51
Bituminous Coal Act, 174
Blumstein, James, 164*nn*2–6
Bonfield, Arthur, 38*n*38
Bowers, James, 266*n*38
Boyer, Barry, 37*n*20, 120*n*46
Breyer, Stephen, 36*n*10, 37*n*11, 47, 86*n*8,
102, 120*nn*41–42, 218*n*78, 267*n*55
Browner, Carole, 128–129
Brownlow Committee, 10–11
Bruff, Harold, 266*n*26, 266*n*28, 266*nn*33–34,
266*n*37, 267*n*46
on imprinting president's principles in
OMB review, 246
on OMB advantages in review process,
241–242

on social regulation by OMB during review process, 236

Bryner, Gary, 37*n*13, 38*nn*34–35, 119*n*6, 119*nn*8–9, 120*n*39, 265*n*5, 282, 296*n*15

Budgets. *See also* Resources
congressional oversight of rulemaking using, 225–226
for rulemaking management, 142–144

Bureaucracy. *See also* Agencies
culture and operating systems and rulemaking by, 277–278
discretion by, rulemaking and, 116–117
institutions of, as sources of rules, 4
principal-agent theory of congressional relations with, 222–223
rulemaking to limit power and discretion of, 32–33

Bureaucratic capacity
e-rulemaking and, 204–205
rulemaking and, 29–31

Bureaucratic dominance school
Bryner on overseers of rulemaking and, 282
conflict in, 281–282
Downs's bureaucratic types and, 279
Lowi and Niskanen on, 222, 278–279
McGarrity on variations in rulemaking structure and cultures and, 280–281
West on professional differences among bureaucrats and, 279–280

Bureaucrats. *See* Career bureaucrats

Bureau of Alcohol, Tobacco, and Firearms, 115

Bureau of Explosives, American Railway Association, 172

Bureau of Land Management, 202

Bureau of Marine Inspection and Navigation, 12, 173

Bush, George H. W.
accountability through review under, 234, 235*t*, 236–237
conflicts with OMB review under, 243
moratorium on rulemaking at start of administration of, 112
participation and, 187–188
percentage of rules approved by OIRA without change under, 245*t*
rulemaking management under, 125, 126, 129, 234, 237

rulemaking statistics under administration of, 16–17, 17*t*

Bush, George W.
accountability through review under, 237–239
on communicating rule ideas to OMB, 78
conflicts with OMB review under, 243–244
e-rulemaking progress under, 203
executive order on devices other than rules to set policy under, 184
homeland security rules and rulemaking under, 43
information requirements for rulemaking by executive order of, 63
moratorium on rulemaking at start of administration of, 112
OSHA's Ergonomic Rule and, 231
participation and, 188
percentage of rules approved by OIRA without change under, 245*t*
public confidence in government under, 89
rulemaking management under, 125, 127, 129, 237–239
rulemaking statistics under administration of, 18–20, 19*t*
"Updated Principles of Risk Analysis" from, 247

Businesses and business interest groups. *See also* Corporate earnings and profits; Financial institutions; Small businesses
agencies' contacts prior to rule proposals with, 200–201
early participation in rulemaking by, 288
mixed record of influence on rulemaking by, 211–212
participation by, 189, 193–195
rules affecting starting of, 23–25
on timeliness of rulemaking, 105
variable factors in relationship between rulemaking agencies and, 212–213

Byre, Clark, 267*n*55

Cabinet officers, early Congressional delegation of authority to, 8, 45

Calvert, Randall, 223, 265*n*4, 265*n*6

Canon, Bradley, 87*n*37

Capriciousness of rules, 55, 56, 256, 257–258
Captured agencies, 174, 182
Card, Andrew H., Jr., 238
Career bureaucrats. *See also* Agency officials
  conflict with political appointees, OMB
    and, 241–242
  Downs on types of, 274–275
  rulemaking and self-interest of, 35–36
  timeliness of rules and conflicts between
    political appointees and, 110
  vertical concurrence for conflict
    management and, 146
  West on professional differences among,
    279–280
Carter, Jimmy
  participation and, 180–185
  principles for rulemaking under, 234
  rulemaking and proposed rules under
    Reagan vs., 17–18
  rulemaking management under,
    123–125, 129
Carter v. Carter Coal Co. (1936), 47–48
Case studies
  of legislative vetoes, 230
  of rulemaking participation, 189, 211–212
Categories, in priority-setting systems, 133
Center for Drug Evaluation and Research, 142
Center for Food Safety and Applied
  Nutrition, 142
Center for the Study of Rulemaking, 130–131
Challenges. *See also* Courts
  to delegation of legislative authority
    during New Deal, 47–49
  negotiated rulemaking and, 207
  participation in rulemaking and, 169
  to rules by interested parties, 115
  work group success or failure and, 159
Cheit, Ross, 217*n*61, 218*n*72, 220*nn*111–114,
  220*n*118
  on business interests and rulemakers'
    decisions, 211
  on participation by regulated
    industries, 195
  participation in rulemaking case studies
    by, 190
Chevron USA v. NRDC (1984), 259–260
Children's Bureau, 171
Citizens. *See also* Constituents
  average, reform of rulemaking and, 293

Citizens to Preserve Overton Park v. Volpe
  (1971), 257–258
Civil Rights Act (1972), Title VIII, 22–23
Clayton Act, FTC and, 9
Clean Air Act Amendments (1990), 78, 94
Clean Water Act Amendments (1977),
  177–178
Climbers, bureaucratic, 274–275, 279, 281,
  286, 290
Clinton, Bill
  accountability through review
    under, 237
  conflicts with OMB review under, 243
  federal workforce cuts under, 113
  information requirements for rulemaking
    by executive order of, 63
  on information technology in government,
    202
  on negotiated rulemaking, 208
  OSHA's Ergonomic Rule and, 231
  participation and, 188
  percentage of rules approved by OIRA
    without change under, 245*t*
  Regulatory Working Group under, 78
  rulemaking management under, 125,
    126–127, 129, 237
  rulemaking statistics under administration
    of, 18, 19*t*
  vetoes Comprehensive Regulatory Reform
    Act, 61
Coalition formation, participation and,
  196, 197*t*, 198*t*
Coast Guard, United States, 101, 133,
  135, 143
Code of Federal Regulations (CFR)
  categorized by function performed by
    rules, 22–23
  at close of New Deal and growth into
    1960s, 12–13
  creation of, 10
  organization of categories by titles and
    chapters, 21–22
  page count by selected presidencies, 22*t*
  page count during Reagan presidency,
    16, 17*t*
  for regulating government, 27
  rules added during Bush II
    presidency, 19
  rules added from 1976 to 1980, 15

Codes, under National Industrial Recovery
Act, 10
Coglianese, Cary, 203, 205, 208, 219*n*95,
219*n*103
Cole, Roland, 119*n*7, 119*n*23
Comments. *See also* Notice-and-comment
rulemaking; Written comments
agency consideration of, 288
Carter on increased period for, 180, 181
rebuttal, in legislative hearings, 68
in use at the end of the 1930s, 171, 172
use by agencies of, 67
usefulness of participation for, 169
Commerce, Department of, 133, 135
Commissions. *See also* Agencies
e-rulemaking used by, 203
as type of agency, 4
Committee on the Status and Future of
e-Rulemaking, 203–204
Common Sense Initiative, EPA's, 188
Communication to general public, during
Carter administration, 181
Complexity of rules
difficulties in measuring, 114
problems with, 99–100
timeliness issues and, 107–108
Compliance and implementation
information, 153, 155
Compliance costs, long-delayed rules and,
240–241
Comprehensive Regulatory Reform Act, 61
Compromise, central importance of,
289–290
Conferences, for participation in rulemaking,
66, 171, 172
Conflict. *See also* Controversy
among rulemaking bureaucrats, West on,
280
concurrence systems for managing,
145–147
management for individual rule
development, 152
between OMB and rulemaking agencies,
241–242, 243
between or among agencies on rules,
233–234
participation in rulemaking and, 116, 169
potential at EPA, work groups and,
162, 163

reform of rulemaking and, 293
rulemaking and, 167
timeliness of rulemaking by agencies and,
109–110
in work groups, 158, 160
Congress. *See also* Administrative Procedure
Act; Delegated authority; Legislation
accountability in rulemaking and,
55, 70–71, 221–222, 264
acknowledgement of power of
presidential oversight by, 246
administrative agreement with OMB
on regulatory review procedures
and, 243
affect of rulemaking on, 291–292
benefits of rulemaking for, 167
budgetary approaches for rulemaking
oversight by, 225–226
bureaucratic capacity and limits of, 29–31
CFR on rulemaking by, 12
culture and operating system and
rulemaking by, 277–278
dialogue during rulemaking with agencies
and, 290
early delegation of authority to president
to issue rules by, 8
interest groups and interest in rulemaking
by, 170–171
interest in rulemaking process of, 214
legislative vetoes for rulemaking oversight
by, 228–232, 230*t*
limiting delegation of authority by,
223–224
managing review of agency rulemaking
by, 148–149
Ninety-fifth, frequency and effectiveness
of oversight by, 229*t*
outside advisors on rulemaking and, 287
oversight of rulemaking performance by,
227–228
in principal-agent model, 222–223,
282–283
priority-setting by, timeliness of agencies'
rulemaking and, 113
procedural approaches to oversight by,
224–225
on processes agencies use to write
rules, 15
promotion of participation by, 176–177

Congress *(cont.)*
  public participation in rulemaking
    expansion by, 66–67, 177–179
  reasons for rulemaking by, 272, 275
  review of draft rules by, 84
  rulemaking, bureaucratic capacity and
    limits of, 29–31
  rulemaking process and, 3
  self-interest by, rulemaking and, 33
  on timeliness of rulemaking, 105
  timeliness of rulemaking by agencies and,
    111, 112
  writing laws as origin of rulemaking
    activity, 75
Congressional Research Service, 196, 231,
  243–244
Congressional Review Act (CRA), 149, 231
Congruency of rules, 97, 98
Consensus
  bureaucratic structures promoting, 290
  negotiated rulemaking and, 207, 208
  on participation in rulemaking, 110
  in work groups, 159
Consensus national standards, OSHA's
  institutional capacity and, 92–93
Conservers, bureaucratic, 274–275, 279,
  286, 290
Constituents. *See also* Interest groups
  demands of, as reason for
    rulemaking, 271
  fire alarm oversight and service for, 227
  rulemaking as opportunity for Congress to
    assist, 292
Constitution
  on legislative power of Congress, 293
  rules in violation of, 255
Consultants, interest groups' use of for
  monitoring rulemaking, 195
Consumer product regulations,
  14, 24–25, 68
Consumer Product Safety Act, 178, 179
Consumer Product Safety Act Amendments
  (1981), 178
Consumer Product Safety Commission,
  211, 282
Contacts with agencies, informal
  congressional oversight of rulemaking
    using, 223, 231, 232
  interest groups on effectiveness of, 199

participation in rulemaking using,
    196, 197*t*
  for pre-proposal participation, 199–200
Content information, 152, 154, 169
Contractors, for rule development, 80
Controversy. *See also* Conflict
  participation in rulemaking and, 116
  timeliness of rules and, 109–111
  work group leaders and, 158–159
Cooper, Joseph, 266*n*38
Cooper, Phillip J., 36*n*5, 37*n*22, 87*n*20
Copeland, Curtis W., 119*n*19, 218*n*76, 225,
  265*n*11, 266*nn*40–41
Corporate earnings and profits, 26, 90,
  103. *See also* Businesses and business
  interest groups
Corrections Day, as legislative veto,
  230–231
Cost-benefit analysis
  as information requirement for
    rulemaking, 62, 63, 125–126, 244
  as presidential accountability tool,
    246–247
  public comments for Obama on, 128
  of regulatory impact of major rules, 117
Cost-effectiveness of rules, 96
Costs. *See also* Resources
  of negotiated rulemaking, 209
  of rulemaking during 1970s, 16
  of rulemaking vs. legislation, 31
Council of Economic Advisers, 123–124
Council of Environmental Quality, 83
Council on Competitiveness, 78, 126,
  187–188, 236–237
Council on Wage and Price Stability, 125
Courts. *See also* Challenges; Judicial review;
    Litigation; Supreme Court
  accountability in rulemaking and,
    221–222, 247–248, 264
  affect of rulemaking on, 292
  agencies rarely affected by, 260–261
  APA on situations appropriate for
    rulemaking vs. adjudication by,
    50–51
  CFR on rulemaking by, 12
  culture and operating system and
    rulemaking by, 277–278
  federal, on timeliness of rulemaking, 105
  interest in rulemaking process of, 214

lower, inconsistent interpretations by
    judges of, 259–260
objectives for overseeing rulemaking by,
    248–251
on presidential management of
    rulemaking, 243
as principals, in principal-agent model,
    282–283
priority-setting by, timeliness of agencies'
    rulemaking and, 113
rulemaking process and, 3
scope of review by, 254–259
social regulation decisions by, 261–263
standing issues for, 251–253
timeliness of rulemaking by agencies and,
    111, 112
Craig, Barbara, 265*n*18
Crane, W. Mark, 120*n*35
Croley, Steven, 87*n*36, 164*nn*2–6, 266*n*33,
    266*n*37
Cross-examinations, in legislative hearings
    on rulemaking, 68, 178
Czars of regulatory policy, under Obama,
    128–129

Dalton, Deborah, 219*n*99, 219*n*102
Data Quality Act (2000), 61, 102
Davis, Kenneth Culp, 38*nn*51–52,
    87*nn*17–18, 215*n*20, 296*nn*2–3
on APA's rules of general applicability, 65
on congressional ability to oversee
    administrative process, 272
on courts and rulemaking, 273
on discretionary power, 32
on rulemaking provisions in APA
    section 553, 52
Deadlines, as oversight mechanism, 226–227,
    255, 264
Defense, Department of, 111
Deficits, timeliness of rules and, 112
Delegated authority
    Brownlow Committee study of, 11–12
    of bureaucratic institutions, 4
    legislative, during New Deal, Supreme
        Court on, 47–48
    legislative, early academic study of, 9
    literature on reasons for, 272
    participation and, 167–168
    as reason for rulemaking, 270–271

Democracy
    affect of rulemaking on, 292
    participation in rulemaking as expanded
        form of, 65–70
    reform of rulemaking and, 294–295
    Schoenbrod on delegated authority as
        unacceptable perversion of, 223
Departments. *See also* Agencies
    e-rulemaking used by, 203
    as type of agency, 4
Derivative authority, of bureaucratic
    institutions, 4
Direct final rules, 74, 288
Directives, rulemaking process and, 3
Discretionary Justice (Davis), 32
Discretionary rulemaking, agency
    priority-setting on mandatory
    rulemaking vs., 134
District courts, 250. *See also* Courts
Diver, Colin, 2–3, 36*n*3, 97–100, 120*nn*29–31,
    120*n*33
Dockets, of rulemaking records, 65, 72, 115.
    See also E-dockets
Douglas, William O., 253
Downs, Anthony, 38*n*54, 274–275, 279,
    296*n*4, 296*n*7
Draft rules
    action on, 84–85
    development of, 81–82
    external review of, 82–83
    internal review of, 82
    responsibility for writing, 149–150
    revision and publication of, 83
Du, Junlin, 296*n*21
Dudley, Susan, 267*n*49
Dunlop, John, 205

Eads, George, 267*n*43
Early influence, 134–136, 171, 288–289, 291.
    See also Participation
East West Research Group, 200, 218*n*82,
    218*n*84, 220*n*122. *See also* West,
    William F.
E-dockets, 84, 115–116, 203, 204–205
Education, Department of, 207, 236
Efficiency in rules, 96
Eisenhower, Dwight, 123
Eisner, Neil, 105, 120*n*49, 142,
    165*nn*20–21

Elections, 33, 295

Eligibility. *See also* Beneficiaries of rules
for government programs, 27

Emanuel, Rahm, 240, 266*n*31

Emery, Fred, 88*n*55, 165*n*25

Employee Retirement Income Security Act
(ERISA), 25

Employees. *See also* Career bureaucrats;
Personnel costs; Task forces; Work
groups
businesses and rules about, 24
federal, shortage of and timeliness of
rulemaking, 113

Endangered Species Act Amendments
(1977), 178

Energy, Department of, 111

Energy Policy and Conservation Act, 179

Enforcement
complexity of rules and, 100
differences in perspective between rule
writing and, 109
draft rule stage considerations for,
81–82
lawyers from, role in work groups
of, 156
negotiated rulemaking and costs of, 207
participation in rulemaking and, 169
of procedural requirements for
rulemaking, 74
rulewriting quality oversight and,
103–104

English, plain, 124, 125

Environmental groups, 105, 194, 253

Environmental impact statements (EIS),
60, 68–69, 177

Environmental Law Institute, 291

Environmental legislation, 13, 14, 15, 24, 25

Environmental Protection Agency (EPA).
*See also specific government entities
reporting to*
Bryner on overseers of rulemaking by, 282
on budgets for rulemaking
management, 143
Common Sense Initiative of, 188
Council on Competitiveness and Clean Air
Act notifications, 187
Council on Competitiveness veto of
regulation by, 236–237
draft communications strategy of, 81

FERC's jurisdiction overlapping with,
110–111
hammer provisions directed at, 226
information for rulemaking on toxic
substances by, 58–59
information technology in rulemaking
used by, 202
lawsuits challenging rules by, 261–263
legal information for source performance
standards of, 153
litigation on definition of air pollution
sources, 259
McGarrity's study of internal
decisionmaking processes by,
280–281
negotiated rulemaking used by, 208
OMB reviews and changes to rulemaking
by, 236, 244
participation during Carter administration
in, 183–184
percentage of rules approved by OIRA
without change, 245*t*
planning documents for rulemaking
by, 136
planning provisions of Clean Air Act
Amendments (1990) by, 78
priority-setting process of, 132
on problems with increased
rulemaking, 96
public participation management by,
147, 148
on regulations for staff writing rules,
102–103
rule initiation in, 135
rulemaking during Bush II presidency
by, 20
rulemaking impact on small business
and, 179
rulemaking training programs of, 155
rulemaking volume as strain on
institutional capacity of, 93–94
rules for multiple and distinct interrelated
programs under, 109
rule-writing specialists at, 150
schedules for rulemaking by, 142
time for rulemaking in its four major
program areas, 106
timeliness of rules by, 107*f*, 108*f*
time period for OMB reviews and, 240

types of groups participating in
rulemaking by, 193–194
work group model evolution at,
162–163
work groups' role for, 145, 156
Equal Employment Opportunity
Commission, 22–23
Era of rulemaking (1970s), 13–16, 32–33
Ergonomic Rule, legislative veto and, 231
E-rulemaking, 84, 202–205
Estreicher, Susan, 37*n*30
Evasion of rulemaking procedures, 73–74
Exceptions to legal requirements, 72–73
Executive branch. *See also* Bureaucracy;
President
rulemaking and bureaucratic capacity and
limits of, 30–31
Executive compensation. *See also* Businesses
and business interest groups
Treasury regulations under TARP on, 1–2
Executive order(s)
as basis for rulemaking, 233
exemption allowances in, 73
information requirements for rulemaking
by, 61–63
public participation and rulemaking
under, 69
rulemaking process and, 3
Executive Order 12044 (Carter), 62, 123–125,
126, 180
Executive Order 12291 (Reagan)
on comprehensive rule analysis
program, 186
evasion through interpretation of, 73–74
provisions of, 125–126
on regulatory impact analysis, 62, 63
on time period for OMB reviews, 240
Executive Order 12372 (Reagan), 69
Executive Order 12498 (Reagan), 62
Executive Order 12612 (Reagan), 62
Executive Order 12866 (Clinton)
accountability through selective review
under, 237
Bush II amendment of, 188
Bush II's use of, 238
exemption allowances in, 73
information requirements in, 63
Obama's use of for rulemaking
management, 128

regulatory impact analysis disclosure
under, 69
on time period for OMB reviews, 240
Executive Order 13175 (Clinton), 62
Executive Order 13258 (G. W. Bush), 63, 127
Executive Order 13422 (G. W. Bush), 63, 127
Exemptions, of legal requirements in
rulemaking, 72, 73
Expertise. *See also* Outside experts
of public and interest groups, 168
for rulemaking, 79–80
for work group membership, 161
for writing rules, regulations on, 102–103
Explosives and Combustibles Act (1908), 39
External interests. *See also* Interest groups;
Participation
litigious vs. non-litigious, 261
Stewart on administrative processes of
government agencies and, 111
External signals model, 282

Fair Labor Standards Act, 45–46, 173,
174, 205
Families, Reagan on federal rulemaking
affecting, 63
Farhi, Paul, 119*n*20
FDMS.gov, 203
Federal Advisory Committee Act (FACA,
1972), 68, 154, 177, 202, 209–210
Federal Aviation Administration (FAA)
airworthiness directives of, 30–31, 42, 153
Aviation Rulemaking Advisory Committee
of, 79
on budgets for rulemaking
management, 143
complexity and timeliness of flight-time
rules and, 107
delays in revisions to flight time rules by,
106
information for rulemaking by, 101
negotiated rulemaking used by, 207–208
priority-setting process of, 132
prohibitions and limitations in rules of,
25–26
public participation management by, 148
rare adverse judicial decisions against,
260–261
rulemaking training programs of, 155
rule writer-editors for, 149–150

Federal Aviation Administration (FAA)
(cont.)
schedules for rulemaking by,
137, 138–141f, 142
timeliness of rules by, 107f
work group model evolution at, 162–163
work groups for, 156
Federal Communications Commission (FCC)
on budgets for rulemaking
management, 143
early participation of interested groups
with, 171
history of participation in rulemaking for,
172
on institutional capacity to implement
new rules, 95
planning provisions of
Telecommunications Act (1996)
by, 78
public participation management by, 147,
148
rulemaking volume as strain on
institutional capacity of, 94
vagueness of rules issued by, 97–98
voluntary hearings of, 173
Federal Docket Management System
(FDMS), 203
Federal Energy Regulatory Commission
(FERC)
complexity of rules of, 100
delay in implementing NEPA in
hydroelectric power licensing
program, 106
EPA's jurisdiction overlapping with,
110–111
hydroelectric power plant licenses
by, 27
pressure to develop rule on NEPA
compliance by, 78
public participation management by, 148
vertical concurrence system of, 147
Federal government. See also Government
expansion in later 19th and 20th centuries
of, 8–9
expansion of, as reason for rulemaking,
271–272
expansion of, rulemaking management
and, 123
Roosevelt and expansion of, 9–10

Federal Insecticide, Fungicide, and
Rodenticide Act (FIFRA), 59
Federalism assessment, as information
requirement for rulemaking, 62–63
Federal Motor Carrier Safety Administration
(FMCSA), 143, 146, 149
Federal Power Commission, 173
Federal Register
actual time to rule authorization from first
notice in, 106–107
agencies' responses to comments
in, 211
chartering of advisory committees
in, 68
on comments for Obama on new
executive order on rulemaking, 128
creation of and purpose for, 10
interest groups' use of for monitoring
rulemaking, 195–196
notice of information required under rules
in, 53
notice on Hazardous Materials Regulations
revision in, 39, 40–41f, 42
notices on abandoning a rule in, 85
page count during Bush I presidency, 17t
page count during Bush II presidency,
18–20, 19t
page count during Clinton presidency,
18, 19t
page count during Reagan presidency,
16, 17t
pages on Treasury rules for executive
compensation, 2
participation reports in, 194
preparation of notice for, 84
for public disclosure of rulemaking
information, 64
Federal Reserve Board, 171, 172
Federal Reserve System, 9, 115
Federal Trade Commission (FTC), 9, 12, 155,
230, 233
Federal Trade Commission Improvements
Act (1980), 178, 179
Federal Water Power Act, 9
Ferguson, Thomas, 216n39
Finality, for judicial review, 254
Final rules, West on direct and interim, 288
Financial institutions, 1–2, 26, 90, 103, 112.
See also Banking rules

Fiorina, Morris, 38*n*53, 272, 296*n*1
Fire alarm oversight, 227–228
  legislative vetoes using, 228–229
Firms. *See* Businesses and business interest
  groups
Fisher, Louis, 38*n*48
Fisheries, Interior Dept. rules in 1930s on, 46
Fix, Michael, 267*n*43
Food, Drug, and Cosmetic Act, 174, 179
Food and Drug Administration (FDA), 107*f*,
  108*f*, 142, 172, 182–183, 230, 282
Food Safety and Inspection Service (FSIS),
  137, 143, 145, 150
Food Standards Committee, 172
Ford, Gerald R., 62, 123
Foreign relations, CFR on rulemaking for, 12
Foreman, Christopher, 228, 230, 265*n*10,
  265*n*17, 265*nn*19–20
Formal hearings, 173–174. *See also* Hearings
Freedom of Information Act, 27–28, 176
Freeman, Jody, 209, 219*n*107
Fritschler, A. Lee, 38*n*34, 190, 193, 217*n*61
Fuchs, Ralph, 37*n*11
Furlong, Scott R., 120*n*45, 120*n*53, 121*n*57,
  121*n*64, 217*n*58, 218*n*65, 218*n*69,
  218*n*85, 219*n*104, 220*n*120
  on agencies' views of interest groups'
    influence, 213–214, 214*t*
  on agencies' views of particpants'
    contacts, 201
  on business groups' domination of
    rulemaking participation, 194
  on differences between legislative and
    executive branch lobbying, 192–193
  on negotiated rulemaking, 208
Future effect, of rules, 6–7
Future rulemaking research, 290–291

Gallup Polls, 89
Galston, William A., 118*n*2
Garrett, Ryan, 296*n*21
Gas Appliance Manufacturer's
  Association, 211
Gatrell, Jay, 296*n*18
Gellhorn, Ernest, 37*n*20
Gellhorn, Walter, 215*n*20, 267*n*55
General Accounting Office (GAO). *See also*
  Government Accountability Office
  on pace of rulemaking at FAA, 162

review of draft rules by, 84
on timeliness of rulemaking, 106, 107,
  107*f*, 108*f*
General applicability, of rules, 6, 65
General Counsel, Office of, 82, 145, 147,
  156, 285
Gersen, Jacob E., 121*n*61, 265*n*13
Golden, Marissa, 218*n*63, 218*n*68, 218*n*73,
  218*n*75, 220*n*116
  on business groups' domination of
    rulemaking participation, 194
  on comments and changes between
    proposed and final rules, 212
  on sources of information for participants
    in rulemaking, 196
  studies on participation by, 192
Gore, Albert, 127, 216*n*55
Government. *See also* Federal government;
  Local governments; State governments
  affect of rulemaking on U.S. system of,
    291–292
  complexity of rules as tactic of, 100
  general condition of, as context for
    rulemaking, 89–90
  other, participation by, 189
  on timeliness of rulemaking, 105–106
Government Accountability Office (GAO).
  See also General Accounting Office
  fire alarm oversight and reports by, 227
  managing review of agency rulemaking
    by, 149
  on OIRA influence, 246
  oversight by, 29
  rulemaking management study by,
    142, 144
  on rules published without prior notice,
    190, 191*f*
  Small Business Regulatory Enforcement
    Fairness Act and, 231
  support for congressional oversight by,
    231–232
Government in the Sunshine Act, 177
Graham, John, 242, 245
Gramlich, Edward, 119*nn*26–27
Gramm, Wendy, 245
Grassroots organizations
  agencies on effectiveness of, 201
  importance to interest groups for
    using, 192*t*

Grassroots organizations *(cont).*
  to influence rulemaking, tactics
    for, 196
  interest groups on effectiveness of,
    198*t*, 199
  participation in rulemaking using, 197*t*
Great Society programs, 177
Groups. *See* Interest groups
Guidance documents
  Bush II on OIRA review of, 127
  Bush II on OMB review of,
    63, 129, 188
  information about agencies' rulemaking
    management in, 155
  as source of understanding rulemaking
    management, 130
  uses for, 153
  West on early rulemaking using, 288
Guidelines, confusion over rulemaking
  agencies' use of, 184

Hammers, 75, 226–227
"Hard look" standard of judicial
  review, 258
Harrington, Winston, 166*n*30, 217*n*61,
  218*n*66, 220*n*115, 220*n*119, 282,
  296*n*16, 296*n*23
Harter, Phillip, 118*n*5, 121*n*68, 215*nn*1–2,
  219*nn*97–98, 220*n*110
  on adversary process of rulemaking, 116
  on consensual basis for rulemaking, 168
  on negotiated rulemaking, 206–208, 210
Hawkins, Keith, 36*n*3, 120*nn*29–31, 120*n*42,
  120*n*46, 276, 296*n*5
Hazardous and Solid Waste Amendments, of
  Resource Conservation and Recovery
  Act (1980 and 1984), 93–94
Hazardous Materials Regulations (HMR)
  complexity of, 108
  interests in and effects of, 43–44
  obligations for companies under, 25
  revision of, 39, 40–41*f*, 42
  volume of, 93–94, 96
Health, Education and Welfare, Department
  of, 125, 182–183
Health and Human Services, Department of,
  236, 245*t*
Health and safety regulations, 14,
  98–99, 101

Health Care Financing Administration, 150
Hearings
  agencies on effectiveness of, 201
  attendance at, as participation in
    rulemaking, 196, 197*t*
  attendance at, interest groups on
    effectiveness of, 198*t*, 199
  informal and formal, 173–174
  legislative, for fire alarm oversight, 227
  legislative, for soliciting public comments,
    67–68
  legislative, mandatory or voluntary,
    173–174
  legislative, social regulation statutes of
    1970s on, 178
  public, advance work for, 80
  public, as adversary process, 116
  public, as outreach for participation, 181
  public, for participation in
    rulemaking, 83
Heffron, Florence, 36*n*9
Hepburn Act, 9
Herrnson, Paul, 218*n*65
Hibblen, H. Kenneth, 119*n*28
Hierarchical model of rulemaking,
  280, 281
Hildreth, W. Bartley, 37*n*17, 86*n*7,
  215*n*19
Holmes, Oliver Wendell, 2–3
Homeland Security, Department of,
  20, 133, 143
Home mortgage crisis, 90
Horizontal concurrence, for conflict
  management, 146
Horizontal review, of draft rules, 82
House of Representatives. *See* Congress
Housing and Urban Development,
  Department of, 194, 236
Hybrid model of rulemaking, 280–281
Hydroelectric power plant licenses,
  27, 100, 106

IBM Center for the Business of
  Government, 131
Immigration and Naturalization Service v.
  Chadha (1983), 230
Impact analysis. *See* Cost-benefit analysis;
  Inflation impact statement; Regulatory
  impact analysis

Impact information, 152, 154
Implementation
  bureaucratic capacity and limits on,
    29–30
  complexity of rules and, 100
  draft rule stage considerations for, 81–82
  field personnel for, role in work
    groups, 156
  internal conflicts and, 110
  participation in rulemaking and, 169
  rules for, 5
  rulewriting quality oversight and,
    103–104
  vagueness of rules and problems in, 98
  volume of rules as disruption to, 94–96
  work group success and, 159
Implementation and compliance information,
    153, 155
Imports, regulation of, 8, 45
Individuals, responsibilities for developing
    rules of, 144
Industry. *See also* Businesses and business
    interest groups
  as sources of information for rules, 102
Industry-specific regulation programs,
    14, 24–25
Inflation impact statements, 123
Informal contacts. *See* Contacts with
    agencies, informal
Informal hearings, 173. *See also* Hearings
Informal rulemaking, of APA section
    553, 52
Information
  ambiguous mandate for rulemaking and,
    285–286
  assessment by work group leader of, 157
  to be used during rulemaking, statutes
    on, 60–61
  bureaucratic monopoly on, 278–279
  Carter on regulatory agenda and calendars
    of, 180
  hearings for gathering of, 173
  investigations for gathering, 171–172
  legal developments related to open
    discovery of, 71–72
  negotiated rulemaking and, 207
  participation and clarity and technical
    difficulty of, 115
  participation in rulemaking and, 57

in principal-agent model, 283
quality, early influence in rulemaking
    and, 289
quality of, Bush II's requirements for
    OMB reviews for, 238
quality of for Clean Air Act, Magat et al.'s
    study of, 291
quality of rules and limitations of,
    101–102
required to disclose to public on
    rulemaking, 63–65
requirements, in rulemaking, 53–54
requirements, in rules for private
    behavior, 26–27
requirements by executive orders,
    61–63
requirements in authorizing statutes,
    58–60
rulemaking budgets for personnel
    interrelated with, 144
sharing of, 155
types to be collected and analyzed,
    152–155
for work groups, assembling of, 158
Information Quality Act (2000), 61, 102,
    180, 188
Inside Bureaucracy (Downs), 274–275
Interest groups
  acknowledgement of power of
    presidential oversight by, 246
  agencies' contacts prior to rule proposals
    with, 200–201
  agencies on effectiveness of, 213–214, 214*t*
  ambiguous mandate for rulemaking
    and, 285
  comparative importance of participation
    to, 191, 192*t*
  competitive, as outside advisors on
    rulemaking, 287
  on congressional budgetary restrictions
    on types of rulemaking permitted,
    225–226
  Congress's interest in rulemaking and,
    170–171
  culture and operating system and
    rulemaking by, 277–278
  on effectiveness of specific participation
    techniques, 198*t*
  importance of participation to, 210

Interest groups *(cont.)*
  information of as influence on
    rulemaking, 274
  lobbying OMB in Reagan era, 186
  participation by, 189, 190
  in principal-agent model, 283
  public, as sources of information for
    rules, 102
  reform of rulemaking and, 293
  rulemaking and self-interest of,
    34–35, 272
  on success in participation by, 213
  types of, involved in participation,
    193–195
  West on early participation by, 288
Interest-representation model, Stewart's,
    210, 214, 282, 290
Intergovernmental issues, federal legislation
    of 1970s and, 15
Interim final rules, 288
Interior, Department of, 11, 46, 171–172, 183,
    245*t*. *See also* Environmental Protection
    Agency
Internal Revenue Service, 99, 253
International Association of State Game, Fish
    and Conservation Commissioners, 172
Internet, e-rulemaking and, 202, 203
Interpretive rules, 5, 22–23, 30
Interstate Commerce Commission (ICC),
    9, 11, 172, 173, 252–253
Investigations, for information gathering,
    171–172
Issue networks, 133. *See also* Interest groups;
    Networks of colleagues

Jackson, Robert, 10
Johnson, Charles, 87*n*37
Johnson, Lyndon, 123, 177
Johnson, Stephen M., 268*n*69
Judges. *See also* Courts
  accountability in rulemaking and, 71
  activism of, and cases in which courts
    took action, 262
  administrative law, 55
  legal and political philosophies, and
    tenure of, 248–249
  of lower courts, inconsistent
    interpretations by, 259–260
  reasons for rulemaking by, 272–274

rulemaking and self-interest of, 34
  rulemaking process and, 3
Judicial review. *See also* Courts
  for accountability of rulemaking,
    55, 56–57
  APA on scope of, 254–256
  public comments as cause for, 67
  public participation promotion during,
    69–70
  of rulemaking during the New Deal,
    47–48
Judiciary. *See* Courts

Kagan, Elena, 266*n*42
Kagan, Robert, 120*n*32, 120*n*48
Kamarck, Elaine C., 118*n*2
Kamieniecki, Sheldon, 194, 199, 217*n*58,
    218*n*69, 218*n*70, 218*nn*80–81
Katzen, Sally, 242, 245, 266*n*24
*Keeping a Watchful Eye: The Politics of
    Congressional Oversight*
    (Aberbach), 228
Kelly, R., 219*n*88
Kelly, Thomas, 216*n*31
Kennedy, John F., 123
Kerwin, Cornelius M., 38*n*46, 120*n*45,
    120*n*53, 121*n*57, 121*n*64, 165*n*17,
    165*nn*23–24, 219*n*104, 219*nn*105–106
  on negotiated rulemaking, 208–209
  sources for information on agency
    rulemaking management for, 130
  on work group leader success, 159
Klass, Michael, 119*nn*11–13
Kraft, Michael E., 87*n*24, 217*n*58, 218*n*69
Krupnick, Alan, 166*n*30, 217*n*61, 218*n*66,
    220*n*115, 220*n*119, 282, 296*n*16, 296*n*23

Labor, Department of. *See also specific
    government entities reporting to*
  OMB reviews and changes to rulemaking
    by, 236, 244
  participation in rulemaking by, 66, 183
  percentage of rules approved by OIRA
    without change, 245*t*
  Regulatory Plan and Regulatory Agenda
    of, 133
  rulemaking by Wage and Hour Division
    of, 45–46
  time period for OMB reviews and, 240

Landis, James, 30, 38*n*49
Langbein, Laura, 119*n*25, 208–209, 219*nn*105–107, 220*n*122
Late hits, by senior managers, 135, 146, 158
Lateral concurrence, for conflict management, 146
Lavilla, Juan, 217*n*62
Law. *See also* Authorizing statutes; Legislation
   in principal-agent model, 283
   rulemaking goals and objectives set by, 276
   as subject matter of rules, 5
Lawyers. *See* Attorneys
Leadership of work groups, 156–159
Legal information, 152, 153
Legal interests test, of standing in judicial review, 252
Legislation. *See also* Authorizing statutes; Law
   ambiguity for rulemaking under, 285
   clear mandate for rulemaking in, 284
   information requirements for rulemaking by, 60–61
   as origin of rulemaking activity, 75, 91
   pork-barrel, 271
   quality of rules and clarity or premises of, 97
   rules and, 7–8
Legislative authority. *See also* Delegated authority
   granted by Congress to agencies, 4
Legislative branch/legislatures. *See also* Congress
   rulemaking and bureaucratic capacity and limits of, 29–31
   rulemaking by administrative agencies similar to, 50
Legislative hearings. *See* Hearings
Legislative rules, 22
Legislative vetoes, 228–232, 257, 264
Legitimacy benefit, negotiated rulemaking and, 209
Levin, Ronald, 88*n*46
Levine, Charles, 36*n*6
Licenses, 23–24, 27, 100
Lieber, Harvey, 38*n*37
Limitations, in rules for private behavior, 26
Linoff, Richard, 88*n*42
Listservs, for rulemaking participation, 202

Litigation. *See also* Challenges; Courts; Judicial review
   ambiguous mandate for rulemaking and, 286
   competing information of interest groups and, 287
   compromise and negotiation forced by, 290
   importance to interest groups of, 192*t*
   negotiated rulemaking and, 207, 208
   threat of, rulemaking agencies and, 249–250
Lobbying, 192–193, 192*t*, 196. *See also* Businesses and business interest groups; Interest groups
Local governments, 35, 111, 189. *See also* Government
Lowi, Theodore, 37*n*33, 38*n*50, 121*n*69, 216*n*52, 218*n*64, 265*n*1, 265*n*8, 296*n*6
   on dominance of bureaucracy in rulemaking, 222, 278–279
   on legislation evolving from general to specific, 223–224
   on participation and Reagan's OMB reviews, 186
   on rulemaking bureaucrats as patrons, 280
Lubbers, Jeffrey, 87*nn*29–30, 87*n*34, 87*n*39, 88*n*46, 88*n*49, 121*n*61, 209–210, 216*n*32, 216*n*48, 219*n*108, 266*n*30, 267*n*63, 267*nn*64–65, 267*n*68, 268*n*75

Magat, Wesley, 166*n*30, 217*n*61, 218*n*66, 220*n*115, 220*n*119, 296*n*16, 296*n*23
   on comments by affected industries, 212
   empirical research by, 291
   on external signals model, 282
Magnuson-Moss Warranty-Federal Trade Commission Improvements Act, 178
Management
   ambiguity for rulemaking and importance of, 285
   of individual rules, 152–163
   information for, 153, 155
   levels of, 122
   presidential, 122–129
Management by individual agencies
   budgets for, 142–144
   concurrence systems, 145–147

Management by individual agencies *(cont.)*
creation and institutionalization of
rulemaking offices and, 150–152
drafting the rule, 149–150
elements of, 129–137, 142–144
liaison with the OMB and Congress,
148–149
planning documents preparation for,
136–137
priority-setting processes for, 131–134
of public participation, 147–148
responsibilities for developing rules,
144–145
rule initiation and early input processes
of, 134–136
schedules for, 137, 138–141*f*, 142
sources for information on, 130–131
"The Management of Regulation
Development: Out of the Shadows," 131
Mandatory hearings, 173.
Mandatory rulemaking, agency priority-
setting on discretionary rulemaking
vs., 134
Manning, Peter, 120*n*42
Maritime Commission, 171
Martinez, Elia, 296*n*21
Mashaw, Jerry, 38*n*39, 119*n*5
Mazmanian, David, 215*n*22
McCubbins, Mathew D., 121*n*59, 215*n*4,
265*n*3, 265*n*4, 265*n*6, 265*n*9, 265*n*16,
265*n*17
on agency policymaking, 223
on procedural approaches to
congressional oversight, 224
on rationales for rulemaking
participation, 170
on types of oversight, 227
McFeeley, Neil, 36*n*9
McGarrity, Thomas, 38*n*39, 87*n*38, 118*n*5,
165*n*27, 166*n*28, 166*n*30, 267*n*47,
296*nn*9–14
on consensus-promoting structures in
bureaucracies, 290
on ossification of rulemaking, 184
on rulemaking structure and cultures,
280–281
McIntosh, David, 243
Medicaid, delays in issuing regulations on
cost-sharing in, 106

Medical Device amendments to Food, Drug,
and Cosmetic Act, 179
Medicare, complexity of rules for, 100
Meier, Kenneth, 284, 296*n*19
Melnick, R. Shep, 121*n*63, 263, 267*n*52,
268*n*82
Membership of work groups
composition and size of, 155–156
functions of, 159–161
leader determination of, 157
Mendeloff, John, 119*n*22
Mercatus Center, George Mason University,
239
Midnight rules, 126, 225, 231, 238
Mihm, Christopher, 217*n*62
Miller, Caitlyn, 296*n*21
Miller, Gerald, 37*n*17, 86*n*7, 215*n*19
Miller, James, 245
Miller, Nancy, 87*n*32, 120*n*54, 215*n*23,
265*n*13, 266*n*36, 267*n*54
Mine Safety and Health Administration
(MSHA), 146, 147–148, 150
Mintz, Benjamin, 87*n*32, 120*n*54, 215*n*23,
265*n*13, 266*n*36, 267*n*54
Mitnick, Barry, 265*n*2, 282, 296*n*17
Mixed-motive bureaucracies, 279
Model Cities Program, 177
Moe, Terry, 220*n*121
Moratoria on rulemaking, 111–112, 125, 126
Motor Carrier Act, 11
*Motor Vehicle Manufacturers Association v.
State Farm* (1983), 258

National Academy of Public Administration,
244, 246
National Academy of Sciences, 247
National defense, CFR on rulemaking
for, 12
National Environmental Policy Act (NEPA,
1969). *See also* Environmental
Protection Agency
citizen participation movement and, 177
as information statute, 60
pressure on FERC to develop rule for
compliance with, 78
programmatic exemptions in, 73
public input requirements under,
68–69
rulemaking due to, 13

National government. *See also* Federal
government
National Highway Traffic Safety
Administration (NHTSA)
business groups' domination of
rulemaking participation with, 194
horizontal concurrence system of, 146
legislative vetoes of rulemaking by, 230
McGarrity's study of internal
decisionmaking processes by,
280–281
priority-setting process of, 132
public participation management by,
147–148
schedules for rulemaking by, 142
timeliness of rules by, 107*f*
National Industrial Recovery Act (1933), 10,
47–48
National Labor Relations Board (NLRB), 12
National Marine Fisheries Service (NMFS),
133, 143
National Organic Standards Board, 79
National Performance Review (NPR), 126–
127, 188, 202, 208
*The Nation's Hazardous Waste Management
Program at a Crossroads*, 93–94
Needham, Mark, 296*n*21
Negotiated rulemaking (*reg neg*), 205–210
Negotiated Rulemaking Act (1990), 68, 179
"Negotiating Regulations" (Harter, 1982),
206–208
Negotiation, central importance of, 289–290
Networks of colleagues, 195–196. *See also*
Issue networks
Neubauer, Jeanne, 215*n*22
New Deal
expansion of national government and, 8
judicial challenges to delegation of
legislative authority during, 47–48
legislative vetoes during, 228
other challenges to delegation of
legislative authority during, 48–49
politics of rulemaking and, 46
Newsletters, professional, for monitoring
rulemaking, 195–196
New York Times, 1
Nichols, Albert, 119*nn*11–12
Niskanen, William, 222, 265*n*1, 278–279,
296*n*6

Nixon, Richard, 61–62, 123, 233
Noll, Roger G., 121*n*59, 170, 215*n*4, 224,
265*n*9, 282
Notice-and-comment rulemaking. *See also*
Comments
under APA section 553, 51–52, 56, 175–
176
degree of regulation and effectiveness of
public influence through, 199
in earliest stages of process, 289
of Interior Department technical or
complex rules, 183
participation and, 196, 197*t*
public participation and, 66–67
using electronic bulletin boards, 202
Notice of proposed rulemaking. *See also*
Public disclosure of information
agencies publishing actions without,
190, 191*f*
participation role prior to, 199–200
Nuclear Regulatory Commission (NRC)
on budgets for rulemaking
management, 143
courts on notice and comment rulemaking
by, 258
electronic bulletin boards of early 1990s
used by, 202
negotiated rulemaking used by, 207
priority-setting process of, 132–133
public participation management by, 147,
148
rule initiation in, 135
schedules for rulemaking by, 137
vertical concurrence system of, 147

Obama, Barack
accountability through review under,
239–240
framework for restoration of American
economy under, 1
information requirements for rulemaking
by executive order of, 63
on making rulemaking more transparent
and open, 196
participation and, 188–189
percentage of rules approved by OIRA
without change under, 245*t*
proposed rulemaking agenda
under, 94

Obama, Barack *(cont.)*
rulemaking management under,
125, 127–129, 239–240
rulemaking statistics under administration
of, 20–21, 20*t*
speculation on rulemaking management
under, 244
timeliness of rulemaking by agencies and,
112
Objectives, for rules, 80, 160
O'Brien, David, 119*n*28
Occupational Safety and Health Act (OSHA),
58, 92–93, 178
Occupational Safety and Health
Administration (OSHA)
Bryner on overseers of rulemaking
by, 282
Carter and revision of fire safety standards
by, 125
concurrence systems of, 146
Congress on goals for, 6
Ergonomic Rule passed as midnight
legislation, 231
lawsuits challenging rules by, 261
limitations in rules of, 26
OMB reviews and changes to rulemaking
by, 236
overinclusive and underinclusive rules
issued by, 98–99
participation during Carter administration
in, 183
public participation management by, 148
responsibilities overlapping with specific
industries, 15
rule drafting at, 149
rulemaking as strain on institutional
capacity of, 92–93
rulemaking impact on business and, 179
rules conflict with Agriculture
Dept., 233
stalling tactics for rulemaking by, 114
O'Connell, Ann Joseph, 121*n*61, 164*n*12,
265*n*13
Office of General Counsel. *See* General
Counsel, Office of
Office of Information and Regulatory Affairs
(OIRA), of OMB
Bush II on transparency of, 188
Bush II's creation of, 127

Clinton's Regulatory Working Group and,
78
impact information and, 154
on negotiated rulemaking, 209
Obama's regulatory policy czars and, 129
public comments for Obama on
interrelationships of agencies
with, 128
return letters under Bush II and, 238–239
rulemaking agencies' relationship with,
241–246
Small Business Regulatory Enforcement
Fairness Act and, 231
standards for contact with the public and
recording communications, 186–187
timeliness of rules and reviews by, 241*t*
Office of Management and Budget (OMB)
Bush II on rulemaking process and,
63, 238
Carter on agency progress evaluations by,
180–182
Carter on rulemaking management by,
124–125
delays due to reviews by, 240–241
"E-Government Strategy" (2002), 203
Hazardous Materials Regulations revision
and, 42
managing review of agency rulemaking
by, 148–149
on nominations of existing rules for
review, change, or elimination, 239
number of reviews and actions taken by,
234, 235*t*, 236
Paperwork Reduction Act and, 243
public opinion on bonuses after collapse
of, 1–2
Reagan's executive order mandating
reviews by, 112, 125–126, 185–186
review of draft rules by, 83, 84, 273
rulemaking agencies' relationship with,
241–246
Stevens Report on regulatory impact of
major rules, 117
Office of Solid Waste and Emergency
Response (OSWER), of EPA, 93–94
O'Leary, Rosemary, 121*n*62, 262–263,
265*n*14, 268*n*77, 296*n*22
Oleszek, Walter, 265*n*22
Olson, Mancur, 216*n*39

OMB Watch, 246

Orders. *See also* Rules

future effect of rules and, 7

O'Reilly, James, 37*n*12, 72, 75, 76–77*t*, 87*n*27, 87*n*40

Organizations. *See* Interest groups

Outside advisor model of rulemaking, 280, 286–287

Outside experts, as sources of information for rules, 102

Overinclusiveness of rules, 98–99

Oversight. *See* Accountability

Overspecificity of rules, 99, 104

Panama Refining Co. v. Ryan (1935), 47–48

Paperwork Reduction Act (PRA)

congressional reauthorization of, 243

exemption allowances in, 73

as information statute, 60–61

OMB review and clearance provisions of, 264

public input requirements in, 68, 69

Participation. *See also* Early influence

additional rounds of, 84

Administrative Procedure Act (1946) and, 175–176

Bush I's reforms and, 187–188

Carter's reforms and, 180–185

Clinton's and Bush II's approaches and, 188

comments for Obama on new executive order on rulemaking, 128

comparative importance to interest groups of, 192*t*

as core element of rulemaking, 54

draft rule development and, 81

early inattention to, 170–171

at the end of the New Deal, 171–175

e-rulemaking and, 202–205

examining actuality of, 190–193

as expanded form of democracy, 65–70

expansion of scope and diversification of forms of, 177–180

frequency or infrequency of, 191*f*

importance of, 210–214

increased, Carter on, 124

information in rulemaking and, 57

limitations on vs. expediency in rulemaking, 74

management by individual agencies of, 147–148

monitoring rulemaking and influencing roles in, 195–196, 197*t*, 198*t*, 199–201

negotiated rulemaking and, 205–210

Obama and, 188–189

planning for, 80

prerequisites for, 189

priority-setting process and, 133–134

problems for public and agencies due to, 114–116

purposes of, 168–170

Reagan's changes and, 186–188

records of rulemaking documentation and, 65

reform of rulemaking and, 293

representative democracy and, 167–168

rise of social regulation and, 176

as stage in rulemaking, 83–84

at the turn of the twentieth century, 171

types of groups involved in, 193–195

Particular applicability, of rules, 6

Patrons, Lowi on rulemaking bureaucrats as, 280

Pedersen, William, 87*n*31

Percival, Robert, 266*n*32

Permits, 27. *See also* Licenses

Perritt, Harry H., 202, 219*nn*89–90

Perry, James, 215*n*21

Personnel costs. *See also* Employees

rulemaking budgets for information interrelated with, 144

Peters, B. Guy, 36*n*6

Petitions, 78–79, 91, 196

Pew Research Center for People and the Press, 89, 90

Pfiffner, James, 266*n*27

Place of proposed rulemaking, information on, 53

Plain English, 124, 125

Planning, for rulemaking, 79–81, 136–137

Police patrol oversight, 227–228

legislative vetoes using, 228–229

Policy, as subject matter of rules, 5

Policy analysts, 156, 281

Policy area rules, 21–22

Policy circulars, confusion over rulemaking agencies' use of, 184

Policy information, 152, 153–154
Political appointees. *See also* Agency officials
  ambiguous mandate for rulemaking
    by, 285
  conflict with career bureaucrats, OMB
    and, 241–242
  guidance on rulemaking by, 80
  priority-setting by, timeliness of agencies'
    rulemaking and, 113
  rulemaking management systems
    and, 151
  timeliness of rules and conflicts between
    career bureaucrats and, 110
  vertical concurrence for conflict
    management and, 146
Political contributions, importance to interest
    groups of, 192*t*
Political information, 152–153, 154
Politics
  ambiguous mandate for rulemaking
    and, 286
  information for rulemaking as currency
    for, 276–277
  Magat et al.'s study of Clean Air Act
    and, 291
  in principal-agent model, 283–284
  of rulemaking process, 46–52
Pork-barrel legislation, 271
Portney, Kent, 185, 215*n*21, 216*n*51
Preambles of rules, 64–65, 67, 81, 84, 125
Prescribing goals for laws or policy, 6, 30
President. *See also* Office of Management
    and Budget; *specific presidents*
  accountability in rulemaking and, 55, 71,
    221–222, 264
  affect of rulemaking on, 292
  CFR on rulemaking by, 12
  cost-benefit analysis issues for, 246–247
  culture and operating system and
    rulemaking by, 277–278
  dialogue during rulemaking with agencies
    and, 290
  federal judge appointments made by,
    248–249
  interest in rulemaking process of, 214
  management of rulemaking by, 122–129
  objectives for overseeing rulemaking by,
    232–234
  as origin of rulemaking activity, 78

  outside advisors on rulemaking and, 287
  as principal, in principal-agent model,
    282–283
  reasons for rulemaking by, 272–274
  relationship with rulemaking agencies
    and, 241–246, 245*t*
  rulemaking and self-interest of, 33–34
  signing statements by, 233, 288
  as source for rules, 3
  timeliness of rulemaking by agencies and,
    111, 112
Principal-agent theory of legislative-
    bureaucratic relations, 222–223,
    282–284
Priority-setting by agencies, 79, 112, 113,
    131–134
Pritzker, David, 219*n*99, 219*n*102
Privacy Act, 27–28, 176–177
Private attorneys general(s), 252
Private behavior
  rules for, 23–25
  types of requirements in rules for, 25–27
Private property, Reagan on federal
    rulemaking affecting, 63
Private sector
  complexity of rules for, 99–100
  information for rulemaking known by,
    104–105
  as origin of rulemaking activity,
    78–79, 91
  overinclusive rules and working
    relationship of public sector with,
    98–99
  on timeliness of rulemaking, 105
Procedural rules, 23, 27
Procedural statutes, general, participation in
    rulemaking under, 110
Procedures
  for congressional oversight of rulemaking,
    224–225
  for issuing rules, 7
  required, difficulties in measuring, 114
  required, timeliness of rulemaking and,
    111–112
  for rule development, APA on, 255–256
  for rule development, litigation
    on, 257
Progressive Era, professionalized
    bureaucracy and, 29

Prohibitions, in rules for private behavior, 25–26
Prompt letters, as rulemaking management device, 239, 244
Proposed rules. *See also* Rules
  agencies publishing actions without notices of, 190, 191*f*
  APA on public participation on, 54
  during Bush I presidency, 16–17, 17*t*
  Carter on advance notices of, 180
  Federal Register notice of information required for, 53
  information in notices of, 64
  legislation on advance notices for, 179
  management issues for revisions to, 115
  during Reagan presidency, 16, 17*t*
  technical or complex, advance notices of, 183
  West on participation role prior to notice of, 199–200
Public agencies. *See* Agencies
Public Citizen, 246
Public disclosure of information. *See also* Notice of proposed rulemaking
  agency discretion on, 53–54
  APA on, 63–65
  executive orders on, 69
  NEPA on, 177
  for proposed rules, 178
Public hearings. *See* Hearings
Public opinion, 1–2, 42, 89, 90
Public participation. *See* Participation
Public Welfare, CFR on rulemaking for, 12–13
Purpose, for rules, 7, 53–54, 55, 96–97

Quality of life, as information requirement for rulemaking, 62, 123
Quality of rules
  Diver on elements of, 97–100
  limitations of information and, 101–102, 276
  limitations of rulemakers and, 102–105
  OSHA's consensus national standards and, 93
  purpose for rules and, 96–97
  standards of, 96–97
  work group success or failure and, 159
Quayle, Dan, 126, 187–188, 236–237

Reagan, Ronald
  accountability through review under, 234, 235*t*, 236–237
  conflicts between political appointees and career bureaucrats under, 110
  conflicts with OMB review under, 243
  information requirements for rulemaking by executive order of, 62–63
  moratorium on rulemaking at start of administration of, 111–112
  participation and, 185–187
  percentage of rules approved by OIRA without change under, 245*t*
  reductions in rulemaking under, 16, 17–18
  rulemaking and power of, 33–34
  rulemaking management under, 125–126, 234, 236–237
  rulemaking statistics under administration of, 17*t*
  Vice President's Task Force on Regulatory Relief under, 78
Rebuttal comments, in legislative hearings, 68
Records, of rulemaking documentation, 65, 72, 189
"The Reformation of American Administrative Law" (Stewart), 210
Reg neg (negotiated rulemaking), 205–210
Regulations.gov, 203
Regulatory agenda program, Carter's, 181
Regulatory alternatives, as information requirement for rulemaking, 62
Regulatory Analysis Review Group (RARG), 123–124
Regulatory Council, 124, 125
Regulatory Flexibility Act (RFA), 60, 61, 82, 83, 84
Regulatory impact analysis, 62, 63, 69, 73–74, 125
Regulatory Working Group (RWG), 78
Reporting requirements, in rules for private behavior, 26–27
Research analysts, 156
Resource Conservation and Recovery Act (RCRA, 1976), 93–94, 226, 262
Resources. *See also* Budgets; Costs
  for rulemaking, changes in priorities and, 113, 134
  shortage of, timeliness of rulemaking and, 112

Return letters, as rulemaking management
device, 238–239, 244
Rinfret, Sara, 200, 212, 218*n*83, 220*n*117
Ripeness, for judicial review, 254
Risk assessment, as basis for rulemaking, 59
Robinson, Glen O., 215*n*2
Rogers, Joel, 216*n*39
Roosevelt, Franklin Delano, 9–10, 48, 49,
123, 175
Rosenbloom, David, 37*n*17, 37*n*21, 46–47,
86*n*7, 87*n*10, 215*n*19
Rossi, Jim, 219*n*96
Rothstein, Mark, 120*n*38, 217*n*61
Rubin, Jack, 37*n*17, 86*n*7, 215*n*19
Rulemakers, limitations of, 102–105
Rulemaking. *See also* Administrative
Procedure Act; E-rulemaking; Rules;
Work groups
accountability mechanisms, 70–71
action on draft rules, 84–85
activities after, 85
affect on U.S. system of government,
291–292
alternative situations for, 284–287
authorization to proceed with, 79, 112
bureaucratic capacity, legislature limits
and, 29–31
bureaucratic discretion and, 116–117
bureaucratic dominance school on,
278–282
under Bush II presidency, 18–20, 19*t*
changes in APA model, 71–72
during Clinton's presidency, 18, 19*t*
at close of New Deal, 10–13
containing administrative discretion using,
32–33
core elements of, 53–57
debates about, 89–90
definition of, 2–3
developing the draft rule, 81–82
earliest stages of, 288–289
early sessions of Congress on, 8
effects of, 117
from end of World War II to mid-1960s, 13
exceptions, exemptions, and evasions to,
72–75
external review of draft rules, 82–83
from first Congress to APA, 45–46
future research on, 290–291

general influences on, 276–278
Hazardous Materials Regulations revision
process, 39, 40–41*f*, 42–43
history of, 7–21
increased legal requirements for
information on, 57–65
inseparable issues and trade-offs in, 118
internal review of draft rules, 82
in late 19th and early 20th centuries, 8–9
management of. *See* Management
negotiated, 205–210
negotiation and compromise as central to,
289–290
New Deal and, 9–10
1970s as era of, 13–16
during Obama presidency, 20–21, 20*t*
origin of, 75, 78–79
participation mandated by law, 65–70
participation problems for, 114–116
planning for, 79–81
politics of process in, 46–52
principal-agent school on, 282–284
process and substance of, 43–53
public participation in, 83–84
quality in, 96–105
during Reagan and Bush I administrations,
16–18, 17*t*
reasons for, 28–36
reform of, 292–295
revision and publication of draft rules, 83
self-interest and, 33–36
stages of, 75–86
theory. *See* Theory, rulemaking
timeliness of, 105–114
timing for lawsuits regarding, 254
for U.S. government programs, 2
variations in sequence of, 85–86
volume of, as strain on institutional
capacity, 91–96, 204–205
Rules. *See also* Draft rules; Proposed rules
agencies as sources of, 3–4
categorized by policy area and originating
agency, 21–22
definition of, 3
differences in scope and importance
of, 28
direct final, 74, 288
draft. *See* Draft rules
enforcement. *See* Enforcement

general and particular applicability of, 6
for government, 27–28
implementation. *See* Implementation
individual, origin of, 75, 78–79
influences on content of, 275–291
interim final, 288
law and policy as subject matter of, 5
managing essential information for,
152–155
methods for regulating private behavior
in, 25–27
for negotiated rulemaking, 207
preambles of, 64–65, 67, 81, 84, 125
for private behavior, 23–25
range of influence over law and policy
of, 5–6
Sept. 11 events and public opinion
on, 89
for those approaching government, 27
volume of, program implementation and,
94–96

Safe Drinking Water Act, 59, 178, 262
Scalia, Antonin, 37*n*32
*Schechter Poultry Corporation v. United
States* (1935), 47–48
Schoenbrod, David, 223, 265*n*7
Scholzman, Kay, 217*n*60
Schwartz, Thomas, 170, 215*n*4, 227, 265*n*16
Securities and Exchange Commission (SEC),
108*f*, 142, 172
Senate. *See* Congress
Senior agency officials. *See* Agency officials;
Political appointees
Separation of powers. *See also*
Accountability; *individual government
branches*
control of rulemaking and, 264
judicial review of rulemaking and, 257
rulemaking and, 30
September 11, 2001, terrorist attacks, 89
Shaiko, Ron, 218*n*65
Shapiro, Martin, 36*n*7, 50, 87*nn*13–15,
268*n*70
Shere, Mark, 88*n*45
Shift responsibility model of legislative
behavior, 272
Shumavon, Douglas, 119*n*28
Side agreements, in rulemaking, 162

Signals from the Hill (Foreman), 228
Significant rules, Clinton administration's
definition of, 126–127
Signing statements, 233, 288
Simplicity of rules, 97, 99–100
Small Business Administration, 83, 100
Small businesses, 82, 95, 99–100, 179. *See
also* Businesses and business interest
groups
Small Business Regulatory Enforcement
Fairness Act (1996), 179, 231
Smoking and Politics (Fritschler), 190
Social regulation
complexity and timeliness of rules
for, 108
lawsuits challenging rules on, 261
limitations of information for, 101–102
participation revolution of 1960s and
1970s and, 176, 177
rulemaking management and, 123
strains on institutional capacity due to
programs for, 92–93
time period for OMB reviews and, 240
Social Security Act (1939), 12
Social Security Administration (SSA),
12, 150
Sommers, Paul, 119*n*7, 119*n*23
Song, Ge, 296*n*21
Spaeth, Harold, 87*n*11
Splotila, John, 245
Standards, in rules for private behavior,
26–27
Standing, principle of, 251–252
State governments, 35, 62, 110, 189. *See also*
Government
Statespersons, bureaucratic, 274–275, 279,
281, 286, 290
Statutes. *See* Authorizing statutes;
Legislation
Stern, Stephanie, 288, 296*n*20
Stevens Report, 117
Stewart, Richard, 36*n*10, 37*n*11, 86*n*8,
121*n*58, 219*n*109, 267*n*55, 296*n*17
on agency's role in negotiations, 290
on external interests and administrative
process in government agencies, 111
on interest representation, 210, 214
on judicial challenges to NIRA in mid-
1930s, 47

Strauss, Peter, 267*n*55
Students Challenging Regulatory Agency
    Procedures (SCRAP), 252–253
Subject of rules, suspension of legal
    requirements in rulemaking and, 72, 73
Substantive rules, 22
Sunset review, Carter on, 124
Sunstein, Cass, 128, 242
Supreme Court. *See also specific cases*
    on delegated legislative authority of New
        Deal, 47–48, 271
    Roosevelt's Court-packing plan for, 48
    rules cases heard in and decisions by,
        250–251
Surveys, on rulemaking participation,
    189–190, 213

Tahler, Bryan, 88*n*45
Task Force on Regulatory Relief, 126, 187
Task forces, 78, 144–145, 275. *See also* Work
    groups
Team model of rulemaking, 280
Technical corrections, confusion over
    rulemaking agencies' use of, 184
Technical information. *See* Content
    information; Legal information
Technology. *See* E-dockets; E-rulemaking
Telecommunications Act (1996), 78, 94
Theory, rulemaking
    on alternative situations, 284–287
    bureaucratic dominance school of,
        278–282
    determination of rules' contents in, 275–291
    on earliest stages, 288–289
    general influences on rules' contents in,
        276–278
    negotiation and compromise in, 289–290
    principal-agent school of, 282–284
    prospects for rigorous content analysis in,
        290–291
    reasons for rulemaking, 270–275
    value of, 269–270
Third Way, 89
Thomas, John, 36*n*3, 120*nn*29–31, 120*n*42,
    120*n*46, 276, 296*n*5
Thompson, Frank, 36*n*6
Thomson, Ken, 185, 215*n*21, 216*n*51
Threshold assessment, of environmental
    impact, 60

Thurber, James A., 38*n*48
Tierney, John, 217*n*60
Timelines
    for budget preparation vs. rulemaking
        development, 143–144
    for proposed rules, 42, 53
    public participation in proposed rules
        and, 67
Timeliness of rules
    complexity of rules and, 107–108
    concerns about, 105–107, 107*f*, 108*f*
    controversy and, 109–111
    information availability and, 276
    judicial review of unreasonable
        delays, 255
    management obstacles and deficiencies,
        112–113
    negotiated rulemaking and, 207, 208
    OMB/OIRA reviews and, 240–241, 241*t*
    procedural requirements and, 111–112
    shortage of resources and, 112
    tactical delays and, 113–114
    volume of written comments and,
        182–183
Toxic Substances Control Act (TSCA),
    58–59, 178
Trade associations. *See* Businesses and
    business interest groups
Transparency, 97–98, 128, 239, 289
Transportation, Department of. *See also
    specific government entities reporting to*
    Assistant General Counsel for Regulation
        at, 137, 149, 150
    Carter and revision of rules managed
        by, 125
    complexity of rulemaking by, 108
    congressional budgets on types of
        rulemaking by, 225
    Hazardous Materials Regulations revision
        by, 39, 40–41*f*, 42
    liaison with OMB by, 149
    percentage of rules approved by OIRA
        without change, 245*t*
    priority-setting process of, 132
    rule initiation in, 135
    rulemaking during Bush II presidency
        by, 20
    schedules for rulemaking by, 142
    timeliness of rules by, 108*f*

Treasury, Department of, 1–2, 8, 115, 133, 135
Tregos, Nancy, 121*n*66
Triano, Christine, 216*n*54
Troubled Asset Relief Program (TARP), 1–2
Truman, Harry, 123
Trust in government, as context for rulemaking, 89–90

Underinclusiveness of rules, 98–99
Unified Regulatory Agenda, 196
"Uniform Guidelines on Employee Selection," 22–23, 24

Vagueness of rules, 97–98
Vermont Yankee Nuclear Power Corp. v. Natural Resources Defense Council (1978), 258
Vertical concurrence, for conflict management, 146–147
Vertical review, of draft rules, 82
Veterans Affairs, Department of, 132, 135
Vetoes, legislative, 228–232
Vice president, Clinton vs. Bush II on rulemaking process and, 63
Vice President's Task Force on Regulatory Relief, 78, 126
Viscusi, W. Kip, 119*n*13
Voluntary hearings, 173

Wage and Hour Division, Department of Labor, 45–46
Walter-Logan bill (1940), 49, 175
Washington, George, 45
Waterman, Richard, 284, 296*n*19
Watzman, Nancy, 216*n*54
Webb Yackee, Jason, 194, 199, 216*n*49, 218*n*71, 218*n*79
Webb Yackee, Susan, 194, 199, 216*n*49, 218*n*71, 218*n*79
Weidenbaum, Murray, 38*n*44, 119*n*23
Weingast, Barry R., 121*n*59, 170, 215*n*4, 223, 265*n*4, 265*n*6, 265*n*9
Weiss, Leonard, 119*nn*11–13
West, William F., 37*n*29, 88*n*52, 121*n*56, 165*n*18, 165*n*27, 166*n*29, 166*n*30, 215*n*3, 215*n*5, 217*n*61, 218*n*77, 266*n*33, 266*n*37, 266*n*38, 296*n*8, 296*n*21
  on participation in rulemaking at FTC, 190

on pre-proposal participation role in rulemaking, 199–200
on priority-setting processes, 134
on professional differences among bureaucrats, 279–280
on rationales for rulemaking participation, 169–170
on tactics used to influence rulemaking, 196
Weyman, Richard, 266*n*29
White House. *See* President
Wilcox, Clyde, 218*n*65
Williams, Stephen, 87*n*35
Wilson, James Q., 193, 216*n*39, 218*n*66, 288
Woll, Peter, 87*n*12
Work groups. *See also* Task forces
  career bureaucrats and, 275
  composition and size, 155–156
  evolution of model for, 162–163
  integration with senior management, 161–162
  leadership of, 156–159
  as mechanisms for horizontal concurrence, 146
  membership in, 159–161
  responsibilities for developing rules by, 144–145
Workplace safety programs, 15, 24, 98–99
World Wide Web, e-rulemaking and, 202, 203
Worsham, Jeff, 296*n*18
Written comments. *See also* Comments; Notice-and-comment rulemaking
  as adversary process, 116
  agencies on effectiveness of, 201
  under APA section 553, 175–176
  for Clean Air Act, Magat et al.'s study of, 291
  establishing system for docketing of, 80
  interest groups on effectiveness of, 198*t*, 199
  managing receipt of, 84
  participation in rulemaking using, 66, 83, 196–197, 197*t*
  in use at the end of the 1930s, 171, 172
  volume of, participation and, 182–183

Zealots, bureaucratic, 274–275, 279, 281, 286
Zeckhauser, Richard, 119*nn*11–12
Zoning rules, businesses and, 24